HARVARD EAST ASIAN STUDIES 1

The Center for East Asian Studies at Harvard University administers postgraduate training programs and research projects designed to further scholarly understanding of China, Korea, Japan and adjacent areas.

China's
Early Industrialization

Sheng Hsuan-huai (1844–1916)

China's
Early Industrialization

SHENG HSUAN-HUAI (1844–1916) AND MANDARIN ENTERPRISE

Albert Feuerwerker

HARVARD UNIVERSITY PRESS

Cambridge, Massachusetts

1958

Distributed in Great Britain by Oxford University Press, London

Publication of this volume was aided by a grant from the Ford Foundation. The Foundation is not, however, the author, owner, publisher or proprietor of this publication and is not to be understood as approving by virtue of its grant any of the statements made or views expressed therein.

Library of Congress Catalog Card Number 58-12967

Printed in the United States of America

In Memory of
My Father

Foreword

This volume, the first of the Harvard East Asian Studies, represents the general aim of this series in several respects. First of all, it makes copious use of the pertinent sources in Chinese, Japanese, and Western languages. Secondly, it applies to these materials concerning East Asia the appropriate concepts of the modern social sciences. In addition, Mr. Feuerwerker makes illuminating comparisons between the experience of China and that of Japan and Western countries. All this, we believe, points in the direction of the multilinguistic, multidisciplinary, comparative studies of the future without, however, losing the traditional virtues of careful historical, monographic research.

This study also touches upon some of the unresolved policy problems inherent in economic development. Mr. Feuerwerker's analysis of early Chinese efforts at industrial growth, the nature of their difficulties and the tardiness of the results, provides a much-needed perspective on the industrial effort now being directed from Peking.

Given the affront to Chinese pride presented by Western contact on terms of superiority, it was no doubt inevitable that the spirit of nationalism should eventually have inspired a massive Chinese industrialization program, no matter at what cost. If the early efforts at industrial growth had had greater success in their day, it is conceivable that the program we now see going forward in mainland China might have been less drastic. Yet the example of Japan, so apparently successful in terms of the industrial process, so disastrous in its political-military accompaniments, does not suggest that there was in fact an easy alternative to China's actual experience in the process of economic modernization.

The present study of the social and institutional context, the personnel and politics, and the economic problems and achievements of China's early industrialization constitutes a first approximation, a base-line from which to chart China's pattern of prolonged retardation and revolutionary advance.

Center for East Asian Studies
Harvard University

Acknowledgments

My principal obligations (to be elevated above all others in the manner of a reference to the Imperial presence in a Chinese official document) are to Professors J. K. Fairbank and Lien-sheng Yang of Harvard University — for guidance generously given over a period of years and for their careful reading of this study in typescript.

Dr. Alexander Eckstein read the typescript and I have profited from his comments on some of the economic problems with which I have attempted to deal. I am grateful, too, to Dr. Kwang-ching Liu for his kindness in allowing me to see his work in progress on Sino-foreign shipping enterprise. The frontispiece photograph is reproduced from Arnold Wright, ed., *Twentieth Century Impressions of Hongkong, Shanghai, and other Treaty Ports of China* . . . , London, 1908, p. 525.

The materials that I have used in preparing this volume are for the most part to be found in the Chinese-Japanese Library of the Harvard-Yenching Institute at Harvard University. As anyone who has sought to use his library seriously will know, this implies an enormous debt to Dr. A. K. Chiu — not only for his direct assistance, but also for the energy and skill with which he has assembled this magnificent research collection. For lesser, but no less appreciated assistance, I am obliged to Mr. Howard Linton, Librarian of the East Asiatic Library at Columbia University, and to Dr. Charles S. Gardner, who generously allowed me access to his fine library of Ch'ing dynasty materials.

I am indebted to Mrs. Betty Wang who prepared the bibliographies and glossary; the reader may well be grateful that it is her calligraphy rather than my crabbed characters that will meet his eye.

Finally, I am pleased to acknowledge the support of the Harvard-Yenching Institute, whose fellowships I held while this study was in progress; and to express my thanks to the Ford Foundation Foreign Study and Research Fellowship Program for supplementary grants.

A. F.

CONTENTS

TABLES

China's
Early Industrialization

1

The *Kuan-tu Shang-pan* System: "Official Supervision and Merchant Management"

I

The Problem of China's Retarded Industrialization

Unlike Japan, China was not transformed from an agrarian society into a predominately industrial one in the decades before World War I. There was nevertheless an industrialization effort in China, albeit on a limited scale, which roughly corresponded in time with the great changes of the Meiji era in Japan.

Modern industry in China began with the modernization of armaments.[1] The desire to acquire Western military technology was one of the principal themes of the decade of the "T'ung-chih Restoration," the first decade following the final treaty settlement of 1860. Such a man as Tseng Kuo-fan (1811–1872), the chief architect of the victory over the Taiping Rebellion and the symbol of the efforts made in these years to check the decline of the dynasty by a reassertion of Confucian principles, first became interested in Western methods in his desire to improve China's defenses. As early as 1855 Tseng established small arsenals in Kiangsi, and in 1861 he opened an arsenal and shipyard at Anking in Anhwei province where he had located his headquarters. Tseng Kuo-fan's principal industrial project was the Kiangnan Arsenal, established by himself and Li Hung-chang (1823–1901), then acting governor-general at Nanking, at Shanghai in 1865. The enterprise eventually produced several small armored naval vessels, as well as rifles, cannon, gunpowder, and cartridges.

It was a natural step, but a difficult one in the face of strong conservative objections to Western learning, to proceed from the manufacture of foreign arms in China to the study of the scientific and engineering principles underlying their production. From 1867, the interpreters' college or T'ung-wen Kuan which had been set up in Peking in 1861 began to add astronomy, mathematics, chemistry, physics, biology, mineralogy, metallurgy, mechanics, anatomy, physiology, political economy, and international law to its curriculum under the camouflage of a newly instituted department of "astronomy and mathematics." Between 1872 and 1881, one hundred and twenty Chinese students studied in the United States while a lesser number were receiving technical training in France and England. In each case the aim was to master the secrets of Western technology in order to further the efforts at "self-strengthening" which officials such as Tseng Kuo-fan and Li Hung-chang had initiated.

It was quickly seen that defense required more than weapons alone. A steamship company and telegraph lines to furnish modern transport and communications facilities were undertaken. In what seems a logical sequence, a coal mine was opened in Chihli (present-day Hopei) in 1877 to furnish fuel for the newly erected arsenals and the steamship line. Transportation of the coal from the pithead to a suitable port led to the construction of China's first railroad. A gold mine was opened in Manchuria in the Amur River region in 1887 which was intended to help pay for Li Hung-chang's Westernization projects. Both Li and the governor-general at Wuchang, Chang Chih-tung (1837–1909), undertook to sponsor textile mills which would furnish cloth for their troops and revenue for their other projects. Chang erected an iron and steel works at Hanyang in central China to provide raw material for his arsenals and to manufacture rails for a trunk line connecting Peking and Hankow. And gradually flour milling, cotton spinning and weaving, silk reeling, and other consumer-goods industries were inaugurated in the principal cities of the coastal provinces.

By the turn of the century a wide variety of industrial projects had been begun, either by Chinese promoters or by foreign interests in the treaty ports. Yet the development had been slow and uneven when compared to contemporary accomplishments in Japan, and even more so when compared to the nineteenth-century industrial growth of England, Germany, or the United States. Measurement of the extent of China's pre-1911 industrialization is made difficult by the shortcomings of the available statistical materials. They may, however, be employed as indicators of very gross trends, which are worth noting here as a preliminary step before we turn to an examination of the nature of the early industrialization effort.

One set of data relating to China's industry and commerce toward the end of the Ch'ing dynasty is of particular interest. These are the statistical tables of the Ministry of Agriculture, Industry, and Commerce (*Nung-kung-shang pu*).[2] By the close of 1908, 227 joint-stock companies had registered with the ministry under the provisions of the "Company Law" promulgated in January 1904.[3] In Table 1 these companies are

Table 1

Companies Registered with the Ministry of Agriculture, Industry, and Commerce, 1904–1908

Type of business	Authorized capital (in taels)					
	100,000 and below	100,001– 500,000	500,001– 1,000,000	1,000,001– 2,000,000	2,000,001 and over	Totals
Cotton spinning and weaving	9	7	2	3	0	21
Silk reeling	4	4	0	0	0	8
Dyeing	4	0	0	0	0	4
Railroads	0	0	0	1	3	4
Steamships and steam launches	6	1	1	0	0	8
Electricity and other utilities	4	4	0	0	0	8
Pottery and glass	8	2	1	0	0	11
Soap and candles	8	0	0	0	0	8
Mining and smelting[a]	7	3	0	1	1[a]	12
Matches	1	1	0	0	0	2
Leather	0	1	0	0	0	1
Cement	0	0	1	0	0	1
Paper	0	1	0	0	0	1
Machinery	0	1	0	0	0	1
Miscellaneous manufacturing	8	0	0	0	0	8
Flour milling and rice husking	9	5	1	0	0	15
Tobacco and cigarettes	9	1	0	0	0	10
Oil pressing, bean-cake	4	4	0	0	0	8
Sundry food manufacturing	6	0	0	0	0	6
Modern-type banks	0	2	2	2	1	7
Native banks	4	2	0	0	0	6
Insurance	0	1	2	0	0	3
Pawnshops	18	0	0	0	0	18
Wholesale and retail commerce	25	3	0	0	0	28
Agriculture and fishery	10	1	0	0	0	11
Land reclamation and river dredging	1	3	0	0	0	4
Building contractors	4	2	0	0	0	6
Publishing, booksellers, stationers	6	0	1	0	0	7
Totals	155	49	11	7	5	227

[a] This includes as a single unit the Han-Yeh-P'ing Coal and Iron Corporation, consisting of three companies whose total authorized capital was $20,000,000 (Chinese).

arranged by type of business and according to the size of their authorized capitals.

In all likelihood, many of the companies which had organized on a joint-stock basis could only formally be counted as modernized enterprises. There is no way to determine to what extent, if at all, adherence to the new law made for rationalization of business practices. It is probably justifiable to assume that the pawnshops, native banks, and petty commercial enterprises, as well as companies engaged in agriculture, fishery, and land reclamation, continued to operate much as they had before their registration. The more clearly industrial enterprises among the 227 were modern in the sense that the employment of power-driven machinery in factories differentiated them from traditional Chinese handicraft production. As we shall see, they too did not entirely escape the traditional patterns of conduct in their operations. These industrial enterprises included the leading privately owned Chinese firms in each field which had registered with the ministry, seeking to take advantage of whatever protection against official interference and exactions they could find in the new Company Law. This may be inferred from the fact that the industrialist Chang Chien, who was a leader among those championing wholly private ownership and operation, had registered his largest enterprise, the Ta-sheng Cotton Mill (capitalized at Tls. 1,130,000), as well as a dozen other companies with which he was associated.[4]

A look at Table 1 reveals the existence of a large number of enterprises using foreign machinery but operating on a very small scale. This is evident too from other data. For example, in the area around Chinkiang in 1917 there were at least a dozen small Chinese flour mills that used Western machinery, but these were generally unable to work the whole year round and their income was unstable.[5] If we take a capital of Tls. 100,000 as a division point, only 72 of the 227 registered companies had authorized capitals in excess of this amount. These included thirteen cotton mills, four coal mines, one iron and steel plant, six flour mills, seven banks, three insurance companies, three pottery and glass works, six oil pressing mills, and two steamship companies. The total authorized capital of all 227 firms was approximately Tls. 97,000,000. Forty-eight per cent of the total, or Tls. 47,000,000, was accounted for by the 22 largest companies, that is, by the 10 per cent of the total number of registered companies having capitals in excess of Tls. 500,000. These figures support the conclusion that the structure of China's "modern" industry at the end of the Ch'ing dynasty was characterized by the prominence of a small number of large enterprises (such as the Han-Yeh-P'ing Coal and Iron Corporation or the Ta-sheng Cotton Mill) against the background of a larger number of companies — but still relatively few — employing Western techniques on a very small scale. Unlike the contemporary situation in Japan, this growth of industry was not supported by structural changes in the economy all along the line. Nor was there the development of an overhead structure of credit and communications comparable to that erected by the Meiji oligarchs in their efforts to modernize Japan.[6] The results of China's industrialization effort can be summed up with the statement that these were isolated cases rather than an epidemic of industrialization.

This view is corroborated by other data. It has been estimated, for example, that in 1912 there were 20,749 "factories" in China, a term left undefined but one whose scope becomes quite clear when we note that only 363 of this huge total employed mechanical power, while the remaining 20,386 were operated with human or animal exertion only.[7] "Factory" as used in this estimate meant any kind of workshop, ranging from the Chinese equivalent of "cottage" industries to cotton mills employing several thousand workers. The average number of workers in these factories was 32 in 1912 with the distribution as shown in Table 2.[8] In this year the mean number of workers in cotton spinning and

Table 2

Distribution of Chinese "Factories" by Number of Employees, 1912

Number of workers	Number of factories	Per cent
7–29	18,212	88.0
30–49	990	4.8
50–99	798	3.7
100–499	514	2.4
500–999	181	0.9
1,000–	54	0.2
Total	20,749	100.0

weaving establishments was 1,122; silk reeling, 286; matches and gunpowder, 131; pottery and glass, 31; flour milling and rice husking, 20; soap and candles, 19; and paper, 14.[9] It must be stressed that these statistics are useful only to indicate large relationships — in this instance to underline the very small place occupied by Chinese-owned modern industry in the economy as a whole, and to mark the prior position of the cotton industry within this small modern segment.

This discussion has so far dealt only with privately operated (shang-pan) Chinese enterprise. Several significant groups of modern enterprises which were not registered with the Nung-kung-shang pu must be brought into the picture in order to give a more complete account of the character and extent of China's industrialization in the late Ch'ing period. In addition to those companies which did not choose to register with the ministry, the most obvious omission was of course that of the foreign-owned industries in China's treaty ports. These were particularly important in the fields of cotton spinning and weaving, dockyards, shipbuilding and engineering, utilities, and banking.[10] For example, in 1913 the eight foreign-owned cotton mills in Shanghai operated 40 per cent of the total number of spindles in China and 69 per cent of those in Shanghai.[11]

It is difficult to determine what proportion of the total foreign direct business investment in China (which is estimated at U. S. $1,084,000,000 in 1914 [12]) was accounted for by modern industrial and commercial enterprises in the treaty ports of the type we are considering. According to one estimate, British investments in China in the fields of shipping, public utilities, mining, and manufacturing totaled U. S. $175,000,000 in 1914.[13] The next largest block after the British was that of Japan, whose nationals as of 1914 are estimated to have invested 98,926,000 yen (the equivalent of U. S. $50,000,000) in public utilities, mining, manufacturing, and banking and finance.[14] In any case, it is clear from these figures that foreign-owned enterprises constituted a large part of the modern sector of China's pre-Republican economy, especially after the signature in 1895 of the Treaty of Shimonoseki, permitting foreign-owned manufacturing enterprises in the treaty ports.

Account must be taken also of government-owned enterprises. These included arsenals, most of China's railroads, and after 1902 the telegraph lines. In 1902 the "government-supervised and merchant-managed" (*kuan-tu shang-pan*) Imperial Telegraph Administration operated 41,417 *li* (13,806 miles) of telegraph lines for which the imperial government paid the shareholders $3,960,000 or approximately Tls. 2,850,000. Some 59,211 *li* (19,737 miles) of lines were owned by the individual provinces, and these were nationalized in 1911. They may be taken as having had the same or a somewhat higher value than the *kuan-tu shang-pan* lines.[15] As for the railroads, between 1894 and 1914, 7,339 miles of lines were constructed exclusive of the Russian-controlled Chinese Eastern Railroad.[16] If we apply the average cost per mile of the Peking-Hankow railroad, Tls. 55,000, to this figure, China's pre-World War I railroads had been constructed at a total outlay of approximately Tls. 406,645,000, which was largely borrowed from foreign creditors.[17]

A further category of unregistered enterprises consisted of companies (such as the China Merchants' Steam Navigation Company with assets in excess of Tls. 10,000,000) which until the end of the dynasty were still formally organized as *kuan-tu shang-pan* undertakings. This group included also the principal semiofficial modern banks: the Imperial Bank of China (*Chung-kuo t'ung-shang yin-hang*), the Hu-pu Bank (later reorganized as the Ta-Ch'ing Bank), and the Bank of Communications (*Chiao-t'ung yin-hang*), the three together having a total subscribed capital of perhaps Tls. 20,000,000.[18]

There would be little point in trying to construct even an approximate total for the capital value of the modern enterprises which have been noted above. That they did not represent an "industrial revolution" radically altering the basis of China's economy needs no demonstration. This is clear from even the scattered figures presented here and is emphasized by the concentration of these new enterprises in the treaty ports and coastal provinces — especially in Shanghai and elsewhere in Kiangsu — where contact with the foreigner and his ways was centered (see Table 3).[19]

Table 3

Location of Companies Registered with the Ministry of
Agriculture, Industry, and Commerce, 1904–1908

Place	Number of companies	Per cent
Kiangsu (except Shanghai)	69	30.4
Shanghai	30	13.2
Chihli	25	11.0
Kwangtung	22	9.7
Chekiang	15	6.6
Honan	11	4.8
Anhwei	10	4.4
Fukien	8	3.5
Shantung	7	3.0
Hupei	7	3.0
Hunan	7	3.0
Kiangsi	4	1.7
Manchuria	3	1.3
Szechwan	2	0.9
Shansi	2	0.9
Singapore	2	0.9
Hong Kong	1	0.4
Yunnan	1	0.4
Kwangsi	1	0.4
Total	227	100.0

In dealing with China's modern-type industries and financial institutions in this period, exclusive concern with statistical measurement would be misleading. The absence of satisfactory time series among the mass of quantitative data to be found in the Chinese sources is of course regrettable. But, in any case, primary attention must be given to the qualitative data which help to explain and interpret the economic performance of the Chinese in the last decades of the Manchu dynasty. A principal assumption underlying this study is the belief that industrialization in the broadest sense was the normative development to be expected if China's traditional society were to adapt to the demands of the modern world. Retardation of change in this crucial area was a major factor in the inadequacy of China's total response to the impact of the West. At the same time the inability of China to accomplish the transition to an industrial society reflected the institutional and ideological obstacles to change which were operative as well in other sectors of the traditional society.

China's modern industry in the late Ch'ing period included, as we have seen, extensive foreign enterprise in the treaty ports and in the shipping lanes between them. Through Shanghai and other points of contact with Europe and America came much of the technology and equipment which made possible the industrial efforts of Chinese promoters. But the crucial issue was not the success or failure of any number of industrial undertakings established under the protection of the foreigner's extraterritorial privileges; what mattered was the fate of the modern industry which, in the last decades of the nineteenth century, the Chinese undertook to establish themselves. Whether or not fundamental economic change would be seen depended in large part on the fertility of these enterprises. If they would be fruitful and multiply, if they would build up enough momentum to break through the barriers inherent in the traditional agrarian economy, they would carry the other sectors of society with them into the modern industrialized world. But if the institutional barriers could not be shattered, it was inevitable that industrialization would be retarded. An investigation of the characteristic patterns according to which the Chinese merchant and entrepreneur undertook and operated modern-type industrial and commercial enterprises should throw light on the causes of this retardation, on the one hand, and on the factors making for change, on the other.

This study is directed to an examination of these characteristics as they appeared in several key enterprises. Together they constituted a system of "official supervision and merchant management" (*kuan-tu shang-pan*) which in varying degrees underlay all efforts toward economic modernization.

II

Origin and Content of "Official Supervision and Merchant Management"

Writers on this subject have tended to devote a great deal of ingenuity to devising systems of periodization for the history of China's industrialization.[20] These are perhaps the products of a desire to increase the weight or density of what might otherwise be a sparse narrative. One work,[21] for example, divides the period from 1862 to 1911 into four subperiods: (1) *1862–1877,* the period of "military industry." Following the Anglo-French occupation of Peking in 1860 and the demonstration of the value of Western-style arms against the Taiping rebels, such leaders as Tseng Kuo-fan, Li Hung-chang, and Tso Tsung-t'ang undertook the establishment of arsenals and dockyards to produce armaments in support of a policy of "self-strengthening" (*tzu-ch'iang*) against the supposed threat from the West. (2) *1878–1894,* the period of *kuan-tu shang-pan* industry. This was characterized by official sponsorship of industrial enterprises, in particular of cotton spinning and weaving, and of mining. Although other forms of organization were employed, that of "official supervision and merchant management" was most widespread. (3) *1895–1902.* Foreign industry established itself firmly in the treaty ports on the basis of the right to engage in manufacturing granted to the Japanese — and by the "most-favored-nation" provision to the other imperialist powers — in the Treaty of Shimonoseki. The Ch'ing government, responding to the threat of foreign capital, took some verbal steps to encourage industry. Among other things, it sanctioned investment in commerce and industry by officials and gentry and thus removed the last formal vestige of opposition to such activities.[22] (4) *1903–1911,* a period of intense foreign economic rivalry in China, active government promotion of industry, and greater response from the populace. There occurred a consequent diminution of the role of officials in the operation of industries and the eclipse of *kuan-tu shang-pan* enterprises by privately owned (*shang-pan*) undertakings.

This chronology has the merit of distinguishing clearly the succession of events as they appear from a surface view, but it is misleading if taken to imply a fundamental alteration in the characteristics of the modern-type enterprises undertaken in the four periods. Strictly speaking, there were only a dozen or so large enterprises formally acknowledged as being operated according to a system of official supervision and merchant management. In the order of their establishment, the most important *kuan-tu shang-pan* companies were the China Merchants' Steam Navigation Company (1872), the K'ai-p'ing Coal Mines (1877), the Shanghai Cotton Cloth Mill (first planned in 1878; later the Hua-sheng Cotton Mill), the Imperial Telegraph Administration (1881), the Mo-ho Gold Mines (1887), the Hanyang Ironworks (from 1896), the Ta-yeh Iron Mines (from 1896), the Imperial Bank of China (1896), and the P'ing-hsiang Coal Mines (1898).[23] But the essential ingredients of the *kuan-tu shang-pan* pattern were to be found in virtually every industrial or commercial undertaking organized by Chinese promoters before the end of the Ch'ing dynasty. There were, to be sure, obvious formal differences among the China Merchants' Steam Navigation Company under Sheng Hsuan-huai, Chang Chien's cotton mills and other enterprises at Nantung, Kiangsu, and the government-owned Peking-Hankow railroad. But, as will be evident, these and many others of the modern-type enterprises noted in the first section of this chapter may safely and profitably be considered as of one species.

Before proceeding, however, it should be stressed that the *kuan-tu shang-pan* system was not an institution legislated into being and possessing legally definable limits. Rather this study treats a series of discrete events and organizations which were recognized by their contemporaries as having certain traits in common. What appears to the hindsight of the historian to have been a "system" had only an *ad hoc* existence for those immediately concerned. If the regulations of the *kuan-tu shang-pan* China Merchants' Steam Navigation Company were a model for those of the Mo-ho Gold Mines or the Hanyang Ironworks, it was more for the reason that they adequately served current needs than that they complied with a fully formed a priori notion of how such enterprises should be organized. Nevertheless the uniformities were there and were prominent enough to justify the treatment of these separate enterprises as examples of one underlying institution.

What then were the characteristics of the *kuan-tu shang-pan* industries? The immediate ancestor of the system of official supervision and merchant management as it operated in the latter part of the nineteenth century seems to have been the government salt monopoly. The chronicles of the salt administration abound with terms such as "official supervision and merchant sales" (*kuan-tu shang-hsiao*) or "official transportation and merchant sales" (*kuan-yün shang-hsiao*), which are analogous to *kuan-tu shang-pan*.[24] It would be a formidable task to summarize the protean forms of the traditional salt monopoly within the confines of a single paragraph.[25] For the purposes of the present discussion, however, the relevant fact is that the government appointed official supervisors, while the rights to manufacture, transport, and sell the salt were farmed out or sold to various groups of merchants. The salt administration may be characterized as a joint official-merchant institution of a tax-farming nature. In the last half of the nineteenth century it was administered on a regional or provincial basis with the Ministry of Revenue (*Hu-pu*) nominally at the top, but with actual control increasingly in the hands of the governors-general and governors.

Profit from the salt gabelle for the officials and merchants who participated took a multitude of forms. At each stage — production, distribution, sales — the merchant was protected by monopoly rights for which, of course, he had paid handsomely in the first place. The licenses of the producers and the salt merchants were often handed down from father to son. For the government in Peking the salt gabelle netted Tls. 6,000,000 annually in the latter part of the nineteenth century, to which must be added Peking's share of the salt *likin* or transit tax. But this was only the expected statutory yield. Over and above these amounts were the sums retained in the provinces and never reported to Peking; the "squeeze" exacted at all levels in return for appointment to the lucrative official posts in the salt administration;[26] and the constant extortion of "contributions" from the salt merchants (generally under the heading *pao-hsiao* or "efforts made to return [the imperial grace]"). Quite explicitly the salt administration was a fiscal institution. It did fairly well what it was designed to do, that is, to provide a stable source of income for the central and provincial governments. The anomaly was that some of the principal features of this institution were carried over into the modern-type enterprises undertaken by the "self-strengtheners" who sought to employ Western-style arms and industrial techniques in an effort to shore up the dynasty against domestic and foreign dangers.

Like their predecessor, the *kuan-tu shang-pan* industries were joint official-merchant undertakings. While they were no longer primarily devices for fiscal administration, neither did these enterprises represent the simple importation of Western-type industries and their superposition onto the Chinese scene. From the past they retained a bureaucratic management and the monopolistic restrictions and official exactions which had characterized the salt administration. These features were combined with such new nineteenth-century developments as the growth of provincial at the expense of imperial power and the appearance of new sources of capital in the treaty ports. The product — the *kuan-tu shang-pan* institution — was deficient in the rationalized organization, functional specialization, and impersonal discipline associated with the development of modern industry in the West. And the enterprises organized according to the *kuan-tu shang-pan* pattern were further burdened by competition for capital from the nonmodern sector of the economy, by the weight of family and local loyalties, and by the pressure of foreign competitors for the Chinese market.

Typically the share capital of these enterprises came from treaty-port merchants and from gentry relatives and friends of the promoters. The companies were organized under the protection of high provincial officials, and official funds might be deposited at interest as they had previously been lent to old-style pawnbrokers. The position of the manager was ambiguous. He usually held official rank, either by purchase or by recommendation of higher officials. At the same time, he was a representative of the shareholders and often among the largest shareholders himself. Thus, both the manager and the enterprise as a whole may be said to have had a semiofficial status. Because of these ties to officialdom, frequent reference to the principal *kuan-tu shang-pan* firms appears in the Ch'ing documents of this period, especially in the memorials and official correspondence of their patrons. With few exceptions, the records of the companies themselves are not available. It is largely from the official documents that we are able to study them.

III

The Industrialization Effort and Regional Foci of Power

The earliest use of the expression *kuan-tu shang-pan* in connection with modern-type enterprises that I have found occurs in a letter, dated December 23, 1872, from Li Hung-chang to the Tsungli Yamen, reporting the establishment of the China Merchants' Steam Navigation Company:

> At present we are giving it a try [i.e., the original organization of the Company under Chu Ch'i-ang], and if there turn out to be any unsatisfactory matters I shall order an investigation and make changes as needed.
>
> As there are now no merchant vessels built by the government shipyards [at Shanghai and Foochow] included among the Company's steamers, we cannot have joint operation by officials and merchants (*kuan-shang ho-pan*); we should continue with official supervision and merchant management (*kuan-tu shang-pan*). While the government will lay down the general principles and keep its eye on the company's merits and demerits, the merchant directors (*shang-tung*) will be permitted to propose their own regulations so that the shareholders will be satisfied.[27]

The circumstances of this letter point to one of the outstanding features of the government-supervised and merchant-managed industries, namely, their place as parts of strong provincial foci of power which developed in the last half of the nineteenth century. In the *kuan-tu shang-pan* formula, the role of the *kuan* or supervising official was typically not filled by the central government in Peking. Li Hung-chang,[28] the governor-general of Chihli, was the protector of the China Merchants' Steam Navigation Company, the Shanghai Cotton Cloth Mill, the Mo-ho Gold Mines, and others. Chang Chih-tung,[29] the governor-general of Hupei and Hunan, stood behind the Hanyang Ironworks, the Ta-yeh Iron Mines, and the P'ing-hsiang Coal Mines.

Although the imperial government, after the defeat of 1894–1895, was converted to the support of efforts to introduce modern industry, its contributions were largely verbal. Provincial "Commercial Affairs Bureaus" (*shang-wu chü*) — such as the one at Nanking to be mentioned below in connection with Chang Chien and the establishment of the Ta-sheng Cotton Mill — were sanctioned. Investment in commerce and industry by officials and gentry received formal imperial approval. A system of rewards for the successful promotion of industry — either monopoly rights or official rank — was established. In 1903 a Ministry of Commerce (*Shang-pu*) was set up; and it drew up a Company Law and later a Bankruptcy Law. Further regulations for rewarding useful inventions and the inauguration of industrial, commercial, and agricultural enterprises were promulgated.[30]

But all of this was of small effect. The Ch'ing government was bankrupt; it could make no capital investments. Because of its political weakness it was unable to abate the transit taxes (*likin*) and commercial levies which plagued newly established ventures but which were largely under provincial control. In fact, Peking itself sought to exact a 10 per cent excise on goods manufactured in China.[31] The "unequal treaties" prevented Chinese enterprises from receiving better treatment than was afforded to foreign factories in the treaty ports. The decline of imperial power and opulence deprived any movement for modernization of a central focus and direction. Such efforts as were made to introduce new industries resulted from the initiative of powerful provincial leaders of whom Governor-general Li Hung-chang was the outstanding example.

Li Hung-chang's position was based first of all upon the *Huai-chün* or Huai Army which he had led against the Taiping rebels. From 1870 to his downfall as a result of China's defeat by Japan in 1894–1895, he was entrenched in the metropolitan province of Chihli. He might have become a prisoner of the Ch'ing court in this post. But Li retained command of the Huai Army and partial control of the finances of the rich lower Yangtze provinces. Through the agency of such strategically placed subordinates as Ting Jih-ch'ang,[32] he was able to extend his power beyond Chihli. For twenty-five years he moved toward single-handed control over foreign affairs, domination of the maritime customs revenue, monopoly of armaments production, and complete control of the military forces in the northern half of the empire. The erection of a regional "bureaucratic machine," which on many points effectively challenged the power of the imperial government, Li accomplished by developing his army further, undertaking a navy, placing his own men in key metropolitan and provincial posts, and by sponsoring industrial ventures such as those that have been mentioned.[33]

These industrial efforts had a marked regional character which can be illustrated by an account of the famous railroad controversy of 1888–1889. In 1885 Li had organized a company to undertake the extension of a short railroad already operating at the K'ai-p'ing Coal Mines.[34] This company was reorganized as a *kuan-tu shang-pan* enterprise in 1887 and took the name Chinese Railway Company (*Chung-kuo t'ieh-lu kung-ssu*). By 1888 a line was in operation from the mine (at T'ang-shan,

Chihli) to Tientsin, about ninety miles distant. Acting on the suggestion of the shareholders in the Chinese Railway Company, Governor-general Li then proposed an extension of the T'ang-shan-Tientsin railroad westward to T'ung-chou (near Peking). The principal reason given for the new undertaking was that it would strengthen the defenses of the capital area by facilitating the movement of troops and supplies. What Li actually had in mind, however, was the eventual extension of the T'ang-shan railroad northward to Shanhaikwan, a route which would yield little commercial traffic, but which would strengthen Li's military position in the north and bring Manchuria under his control. He was ready to support the Tientsin-T'ung-chou line since it would furnish revenue which could be used for the Shanhaikwan extension.

Violent opposition was aroused to the threatened intrusion of a railroad into the capital precincts. Peking was flooded with memorials from Li's political enemies and from conservative officials who were opposed to railroads on any grounds. This was the last great fight over the principle of railroad building which had been debated by the court and the bureaucracy since MacDonald Stephenson's proposals of 1863–1864. It was settled by a memorial from Chang Chih-tung, then the Liang-Kuang governor-general, which was intended as a compromise between Li and his opponents. Chang suggested a line from Lu-kou-ch'iao ("Marco Polo Bridge" on the outskirts of Peking) to Hankow, and he was transferred to the post of governor-general of Hu-Kuang in order to take charge of the construction. The Hu-pu was ordered to appropriate Tls. 2,000,000 for the Peking-Hankow (Lu-Han) line, but the opposition from Li Hung-chang and his supporters continued to be so strong that the project was pigeonholed and not revived until after the Sino-Japanese War. In the meantime an edict of April 11, 1891, sanctioned Li's request that the Tls. 2,000,000 appropriated to the Lu-Han railroad be transferred to his control for the purpose of extending the T'ang-shan line to Shanhaikwan and beyond the pass into Manchuria. Some progress had already been made beyond the pass (on what was later to be the Peking-Mukden railroad) when Li fell from power in 1895.[35]

In this instance, as in others, Li Hung-chang was careful to keep in mind the potential value of the proposed industrial project to the extension of his regional power. Li's influence in Peking, we may conclude from the above, was adequate for him to obtain imperial sanction for measures which would strengthen his position. The *kuan-tu shang-pan* enterprises of which he was the patron at once conformed to the "self-strengthening" ideology that he propagated, and were institutions providing services (for example, transportation for his troops), income (legitimate and illegitimate), and sinecures for Li Hung-chang's own satrapy.

The relation of modern industries to regional foci of political power was not restricted to undertakings formally organized according to *kuan-tu shang-pan* regulations. This may be seen in the case of Chang Chien, who has already been mentioned in passing as an advocate of the private ownership and operation of new-type enterprises. Chang, a private entrepreneur, was nevertheless dependent on assistance from Governors-general Chang Chih-tung and Liu K'un-i [36] in establishing his Ta-sheng Cotton Mill.

At the end of hostilities with Japan in 1895, while Chang Chih-tung was still acting governor-general in Nanking, he sought to promote cotton mills in Kiangsu province in order to counter the huge incursion of foreign goods which he feared would result from the Shimonoseki treaty. Chang Chien was invited to undertake the establishment of a mill and accepted.[37] When Chang Chih-tung returned to his regular post at Wuchang, Chang Chien received authorization from his successor, Governor-general Liu K'un-i, to open a mill at Nantung. Liu was of little assistance, however, in the crucial matter of raising funds, and Chang Chien's original "merchant" [38] associates in Nantung and Shanghai were unable to provide sufficient capital to purchase machinery for the plant. Chang was therefore forced to give up his original intention of keeping the enterprise entirely in private hands. He entered into an agreement with the head of the Nanking Commercial Affairs Bureau (*shang-wu chü*) to accept Tls. 500,000 worth of textile machinery — originally purchased by Chang Chih-tung before the Sino-Japanese War to equip a projected mill at Wuchang — as official capital in the new project. The cotton mill was now to be operated under joint official-merchant management (*kuan-shang ho-pan*). But Chang Chien's leading backers withdrew late in 1896 after a dispute over the question of the interest to be paid on the official investment, and the agreement fell through.

Chang now turned to Sheng Hsuan-huai, who, in addition to heading the largest Chinese cotton mill in Shanghai, was an official of some importance and closely associated with Chang Chih-tung's political power in Hupei and Hunan (see Chapter 3). In the spring of 1897 Sheng agreed to take over one half of the Tls. 500,000 in textile machinery, and Chang Chien the other half. So as not to frighten away the potential merchant investors from whom Chang hoped to raise the additional Tls. 250,000 needed to establish his mill, it was agreed that the company would be entirely merchant-operated (*shang-pan*), notwithstanding the official investment in the form of machinery. Sheng Hsuan-huai also engaged to assist Chang in raising working capital as did the taotai Kuei Sung-ch'ing, head of the Nanking Commercial Affairs Bureau. Neither of these promises yielded any fruits, however, and in the next two years Chang Chien repeatedly and with little success sought assistance from Chang Chih-tung and Liu K'un-i. When the Ta-sheng Mill at last began operations in May 1899, Chang had raised less than Tls. 250,000. Fortunately, since the firm showed itself a successful venture, Chang was able to raise further capital from nonofficial sources. Yet the largest single increment came in 1902 when Liu K'un-i turned over the Tls. 250,000 of machinery which Sheng Hsuan-huai had contracted for in 1897 but had not used.[39]

This brief account is far from the complete story of Chang Chien as a textile entrepreneur, but it should be sufficient to demonstrate that even his attempts to establish wholly private enterprises could be undertaken only with regard to the existing political framework, that is, with the sanction and assistance of the powerful provincial leaders who dominated late nineteenth-century China. While the Ta-sheng Mill gradually passed out of official purview, its inauguration and early history can still be most profitably examined as part of the story of the promotion of modern industry in the areas of their political control by Governors-general Chang Chih-tung and Liu K'un-i.

What I have indicated with regard to Chang Chien's *shang-pan* industry is applicable as well to such wholly government-operated (*kuan-pan*) enterprises as China's railroads. Without going into detail at this point, it is clear, for example, that the Peking-Hankow and Canton-Hankow railroads were Chang Chih-tung's special province by virtue of his dominant position in central China. And in regard to modern banking, it is apparent that the Hu-pu Bank, established in 1904, was originally an organ of the Chihli governor-general Yuan Shih-k'ai in opposition to the Imperial Bank of China which was operated by Sheng Hsuan-huai in Shanghai with the backing of Chang Chih-tung and his regional power.

IV

Capital from Treaty-Port Merchants

In the official-merchant undertakings of the period before the Opium War, the largest part of the capital employed came ultimately from the land, whether as taxes and tribute to the government or as rent and interest to landlords and moneylenders. The development of commerce in the treaty ports after the Treaty of Nanking in 1842 provided a place and an opportunity for the growth of "compradore capital" (*mai-pan tzu-pen*), that is, the accumulation of funds by Chinese merchants from foreign trade and its ancillary services, first as adjuncts to Western trading firms and then on their own account.[40] A second characteristic of the *kuan-tu shang-pan* system was that it was designed to tap this new source of capital.

The participation of merchants in the financing and operation of new-style enterprises was a crucial fact even though the Chinese merchant was neither willing nor able to support a full-scale industrialization effort. The term *shang*, translated "merchant," was used quite loosely in the documents of the late Ch'ing period. Within its scope were included persons who engaged in any sort of commercial (for example, import and export, wholesale and retail sales), financial (for example, banking and brokerage) or industrial (for example, manufacturing) pursuit. Thus the money-changer was a "merchant," as was the old-style Shansi banker, the compradore for a large foreign firm such as Jardine, Matheson and Company, the tea exporter, the salt retailer, and the promoter of a Western-type steam-powered textile mill. Li Hung-chang and Sheng Hsuan-huai expected merchants (*shang*) to invest in their enterprises. But such a diverse group as here described, having strong ties to the traditional economy and its values (some of which are discussed in the next chapter under the heading "Trade and Commerce"), could not be a stable source of capital. Presumably only the merchant who had had extensive contact with foreigners, foreign products, and foreign methods in the treaty ports — the compradore class — would look upon the promotion of Western-type industries as a desirable thing in itself. Such a man, for example, was Cheng Kuan-ying, once a compradore for the British firms of Dent and Company and Butterfield and Swire, whose part in a number of new enterprises will be described later. Cheng's book, *Sheng-shih wei-yen* (Warnings to a seemingly prosperous age), which saw several editions between 1862 and 1900, contains many observations on the need for economic changes.[41]

For the rest, their investment in modern-type industrial and commercial ventures differed little from that of the gentry, landlord, and official investors whose liquid funds were attracted into these enterprises. These "backward" economic elements were not concerned with promoting industrialization; they were seeking as high a return as possible on their funds which they would normally invest in land, native banks, and pawnshops. At times the new industries would pay handsomely: the Shanghai Cotton Cloth Mill (*Shang-hai chi-ch'i chih-pu chü*) declared a 25 per cent divided in 1893;[42] the Ta-sheng Cotton Mill paid 80–90 per cent to its shareholders in 1905–1907.[43] Then "official and gentry" (*shih-ta-fu*) capital would be attracted from more traditional investments into textile mills, shipping, or mines. But when these industrial enterprises were not so profitable, their funds would no longer be forthcoming, and if possible they would be withdrawn.[44]

Because the stable investment of those merchants who had confidence in the long-run profitability of industry was insufficient to meet their needs for capital, the *kuan-tu shang-pan* industries were forced to resort to practices which often adversely affected their chances of success. These included short-term borrowing at high rates of interest, guaranteed dividend payments without regard to the company's earnings, and inadequate allowance for depreciation and insurance. Short-term borrowing is illustrated in the case of the Yü-chin Spinning Mill which was founded by Sheng Hsuan-huai in 1895 as a subsidiary to the *kuan-tu shang-pan* Hua-sheng Cotton Mill. In 1897 this plant was reorganized as the Hsieh-lung Cotton Spinning Company. The total cost of its buildings and machinery came to Tls. 736,000, but the subscribed capital was only Tls. 571,600. To make up this deficit the company was forced to borrow funds as best it could. The resulting situation was described by a contemporary observer:

> In a word there is not a better equipped cotton mill, either in China or elsewhere. Its chequered career dates from its inception. Why? Largely because the capital was not fully subscribed. . . . Not only did the mill commence running without sufficient working capital, but in order to procure necessary working capital it had to pay exorbitant rates of interest, as much as eight or nine per cent. In four years the company have paid in interest alone Tls. 108,000. . . . The working account showed a fair profit. . . . Alas! that was swallowed up in interest.[45]

The Yü-chin mill, despite reorganization in 1897, failed completely in December 1901 and passed into Japanese hands.[46] Chang Chih-tung's Hupei Government Textile Mill (*Hu-pei chih-pu kuan-chü*) followed a similar pattern by borrowing Tls. 200,000 at 9 per cent from Shansi bankers on which it paid interest of Tls. 138,000 in six years.[47]

Guaranteed dividends (*kuan-li*) were deducted from the gross income before the profit-and-loss account was drawn up and constituted, in effect, part of the regular operating expenses of the companies which followed this practice in order to attract merchant capital. If the firm's profits were inadequate or if it operated at a loss, the *kuan-li* was taken from the capital or additional funds were borrowed. The dividend was usually 8 or 10 per cent on the subscribed capital. For example, the Ta-sheng Cotton Mill referred to earlier promised a guaranteed return of 8 per cent in order to attract investors. In the period 1895–1899, before the factory was even built and production begun, it paid Tls. 17,000 in *kuan-li* from its capital — in order to attract more capital.[48] While Chang Chien's plant eventually succeeded, many others succumbed under such difficulties.

By not allowing adequately for the depreciation of fixed capital, a

company could show a false surplus in its accounts. Thus it was reported of the Han-Yeh-P'ing Coal and Iron Company:

> While foreign factories and mines make an annual deduction for the de-
> preciation of their fixed assets, except land, the old equipment which this
> plant installed over ten years ago is still carried on the books at its original
> value. . . . Therefore although everyone knows of the company's losses and
> that the market value of its shares is not 50 per cent of the face value, yet
> in its accounts there is always a surplus and never a deficit.[49]

With this "surplus" the company could pay guaranteed dividends to the
shareholders, and bonuses to the management. But its authorized capital
was never fully subscribed, despite these practices, and Han-Yeh-P'ing
became more and more dependent on Japanese capital.[50]

The participation of men coming from compradore backgrounds in
the China Merchants' Steam Navigation Company, the Hua-sheng Cotton Mill, the Imperial Bank of China, and the Imperial Telegraph Administration will be treated in detail in the chapters dealing with these
kuan-tu shang-pan enterprises. They were a source both of funds and
of managerial personnel and constituted the *shang* or merchant in the
kuan-tu shang-pan formula. Some of these individuals obviously had
considerable managerial skill. H. B. Morse, who was "assistant to the
Directors" of the China Merchants' Company in 1886–1887, lamented
the fact that the services of Tong King-sing (T'ang T'ing-shu), ex-
compradore for Jardine, Matheson and Company, whom Li Hung-chang
had selected as the first manager of the new steamship company, were
no longer available to the company: "I have always thought it a pity . . .
that we could not connect Tong King Sing with the Company, so as to
have the advantage of his business capacity; he need not have absolute
control; meeting a board of Directors twice a week would have secured
that." [51] Such competence was unfortunately not universal, and Morse
could blame Tong's colleague, Hsü Jun, for "a sinful waste of money"
in building godowns at Chin-li-yuan wharf in Shanghai with a "third
storey [which] is and will be useless." [52]

The number of potential investors was small, and even if the treaty-
port merchants had not stood half-facing the past it is doubtful whether
their resources could have supported a genuine industrialization movement. Thus it would appear from Sheng Hsuan-huai's statements that
the merchant investors in the China Merchants' Company and the Imperial Telegraph Administration were for the most part the same men
whom he convinced in the following years to put their money into the
Hua-sheng Cotton Mill, the Hanyang Ironworks, the P'ing-hsiang Coal
Mines, and others of Sheng's projects.[53] Their support of the latter industries — as Sheng claimed when he sought to counter an attempt by

Peking to levy new contributions on the China Merchants' Company and the Telegraph Administration — [54] was dependent on the continued profitability of their shipping and telegraph investments.

As examples of treaty-port merchants who were prominent in the organization of *shang-pan* or wholly private enterprises of a Western type, the careers of Yeh Ch'eng-chung, Yü Ho-te, and Jung Tsung-ching may be cited.[55] Beginning from a ship chandlery and sundries shop in Shanghai in 1861, Yeh's business grew quickly until he had establishments in every large treaty port. In the interior his name became synonymous with kerosene oil. Some of the profits from these commercial efforts he put into silk filatures and match factories.[56] The second man of this group, better known as Yü Ch'ia-ch'ing, was for some ten years employed by foreign commercial firms in Shanghai before he became compradore of the Nederlandsche Handel-Maatschappij (*Ho-lan yin-hang*) when it opened offices in China in 1903. In 1908 Yü and nine other men from the Ningpo area founded the Ssu-ming Commercial Bank with a capital of Tls. 1,500,000; this bank and the Chekiang Industrial Bank (*Chekiang hsing-yeh yin-hang*) which opened in 1907 were the first *shang-pan* modern banks in China. Together with the Nanking governor-general Tuan Fang, Yü undertook to promote a Southeast Asia Industrial Promotion Bank (*Nan-yang ch'üan-yeh yin-hang*) — in this case a joint official-merchant enterprise — which proved abortive. Before the 1911 revolution Yü also played a major role in organizing a steamer line between Shanghai and Ningpo; but his principal efforts in the shipping business came in the Republican period.[57] The last of the trio, Jung Tsung-ching, was a local banker in Wusih, who founded a flour mill in 1898, and from this beginning he developed an "empire" of twelve flour mills and six cotton mills.[58]

But as in the case of the China Merchants' Company and other *kuan-tu shang-pan* firms, investment of merchant funds in private industrial enterprises was slow in forthcoming. This is demonstrated by Yen Chung-p'ing in his study of the Chinese cotton textile industry. Yen found that of nineteen mills organized before 1911 which he considered, fourteen were promoted by "official and gentry" (*shih-ta-fu*) elements, and only three by merchants or compradores.[59] He is doubtless correct in stressing the importance of what he terms "bureaucratic capital" (*kuan-liao tzu-pen*) originating from the *shih-ta-fu* class. But the character and origin of the funds invested in these enterprises were often complex matters, and Yen's conclusions may well underrate the role of merchant investment in the pre-1911 period. Aside from the consideration that there were usually other investors as well, the titles or rank held by the promoters could be misleading as an index to their actual status and activities.

Thus one of the largest companies listed by Yen was the T'ung-chiu-yuan Cotton Mill in Ningpo, founded in 1895 by Yen Hsin-hou (or Yen I-pin), Chou Chin-piao, and others. Yen Chung-p'ing notes that Yen Hsin-hou was an expectant taotai, that he apparently was at one time part of Li Hung-chang's entourage, and that he held a brevet third rank (san-p'in hsien). He therefore concludes that the capital of the T'ung-chiu-yuan company was of shih-ta-fu origin. But what was more important about Yen Hsin-hou than his assimilated official rank — although that must certainly have affected his outlook — was his association with numerous other modern, Western-type, industrial undertakings in this period. Yen Hsin-hou was one of the promoters of the Tientsin-Taku railroad in 1883.[60] He operated customs banks (hai-kuan kuan-yin-hao) in several treaty ports whose assets he joined to the Imperial Bank of China when it was organized in 1896. Yen became a director of this bank and the head of its Shanghai office. He was a shareholder and, in 1909, a director of the China Merchants' Company. He was one of the founders of the Ssu-ming Commercial Bank which we have already mentioned in connection with Yü Ho-te. Together with Chang Chien he organized a pottery factory in Kiangsi; and in collaboration with Hsü Jun, the well-known compradore and merchant, he was a founder of the Hua-hsing Insurance Company in Shanghai capitalized at Tls. 1,000,000. Yen also organized flour mills in Kiangsu and at Ningpo; and an oil pressing mill in Kiangsu (with a capital of Tls. 300,000) in association with Chang Chien and others.[61]

This long record of industrial promotion was shared by his fellow provincial Chou Chin-piao, also a founder of the T'ung-chiu-yuan company.[62] The two men came from the area around Ningpo in Chekiang province. Although both had official rank, this seems secondary to their long attention to commercial and industrial matters in the treaty ports. Both, for example, were officials of the Shanghai Chinese Chamber of Commerce (shang-hui) organized in 1902.[63] The initial capital which they put into the T'ung-chiu-yuan mill may well have come from traditional sources; Yen, after all, had been at one time an old-style customs banker. But the record of industrial promotion just cited does not support the conclusion that Yen and Chou were merely "officials and gentry" speculating with funds which normally would have been invested in land or usury. Rather they seem in some degree to have been transformed into industrial entrepreneurs, on however small a scale, in the environment of the treaty port.

V

Bureaucratic Management

In addition to share capital from treaty-port merchants and gentry friends and relatives of the promoters, official funds might also be invested in *kuan-tu shang-pan* enterprises. This was particularly true when a firm was first being established and might take any of several forms. Thus in 1872 Li Hung-chang deposited Tls. 135,000 at interest with the newly organized China Merchants' Steam Navigation Company; these were Chihli provincial military training funds which the governor-general now lent to a modern enterprise in the same manner as they had previously been deposited with old-style pawnbrokers in Kiangsu and Chekiang.[64] The Imperial Telegraph Administration built its first lines in part with government funds which were repaid by deductions from the official telegraph bill.[65] The Hu-pu provided Tls. 1,000,000 of the initial funds of the Imperial Bank of China in 1896.[66] And when Sheng Hsuan-huai took over the Hanyang Ironworks in 1896, he pledged to repay the official funds invested in the plant by means of a levy of one tael on each ton of iron produced.[67]

How official investment might occur even in an entirely *shang-pan* enterprise has been indicated above in connection with Chang Chien and the establishment of the Ta-sheng Cotton Mill.

Despite these examples, it was not so much the investment of official capital that was characteristic of the *kuan-tu shang-pan* industries as it was the official or bureaucratic features of their management and operation. As is shown in the section on "Government Finance" in the next chapter, the Ch'ing government was in no position to make extensive or continuing financial contributions toward the establishment of industry. Such funds as were forthcoming reflected the ability of powerful provincial leaders to extract subventions in support of the enterprises of which they were the patrons, but there was no concerted policy of official investment in industry comparable to that of Meiji Japan.[68] By their patronage, Li Hung-chang, Chang Chih-tung, and Liu K'un-i were performing part of the function of "official supervision" which was called for by the *kuan-tu shang-pan* formula. Their exertions, however, were one step removed from the actual operation of the enterprise, which was left to officials of a lower rank theoretically in conjunction with representatives of the shareholders.

It was at this level of bureaucratic management that the limitations of the *kuan-tu shang-pan* industries were most manifest. The official appointees to the management were often unqualified to operate a business enterprise as anything other than a traditional government *yamen.* And the Chinese official *yamen* was the seat of attitudes and practices which stood in direct contradiction to the requirements of modern industry and commerce. These included the dominance of "particularistic" social values rather than "universalistic" ones, with the result that personal ties such as kinship or common geographical origin tended to be as important considerations as competence or experience in obtaining a place on the management of these enterprises.

There was also the well-known official proclivity for graft or "squeeze." The legal salary of the traditional official was small, and out of it he had to provide not only for himself and his family but also for a body of quasi-officials, secretaries, and retainers who were an indispensable part of his *yamen.* It was an accepted if not a formally sanctioned fact that the incumbent would be able to "squeeze" a larger monetary return out of his post than the official statutes authorized. This tendency was helped along by the circumstance that the official's tenure in a potentially lucrative post, to obtain which he might have made heavy expenditures in gifts and gratuities, was usually strictly limited. By no means were such practices considered "dishonest" so long as they were not carried to extremes. They represented the normal nonrationalized procedures by which official business was carried on in China. But they were inappropriate to modern-type enterprise which demanded a complete rationalization of all activities.

The official *yamen* was also characterized by a willful absence of initiative which contrasts sharply with the enterprising conduct expected from a business executive in the West. This might profitably be traced to the underlying Confucian values or orientations to life, a task which lies beyond the scope of this study. But its immediate cause, at least in part, lay in the doctrine of responsibility which permeated the legal and governmental structure of China. Every official from the emperor down to the lowest local officer was responsible for all happenings within his sphere of competence. At the highest level this was manifested in the long series of penitential edicts through which the rulers of China have declared themselves accountable not only for human disorders, but also for famine, floods, epidemics, and other natural disasters.[69] The local magistrate was likewise accountable for every disorder in his territory. Whatever the cause of a rebellion, for example, he was held responsible for it until he had either suppressed it or had driven it across the border into the territory of his neighbor and thus out of the scope of his own responsibility. In these circumstances the natural tendency was, whenever possible, to refrain from reporting to one's superiors any untoward occurrence; or if it was not possible to keep the matter under cover, to get one's own version of the facts into an official report before one's rivals or enemies could present them in a

less favorable light. The resulting attitude among the majority of officialdom was one of great caution lest they take any action or initiate
any project which departed from traditional practice and the consequences of which could not be clearly foreseen. When this conservatism
was carried over to the management of industry or modern financial
institutions, it stood at a great disadvantage before the initiative and
willingness to take risks which (as is noted in the next chapter) was
so prominent in the Japanese industrialization effort of the Meiji period.

Let us consider the China Merchants' Steam Navigation Company.
H. B. Morse's exasperation with the management is expressed in this
excerpt from a letter written while he was employed by the firm in
1886–1887:

> Ma [Chien-chung, a protégé of Li Hung-chang and one of Sheng Hsuan-
> huai's assistants in the company] would make the best Managing Director
> for the head office. I doubt if his influence is great enough to enable him
> to *tu-pan* and conduct the official business; but he is the only one who has
> any experience in business affairs, and really understands that a steamer
> company is not necessarily conducted on Chinese official lines.[70]

At the height of its prosperity, in the decade before the Sino-Japanese
War of 1894–1895, the director-general (*tu-pan*) of the China Merchants' Company was Sheng Hsuan-huai, who had been appointed to
that post by Li Hung-chang. Sheng was concurrently director-general
of the *kuan-tu shang-pan* Imperial Telegraph Administration and substantive customs taotai first at Chefoo and later at Tientsin. At Shanghai
in charge of day-to-day operations were assistant managers (*hui-pan*)
in varying numbers, but invariably holding official rank and all appointed by Li Hung-chang on Sheng's recommendation. Even the three
merchant directors (*shang-tung*) who were added in 1891, ostensibly
to represent the shareholders, were designated by Li Hung-chang. Until
1910 the company's management was nominally composed of "three
officials and three merchants," but in fact only one of the six was not
an official appointee.

The dominance of the official element even in enterprises in which
much of the capital came from merchants was attacked by a contemporary writer, Wu Tso-ch'ing, in these terms:

> Among the spinning and weaving establishments in China there are some
> which are termed *kuan-pan*, but in fact merchant capital has been invested
> in these. And in the management of those companies which are supposed to
> be *shang-pan*, there are actually officials of many kinds to be found. . . .
> Although the merchant has invested his capital, he is no more than a stranger.
> At the year's end when the profits are distributed, he is entirely dependent
> on the whims of others. He is not even consulted about the expenditures of
> the enterprise nor about the hiring of managers. Although there is a general
> meeting at the close of the year, following the Western example, yet the

merchant shareholders and the management are as far apart as heaven and earth.[71]

It would be erroneous to conclude, however, that the available "merchant" personnel would necessarily have operated the China Merchants' Company or the other enterprises to be examined in the following chapters in a more enlightened manner than the quasi-officials who actually controlled them. They were all party to the same shortcomings which are illustrated in the career of Sheng Hsuan-huai in Chapter 3. Perhaps these were only more egregious in the case of officials of the old style.

Not many enterprises were so favorably situated as the China Merchants' Company, which paid uninterrupted dividends despite the deficiencies of its management. The number of failures among newly established industries was high, and the fact that many of these were largely official undertakings is cited by one writer as proof of the corruption and incompetence of official management.[72] The failure of Chang Chih-tung's *kuan-pan* commercial enterprises at Wuchang and Hanyang stands in contrast to the relative success of the *kuan-tu shang-pan* enterprises sponsored by Li Hung-chang. Thus in 1902 Chang was forced to "lease" a cotton weaving mill, a spinning mill, a silk filature, and a hemp factory (which were the principal divisions of his Hupei Government Spinning Mill [*Hu-pei fang-sha kuan-chü*]) to a syndicate of merchants headed by one Wei Chih-ch'en, a Cantonese tea merchant doing business in Hankow.[73] Earlier, in 1896, Chang had transferred the Hanyang Ironworks to a group of merchants headed by Sheng Hsuan-huai after his efforts to raise further official funds had failed.[74] In general Li's enterprises were more fortunate, although the Yü-chin Spinning Mill, a subsidiary of the Hua-sheng Cotton Mill, failed in 1901 and passed into foreign hands; and the Mo-ho Gold Mine, which was founded in 1889, failed after a few years, came under Russian control, was repurchased by the Ch'ing government in 1901, and failed again.[75] While these examples may indicate that even the small amount of merchant blood to be found in the K'ai-p'ing Coal Mines, the Hua-sheng Cotton Mill, the Telegraph Administration, and the China Merchants' Company was an enviable asset, it should be remembered that the margin between success and failure in any case was a narrow one, given the economic and political context in which these enterprises were undertaken.

The initial unprofitableness of, for example, the foreign textile mills established in Shanghai between 1896 and 1901 has been explained as being chiefly due to "the enormous rise in the price of raw cotton." [76] It may be, however, that some inauspicious business practices were common to Chinese and foreign firms alike in this period — perhaps a product of the baleful influence of treaty-port life. In the pages of the *North-China Herald,* the leading British paper in Shanghai, one can often find correspondence complaining about "company management in the East." For example, the directors of the Indo-China Steam Navigation Company, Ltd. (operated by Jardine, Matheson and Company) were accused of taking £70,000 from the earnings of 1900 to open a "General Reserve Fund" and being "diplomatically vague as to what was going to be done with it." [77] The Shanghai Dock and Engineering Company was attacked for the practice in its accounts of setting off the appreciated value of land ("the supposed appreciation of land is *not realized*") against the depreciation of machinery and installations ("depreciation is a regular working charge which *has taken place* and your costs are misleading if you do not provide for it").[78]

VI

Official Exactions

The *kuan-tu shang-pan* enterprises were always open to demands for funds from one part or another of the official bureaucracy. These exactions constituted a crippling burden on whatever there was of a modern sector in the Chinese economy and stood in sharp contrast to the official subsidization of industry which was a key feature of the economic policy of Meiji Japan. At the top, the imperial court expected to reap the fruits of whatever success the new industries showed. Thus in 1899 no less a personage than a grand secretary, Kang-i, came south to Shanghai to look into the accounts of the China Merchants' Company and the Telegraph Administration in an effort to claim for the imperial coffers what surpluses or reserves had accumulated (see Chapter 2). Such payments often went under the old rubric of *pao-hsiao* or "efforts made to return [the imperial grace]," which had been used earlier for the contributions of the salt merchants.

The levy might also be in the interest of provincial or local officials. As an instance of the former, the establishment of the Chinese Cotton Cloth and Yarn Administration (*Fang-chih chi-ch'a kung-so*) in 1894 may be cited. This was an organ of Li Hung-chang and Sheng Hsuan-huai which for a number of years "continued to levy the royalty of Tls. 1 per bale on the products of the various mills, and also exercised more or less control over all of them, such as passing their materials and products through the Customs, and carrying on all negotiations with the Government or officials in connexion with their operations generally." [79] It had been established to carry on the ten-year monopoly of the manufacture of cotton cloth and yarn which had been granted to Li Hung-chang's Shanghai Cotton Mill before it was destroyed by fire in September 1893 (see Chapter 6). Local exactions may be illustrated by the continued demands made by the Ta-yeh *hsien* government for contributions from the Ta-yeh Iron Mines. At first the excuse was the support of local self-government; later the *hsien* officials gave the support of local police as a pretext. Some Tls. 4,000 was sought annually.[80]

In the absence of any commercial code the shareholders had no legal appeal against these exactions. Their only protection was the power of one official or group of officials who might have a particular interest in the company against the demands of outsiders. Thus the following statement by Tong King-sing, manager of the China Merchants' Company, cannot be taken at face value as implying a clearly defined concept of purely business practice in contrast to the institutionalized inefficiency and "squeeze" of the official *yamen:*

the business of the Company must be entirely and purely commercial. No officials [are] to be appointed, no official clerks or runners to be employed; the custom of making official reports and forwarding accounts for official inspection [is] to be discontinued; nothing but what [is] purely commercial [is] to have a place in the Company's transactions.[81]

Rather it was a warning to all comers that the company was under Li Hung-chang's protection; and Governor-general Li seconded this warning on repeated occasions. His assertion that "the gains and losses of the company are strictly the merchants' affairs, and are not the concern of the government," [82] in reply to indictments of his enterprises by officials in Peking, clearly had this meaning.

In these circumstances it is evident that rather than leave the pickings to the waiting despoilers, the officers of the *kuan-tu shang-pan* enterprises willingly shared the profits among themselves. We have therefore the paradox that the companies were often in financial straits and appealing for official assistance, while the personal wealth of their managers was being constantly augmented.

Presumably the burden of official exactions was less in the case of entirely *shang-pan* enterprises than in the case of those industries in which the government might have a formal claim. There was nevertheless the scheme to introduce a 10 per cent levy on manufactures, which has already been mentioned. This was proposed in July 1896 by the Tsungli Yamen and was to be assessed on all goods manufactured in China, whether by Chinese or foreigners, at the place of manufacture. These goods, whatever their destination, would then be exempt from all *likin* charges.[83] It was explicitly stated to be a measure to raise revenue for the imperial government, and it was designed to counter the decline in import duties which was expected to follow from the institution of foreign manufacturing establishments in the treaty ports. The comment of the *North-China Herald* on this tax is instructive:

The ten per cent excise [on goods manufactured in China] seems to most of us a very great mistake. It is evident to us that the extension of cotton mills and other industries must be of great advantage to China as giving employment to her surplus population and increasing her wealth, but we can understand the difficulty of making Chinese officials realise this. . . . Their vision is limited to the effect of the extension of these industries on the revenue; if 1,000 bales of cotton yarn are manufactured in Shanghai, 1,000 bales less are wanted from India and Japan, and the revenue loses the duty on these 1,000 bales.[84]

As far as foreign manufactures in the Shanghai area and elsewhere were concerned, the proposed 10 per cent excise was of course inoperative unless the treaty powers were to agree to a revision of the commercial treaties, which they did not do.[85] But Chinese manufactured goods, which previously in many cases had been exempted from all but export duty and a 5 per cent tariff if they were shipped into the interior,[86] were ordered to pay the excise. That this order was at least nominally enforced is, I believe, a valid conclusion from the petitions by Chang Chih-tung[87] and Sheng Hsuan-huai[88] in 1896, and by Sheng again in 1901 [89] and 1906 [90] asking that the products of the Hanyang Ironworks be exempted from the 10 per cent levy on the grounds that the smelting of iron differed from the manufacture of consumption goods and that the government itself had an interest in the ironworks, which was a *kuan-tu shang-pan* enterprise.

VII

Restrictive Monopoly Rights

There is no doubt about the sincerity of Li Hung-chang's claim that the mines, textile mill, shipping company, and other enterprises which he sponsored were intended to oppose the steady increase of foreign imports into China and the virtual foreign monopoly of the coastal carrying trade. He suggested that the most efficacious means of withstanding foreign economic pressure would be to have Chinese merchants organize companies which would be supervised by officials and granted concessions or monopoly rights in order to guarantee their success. This was quite explicit in his famous memorial of 1872 in defense of building steamships.[91]

In the same manner that a concession to carry tribute rice was granted to the China Merchants' Company, each of the other early *kuan-tu shang-pan* enterprises received some sort of patent or monopoly intended to protect its position against foreign competition. Thus the Shanghai Cotton Cloth Mill was given a ten-year monopoly for the manufacture of cotton cloth and yarn;[92] the Imperial Telegraph Administration controlled the dispatch and receipt of overseas telegrams, having connections with foreign cables at Shanghai and on the Yunnan and Manchurian borders;[93] and the Hanyang Ironworks was granted a monopoly for the manufacture of rails for the Peking-Hankow and Canton-Hankow railroads.[94]

Monopoly privileges should not, however, be thought of solely as means to support a Chinese firm in the face of severe competition from foreign-owned enterprises in the same line of business which profited from extraterritorial privileges and an artificially low tariff. Like other features of the *kuan-tu shang-pan* pattern — for example, the guaranteed dividend payments already referred to — these privileges were also necessary inducements to attract private capital to the company. The difficulty was that a monopoly which had originally been granted to aid the development of Chinese industry tended to become a monopoly which functioned primarily to protect the interest of those persons who had invested in modern enterprises under the aegis of the principal official promoters. In the last analysis, instead of furthering economic expansion, the monopoly rights granted to *kuan-tu shang-pan* industries acted as a prop for "bureaucratic capital." This situation was relieved in part by two circumstances growing out of the defeat suffered at Japanese hands in 1894–1895. On the one hand, the appearance of foreign-owned firms in the treaty ports undermined the monopoly position of such Chinese enterprises as the Hua-sheng Cotton Mill. On the other hand, the efforts of the Ch'ing government to support industrial development after 1895, however limited and restricted to paper decrees, did result in the establishment of a number of firms outside of the *kuan-tu shang-pan* enterprises which earlier had dominated their respective fields. The importance of monopoly and quasi-monopoly status in the case of the China Merchants' Company and the Hua-sheng Cotton Mill in particular will be examined in detail in later chapters.

To recapitulate, China's industrialization effort in the last four decades of the Ch'ing dynasty did not result in a fundamental transformation of the country's economy. Some insight into the reasons for this failure may be obtained from a study of the way in which such modern-type industries as did take root were organized and operated. In particular, a pattern characterized as "official supervision and merchant management" (*kuan-tu shang-pan*) underlay the entrepreneurial efforts of this period. Five aspects of the *kuan-tu shang-pan* system have been discussed as a preface to a detailed examination of the career of the leading industrial promoter in late Ch'ing China and the enterprises with which he was connected:

1. The close relationship of the *kuan-tu shang-pan* industries to the regional foci of political power which developed after the Taiping Rebellion;

2. The dependence of these enterprises on capital and, to a lesser degree, personnel from the merchants of China's treaty ports;

3. The role of officials and traditional bureaucratic methods in their management, and the corollary deficiency in rationalized business practices;

4. The vulnerability of this modern sector of China's economy to official exactions;

5. The importance of the grant of officially protected monopoly privileges.

Before proceeding to Sheng Hsuan-huai and his enterprises, it seems advisable to consider these characteristics of the *kuan-tu shang-pan* industries in the context of the economic situation of late nineteenth-century China. Although the account is far from exhaustive, some of the causes of the inadequate response of both government and merchants to the challenge of economic modernization are treated in Chapter 2.

2

Economic Conditions in the Late Ch'ing Period

I

Economic Thought

This is a subject which has not been adequately studied. The most recent comprehensive Chinese monograph, which bears the translated title *Economic Thought During the Last Fifty Years of the Ch'ing Period*,[1] would more accurately have been called Proposals for Economic Reform During the Last Fifty Years of the Ch'ing Period. The author, Chao Feng-t'ien, confronts us with a compendium of lengthy excerpts from the memorials and essays of officials and gentry in some degree sympathetic to the idea of modernization and reform. Typically their economic content is relatively undifferentiated from ethical or political formulations. The substance of these writings is a compounding of traditional formulae from the *Chou-li, Kuan-tzu,* and other classical works with ideas drawn from translations of Western books, contact with foreigners in China, and personal observation of Europe and America.[2]

Unfortunately, material illustrating the economic thinking of the more conservative members of the metropolitan and provincial bureaucracy which ruled China[3] has been excluded from Chao's work. The core of the divergence between the dominant conservative outlook and that of the reformers[4] must have lain as much in conflicting interpretations of classical writings as in the relative ignorance of Western experience on the part of the conservatives. Neither variety of Chinese economic thought has been studied by Occidental economists in the light of their more rigorous theory.[5]

The following, then, is perforce limited to a consideration of the reformers and their quasi-economic programs. These are useful, however, not merely because they are accessible. If the thinking of these men was the most advanced of their time, it may be assumed that it was inclusive of the outlook of those who undertook to inaugurate enterprises modeled on the West. Therefore both the insight and the naïveté which they reveal can illuminate the climate of opinion into which the *kuan-tu shang-pan* industries were introduced.

Despite the burden of traditional terminology and probably without being aware of the full significance of their insights, the reform writers as a group were able to point to the most important factors on which the successful economic transformation of China would depend. No one writer was able to combine all these points into a coherent program, nor was there any trace of systematic theorizing. But the sum of their practical suggestions is evidence that the Chinese had at hand some of the same intellectual fuel, though they may not have been able to ignite it, which the Japanese used to propel themselves from an agrarian to an industrial society.

1. *Awareness of the Importance of Adequate Motivation.* Within the limitations of his vocabulary and concepts, Hsueh Fu-ch'eng,[6] who served as China's minister to London and Paris from 1890 to 1894, was certainly touching on the crucial question of motivation in this passage from his discussion of the small success of joint-stock companies in China. Hsueh wrote while in Europe:

> Recently, following on Sino-foreign trade, there have been attempts to imitate the Western method of issuing shares [in order to form companies]. Those efforts which have been successful include the China Merchants' Steam Navigation Company, the Telegraph Administration, the K'ai-p'ing Coal Mine, and the Mo-ho Gold Mine. But compared to foreign companies, they are infinitesimal in size and pitifully weak. . . . Foreign companies are sure of success because their people are determined, the regulations [of the companies] are thorough, prohibitions [against malpractices] are strictly enforced, and their planning is careful. Chinese joint-stock companies have failed because of a lack of determination, confused regulations, lax prohibitions, and careless planning. The reason that we are so far behind the foreigners in these four regards is that the proper spirit has not yet been initiated (*feng-ch'i pu-k'ai*). . . . If the general attitude (*feng-ch'i*) does not change, joint-stock companies will not be successful; if they are not successful, not one line of industrial or commercial enterprise will prosper with the result that China will be unable to become rich, or to become strong.[7]

The traditional phrase *feng-ch'i pu-k'ai,* roughly translatable as "the proper spirit/attitude has not yet been initiated," has been used time and again to "explain" the failure of the populace to respond to some new measure. While it often explains nothing, in the right context it goes to the core of the problem.

It was because the right spirit was in the air that the experience of Meiji Japan differed so much from that of late Ch'ing China. The most recent comprehensive study of the economic development of Japan concludes that "the real drive and momentum lay in large measure outside the realm of national political ambition and State activity." It was to be found in "the exercise of personal initiative and entrepreneurial responsibility in increasingly pervasive fashion, and not merely at the top." [8] In the next chapter, the adverse and limiting effects of his family, local, and bureaucratic roles on the performance of Sheng Hsuan-huai's business role are considered in some detail. Each of these was a powerful bond tying him to traditional values and limiting his motivation and ability to do new things or to deal with old problems in a new way. Hsueh Fu-ch'eng and the others may not have been able to account for the relative absence of the "entrepreneurial spirit" in that combination of Confucian officials and treaty-port compradores who were responsible for the effort that was made to introduce modern industry and commerce into China, yet they were aware that it was missing. This I take to be the most important meaning of the passage by Hsueh cited above.

The same insight into the importance of motivation is found in the writings of the scholarly compradore, Cheng Kuan-ying,[9] although he approached the problem by a different route, through the traditional formula that the root of the trouble lies "merely in the lack of men" (*wu-jen erh*). Cheng wrote:

> Look now, how is it that tiny Japan increasingly is benefiting [from commerce] while China for all its large size repeatedly has been distressed by it? The trouble stems merely from the lack of [competent] men who devote themselves to commercial matters (*shang-wu*). Responsibility for this lies both with the officials above and with the merchants below. . . .
> The officials do not protect the merchants, on the contrary they do them harm by regarding the merchants' wealth in the same way as Ch'in looked at Ch'u's prosperity. Although they fill their private purses, the sources of general wealth (*li-yuan*) are blocked up. This is the evil of those above.
> As for the merchants, there are many who are ignorant and few with knowledge; many who are false and few who are truthful; many divisive men and few who contribute to unity; many followers, but few innovators; many who are dishonest and few who can be trusted; many who look to their own small profits, but few who are guided by the whole situation. . . . Therefore shares are collected [to start companies], but there are losses of capital; joint-stock enterprises are inaugurated, but they fail. This is the evil attributable to those below.[10]

Cheng is dealing in this passage with what he must have seen at first hand as compradore for the English firm of Butterfield and Swire, as founder of China's first cotton mill, as assistant manager of the China Merchants' Company, and as manager of the Hanyang Ironworks. He is acutely aware of the inadaptability of either the Confucian official or the traditional merchant class to the risk-taking, decision-making, innovating entrepreneurial activity which was the basic motor of economic development both in Japan and in Western Europe. In other words, he is describing the absence of adequate motivation or desire for fundamental economic change.

2. *The Need to Develop the Traditional Bases of the Economy.* Because of the striking contrast it offered to pre-Meiji Japan, the foundation of Japanese large-scale industry in the four decades before World War I has received much attention. "But," says Lockwood, "it was the expansion of Japan's basic economy — agriculture and small-scale industry built on traditional foundations — which accounted for most of the growth of national productivity and income during this period." [11] It hardly needs to be stressed that in China, on the contrary, the situation of agriculture remained relatively unchanged from the period of "self-strengthening" down to the recent past. To some degree the reform writers showed an awareness of the importance of agricultural reforms as a basis for the development of commerce and industry. As will be pointed out, however, their insights in this regard were quite limited.

Liang Ch'i-ch'ao,[12] for example, wrote that even in Europe agriculture was more important in the economy than commerce. The trouble with China was that with respect to technique and productivity her agriculture was hopelessly behind Europe and even more behind the United States. Commerce depended on exports, and these in turn called for agricultural development. Therefore Liang urged the opening of new land to cultivation, efforts to increase the yield of the present acreage, and a strong emphasis on agricultural science and education. He concluded:

> China's distress lies only in insufficient attention to agriculture. If she were to emphasize her agriculture, how could she suffer from impoverishment! Of those who today discuss the governing of a country, many advocate strength and few speak of wealth; and of those who do advocate enriching the country, the majority speak of commerce and few speak of agriculture. This is slighting what is basic, without being aware that when one is poor then one is already weak.[13]

The exclusive emphasis on agriculture in Liang's case was to a large degree rhetorical, but the program he offered — cultivation of new land, improvement of agricultural techniques, and the like, with no reference to tenancy, tax, credit, or marketing problems — was typical of the comments of the other reform writers.[14]

It might even be hazarded that only in tone and in the context of their proposals in other areas did the agricultural program of these men differ from the statements of the conservative memorialists who scoffed at industry and commerce and pointed to the promotion of agriculture, sericulture, and water conservancy (*shui-li*) as "the great principle of the ancient sage kings." The following from a memorial presented in October 1896 by the censor Hui-hua may be taken as representative of this latter viewpoint:

From where do the country's necessities come? They come from the people. From where does the populace obtain wealth? They get it from the land. From where does profit (*li*) derive? It derives from natural products. It is the function of industry to manufacture goods [from raw materials], of commerce to circulate them, of ships and railroads to transport them. . . . Even though there are factories, if they are without raw materials, how will they be able to operate? And although there are ships and railroads, without goods what will they transport? . . . Therefore promoting agriculture and sericulture and fostering the production of natural products was the great principle of the ancient sage kings for producing wealth, and today is the true means of nourishing the people to prosperity. . . .[15]

The reformers were able to see far enough to acknowledge that officialdom was as parasitic on the secular development of the traditional economy as it was on the modern sector. They pointed out, for example, that the actual cost of newly opened land was three times the basic cost as a result of "fees" exacted by various officials.[16] But the reformers were not able to go beyond this observation to advocate the removal of the "feudal," antiquarian obstacles to agricultural improvement afforded by *de facto* tax-farming, usurious loan practices, and restricted local markets.

The principal limitation of the agricultural programs of Liang Ch'i-ch'ao and similar writers was to be found in their chief concern with technological considerations to the neglect of the political and economic facts which in the end decided what the outcome for China would be. Chinese agriculture could serve the cause of industrialization only if, as in Japan, the government had the effective power to mobilize the surpluses of agriculture by means of taxation. Moreover, to increase the size of the surpluses it was necessary that the traditional structure of credit and marketing be replaced by one more suitable for the extension of capitalism into agriculture.

3. *The Need to Regain the Domestic Market.* The writers who are being considered here were unanimous in attributing China's economic weakness to the adverse effects of foreign trade as it had developed under the treaty tariff, and to the right to open manufacturing enterprises in the treaty ports granted to foreigners in the Treaty of Shimonoseki. With these advantages Europe, joined later by Japan, had come to dominate China's domestic market for manufactured commodities and had effectively undermined traditional handicraft industry. It was agreed that no return to pre-1842 conditions was possible or desirable. The reform advocate Ch'en Chih declared in 1897, "Can we prohibit the people from using foreign commodities? I say we cannot. Then what can we do? We can promote industry." [17] The only alterna-

tive was to promote industry or, more broadly, *shang-wu,* an inclusive term for mining, manufacture, trade, and transport, so as to regain the domestic market for China's own products.

While the actual extent as well as the mechanism of the impact of foreign manufactured imports on China's native handicraft production still awaits investigation, the apparently striking contrast between the effect of foreign trade on China and Japan is brought out by Lock-wood's summary of the Japanese experience in this regard. "On the whole . . . the destructive impact of imported foreign manufactures seems to have been neither very pronounced, nor very widespread. It was slight compared with the inroads made in later years by Japan's own developing factory industries." [18] The ability of Japan's consumption-goods industries, despite the lack of tariff protection throughout most of the Meiji era, to win a competitive position against foreign goods was one of the pillars on which Japanese economic development was built.

Undoubtedly the reformers' concern to regain China's domestic market to some extent reflected an awareness of the importance of this step for establishing viable manufacturing industries and beginning the transformation of China's economy. Hsueh Fu-ch'eng was explicit in stating that China must follow the Japanese example. Without machine production Chinese goods could not compete with those made in the West either in quality or cheapness. Handicraft industry would be completely destroyed and the entire profit (*li*) would go to the foreigners. Recently Japan had been able to seize some of the Chinese market from the Westerners; could not China do as much? [19] One writer was so optimistic about the future of Chinese goods, which he said would be as good as but cheaper than foreign manufactures, that he looked beyond recapturing the domestic market to ask, "We can't prevent our people from using Western manufactured goods; can they prevent their people from using Chinese goods?" [20]

4. *The Importance of Technology.* A constant theme running through the economic proposals of the reformers was an emphasis on "study" (*hsüeh*), particularly study of Western technology in agriculture, mining, industry, and commerce. All would begin their reform of any specific institution with education, schools, translations. In 1897 K'ang Yu-wei,[21] for example, wrote:

> If we desire today to open the mines that are in the earth, we must first open the mines that are in our minds, the mines that are in our eyes. What are these mines in our minds, in our eyes? They are the opening of mining studies, the translation of mining books. If we do not do so, it is like wanting to enter a room and keeping the door closed.[22]

Study of Western technology was almost a panacea for China's economic backwardness. One writer in 1898 proposed to overcome the lack of trained technical personnel by a grandiose plan to send 2,000 students abroad, forty to fifty in each of the forty main fields of study, for a ten-year period. When the initial 2,000 returned, 2,000 more would be dispatched, and this would be repeated a third time to give a total of 6,000 technicians in thirty years! [23] The problem would not be so easily solved, yet this attention to the importance of acquiring Western technology was not misplaced.

In regard, again, to Japan's experience in her transition to industrialization, the catalytic effect of Western goods and machinery, of foreign travel and study by Japanese nationals, of technical education and foreign advisers is a well-known story. "Fortunately for Japan this was an era in which machinery and technique were made available freely by the advanced industrial nations. . . . Thus the Japanese could tap the most advanced technology of the West wherever it might serve their needs. Within the limits of their buying power they could import capital, producer goods, and technical services in whatever combination they saw fit." [24] Western technology was available to the Chinese as well, but certainly with respect to its quantitative impact, and very likely in regard to the quality of its effect, the contrast with Japan was striking.

In some measure the relatively poor performance of the Chinese must have been due to the strong hold of traditionalism even on the reform writers who were wont to consider the introduction of modern technology in the context of a lamentation for the decay of the ancient "industrial arts" (*kung-i*).[25] Further responsibility must be assigned to the inability of the old order to find a place for even those relatively few in number who acquired technical training in the West or in Japan. The advocacy of technology in isolation, in the absence of an initial generally agreed upon purpose of industrialization, was futile.

5. *The Role of the Government and Officialdom.* Throughout these writings there runs a marked ambivalence as to what role should be assigned to the state in bringing about the desired economic reforms. This attitude is especially noticeable in the work *Sheng-shih wei-yen* (Warnings to a seemingly prosperous age) by Cheng Kuan-ying. On the one hand Cheng was highly critical of the role of officials in commercial and industrial undertakings:

> Moreover, it is my experience that when commercial undertakings are exclusively controlled by officials they rarely produce profits. . . . The profits of the Shanghai Cotton Cloth Mill [26] are very rich, while the Hupei textile mill [27] still is on the point of failure. What is the reason for this difference?

I fear that it is due to nothing else but the officials in charge (*wei-yuan*) [of the Hupei mill] continuing to follow the practices of the official *yamen*. Not only do they not understand commercial matters, but they cannot adapt to circumstances.[28]

Graft and exactions by official managers put Chinese enterprises at a serious disadvantage before their foreign competitors:

In China when a factory is to be established, an official bureau (*chü*) is first set up; it is managed by officials (*kuan-pan*). There is a supervisory officer (*tu*[-*pan*]), and a general manager (*tsung*[-*pan*]); and even more certainly there are assistant managers (*hui-pan*) and secretaries (*t'i-t'iao*), and other officials. The reported annual expenditure is very considerable, while the funds going into their private purses from multifarious malpractices is tremendous. Therefore the goods manufactured are more than half again as expensive as foreign goods, and as a result of inadequate machinery their quality is poor and they are difficult to sell. And so the profits of trade go to the foreigners alone.[29]

On the other hand Cheng came to the conclusion that direct government aid and support of Chinese commerce and industry was a vital necessity. He defined his position as advocating "the use of official authority (*ch'üan*) to compensate for the weakness of the merchants." Rather than official interference in individual enterprises, Cheng called for the government to establish technical schools, invite foreign experts to come to China, grant patent rights, reduce the export tariff and increase the import tariff, and establish regional chambers of commerce. But as most important he stressed the need of government support for the development of manufacturing. The production and export of silk and tea and other native products were inadequate bases for China's economic development. By lending official funds to new enterprises and by reducing the burden of *likin* and other taxation, the government was to promote the domestic manufacture of cotton yarn and cloth, of paper, tobacco, sugar, and wine, and of kerosene, matches, and ceramics. To provide a base for these consumption-goods industries, heavy industry such as coal, copper, and iron mining was to be fostered.[30]

A position similar to that of Cheng Kuan-ying was held by Chang Chien,[31] who expressed the need for active state support for the opening of new land to cultivation. This was to take the form of long-term tax exemptions, reforestation projects, and education. But the actual projects were to be carried out by mercantile joint-stock companies (*kung-ssu*), and by agricultural associations (*nung-hui*) whose establishment Chang proposed.[32]

Cheng, Chang, and the others could appeal to a long tradition of government interference with the economy. We even find an example of two authors using terminology going back at least to the T'ang dynasty (618–907), when they suggest that the government grant mining land to the populace as *yung-yeh*, or "hereditary allotments." [33] They also had before them the experience of Japan in which the Meiji oligarchs were able to carry out just such a program as Cheng Kuan-ying suggested.[34] But in these writings at least they gloss over the decay of the Ch'ing state power, with the result that their estimate of what might in reality be expected from the Chinese government at the end of the nineteenth century is considerably exaggerated.

To sum up this quick survey of reformist economic thought in the last decades of the Ch'ing dynasty: if, in fact, the Chinese merchant and official had been inspired with the same motivation as their Japanese peers, if there had been an agricultural surplus and if it could have been harnessed for the purposes of industrialization, if Chinese home industry had been able to win back the domestic market for manufactured consumption goods so as to obtain a secure base for further growth, if Western technology and organizational forms had been adopted on a scale and at a pace comparable to that of Japan, and if, finally, the Ch'ing government had been able to play a positive part in the realization of the foregoing program — if these five points of the reformers' economic proposals had been realizable, there is no question that the economic development of China would have assumed a far different form than that which is described in this study.

The insights which have been ascribed to the reformers were inadequate in several crucial respects. Most obvious is the fact that as a group these writers were not those who had the position and power to put their proposals into effect. Secondly, while they were in varying degrees aware of each of the key problems discussed above, their awareness was clouded by traditional terminology and naïve conceptions. They were not, after all, considering in retrospect the problem of why China's industry did not develop. To draw together their several insights into a more coherent whole than they themselves did is perhaps justifiable more on heuristic than on strictly historical grounds. In the third place, there were enormous gaps and misconceptions in their writings of which the following are examples: (1) there is no indication that they understood the structure of the traditional economy and the influence of traditional values as they affected the inadequate supply of capital for the new ventures they proposed; (2) they were weakest on the key question of the relation of agriculture to industrialization, showing no awareness of the necessity for forced saving in agriculture as a basis for the initial growth of industry; (3) their understanding of the political situation — that is, the progressive decay of the Ch'ing governmental structure at least from the time of the

Taiping Rebellion — was apparently limited by the closeness of events, for they assigned a major role to the state in the execution of their program.

II

Government Finance

It has been estimated that between 1868 and 1881 the Meiji government transferred over 34 million yen from current agricultural taxation into industrial investment. This amount was only 5½ per cent of the ordinary revenue for the period. But a better idea of its significance emerges from the fact that 34 million yen came to 13 per cent of government expenditure exclusive of the fixed costs of liquidating the Tokugawa regime, and that it amounted to over one third of the total outlay for the army and navy.[35] And "significantly the first [government] bonds issued for public sale, in 1878, were to finance new industrial enterprise."[36] Lockwood's study of the economic development of Japan has, I believe, done a service in correcting the common view that the remaking of Japan as an industrial power was entirely the work of the Meiji state. It nevertheless remains true that, especially in the early period, government effort and assistance were factors of supreme importance.

Moreover, even when the initial phase of direct government participation in the establishment of industrial enterprises had passed, the Meiji state made the largest contribution to the creation of the framework of communications and credit on which the growth of Japanese industry and commerce depended. This section is concerned with the financial inability of the Ch'ing government to follow the Japanese example and contribute directly or indirectly to the economic modernization of China.

Scholars who have examined the fiscal situation of the late Ch'ing period have tended to take the view that although the central government's financial position may have been deteriorating from the beginning of the Kuang-hsü reign (1875), it was only following the Sino-Japanese War of 1894–1895 that huge deficits which the government could not meet began to accumulate. After 1895 the triple pressure of indemnity payments, servicing foreign loans, and military expenditures totally wrecked the rough balance between income and outlay which Peking had maintained until that time.[37] The increase in China's fiscal distress after 1895 is of course true, but unqualified emphasis on this point could lead to such extravagance as the following:

Before the Sino-Japanese War, China's finances were moving toward greater stability. The foreign debt was no more than several hundred thousand taels, and with the growing receipts from the maritime customs and the flourishing of *likin,* the government's finances were able to show an annual surplus. The founding of a navy, the building of railroads, the establishment of shipyards, and the inauguration of telegraph and telephone lines all were new undertakings which were based on the fiscal improvement of this period.[38]

In fact, as Lo Yü-tung has shown,[39] the annual surpluses reported by the Ministry of Revenue (*Hu-pu*)[40] must have been illusory. Throughout the period from 1874 to 1894, the ministry was engaged in a series of largely unsuccessful efforts to raise funds in order to meet a continuing series of crises — the dispute over Ili with Russia, the Sino-French War, floods and famine, and the Sino-Japanese War. For emergencies such as Tso Tsung-t'ang's western expeditions and reconstruction in the northwest the government was forced to depend on foreign borrowing.[41] Before 1894 nine loans totaling Tls. 40,000,000 were made, mostly for defense and immediate needs. These funds came from foreign firms in the treaty ports, not from foreign governments.[42] It is also a fact, however, that some Tls. 33,000,000 had been repaid on these loans before the Sino-Japanese War.[43] This repayment is an indication that the problem was not merely the very real one of the inadequate resources of the Chinese economy as a whole. In large measure the financial straits in which the Peking government found itself were due to the decay of the fiscal institutions by means of which it could command such financial capacity as there was in its empire.

To suppress the Taiping Rebellion (1851–1864), Peking had been forced to grant a large measure of authority to leaders of gentry-official cliques, such as Tseng Kuo-fan and Li Hung-chang, who had organized the only Chinese forces able to contend with the rebels on equal terms. These new military leaders tended to dominate the key posts of governor-general and governor until the end of the century, marking not only a shift of power in the provinces from Manchus to Chinese but also an augmentation of the power and influence of the provincial governors-general and governors as against the imperial government in Peking.[44] These local leaders tended to form regional "bases" or "machines," founded on the military forces they had organized against the Taipings, which were able to drive hard bargains with Peking. The clearest case of this development was that of Li Hung-chang, who with his Huai Army (*Huai-chün*) dominated northeastern China for almost a quarter of a century, until his army and navy were disastrously defeated by the Japanese in 1894.[45]

The Taiping Rebellion was a fiscal as well as a political turning point for the Manchu dynasty. This change was symbolized by the eclipse of the provincial treasurer (*pu-cheng shih*) who had been the official in the provinces responsible to the Hu-pu for the taxes collected by the local magistrates. The new sources of taxation developed originally by the provincial leaders to support their campaigns against the Taipings were under the direct control of the governors-general and governors; only the traditional land and "miscellaneous" taxes continued to be administered by the provincial treasurer.[46] Among the new revenue sources the most important was *likin*, which was first instituted in 1853 in Kiangsu as an internal transit tax on grain passing through the Grand Canal. By 1862 it had been applied to nearly all commodities and had been copied by every province except Yunnan, Heilungchiang, and Formosa. In some cases *likin* had come to be charged not only along the route of transit but also as a production tax at the point of origin and as a kind of sales tax at the destination. The rate varied widely, from 1 to 20 per cent *ad valorem*. The share of this new income that the provinces remitted to Peking was only a fraction of the annual yield, perhaps 20 per cent.[47]

In a typical year in the last two decades of the nineteenth century, Peking's revenue from all sources was probably something like the estimate shown in Table 4.[48] This total does not represent the actual physical

Table 4

Estimated Annual Revenue Reported to Peking

Land tax	Tls. 25,088,000
Grain tribute	6,562,000
Salt gabelle (including salt *likin* of approximately Tls. 7,500,000)	13,659,000
Likin	12,952,000
Maritime customs (1893)	21,989,000
Native customs	1,000,000
Duty and *likin* on native opium	2,229,000
Miscellaneous taxes, sale of office, "contributions," etc.	5,500,000
Total	Tls. 88,979,000

remittance of tax receipts to the capital. It is the amount reported yearly (in two installments) by the provinces to the Ministry of Revenue, which was then stored in money or in kind in the several provincial treasuries to await allocation by the ministry. Eventually one part of the reported total was retained by the province in question to cover local expenses for the ensuing period, a second portion was remitted to Peking (or elsewhere at the direction of the Hu-pu), and in some cases a third part was shipped as grants-in-aid to other provinces.

As already noted in the case of *likin,* the revenue reported annually to Peking was very far from being the same thing as the total tax collection of the empire. This theory was made more flagrantly fictitious by the developments that have just been described as following from the Taiping Rebellion, in particular the growing power of the provincial high officials vis-à-vis the imperial institution and the metropolitan bureaucracy. Whatever the potential fiscal resources of the country, the share which came under the control of the central government was largely inelastic. The quotas due from the land tax and grain tribute had been fixed since the Ch'ien-lung period (1736–1796). *Likin* and the native customs were in fact under the control of the governors-general and governors who were often able to resist demands from the Hu-pu for increased remittances on the plea that Peking was ignorant of the true financial situation in their provinces.[49] The import tariff was fixed by international treaty, leaving only the salt gabelle and miscellaneous minor taxes which could to some extent be manipulated by the central government. H. B. Morse, for example, in a work published in 1908 offers the synthetic figure Tls. 284,154,000 as a grand total of "the amounts presumed to be paid by the taxpayer." [50] Lo Yü-tung notes that according to the provincial *Ts'ai-cheng shuo-ming-shu* (Descriptions of financial administration), which are the reports of Financial Reorganization Bureaus set up by imperial decree in each of the provinces in 1909, the total revenue for 1908 (Kuang-hsü 34) came to more than Tls. 200,000,000 — twice the amount reported to Peking.[51] The discrepancy between the totals suggested by Morse and Lo and the revenue actually reported to the central government represents that part of the financial capacity of the empire which was retained by local and provincial authorities either for legitimate needs or as part of the universal "squeeze" that characterized every financial transaction. Provincial retention of land-tax and *likin* collections made up by far the largest share of this amount; perhaps only 20–25 per cent of the revenue under these heads was reported to the capital.[52]

For the sake of comparison, the Japanese land-tax revision of 1873 should be noted briefly. The Meiji oligarchs in their concern for stable government revenue saw that they must provide a unified system of taxation with a yield which would not fluctuate with the size of the harvest. Their basic scheme was a change from the diverse levies, usually in kind, which had been imposed arbitrarily or by custom by both the *Bakufu* and *han* governments, to a unified money tax under the direct control of the new central government. This tax was fixed at a uniform rate of 3 per cent of the land value, which in turn was assessed at 8.5 times the average annual crop yield. Its collection thus amounted to about 25–30 per cent of the annual crop value. At the outset the new land tax provided 94 per cent of the government's revenue, and it continued to account for over 50 per cent until almost the turn of the century.[53] The key role of land-tax revision in the success of the Meiji reforms is summarized by E. H. Norman:

The revision of the land tax was not a hasty make-shift measure but a reform which occupied the best minds in the government over a long period of time. . . . By providing for a *constant* source of revenue, they [the Meiji oligarchs] were making possible a modern budgetary financial system. In a country still agricultural and lacking tariff autonomy it was natural that the very considerable burden of military expenditures as well as of capital outlay for model industries and the maintenance of a large body of bureaucrats should be made dependent on the land tax, and it was important that this revenue should not fluctuate.[54]

This demonstrated ability of the Meiji government to make the best possible use of the financial resources available to it stands in striking contrast to the difficulties of the Ch'ing government which we have outlined.

If the Ch'ing government was already a sufferer from financial disability before 1895, consider what the effects of the Sino-Japanese War and the Boxer Rebellion must have been. To repay the Russo-French and Anglo-German loans which were contracted in order to meet China's Tls. 230,000,000 indemnity to Japan, the Hu-pu was called upon to produce some Tls. 20,000,000 annually above its prewar outlay. From 1902 payments on the principal and interest of this debt, together with the Boxer indemnity payments, required more than Tls. 42,000,000 annually.[55]

Whence did the funds come? In the case of the Russo-French loan of 1895 and the Anglo-German loan of the following year, payments were made from the maritime customs receipts. The supplementary Anglo-German loan of 1898 was also formally secured by the customs revenue. However, in order to meet the annual payment of Tls. 5,000,000 the Hu-pu was also obliged to pledge revenue from salt and *likin*, six collectorates in the Yangtze basin being placed under the supervision of the Inspectorate of Customs.[56] This is only the beginning of the matter. The important problem is to determine from what sources the Hu-pu was able to raise funds with which to offset the deficit in its regular income resulting from the diversion of customs and *likin* receipts to the service of the foreign debt.

The answer in part lies in the steady increase of China's foreign trade which produced augmented customs and *likin* revenue. In the period 1871–1885, the average annual value of exports and imports together was Tls. 144,000,000. This average jumped 76 per cent, to Tls. 254,000,000, for the years 1885–1898. For 1899–1913 the annual average increased to Tls. 657,000,000.[57] As they bear on the payment of foreign indebtedness, however, these figures must be qualified with the statement that in the same period the decline in the price of silver meant that some of the increased customs revenue was offset by the necessity to pay more taels per gold franc or pound.[58] For the rest, Lo Yü-tung details a whole series of efforts by the Hu-pu to increase the yield from the traditional sources of revenue, but they seem to have produced very uncertain results. Provincial opposition to increased salt prices, to the reduction of salaries and emoluments, to higher tax quotas on native opium, and to increased central control of opium brokers was very strong, with the result that Peking's gains under these categories were small and temporary.[59]

Of some interest was an attempt by the Hu-pu to float a domestic loan at the beginning of 1898. One hundred million taels of *Chao-hsin p'iao*, or "Sincerity Bonds," were to be marketed in Peking and the provinces. The bonds paid 5 per cent per annum and were redeemable in twenty years.[60] This attempt at modern financing was unable to escape the fate of assimilation to the traditional practices of Ch'ing finance. In January 1899 an imperial edict stated:

Owing to the many cases of extortion complained of, arising from dishonest officials compelling people to subscribe to *Chao Hsin* Bonds we commanded that, with the exception of officials in the provinces and wealthy merchants and gentry who had already subscribed and paid for the said Bonds, no more canvassing was to be made among the gentry, traders, and masses, nor was payment to be forced from those who had subscribed but were unable to meet their obligations. In fact it was our intention to put a stop to any further sale of *Chao Hsin* Bonds. . . . Now we again issue this command to all. . . .[61]

Probably no more than Tls. 10,000,000 of the bonds were sold.[62]

Yet, for the payment of the Boxer indemnity, and in one other very different case which will be discussed later, the Peking government was

Table 5

Sources of Boxer Indemnity Payments, 1902–1910

	Maritime customs	Provincial assessments	Hu-pu (Ministry of Revenue)	Total
Tls.	33,000,000	164,000,000	27,000,000	225,000,000
Per cent	16	72	12	100

able to compel the provinces to contribute very large sums above their customary quotas. Table 5 gives a breakdown of the sources of the payments that were made on the Boxer indemnity for the nine years 1902–1910.[63] Perhaps two thirds of the Tls. 33,000,000 obtained from customs receipts could be attributed to increased collections following from the 1902 tariff revision; the remainder for the most part came from the receipts of the native customs stations within fifty *li* of each treaty port which had been placed under the Inspectorate of Customs by the Boxer Protocol.[64] The Hu-pu's annual contribution of Tls. 3,000,000 (Tls. 27,000,000 for the nine years) was obtained by ceasing payments to certain old-style military units and by "temporarily" ending rice grants to Manchu and Chinese officials and to the Eight Banners.[65] But the truly remarkable fact is that Peking was able to extract more than Tls. 18,000,000 annually (Tls. 164,000,000 for the nine years) from the provinces.

How was this done? We know that the provinces protested very strongly against the schedule of payments which the Hu-pu drew up for them. Five governors-general and eleven governors joined in a telegram to Peking in which they beseeched the "Imperial favor . . . that the throne permit the indemnity payments due from the provinces to be reduced by 30 per cent." [66] But with the backing of Prince Ch'ing (I-k'uang), who had conducted the Boxer peace negotiations together with Li Hung-chang and had continued in charge of liaison with the foreign powers, the court stuck to its original position and ordered full payment of the assessments.[67] The intervention of Prince Ch'ing supports the conclusion that the major threat which the court held over the provinces in order to force compliance with its demands for funds was that of possible foreign intervention if the Boxer payments were not met. While previous demands for funds had been more in the manner of negotiations, with the local authorities able to resist with some success, in this instance the central government was able to take a firmer stand. Provincial payments had to be deposited monthly in Shanghai, and there was no room allowed for bickering as to the amount.[68] With one minor exception, the payments were made on schedule and in full.[69]

Whence came these provincial funds — the annual quotas ranged from Tls. 2,500,000 each for Kiangsu and Szechwan to Tls. 200,000 for Kweichow? The chief sources were the land tax, an increase in the price of salt, and *likin*. That is, the provinces were required to remit funds under these categories in addition to their regular quotas as shown in Table 4 above.[70] It is not clear to what extent this was accomplished by heavier taxation on the populace rather than by a diversion of Tls. 18,000,000 annually in existing revenues which had previously been outside of the control of the Peking government.[71]

The fact that such a large sum could be raised, albeit in the very special circumstances of the occupation of North China by the Allied armies, invites comparison with the felicitous results to Japan of the 1873 land-tax revision. In a sense the Tls. 164,000,000 which the provinces paid regularly and in full over a nine-year period, and in addition to the customary taxation which they reported each year to Peking, was parallel to the increased resources which the Meiji government was able to command after it had reformed and centralized the land tax. Of course the differences were profound. In China the arrangements were makeshift and assimilated to the traditional fiscal structure; in Japan, the new revenue of the central government was the result of a conscious act of policy which had "occupied the best minds in the government over a long period of times." Of even greater immediate significance was the disparity in the uses to which these resources were put: for a modern army and the beginnings of modern industry in Japan; for the totally nonproductive payment of indemnities to foreign powers by China. To state the matter in its darkest terms, the effect of the Tls. 164,000,000 in question was actually negatively productive inasmuch as these payments were a net loss to China's total available resources.

This comparison is not meant to imply that the economy of nineteenth-century China was potentially able to provide either the capital or the technology for rapid and extensive economic changes. But within the limits of what might have been done in the given circumstances, the question must be posed: if the Ch'ing government could exert enough pressure to force the provinces to remit the large sums that were required for the Boxer payments, why could it not act likewise to mobilize funds in order to carry out a program of military reform and pioneer industrialization? Among the impediments to such action was the decline of the effective power of the central government, which has already been noted. But this, after all, was only relative so long as the imperial system survived. The obstacles are made clearer by a second instance of successful money-raising. This was the "mission" of the grand secretary Kang-i.

In June 1899 Kang-i, later infamous as a sponsor of the Boxers, left Peking for a tour of the southern provinces with the purpose, according to the Peking correspondent of the *North-China Herald,* of raising Tls. 2,000,000 "to aid in filling up the Imperial Treasury." [72] The grand secretary's attention was first directed to the *likin* collections, the salt gabelle, and the offices of the China Merchants' Company and Imperial Telegraph Administration in Shanghai. In all, he extracted some Tls. 1,200,000 from Kiangsu province[73] before turning his attention to Kwangtung, where his reorganization of the *likin* collection was nominally to have produced Tls. 1,600,000 annually for the empress dowager's coffers.[74]

Contemporary opinion in the treaty ports was uncertain as to the meaning of Kang-i's mission. Did his successful extraction of large sums from the provinces indicate that Tz'u-hsi and the Manchu conservatives had finally realized that "reform" was necessary, and were therefore seeking to centralize China's finances in an effort to make up the Tls. 20,000,000 annual deficit in Peking? Or was it that the empress dowager and her followers were seeking funds for their private purposes and to strengthen themselves against the reform party? [75] This uncertainty is resolved when we consider that the leading victims of Kang-i's money-raising trip were the China Merchants' Steam Navigation Company and the Imperial Telegraph Administration. These enterprises and a handful of others represented whatever there was of a modern sector in the Chinese economy, that sector which, in contrast to the crippling burden imposed by Chinese officialdom, the Meiji leaders were doing their utmost to foster in Japan. Despite Sheng Hsuan-huai's warning to the court that the Hanyang Ironworks, the P'ing-hsiang Coal Mines, the Hua-sheng Cotton Mill, and other modern enterprises which he headed were dependent on the China Merchants' Company and the Telegraph Administration, Kang-i forced Sheng to pledge at least Tls. 100,000 annually from these two companies as a "contribution" to the imperial treasury.[76] Almost simultaneously, another grand secretary, Hsü T'ung, was proposing that the liquid assets of the China Merchants' Company, the Telegraph Administration, and the K'ai-p'ing Coal Mines be appropriated by the court on the grounds that they represented surpluses which should have been used "for the benefit of the government." [77]

Thus even if the central government had been able to improve its financial position, it is unlikely that it was ideologically able to support an extensive program of economic modernization. Such enterprises as those that were the victims of Kang-i's mission were conceived of by the dominant political power as one more source of funds, analogous to additional *likin* stations or a higher price for salt. They were fiscal units always open to official exactions, rather than prototypes of a new and sought-for economic order. The vision necessary to carry out a fundamental transformation of society was all too absent in Peking as compared with Tokyo.

III

Trade and Commerce

Much of the discussion of the enormous contrast between the experience of China and Japan has centered on the alleged strategic differences in the role of the merchant in these two countries. For example, the relatively "open" class structure of China is contrasted with the "closed" class structure of Japan. The former allowed the wealthy merchant or his sons to rise into the gentry class by the purchase of land and rank or by competition in the civil service examinations. In Japan the merchant was forced to maintain his mercantile identity and, like the French bourgeoisie of 1789, became anxious to overthrow the Tokugawa feudal regime.[78] The fact is, however, that a fundamental characteristic of the traditional merchant class in both Ch'ing China and Tokugawa Japan was its close and even parasitic relationship to the agrarian economy and indirectly to the conservative political structure.

In Japan, it is true that the *daimyō* and *samurai*, with the growth of a money economy in the Tokugawa period, became increasingly dependent on a merchant class to convert their feudal rice incomes into money. This is seen in the commercial relations which developed between the *samurai* and a class of rice brokers, the *fudasashi*, and in the growing importance of the *kuramoto*, the financial agents of the *daimyō* in Edo and Osaka.[79] There were many instances in which the wealthier merchants became tied to *samurai* families by marriage or adoption. But the important fact to note for the present discussion is that the point at which the wealth and influence of these merchants was growing was precisely that point at which the *samurai* and *daimyō* were articulated to the Tokugawa feudal system. It was only after the Meiji government had replaced the collection of rice in kind by a uniform money tax, and had carried out the compulsory commutation of the *daimyō* and *samurai* pensions with which it had initially replaced their rice revenues, that the way was cleared for economic development in the direction of industrialization. These measures in fact must have had an untoward effect on the *chōnin* (the term generally applied to the merchant class during the Tokugawa period) who had been the commercial agents and the creditors of the feudal classes.

In the light of Japan's actual success in transforming her economy, these observations point, at least tentatively, to the conclusion that what was important in the situation of late Tokugawa Japan was not only the position occupied by the merchant class, but also the actual degree to which the economy had become commercialized. This subject still awaits adequate comparative study. But might it not have been the case that, despite the weakness and vulnerability of the merchant's position, the industrialization process of the Meiji period was facilitated by the prior development of a market orientation considerably in excess of that present in late Ch'ing China? [80]

In traditional China the merchant was simultaneously devalued and needed. The low valuation of mercantile activity was in part a reflection of the role of commerce in an agricultural society in which the dominant values were those of the Confucian gentry-official. In essence it was the lack of development of the market — the inability of the peasant producers to effect an exchange of their products on any more than a parochial scale — which enabled the merchant to realize substantial profits. By taking advantage of local variations in market price to buy rice where it was cheap and to sell it dearly in areas of local famine, he drained from the peasant the surplus above the minimum needed for survival. At the same time the merchant was competing for that surplus with the gentry-landlord, and with the entire official bureaucratic structure which was ultimately supported by taxation and multiple customary exactions on the total agricultural product. It followed that in the dominant ideology the merchant was seen as essentially parasitic on the two classes accorded the highest positions in the traditional rank-order of gentry-official, peasant, craftsman, merchant (*shih, nung, kung, shang*).

On the other hand, even in an underdeveloped economy, there were essential exchange operations, public and private, for which the merchant was indispensable. For example, despite the low prestige of business enterprise and the prohibitions against officials taking part in it, clandestine business relations between members of the bureaucracy and merchant associates in such fields as overseas trade and rice transport seem to have been a persisting practice.[81] And, of course, the prevailing monetary system was dependent on the arbitrage of middlemen. We might also suggest that the traditional merchant — in addition to the commercial transactions of the kind already noted — functioned as part of a vast decentralized system akin to tax-farming which characterized the financial structure of early modern China. How pervasive this institution was is revealed by recent studies of the *ya-hang* (brokers) system, the country-wide practice of licensing brokers by local officials to collect commercial and market taxes in the many hundred market centers of China.[82]

The ties between the government bureaucracy and commercial enterprises are seen most clearly in the salt administration, perhaps the largest single economic enterprise in Ch'ing China. For example, in the lower Yangtze provinces (the Liang-Huai salt district, which was the most important of eleven in eighteenth-century China) the production of salt was dominated by some thirty "factory merchants" (*ch'ang-shang*) who owed their positions to government recognition. Distribution and sales were farmed out to an equal number of "transport merchants" (*yün-shang*) who had been able to pay the salt gabelle in advance and who received monopoly rights in designated areas. These large merchants and hundreds of smaller ones were part of an elaborate tax-farming institution which produced rich profits for themselves as well as revenue and "squeeze" for the court and the metropolitan and provincial bureaucracy. The annual aggregate profits of the transport and factory merchants of the Liang-Huai salt district alone have been estimated at between six and seven million taels (equal at the very least to the equivalent number of dollars).[83] But despite the large capital involved in salt production and storage and the substantial profits that were realized, the salt merchants developed no distinctive bourgeois consciousness which would have set them apart from the traditional social structure. They definitely shared in the dominant values of the old order, and were not opposed to it even under the burden of official exactions which amounted to nearly Tls. 40,000,000 to the imperial treasury alone between 1738 and 1804. Their adherence to Confucian values, which include the subordination of purely economic motivation to considerations of kinship and status, is evident from the efforts of successful merchants to rise into the gentry class by putting their profits into land, purchasing official rank, and cultivating literature and art.

The obligation to assist less fortunate members of one's clan and the absence of primogeniture were further factors making for what in an economic sense was the dissipation of accumulated mercantile capital.[84] Above all, the existence of monopoly profits depended on the continuation of the traditional fiscal system of the Ch'ing state and thus on the whole complex of conservative institutions of which these refractory finances were but one aspect. The traditional merchant, of whom the salt monopolist was a prime example, was as unable as the majority of the bureaucracy to play a positive part in developing China's economy. As one final consideration, it might be observed that their accumulations of capital were, after all, large only by the standards of an agrarian economy. The requirements of modern industry and communications could never have been met out of the proceeds of the salt gabelle even if those profits had been collected for that purpose.

If such was the inability of the traditional Chinese merchant, what of the new class of merchants, the "compradores" (*mai-pan*), who were a product of the development of commerce in the treaty ports after the Treaty of Nanking? Or, more broadly, if Chinese domestic commerce and trade were irrevocably linked to the old order, could more be expected from foreign commerce, which Lockwood has described as having had such a marvelous effect in Japan?

For Japan herself foreign commerce proved to be the key unlocking the door of economic opportunity. Initially it provided a highway over which new impulses and a new technology came to revolutionize much of her economic life. Later it enabled her to draw increasingly on the world's industrial resources to compensate for her own basic deficiencies. As a result she came to acquire a degree of dependence on the world economy exceeded by that of few other nations in modern times.[85]

As I have shown in the first chapter, to some extent the *kuan-tu shang-pan* system was designed to tap "compradore capital," the accumulation of funds by Chinese merchants from foreign trade and its ancillary services in the treaty ports, first as employees of Western firms and later on their own account. Several former compradores, including Tong King-sing, Hsü Jun, and Cheng Kuan-ying, whose participation in the enterprises most closely associated with Sheng Hsuan-huai will be examined in the following chapters, played major roles in the earliest industrial undertakings. But these men, despite their participation in foreign trade, their residence in the treaty ports, and their association with foreigners, were never wholly free of the past. They were, in the first place, assimilated to the traditional official system, holding official rank and usually the title of expectant taotai. When Hsü Jun, for example, was cashiered in 1884 for misappropriation of China Merchants' Company funds, he held a "brevet rank of the second grade" and was an "expectant taotai in Chekiang." [86] Hsü was greatly concerned to regain Li Hung-chang's favor, and finally in 1890, after he had repaid his defalcations in full, Li memorialized requesting that Hsü receive "the button of the third class" and be restored to the position of expectant taotai.[87] Tong and Cheng of course also were expectant taotais.

Secondly, even those treaty-port merchants who also had a hand in modern industrial or financial enterprises were not exclusively occupied with such undertakings. Hsü Jun, while assistant manager and a large shareholder in the China Merchants' Company and an official of the K'ai-p'ing Coal Mines, made a fortune in real estate and the tea trade, more traditional objects of investment and speculation.[88] When the Imperial Bank of China was opened in 1897, its first directors were leading merchants of Shanghai, including Yen Hsin-hou, originally of Chekiang and an expectant taotai. Yen operated "customs banks" (*hai-kuan kuan-yin-hao*)[89] in Canton, Foochow, Shanghai, Hankow, and other treaty ports which he agreed to join to the modern-style bank that Sheng Hsuan-huai was inaugurating.[90] The first Chinese manager of the new bank was Hsieh Lun-hui, who had operated an old-style "money banking shop" (*ch'ien-chuang*)[91] in Shanghai.[92] Although Yen, at least, in the next decade was the promoter of several industrial enterprises in Ningpo and in Kiangsu (see Chapter 1), it is hardly likely that the operations of the Imperial Bank escaped being influenced by the traditional background of its directors. This was the case, notwithstanding its regulations, which were patterned after the British-operated Hong Kong and Shanghai Banking Corporation. If men like Yen Hsin-hou and Hsieh Lun-hui who were willing to back a modern-type bank were themselves tinged with the old, many more refused the challenge of the new entirely. The example of Hu Kuang-yung, the silk merchant and customs banker who was instrumental in arranging China's earliest foreign loans,[93] is a good one in this connection. He turned down Li Hung-chang's invitation in 1873 to participate in the financing and management of the

China Merchants' Steam Navigation Company, which was being organized at that time.[94]

Further, the inducement was small for those merchants who had accumulated funds from the export of tea and silk, the distribution of foreign imports, or from customs banking and the like to put their wealth into textile mills, shipping, or mines. On the one hand they were attracted by the prestige (and relative safety from official exactions) of owning land. The tendency for merchants to purchase land and fuse with the local gentry is implicit in the ubiquitous reference to the "gentry and merchants" (*shen-shang*) of such and such a locality in late nineteenth-century documents.[95] Possibly in the chambers of commerce (*shang-hui*), such as that established in Shanghai by Sheng Hsuan-huai,[96] the local merchants and gentry may have had a meeting place. On the other hand high returns could be realized from investing in usury, native banks, and pawnshops. The guaranteed interest (*kuan-li*) on shares in the China Merchants' Company and in the Hua-sheng Cotton Mill seems high at 8 or 10 per cent, but even this amount could not compete with the 20–50 per cent per annum which could be earned by traditional-type investments.[97]

As to the effect of foreign commerce, more broadly considered, it may be argued that what took place in the treaty ports of the China coast differed qualitatively as well as quantitatively from developments in Japan. In fact, before the Sino-Japanese War the disparity between the degree of modern economic development in these two countries was not yet flagrant. Take the specific case of the import of machinery. For the years 1889–1893, Japanese imports of machinery, instruments, and vehicles totaled about 6,000,000 yen.[98] In these five years China's machinery imports were valued at Tls. 3,181,000,[99] approximately the same value as the Japanese total if we take one tael as equal to two yen during this period. Skirting the issue of the significance of the large per capita differences hidden by these totals, it is enough for the present discussion to point out that until nearly the end of the century the absolute amount of capital goods imported was a secondary consideration in accounting for the difference between Chinese and Japanese experience.

In homely terms, the situation in China was one of having led the horse to water but being unable to make him drink it. Foreign commerce, as in the case of Japan, was a highway for the introduction of modern science, machine technology, and Western forms of business organization: in the treaty ports and foreign concessions enterprising Chinese merchants or officials would have had ample access to Western experience.[100] In those exceptional cases when the horse did drink, he apparently did so in some style. A commercial mission of the Blackburn Chamber of Commerce which toured China in 1896–1897 reported that the equipment of the few Chinese-owned cotton mills which they had visited was "as complete in every respect as the most modern of our English factories, and no expense has been spared in buying machinery and appliances of the latest and most approved designs." [101] The Chinese were producing iron and steel at Hanyang with modern equipment purchased in Europe by Chang Chih-tung two years before the Japanese government began its iron and steel works at Yawata in 1896 — a fact about which Chang and Sheng Hsuan-huai were not slow to boast.[102] These instances are evidence at least of the accessibility of modern technology, but there were few takers.

Nor does it appear that the privileged status of foreigners and the treaty tariff were differentiating factors of any importance, for these were not abrogated in Japan until 1899. And although the trend was toward eliminating or reducing the role of the foreigner, it has been estimated that even in 1887 nearly 90 per cent of Japanese foreign trade was handled by foreign merchants. This proportion fell to 80 per cent in 1890, but was still more than 60 per cent in 1900.[103] While corresponding figures for late nineteenth-century China would show the foreigner in a larger and undiminishing role, before 1895 the difference was not yet so prominent.

The essential qualitative distinction between the effects of foreign commerce on China and Japan was, as Lockwood has put it, that Japanese foreign trade was an "activator of change." [104] That is, in addition to providing the means for the importation of technology from the advanced industrial nations, it supplied a motive or an impulse for new investment of the modern type. The development of the foreign market for Japanese exports hastened the growth of industry by making possible large-scale production and its attendant economies even with an initially limited domestic market. Why was this possible for Japan and not for China? For an explanation we turn again to the shadowy but crucial question of motivation, and then to the myth of the unlimited Chinese market.

Japanese aggressiveness and resourcefulness in foreign trade and the active part played by the Japanese government are described by Englishmen from Lancashire who were in China in 1896:

This conduct in business is well illustrated by Japan's action in regard to Shashih [Shasi], a Yangtsze city, made a Treaty Port by the Shimonoseki Treaty. Here the Japanese have secured premises which have already been converted into a Trade Museum, where are shown articles suitable to Chinese wants, particularly textiles. To all samples are attached full particulars, and on these the persons in attendance are prepared to quote and book orders.

The Museum is under the auspices of the Japanese Government, and is directly controlled by their Consul, already established in buildings acquired for the purposes of a Consulate.

In strong contrast to this is the fact that at this time an English Consul had been assigned to the port, but had not taken up residence there, our "Consulate" being a large Chinese house boat, moored to the city shore of the river! [105]

These are manifestations of the forces of modernization and growth set in motion after the Meiji Restoration. Foreign commerce could function as an "activator of change" only within a situation in which the government and mercantile classes were prepared to utilize it actively for certain generally accepted national goals. If, as in the case of China, international trade was largely a means wherewith the powers were acting upon China rather than a conscious instrument in the hands of an "enlightened" ruling class, it could not contribute greatly to modernization. These remarks have particular reference to the period before 1899 when both China and Japan were still burdened with a conventional 5 per cent tariff imposed by international treaty, and may be illustrated by the fate of traditional-type exports in the two countries.

Although by 1900 cotton yarn and piece goods and silk fabric accounted for 22 per cent of Japanese exports, indicating that industrialization was beginning to make considerable headway, down to the end of the century traditional-type exports occupied the first place in Japan as well as in China. For China exports of tea and silk were 92 per cent of the total in 1871, dropped to about 80 per cent during the 1880's, and were approximately 50 per cent in 1898.[106] In Japan raw silk was responsible for roughly two thirds of the total exports in the period 1868–1893. Even in 1908 raw-silk exports were nearly double the value of manufactured cotton and silk exports.[107] Raw silk then was a key commodity, the sale of which abroad provided a large portion of the foreign exchange in China and Japan. But Japan was rapidly gaining on China as a supplier of silk: in 1905 each provided one third of the world's supply, by 1913 Japan was well ahead, with 44.3 per cent to China's 31.1 per cent.[108] China lost her leading position as a supplier of silk because of the elephantine conservatism of her traditional peasant producers and merchanting bodies. International trade demanded a better product and a standardized one, which could be achieved only if large-scale centralized organization were introduced from outside the peasant economy to superintend cocoon production and silk reeling. In Japan this organization was provided by the government and the large mercantile houses, such as the Mitsui Bussan Kaisha, through the licensing of egg suppliers, improvement of the methods of the silk raisers, operation of modern filatures, and large-scale marketing of the silk.[109] But in China there was neither a government actively concerned with promoting modernization of the economy nor merchants willing or capable of revolutionizing production and marketing practices. There was little of that intense activity which we have noted of the Japanese in Shasi, apparently little motivation to cope with the challenge of Japanese competition.

Aggravating the inadequacies of the Chinese themselves was the greater political and economic pressure of the foreign powers on China than on Japan. This, I submit, was in large part a function of the myth of the Chinese market. Japan's economic development owed a great debt to the existence of opportunities for the profitable export of Japanese manufactured goods. The principal markets for these were in China and southeast Asia. China, however, would have to depend entirely on the demand of its domestic market to take up the products of its infant industries. But the foreign powers, including Japan, were themselves very much concerned about the potentialities of the Chinese home market. This is a theme extending back to Lord Macartney's embassy of 1793 and continuing through the nineteenth century down to the present time. The lure of "400 million customers" was a potent one, however illusory it might have been in fact.[110] Perhaps a factor contributing to Japan's ability to free herself from the unequal treaties and protect her sovereignty and economy from foreign incursions was the relative neglect by the European powers of what seemed a small prize beside the imagined fruits of the China trade. As late as 1897, these were described in such glowing terms as the following:

China's trade possibilities are immeasurable. The sparing use and non-presence of foreign commodities are warrant enough of future expansion if a policy could be adopted which shall open up the entire country to the advantages of unrestricted commercial intercourse. . . .[111]

Strenuous foreign efforts to promote the sale of their manufactures in the interior of China, combined with the right to undertake manufacturing in the treaty ports — employing relatively cheap Chinese labor and without the expense of transporting goods from Europe or Japan, made deep inroads into the limited Chinese domestic market. The gap left by the breakdown of handicraft production, which should have been the basis for the growth of China's own infant industries, in large measure was filled with the products of European factories.

Thus China's political and psychological inability to adapt her traditional peasant economy to the demands of international trade was coupled with economic pressure from the European powers to reduce greatly the positive effect that commerce had in China as compared with the case of Japan.

It was out of these conditions that the system of official supervision and merchant management developed. The economic outlook of his contemporaries, the fiscal weakness of the Peking government, and the structure of Chinese trade and commerce constituted the environment within which Sheng Hsuan-huai, the leading promoter of *kuan-tu shang-pan* industry, operated. Together with the facts of Sheng's personal life and public career, which will now be examined, these factors helped determine the form of organization and the manner of operation of the enterprises to be discussed in the succeeding chapters.

3

Sheng Hsuan-huai (1844–1916): Official and Industrialist

The late Professor Joseph Schumpeter has used the words "entrepreneurial function" to refer to the risk-taking, decision-making, innovating activity which he has characterized as the basic motor of economic development in Western Europe.[1] Analytically the entrepreneurial function may be performed by an individual, by a corporate group, by the state itself, or by any combination of these. The distinctive characteristic of the entrepreneur is the "doing of new things or the doing of things that are already being done in a new way."[2] Thus there is a good deal of evidence that the Industrial Revolution in Europe was accomplished by newly self-made men and at the expense of the merchant capitalists who had been entrenched since the sixteenth century behind the mercantilist regulation of the state.[3] In Japan, a "creative response" to both the intrusion of the Occident and the internal changes of the Meiji Restoration was characteristic of the economic activities of many ex-samurai, small industrialists or traders, and farmers. This response led to the real economic growth of Japan within the framework of communications and credit largely created by the Meiji state.[4] In particular the major role of declassed samurai in Japan's early industrialization has been well substantiated.[5] The task of introducing economic enterprise of a Western type into nineteenth-century China, in so far as it was attempted, fell to a combination of the Confucian official and the treaty-port businessman, with a resultant compounding of the shortcomings of each.

In the preceding chapters, inadequate motivation or desire for economic change has been referred to several times as a primary deterrent to the success of the kuan-tu shang-pan industries. This chapter will examine in detail the career of one man, Sheng Hsuan-huai, who both as an official and an industrialist played a signal part in the establishment and operation of some of the most important of the enterprises mentioned in Chapter 1. A study of Sheng's life should help, in part at least, to account for the relative absence of the entrepreneurial spirit among those men who led the industrialization effort of late Ch'ing China.

I

The Career of Sheng Hsuan-huai

The principal source for Sheng's life is a biography by his sons and grandson written in the traditional style and printed in the prefatory volume of Sheng's collected works.[6] Since Sheng lived to 1916, he has no biography in Dr. Hummel's *Eminent Chinese of the Ch'ing Period,* which excludes all persons who survived the end of the dynasty. The *Hsing-shu,* as the work by Sheng's sons is called, must, however, be taken with some caution: first, because his filial descendants often tend to exaggerate the part played by their ancestor in the events which made up his career. It seems, for example, that Sheng's role in initiating the China Merchants' Steam Navigation Company is enlarged beyond its true proportion in the *Hsing-shu.*

A second and more important deficiency of this family biography is that it contains almost no information about Sheng's private financial and managerial activities. While there is considerable detail regarding his conduct of negotiations for tariff revision in 1902, nothing is told of the affairs of the Hua-sheng Cotton Mill or of the financial relations of the Han-Yeh-P'ing Coal and Iron Company with the Japanese. The reasons for this omission are not hard to find: it need only be said that such matters found no place in the traditional style of biography, that the prestige assigned to even a minor official post far exceeded that of any mercantile or industrial activity, however extensive. I stress this point because it epitomizes the difficulty of gaining recognition faced by any potential industrial promoter even at the end of the Ch'ing period.

For the years down to 1895, Sheng's industrial activities can be traced in the numerous references to him which occur in the collected papers of Li Hung-chang.[7] From 1896 to the end of the dynasty, Sheng's own memorials and telegrams and those of Chang Chih-tung[8] are the principal sources, to be supplemented by other official and nonofficial contemporary materials.

1. *Early Life and Entrance into Li Hung-chang's Entourage.* Sheng Hsuan-huai was born on November 4, 1844, in Wu-chin-hsien, Ch'ang-chou-fu, in the province of Kiangsu, about 150 miles inland from Shanghai. He was born in the same year in which his father, Sheng K'ang (1814–1902), received the *chin-shih* degree.[9] Sheng K'ang was the second of four sons, all of whom were minor provincial officials. Their

father, Sheng Lung (d. 1867), had been a *chü-jen* of 1810 who served as a department magistrate (*chih-chou*) in Chekiang.[10] Sheng Hsuan-huai thus came from a family of gentry and officials which, although it could claim no national eminence, was prominent in its native Ch'ang-chou.

Sheng K'ang[11] took an active part in the campaign against the Taiping rebels. For four years he participated in the unsuccessful siege of Nanking, the Taiping capital, as a member of General Hsiang Jung's[12] "Great Camp of Kiangnan" (*Chiang-nan ta-ying*). Then in 1856 he returned to Ch'ang-chou and organized a local militia as other gentry leaders were doing under the inspiration of Tseng Kuo-fan and his Hunan Army (*Hsiang-chün*).[13] In 1858 Sheng K'ang entered the service of Hu Lin-i,[14] Tseng Kuo-fan's principal lieutenant, and was given charge of the Hupei "Tax and *Likin* Bureau" (*ya-li tsung-chü*), that is, of the agency for collecting the newly instituted *likin*, or transit tax, which financed Hu's military efforts against the Taipings. Hu Lin-i died in September 1861 after the capture of Anking, and his successor as governor of Hupei, Yen Shu-shen,[15] appointed Sheng K'ang to be Wuchang salt taotai, a post in which he had charge of the Hupei division of the lucrative Liang-Huai salt district.[16]

After his retirement in 1867 to fulfill the mourning obligations for his father, Sheng K'ang held no other substantive posts. But in recognition of his contributions to flood and famine relief in Chihli in 1871, he was made a brevet provincial treasurer (*pu-cheng shih*) on the recommendation of Governor-general Li Hung-chang. He received additional honors in later years, apparently as a result of Sheng Hsuan-huai's close association with Li. Thus in 1881, Sheng K'ang was received in imperial audience, made a taotai for Chekiang, and recorded to fill the next vacancy.[17] When Sheng Hsuan-huai became substantive Chefoo taotai in 1886, Sheng K'ang retired fully and devoted himself to scholarly activity. He died in 1902 at the age of 89.

Sheng Hsuan-huai was the eldest of six sons, of whom four survived infancy. He was the only one of the four to play an important political role in the last decades of the Ch'ing dynasty. There is little credible information about Sheng's early life, except that he is reported to have been a bright youngster and is known to have undertaken the traditional studies in preparation for the civil service examinations as his father and grandfather had done before him. In 1866, Sheng Hsuan-huai and his brother, Sheng Chün-huai, passed the first examination, for the *hsiu-ts'ai* degree, in their home district in Kiangsu. Sheng Hsuan-huai took part in the provincial examinations for the *chü-jen* degree in 1867 but failed to pass; this was the first of three unsuccessful trials.[18] He failed again in 1873; and for a third time in September 1876 when he was already on the way to becoming an important personage. After this last attempt, Sheng abandoned this means of seeking office, but it was to be one of his chief regrets at the end of his life that he had not succeeded in the provincial examinations.

Like Yuan Shih-k'ai and several other important figures at the end of the Manchu dynasty, Sheng Hsuan-huai entered public service as part of the entourage of Li Hung-chang. In May 1870, Li, then governor-general at Wuchang, was ordered north to deal with a Muslim uprising. At the invitation of Yang Tsung-lien, an advisor to Li, Sheng joined the governor-general's headquarters and accompanied him to Sian in July 1870. According to the *Hsing-shu*, Sheng was soon on good terms with Li.[19] This marks the beginning of their close association, which lasted until Li's death in 1901.

Sheng stayed with the Anhwei Army (*Huai-chün*) when Li and his forces were transferred to Chihli and Li relieved Tseng Kuo-fan as Chihli governor-general following the "Tientsin massacre" of June 21, 1870. During the period of more than a year in which Sheng was connected with the Huai-chün, he acted in a secretarial capacity and was occupied with matters of supply for the army. In 1871 he left military service and for a time was engaged in flood and famine relief in Chihli, an activity for which he later gained a considerable reputation.[20]

2. *Sheng as a Subordinate of Li Hung-chang, 1871–1895.* Down to the Sino-Japanese War of 1894–1895, Sheng's position might be described as deputy to Li Hung-chang for economic matters. In a sense his career was parallel to that of Yuan Shih-k'ai, who acted for Li in military and foreign affairs, as, for example, in Korea from 1882 to 1894.[21] Sheng's role in the direction of the China Merchants' Company and the Telegraph Administration, his mining and textile ventures, and his holding of the key posts of taotai at Chefoo and then at Tientsin — all were important assets to the regional power structure which Li Hung-chang was developing in North China.

Throughout his career, Sheng was associated both as shareholder and as manager with China's premier steamship line, the China Merchants' Steam Navigation Company. This association dated from the founding of the company in 1872. Li Hung-chang and Shen Pao-chen,[22] director-general of the Foochow Shipyard, had memorialized opposing the suggestion by certain officials that shipbuilding at Foochow be abandoned, and had proposed that the Shipyard build merchant ships as well as war vessels.[23] On learning of this, Sheng is reported in the *Hsing-shu* to have petitioned Li that the government organize a joint merchant-official company to operate a fleet of steam vessels which would compete with the foreign firms that then dominated the carrying trade on the China coast. To subsidize the new venture, the ships would be permitted to carry government tribute rice from the Yangtze delta to Tientsin for the supply of Peking.[24]

While the *Hsing-shu* assigns to Sheng alone the authorship of this petition, and thus the major responsibility for suggesting to Li Hung-chang the organization of the China Merchants' Company, in Li's memorial reporting the beginning of the company, the petition is said to be from "Chu Ch'i-ang and others." [25] And three years later, in 1875, Li again assigned the major credit for the initiation of the company to Chu Ch'i-ang.[26] While it seems likely that Sheng participated in the general planning, Chu Ch'i-ang and his brother, because of their contacts with the shipping business, played the principal parts in actually getting the China Merchants' Company under way.[27]

When Tong King-sing replaced Chu as manager of the enterprise in 1873, Sheng Hsuan-huai became an assistant manager. Sheng gave his major attention to the C.M.S.N. Co. until the spring of 1875 when he was deputed to take charge of the development of coal and iron mines in Hupei. At the end of 1876 he was instrumental in convincing Shen Pao-chen, now Nanking governor-general, to lend the China Merchants' Company Tls. 1,000,000 of official funds with which an initial payment was made for the ships and other property of the American-owned Shanghai Steam Navigation Company, thereby more than doubling the C.M.S.N. Co.'s fleet.

Li Hung-chang was high in praise of Sheng's role in the purchase of the Shanghai Steam Navigation Company. He also commended the part Sheng had played in negotiations with the British consul at Shanghai, W. F. Mayers. These led to an agreement signed on October 24, 1876, whereby the Chinese government paid Tls. 285,000 to recover an unauthorized ten-mile railroad running from Woosung to Shanghai which had been completed in 1876 by Jardine, Matheson and Company and other foreigners.[28] Li requested an imperial audience for Sheng, who was put high on the list for promotion to the post of taotai in Chihli. In the tenth moon of 1879 (November 14–December 12), Sheng was rewarded with an appointment as acting military administrative taotai (*ping-pei tao*) for the Tientsin-Hochien district, his first regular administrative post. Apparently he carried out the traditional duties of his office in a commendable fashion, if we may judge from Li Hung-chang's memorials to the throne praising Sheng for raising several hundred thousand taels of relief funds, and establishing charitable institutions and an "opium prevention bureau" (*chieh-yen chü*) in which thousands were reputed to have been cured.[29]

This appointment, however, was incidental to Sheng's major activity in the remaining years before the Sino-French War. He was occupied primarily with the planning and construction of telegraph lines, and the organization of a *kuan-tu shang-pan* telegraph company.[30] It was not until the crisis with Russia over Ili in 1879–1880 had sharply demonstrated the inconvenience in negotiations caused by the absence of telegraphic connections between Peking and Shanghai (where the foreign-owned cable connecting with Europe ended) that serious Chinese efforts were made to build telegraph lines.[31] According to the *Hsingshu*, in the spring of 1880 Sheng urged Li Hung-chang to follow the example of the China Merchants' Company and raise funds by the public sale of shares in order to construct a telegraph line from Tientsin to Shanghai.[32] Li's memorial proposing this line to the court does not give Sheng credit for the suggestion,[33] but Li did depute Sheng to negotiate with a Danish firm, the Great Northern Telegraph Company, for the construction of the line. And he was to undertake to raise funds from Chinese merchants with which to replace the official funds advanced for the initial construction.[34] When the Tientsin-Shanghai line was completed in December 1881, a telegraph company — known in English as the Imperial Telegraph Administration — was established at Tientsin with Sheng in charge as director-general (*tu-pan*). In April 1882, following an initial payment to the government of merchant funds raised by Sheng Hsuan-huai, the company was formally recognized as a *kuan-tu shang-pan* enterprise. Under Sheng's direction — he was simultaneously director-general and a large shareholder until 1902 — the telegraph company raised funds for the construction of other lines, conducted extensive negotiations with the Danish and English cable companies, and arranged for the junction of China's telegraph lines with those of the French on the Yunnan and Kwangtung borders and with Russia on the Manchurian border. Of special importance are the frequency and variety of the contact with Westerners which Sheng experienced as a result of these manifold negotiations.[35]

The aggravation of the trouble with France over Annam in the summer of 1883 caused Li Hung-chang to depute Sheng to assist in the management of the China Merchants' Company until Tong King-sing, who had left for Europe in April of that year, should return. Sheng forced the assistant manager, Hsü Jun, to leave the company early in 1884 under charges of irregular financial dealings. Tong King-sing and his younger brother, T'ang T'ing-keng, were themselves dismissed shortly thereafter because of "heavy deficits" discovered in their accounts, and the C.M.S.N. Co. was left largely in the hands of Li's protégé, Ma Chien-chung, during the war with France. Then at the end of hostilities, in 1885, Li Hung-chang ordered a complete reorganization of the company and appointed Sheng Hsuan-huai as director-general (*tu-pan*). From August 1885 until the end of 1902 Sheng was in complete control of the C.M.S.N. Co. He was its principal executive as he was its largest shareholder. The two companies, shipping and telegraph, were recognized by Chinese and foreigner alike to be Sheng's personal domain, subject only to the authority of Li Hung-chang in his capacity as commissioner for the northern ports (*Pei-yang ta-ch'en*).

Concurrently with his responsibility for the two *kuan-tu shang-pan* enterprises, Sheng continued to hold posts in the regular provincial hierarchy. In July 1886 he received a substantive appointment as military administrative taotai and superintendent of customs for Chefoo in Shantung. He remained at Chefoo for six years, again carrying out efficiently the traditional responsibilities of his office. Thus in 1891 he was awarded a "button of the first rank" on the recommendation of his superior Chang Yao, the governor of Shantung, in recognition of his having raised more than Tls. 500,000 in relief funds.[36] Sheng also undertook several flood-control projects, the most important of which was the dredging of the Hsiao-ch'ing river; this was begun in 1891 and was financed principally by Tls. 700,000 raised by Sheng from the local gentry. Sheng's successful record as a provincial official should be considered together with the contemporary treaty-port view that he "achieved a national — almost an international — reputation for grasping avarice and venality."[37] The charges of graft and unscrupulous methods which accompanied Sheng's career as an industrial promoter, and which will be discussed later, were not without basis. But he was operating in a context in which "squeeze" and personal influence were a generally accepted means of conducting business. Of greater significance, perhaps, than his corruption, however deplorable, was Sheng's apparent ability to operate successfully in both a traditional Chinese role as taotai and as the director of a succession of Western-type industrial enterprises of which the China Merchants' Company and the Telegraph Administration were the earliest. The deleterious effects of traditional values and methods in these enterprises have been discussed in the previous chapters and will be pointed to again. But of Sheng himself, even the author of the above remarks about his reputation for avarice and venality admitted that "his ability was recognized by foreigners and Chinese alike — he is one of the few Chinese officials living who understand the inner workings of European finance."[38]

In June 1892 Sheng reached the apex of the administrative pyramid under Li Hung-chang with his appointment to the post of Tientsin customs taotai.[39] He had held that post briefly in the summer of 1884 as acting incumbent, but now his appointment was a substantive one. The office of Tientsin customs taotai (*hai-kuan tao*) was a new one which had been created at the instance of Li Hung-chang in 1870. Li secured the abolition of the office of commissioner for the northern ports as an independent post and made it a concurrent responsibility of the governor-general of Chihli, thereby consolidating his own power. To aid the governor-general with the additional heavy responsibilities, a new office based on specific duties rather than omnicompetent territorial responsibility was created. The Tientsin customs taotai was occupied with "foreign matters" (*yang-wu*), defense, and the customs collection. Through his office the Chihli governor-general gained control of the commerce and revenue of the chief port serving the capital area. This was a major set-back for the imperial court, and opened the way for Li Hung-chang to preempt the revenue of Chihli as he had done before in Kiangsu.[40]

Sheng was now the top financial official in Li Hung-chang's satrapy. In addition to controlling the Tientsin customs, the China Merchants' Company, and the Telegraph Administration, in October 1893 he undertook the reorganization of Li's Shanghai Cotton Cloth Mill, which had been completely destroyed by fire. As the government was unwilling to appropriate additional funds, Sheng, together with Nieh Ch'i-kuei, the Shanghai customs taotai, raised capital from private Chinese sources. Joined to the remaining assets of the old company, this was used to form a new *kuan-tu shang-pan* enterprise known as the Hua-sheng Cotton Mill.[41] As the head of the first successful modern cotton mill in China, and of the shipping and telegraph companies, Sheng became the leading industrialist in the empire.

Even while he was Li Hung-chang's subordinate, Sheng Hsuan-huai was steadily proceeding to build a power of his own. The Tientsin customs reputedly netted him some Tls. 200,000 a year privately in addition to the proceeds of the several industrial enterprises which he controlled.[42] With this wealth in hand, Sheng was not entirely dependent on Li. As early as 1890 the economic substructure within Li's regional "machine" which Sheng controlled began to have relations with the competing regional power of Chang Chih-tung, the Hu-Kuang governor-general. In that year Chang purchased from Sheng iron and coal deposits in Ta-yeh-hsien, Hupei, in order to provide ore and fuel for the projected Hanyang Ironworks.[43] Sheng had secured control of this ore-producing land sometime after 1875, following his appointment by the governors-general Li Hung-chang, Liu K'un-i, and Li Han-chang to take charge of the development of coal and iron resources in the Yangtze valley. The Ta-yeh iron deposits had been especially noted for their quality by English geologists whom Sheng employed in 1877.

The collapse of the Peiyang Army and Navy in 1894–1895, and consequently of Li Hung-chang's whole position, must have been a real crisis for Sheng, who had depended so much on Li's backing. If so, he was nevertheless able to weather it successfully. An extreme view — that of United States Consul Read in Tientsin — makes Sheng out as the villain in the fall of Li Hung-chang. Read's dispatches allege that Sheng, who had been delegated to purchase munitions for Li's forces, together with Mandl, a German commercial agent through whom Sheng had placed orders, Gustav Detring, Imperial Maritime Customs Commissioner at Tientsin and an intimate of Governor-general Li for many years, Major von Hanneken, a German military instructor in Li's employ, and the Russian minister, Count Cassini, persuaded Li to resist Japanese demands regarding Korea and thus brought on the war in 1894. War meant heavy munitions purchases for Mandl, a growth of German military influence for von Hanneken, an increase of Russian diplomatic influence at Peking at the expense of the English for Cassini, while Detring hoped through Li's favor to replace his chief, Sir Robert Hart. As for Sheng, he stood to gain from the gratitude of all these gentlemen. Read believed that this group hoped to use the war as a means to gain paramount influence in China through the power eventually to manage public improvements, railroad construction, and the like.[44]

As an explanation of the origins of the Sino-Japanese War, Read's story leaves something to be desired.[45] The allegations of the American consul, do, however, reflect the notoriety which Sheng Hsuan-huai had acquired as well as Li Hung-chang's hesitations, knowing as he did the weakness of his own military forces. That something was amiss is clear even from the *Hsing-shu*. Sheng's biography reports that he was on leave because of illness when hostilities with Japan broke out in June 1894. He returned to Tientsin to serve as "director-general of army transport" (*pan-li tung-cheng chuan-yün*), charged with supplying and moving Li's troops. While filling this post, Sheng, with Yuan Shih-k'ai, was indicted for alleged corruption in the provision of rice for the troops defending the capital area. Governor-general Li came to the defense of his subordinates and, as in other cases, the charges were dropped.[46]

For Sheng, the principal consequence of the cataclysm of 1894–1895 was the splitting of Li Hung-chang's Chihli machine into its component parts. Wang Wen-shao, governor-general of Yunnan and Kweichow, *ad interim* inherited Li's political post as Chihli governor-general and commissioner for the northern ports. Yuan Shih-k'ai was ordered to build a new, modern army in Tientsin. And Sheng's industrial and commercial enterprises, which had had their start under Li Hung-chang's auspices, gradually were transferred under the wing of Chang Chih-tung. The process of acquiring a new patron for his *kuan-tu shang-pan* enterprises was not completed until Li's death in 1901; it was accompanied by a rapid and significant growth of Sheng's personal power.

3. *Sheng and Chang Chih-tung, 1896–1908.* Wang Wen-shao seems

never to have aspired to inherit Li Hung-chang's empire *in toto*.[47] It may be that Wang lacked the military power which had been Li's before the defeat by Japan and which had allowed Li to achieve a semi-independent position vis-à-vis the Manchu court. Wang held the office of Chihli governor-general from August 1895 to June 1898. During this period Sheng and his industrial enterprises (which Li Hung-chang had guarded jealously) were in fact detached from Wang's control, although he remained nominally in charge by virtue of his office as commissioner for the northern ports. This abridgment of the economic power of the Chihli governor-general went even further under Wang's successors, Jung-lu and Yü-lu.[48] When Sheng Hsuan-huai was indicted in 1899 for mortgaging the godowns and landed property of the China Merchants' Steam Navigation Company to the German firm of Carlowitz and Company, the matter was referred to Chang Chih-tung, the Hu-Kuang governor-general, rather than to Yü-lu.[49]

The increase of Sheng's personal power and influence during the decade in which he was closely associated with Chang Chih-tung was based primarily on his direction of railroad matters and his control of the Hanyang Ironworks and its subsidiary mines. Sheng's new position was supported by his continued hold on the enterprises he had headed before the Sino-Japanese War and was augmented by his sponsorship of a series of new ones, including the first Chinese modern bank, Western-style schools, and chambers of commerce.

On May 23, 1896, the Hanyang Ironworks, which Chang Chih-tung had first undertaken in 1889 as a government industry, was turned over to Sheng Hsuan-huai by Chang and became a *kuan-tu shang-pan* enterprise. In the same year, on October 20, having been received in imperial audience, Sheng was made a "fourth-rank official of the Court of Sacrificial Worship" (*ssu-p'in ching-t'ang*) and was appointed director-general (*tu-pan*) of the newly formed Imperial Railway Administration (*T'ieh-lu tsung kung-ssu*).[50] These two new industrial responsibilities were closely related. According to one account,[51] Sheng agreed to take the Hanyang Ironworks off Chang Chih-tung's hands only reluctantly, in return for Chang's protection of Sheng against charges of corruption and betrayal. The ironworks was in need of funds for new furnaces and the development of coal supplies, and was as yet without an adequate market for its projected output. As a condition for his assumption of responsibility for it, Sheng asked that Chang Chih-tung nominate him to take charge of the program of railroad construction which was being undertaken after the war with Japan. To this Chang consented. On the recommendation of Chang and Wang Wen-shao, who in the winter of 1895 had been ordered to hasten the construction of the Peking-Hankow railroad (or Lu-Han line, shortened from the names of the northern terminus, Lu-kou-ch'iao, near Peking and the southern terminus, Hankow), Sheng became director-general of railroads.[52] As the head of the Imperial Railway Administration he arranged a prepayment of Tls. 1,900,000 to the Hanyang Ironworks for the purchase of steel rails and other materials to be used in railroad construction.[53] With the backing of Chang and Wang he was able to secure for the ironworks an imperial edict ordering all government railroads and arsenals to purchase their iron and steel from Hanyang only.[54]

The history of the Hanyang Ironworks, the Ta-yeh Iron Mines, and the P'ing-hsiang Coal Mines as kuan-tu shang-pan enterprises under the control of Sheng Hsuan-huai is being prepared as a separate study by the author. Briefly, Sheng had had an interest in Chang Chih-tung's ironworks from its inception as a consequence of his control of the Ta-yeh Iron Mines which furnished ore for the plant. It was therefore natural that Chang should turn to Sheng, who had successfully undertaken ventures in the fields of shipping, telegraphs, and cotton spinning and weaving, when the exhaustion of official funds forced him to turn Hanyang over to "merchant management." Under Sheng's control, the P'ing-hsiang Coal Mines in Kiangsi were developed as a source of coking coal for the ironworks, in part with funds borrowed from Sheng's other enterprises and in part with loans from the German firm of Carlowitz and Company. Much larger loans were obtained from Japanese sources for the installation of open-hearth steel-making equipment and additional blast furnaces. The Japanese financial interest in the ironworks grew apace on the basis of these agreements and the continued inability of the company to obtain capital from Chinese sources. In 1908 Sheng obtained imperial approval for the amalgamation of the Hanyang Ironworks and the Ta-yeh and P'ing-hsiang mines to form the Han-Yeh-P'ing Coal and Iron Company Limited (Han-Yeh-P'ing mei-t'ieh ch'ang-k'uang yu-hsien kung-ssu). This limited liability joint-stock company was registered with the Ministry of Commerce as a wholly commercial enterprise, thus bringing to an end its existence as a kuan-tu shang-pan undertaking. Sheng remained at the head of the Han-Yeh-P'ing Company, which continued to be dependent on loans from the Yokohama Specie Bank and other Japanese firms. The strength of Japanese interests led finally to the inclusion of a demand for control of the company in the "Twenty-one Demands" of 1915.

Sheng filled the post of director-general of the Imperial Railway Administration until the end of 1905.[55] Under his direction the Railway Administration arranged for loans from European powers amounting to nearly $300,000,000 (Chinese) for the construction of nearly 3,000 miles of railroads. The most important of these were a concession to a nominally Belgian syndicate for the building of a line from Peking to

Hankow;[56] an agreement, later canceled, with the American China Development Company for a railroad from Canton to Hankow;[57] and concessions to the British and Chinese Corporation for construction of the Shanghai-Nanking and Soochow-Hangchow-Ningpo railroads.[58] When the administration was dissolved in 1906, the Peking-Hankow trunkline had been completed and work on the Shanghai-Nanking line was well under way. The ten years that he headed the Imperial Railway Administration were for Sheng a period of extensive contacts with foreigners during which, under the formal supervision of Chang Chih-tung and the successive governors-general of Chihli, he negotiated the basis of China's railroad system.

At the time that he assumed the post of director-general of railroads, Sheng presented to the emperor a proposal for the establishment of a modern-type bank. Its capital of Tls. 5,000,000 was to be subscribed entirely by Chinese investors, and it was to have the right of coinage and note issue.[59] Although he intended the bank to play a major role in foreign-exchange transactions — as is apparent from its Chinese name, *Chung-kuo t'ung-shang yin-hang,* literally "Chinese Foreign Trade Bank" — Sheng also saw this enterprise as contributing to the industrial empire he was steadily building. The Imperial Bank of China, as it was generally known to Westerners, opened in Shanghai in 1897 with assets of Tls. 3,500,000. Of this amount, Tls. 1,000,000 was lent by the Ministry of Revenue, and the rest was subscribed by individual Chinese investors and the enterprises, such as the China Merchants' Company, which Sheng Hsuan-huai controlled. It was the first Chinese-owned bank to be organized on Western lines and was operated as a *kuan-tu shang-pan* enterprise under Sheng's direction.[60]

Sheng's use of the surplus funds of the China Merchants' Company and Telegraph Administration was not limited to the support of his new bank. Contributions from these enterprises were also employed to finance two important projects of Western-style education. The first was undertaken in September 1895, while Sheng was still in office at Tientsin. He petitioned the Chihli governor-general, Wang Wen-shao, for the establishment of a school teaching Western subjects, to be known as the Tientsin Sino-Western Academy (*Chung-hsi hsüeh-t'ang*).[61] Wang's memorial embodying Sheng's proposals received imperial approval, and a school with preparatory and collegiate departments was undertaken.[62] Twenty thousand taels were contributed annually for its support by the China Merchants' Company and a smaller sum by the Imperial Telegraph Administration. Charles D. Tenney,[63] an American, served as the first president of the institution, which later became Peiyang College (*Pei-yang ta-hsüeh*).

Sheng also founded a school at Shanghai in the winter of 1896 after he had established the offices of the Railway Administration in that city.[64] Known first as the Nanyang Public Institute (*Nan-yang kung-hsüeh*), this school was supported by annual grants of Tls. 50,000 each from Sheng's shipping and telegraph companies. The buildings, which were completed in 1899, housed primary, preparatory, and commercial departments, and the first modern normal school in China. Dr. John C. Ferguson,[65] a close friend and adviser to Sheng, was president of the school until 1902; thereafter the administration was completely Chinese, although some foreign teachers were employed. In 1905 it was made a school of technology and placed under the Ministry of Commerce, and in 1907 it became an imperial polytechnic school under the Ministry of Posts and Communications.[66] Associated with the school was a translation office which first produced only textbooks, but from 1902 also translated more advanced political and technical works.[67] Outstanding graduates were sent abroad to continue their studies.[68]

The school in Shanghai, which came to be called Nanyang College (*Nan-yang ta-hsüeh*), and that in Tientsin developed into good technical institutions at which many Chinese engineers as well as political leaders such as Wang Ch'ung-hui and Ch'en Li-fu were trained.[69] As for Sheng's motivation in supporting these institutions, he is reported to have stated to the grand secretary Kang-i (who in 1899 attempted to get Sheng to give up his support of the schools and turn over the funds saved to the empress dowager's treasury) that

China needs to be independent of the foreigners. China can only acquire that independence by technical education. If pupils learn to do what foreigners do, the hire of foreigners may be dispensed with. It would be better policy to train electricians, engineers, and shipbuilders than to continue to be beholden to the foreigners. China ought to train her own engineers and shipbuilders. Is it not your own wish that China should not engage the services of foreigners? The best way to carry out this idea is to encourage such an institution as mine.[70]

The emphasis of this statement, which was certainly designed to appeal to Kang-i's known anti-Western feelings, is on technical studies, but Sheng's conception of the function of the schools was not limited to this, as is apparent from his outline of their curricula.[71] To some extent he was seeking to promote Western education more broadly conceived. Regardless of how conscious his intentions were in this matter, by establishing and supporting the Tientsin and Shanghai schools Sheng contributed notably to the spread of Occidental learning and ideas which were gradually undermining the traditional order.

Although it was undertaken some years later, one other institution for whose initiation Sheng Hsuan-huai was largely responsible might be considered at this point. That was the Chinese "chambers of commerce," the first unit of which was opened in Shanghai in 1902. In October 1902, Sheng, who had been appointed imperial commissioner for negotiating commercial treaties, memorialized on the condition of China's commerce, stating:

> The reasons why China's commerce has not flourished are three: commercial studies are not taught, the commercial laws are inadequate, and chambers of commerce have not been established. Of the three, the most important place at which to begin is with the organization of chambers of commerce.[72]

Sheng then drew attention to the role of private commercial organizations in the West and to their recent organization in the major cities and ports of Japan. The *shang-wu chü*, or commercial affairs bureaus, which had been established during the "Hundred Days Reform" of 1898, were actually semiofficial organs. "They employ expectant officials, not merchant directors." And while the foreigners had a general commercial organization in the chief trading city, Shanghai, the Chinese had only their old-style guilds, each restricted to one line of trade. They were not organized as a whole to face the competition of the foreigners.

To remedy this situation, of which he had become acutely aware in his negotiations for treaty revision, Sheng ordered the Shanghai customs taotai and the manager of the Imperial Bank of China, Yen Hsin-hou, to convene the merchant leaders of Shanghai and organize a general Chinese chamber of commerce. Yen raised funds, a building was secured and the Shanghai Commercial Association (*Shang-hai shang-yeh hui-i kung-ssu*) was opened with Yen as director (*tsung-li*) and Chou Chin-piao as assistant director. Sheng also discussed with Chang Chih-tung and other high provincial officials the extension of this kind of organization to other provinces and cities.[73] By 1908 there were similar organizations, generally called *shang-wu hui*, established in 31 major places in China, 13 in overseas Chinese communities, and 135 more in smaller localities.[74] Although the chambers of commerce did not replace the old-style guilds, they were an attempt to bring the guilds together for cooperative action in the encouragement and protection of Chinese commerce.

In these years, as his industrial and commercial activities flourished, Sheng's official position and court rank were steadily rising, a sign of his increasing power and affluence. In November 1896 Sheng was appointed sub-director of the Court of Sacrificial Worship (*T'ai-ch'ang-ssu shao-ch'ing*),[75] and in December 1897 he was made sub-director of the Imperial Court of Revision (*Ta-li-ssu shao-ch'ing*)[76] — sinecures so far as the duties involved, but carrying with them a high court rank. Then in December 1900 Sheng became vice-director of the Imperial Clan Court (*Tsung-jen-fu fu-ch'eng*) and reached the upper third rank.[77] In January 1901, the empress dowager, living in self-imposed exile in Sian, appointed him associate imperial commissioner for negotiating commercial treaties (*hui-pan shang-wu ta-ch'en*), and in September he was promoted to imperial commissioner.[78] In recognition of his role in arranging the "Yangtze Compact" which secured the pacification of South China during the Boxer uprising, Sheng was made a junior guardian of the heir apparent (*t'ai-tzu shao-pao*) in December 1901.[79] It is due to this title that he is usually referred to in Western sources as Sheng Kung-pao. Then in February 1902 he was given the post of senior vice-president of the Ministry of Works (*Kung-pu tso-shih-lang*) and the upper second rank.[80]

Sheng's activities during the Boxer Rebellion and the subsequent negotiations for revision of the commercial treaties with the Western powers are reflected in these appointments. In November 1899, as the time approached when the treaties embodying the 5 per cent conventional tariff could be renegotiated, Sheng Hsuan-huai and Nieh Ch'i-kuei, the Shanghai customs taotai, were deputed to consult with Robert Hart, the inspector-general of the Imperial Maritime Customs, and to draft a plan for revising the tariff. Sheng presented a scheme providing for a tariff increase on foreign imports coupled with the elimination of *likin* payments on these goods.[81] Before this proposal could be discussed with the European powers, however, the Boxer holocaust intervened.

Sheng was in Shanghai conducting an investigation of customs affairs in that port when, on June 20, 1900, the imperial court issued a proclamation of war against the Western powers in response to their seizure of the Taku forts. The Yangtze and coastal provinces were ordered to rise against the foreigners. Along with most officials outside of Chihli and Shansi, including Li Hung-chang in Canton, Sheng for practical reasons disregarded the proclamation. He treated it as a forged document and urged the chief provincial officials in the south not to give it circulation. When the antiforeign outbreaks threatened to spread into the Yangtze provinces, Sheng was instrumental in formulating a dual policy, of neutrality toward affairs in the north and loyalty to the Manchu court, a policy which Governors-general Chang Chih-tung and Liu K'un-i adopted. Sheng drafted the terms of the agreement which was concluded with the foreign consuls in Shanghai on June 27, providing for the protection of life and property in the Yangtze area by the two governors-general. This was the so-called "Yangtze Compact" (*Tung-nan hu-pao*). In a joint telegram on July 3 to the Chinese ministers in the various foreign capitals, Chang and Liu formalized this agreement by undertaking to protect lives and property in the areas under their control so long as no foreign troops were landed. This example was followed by the authorities in the other southern provinces with the result that the fighting and destruction in the north were effectively kept out of South China.[82]

The Boxer Protocol signed in September 1901 provided that the specific customs duties on imports should be increased to an effective 5 per cent in order to facilitate payment of the indemnities secured on the customs revenue (Article 6). The International Tariff Revision Commission met from May to August 1902, and concurrently negotiations for revision of the commercial treaties were opened with each power separately, first with Great Britain.[83] Sheng and Lü Hai-huan, formerly minister to Germany, were appointed the Chinese plenipotentiaries at these negotiations.[84] Although an agreement for an effective 5 per cent tariff was safely concluded,[85] the treaty-revision negotiations dragged on. An agreement, the Mackay Treaty, was signed with England in September 1902, containing a complex scheme for the abolition of *likin* in exchange for a special surtax of one-and-a-half times the regular duty. This was in essence the plan which Sheng had proposed in 1899. Treaties with the United States and Japan which were modeled on the British agreement followed in October. Negotiations were then opened with Germany and Italy, but all talks were suspended and never resumed when the Chinese discovered that each of the others among the nineteen treaty powers intended to exact its special price for assenting to the general agreement. Therefore the stipulations for the abolition of *likin* in the British, American, and Japanese treaties, which had been dependent on the unanimous consent of the treaty powers, remained inoperative.

Sheng, however, was at the peak of his power during the negotiations and received the recognition due him from his foreign counterparts. The *North-China Herald*, leading British organ in Shanghai, was high in praise of Sheng's abilities, one leader declaring that "better men could hardly have been selected than the Commissioners appointed by China to arrange the new tariff. Director-General Sheng was brought up in a bad school, in Tientsin, but he has a thorough grasp of such economical questions as will now come before him." [86] It was just at this point, on October 24, 1902, that the death of Sheng K'ang, Sheng Hsuan-huai's octogenarian father, set loose a train of events which deprived him of his official posts, of the direction of the China Merchants' Company and Telegraph Administration, and ultimately of his control of railroad affairs.

The collapse of Sheng's position is dramatized in a brief item in the *North-China Herald* under the headline "How are the Mighty Fallen!" It reads:

At the last series of the funeral ceremonies in memory of the late Sheng Hsio-jen, father of Sheng Kung-pao, which were held yesterday at His Excellency's residence on the Bubbling Well Road, there were not one-half of the callers present as compared with the number of those who attended upon the death of the late nonagenarian [*sic*], when it was not then known how his son, Sheng Kung-pao, was to be treated by the powers that be in Peking.[87]

According to official etiquette, Sheng was expected to give up all his posts in order to observe twenty-seven months of mourning for his father. He immediately resigned his two highest positions, commissioner of commerce and vice-president of the Ministry of Works. Customarily an imperial edict should have followed, expressing regret at the death of Sheng K'ang and declaring that as Sheng Hsuan-huai's services and talents were such that they could not well be replaced on the spur of the moment, it was the desire of the empress dowager that he remain as "acting incumbent" of these two posts.[88] But instead the court indicated no awareness of the death of Sheng's father, while it abruptly gave the two posts in question to Wu T'ing-fang and T'ang Chin-ch'ung, respectively, in decrees dated October 26 which did not even mention Sheng.[89] There was speculation in Shanghai that this unexpected action, which did not immediately replace Sheng as *tu-pan* of the China Merchants' Company and the Telegraph Administration, was intended to show him now precarious his position was, probably with the expectation that Sheng would take the hint to "settle matters" in a monetary manner.[90] Only on October 30 was an edict sent to Sheng acknowledging the death of his father.[91]

Despite considerable exertions, Sheng was not able to retain his direction of the shipping and telegraph companies. At the end of November 1902 Yuan Shih-k'ai had come on what was ostensibly a visit of condolence to Sheng in Shanghai, and had made it clear that these two enterprises would be taken out of Sheng's hands.[92] An edict of January 15, 1903, "nationalized" the Telegraph Administration and placed it under Yuan's control. The China Merchants' Company, however, remained a *kuan-tu shang-pan* enterprise. Although Yuan's deputies, Yang Shih-ch'i and Hsü Jun, were its principal managers, Sheng was still a major shareholder, and many of his appointees remained with the firm. With this ground secured, he was able at a later date to recover his control of the shipping company. But the shares of the Telegraph Administration were ultimately purchased by the imperial government and the company passed completely out of Sheng's control.

When we note which of his multiple positions and enterprises Sheng was able to retain despite the efforts of his many enemies, the nature of the conflict which threatened the empire he had built for himself since the 1870's will be somewhat clearer. Sheng maintained his control of the Hanyang Ironworks and of its subsidiary iron and coal mines; neither the Imperial Bank of China nor the Hua-sheng Cotton Mill was threatened. With the exception of his textile interests, which had gradually passed out of official purview as they lost their *kuan-tu shang-pan* character, in all these enterprises Sheng Hsuan-huai was in some degree responsible to Chang Chih-tung in the latter's capacity as Hu-Kuang governor-general. In fact, they had each been undertaken by Sheng with the backing and assistance of Chang in much the same manner as the China Merchants' Company and Imperial Telegraph Administration had been sponsored by Li Hung-chang when he was governor-general of Chihli and commissioner for the northern ports. It was, moreover, through the intercession of Chang Chih-tung that Sheng Hsuan-huai was able to keep his position as director-general of railroads, although he was forced to give up his control of the shipping and telegraph companies.[93] Thus those enterprises which Sheng had undertaken and controlled under the protection of Governor-general Chang's powerful "machine" in central China and the Yangtze valley remained securely in his grasp, while the companies which he had inherited from the breakup of Li Hung-chang's Chihli "machine" were now finally wrested from Sheng's control by Li Hung-chang's successor.

Clearly Yuan Shih-k'ai was one of the prime movers behind Sheng Hsuan-huai's discomfitures in the period following the death of his father. As noted above, when Li Hung-chang's Chihli satrapy fell in 1895, its component parts were distributed among Wang Wen-shao, who followed Li as Chihli governor-general, Sheng Hsuan-huai, who took over the industrial and commercial enterprises which Li had sponsored, and Yuan Shih-k'ai, who undertook to build a new army at Tientsin. Yuan retained command of his army, the *Wu-wei yu-chün*, while, having gained the favor of Jung-lu and the empress dowager, he rose rapidly through the positions of Chihli provincial judge and governor of Shantung to the key post in North China, Chihli governor-general and commissioner for the northern ports.[94] Now that he had in his hands both the military and political power which Li Hung-chang had once possessed, Yuan sought to gain control also of what had been the economic component of Li's machine. It was for this reason that he was ready to take advantage of the death of Sheng K'ang and of attacks on Sheng Hsuan-huai from other quarters in order to ease his own men into positions which Sheng had held.[95]

Sheng's position during the next six years, until the dismissal of Yuan Shih-k'ai in 1909, might be compared to that of a man on a roller-coaster. It was marked by a series of sharp ups and downs as he struggled to regain his power with the aid of his enormous wealth and the assistance of Yuan's enemies in Peking. The paradox is that both

Sheng and Yuan were among that group of officials at the end of the dynasty who welcomed the introduction of economic and political methods and institutions modeled on the West. They were, in a word, "reformers," although Sheng had a reputation for sharp dealing and had been only mildly sympathetic to the "Hundred Days" of 1898, while Yuan was an anathema to the followers of K'ang Yu-wei and Liang Ch'i-ch'ao for his alleged betrayal of their cause.[96] Yet each was quick to join with the "reactionary" enemies of the other in order to take advantage of his rival. Thus Sheng first joined hands with the empress dowager's chief eunuch, Li Lien-ying, against Yuan;[97] later he was identified with T'ieh-liang and the Manchu conservative party who were apprehensive about the concentration of power in Yuan's hands.[98] For his part, Yuan Shih-k'ai could make full use of the repeated denunciations of Sheng's activities (particularly the opposition to Sheng's railroad negotiations which attacked him for misappropriation of funds and for making too great concessions to the foreigner) so as to put forward his own follower, T'ang Shao-yi, for Sheng's important railroad posts.[99]

The details of Sheng's setbacks and recoveries which were repeated several times over in these few years are not in themselves of great interest. But one instance may be cited to give some idea of how the struggle went on. In March 1903 Sheng traveled north to the capital, ostensibly for the purpose of personally looking after the arrangements for Tz'u-hsi's trip by railroad to the Western Mausolea. But the real meaning of the trip, as the *North-China Herald* reported at the time, was "nothing less than a determined effort to wrest back the power and prestige of which he was lately so unexpectedly and ruthlessly shorn through the instrumentality (perhaps a harsher term may be used) of Viceroy Yuan Shih-k'ai." [100] With the aid of Li Lien-ying ("actuated thereto by . . . self interest, jealousy, fear and hate . . . against Viceroy Yuan Shih-k'ai, who was the chief author of Sheng's fall and might at any day cause the fall also of that eunuch himself" [101]) and valuable presents presented in the right quarters, Sheng was apparently successful. His restoration to imperial favor was publicly manifested as Sheng stood among a large assembly of officials at Paoting station to receive the imperial train from Peking en route to the Mausolea:

> The Empress Dowager was on the alert and her sharp eyes roving along the long lines of officials waiting for her to leave the train to bend their knees quickly singled out Sheng who, more out of courtesy than right had been permitted to take a stand amongst the half-dozen or so Vice-Presidents of the Six Boards present. Probably she was egged on by her chief eunuch who stood by her side in the railway carriage; at any rate her action was characteristically prompt. Her Majesty immediately commanded that Sheng Kung-pao be permitted to stand at the head of the line of Vice-Presidents of

Boards, although there were others present much senior to him in terms of service . . . and this was the signal to the official world that Sheng's former peccadilloes had been pardoned and his restoration to his former and even higher rank was a mere question of time.[102]

Sheng was also favored in an edict from the empress dowager declaring her pleasure with the imperial train which carried her to the Mausolea and indicating her desire to reward the officials in charge.[103] Yet immediately afterwards he was quite taken aback by what he considered to be the disgrace of an order appointing him a mere deputy to Yuan Shih-k'ai, Chang Chih-tung, Lü Hai-huan, and Wu T'ing-fang in the negotiation of commercial treaties with the powers.[104]

In this trying situation Sheng could rely on Chang Chih-tung, who himself had no love for Yuan Shih-k'ai. Thus in May 1903 Chang and Sheng conferred in a railroad carriage on the outskirts of Peking as Sheng was leaving the capital after the above events.[105] Chang, who had been ordered to investigate charges of graft and corruption levied against Sheng in connection with his handling of rice shipments to the capital, completely exonerated him of the alleged malpractices.[106] Chang's successful effort to keep Sheng in his railroad posts has already been noted. When Sheng was finally ousted as director-general of railroads at the end of 1905, to be replaced by Yuan Shih-k'ai's protégé, T'ang Shao-yi, it seems likely that it was due to the withdrawal of Governor-general Chang's support. This change was undoubtedly the result of disagreements over the disposition of the Canton-Hankow Railroad concession in 1904–1905, with Chang and the "Hunanese party" successfully opposing Sheng's policy of continuing the American concession.[107]

Sheng, realizing that his position was a weak one, had in fact sought to give up his railroad responsibilities as early as May 1905, when he was received in audience at the end of his period of mourning.[108] He was in Peking through the spring and summer of 1905, seeking to name his own successors as *tu-pan* of the Peking-Hankow and Shanghai-Nanking railroads,[109] but his efforts were without success and in October he was back in Shanghai.[110] In July the empress dowager had, however, granted him the high honor of "riding on horseback or in a sedan-chair within the precincts of the Imperial City" (*tzu-chin-ch'eng ch'i-ma*).[111] Sheng did not give up the attempt to arrange the succession to his railroad posts that autumn, but time had run out.[112] Provincial opposition to Sheng's railroad policies had reached a peak, while his reputation for unsavory financial dealings stood him in no good stead in the face of accusations from the Ministry of Commerce. In November 1905, soon after he had inspected the completed Peking-Hankow railroad and accepted it on behalf of the Chinese government,

Sheng was dismissed from the administration of the Shanghai-Nanking railroad and replaced as *tu-pan* by T'ang Shao-yi.[113] The *T'ieh-lu tsung-kung-ssu* was abolished in 1906, and the control of the railroads it operated or was constructing was turned over to the Ministry of Commerce.[114] Sheng presented his last report on the finances of the Railway Administration in October 1906;[115] for the time being the management of railroad matters passed out of his hands. Some of his appointees — for example, K'o Hung-nien, who had been Sheng's French translator and interpreter and superintendent of the northern section of the Peking-Hankow railroad [116] — were removed from their posts by the ministry, while indictments of Sheng's railroad policies (particularly with regard to the Shanghai-Hangchow-Ningpo railroad loan) continued to be submitted to the throne.

From the end of 1905 Sheng devoted himself principally to his own industrial enterprises and to extensive relief work.[117] The one major interruption was his recall to Peking in November 1907 to assist in negotiations with the British and Chinese Corporation with regard to the Shanghai-Hangchow-Ningpo railroad.[118] When a settlement was finally reached in March 1908, after negotiations which often had Sheng in a difficult position between the Chekiang gentry and the English company, he was rewarded with the post of junior vice-president of the Ministry of Posts and Communications (*Yu-ch'uan pu*).[119] But before he had the opportunity to assume his new office, on March 11 — two days after his appointment — Sheng was dispatched to Shanghai to take charge of commercial negotiations.[120] This action was in fact a veiled dismissal from the ministry. Sheng remained the nominal incumbent, while one Shen Yün-p'ei served as acting junior vice-president, but only in 1910 did Sheng for the first time actively occupy this post.

Throughout 1907 the Manchu conservatives in Peking, in particular T'ieh-liang, president of the Ministry of War, had sought to reduce Yuan Shih-k'ai's military power. In September Yuan was suddenly summoned to Peking and made a member of the Grand Council and concurrently president of the Ministry of Foreign Affairs (*Wai-wu pu*). At the same time Chang Chih-tung was removed from Wuchang and also appointed to the Grand Council. The military forces which these two Chinese provincial leaders had trained were transferred to the Ministry of War, which was headed by T'ieh-liang and two other Manchus.[121] Thus both Sheng's chief rival and his protector were effectively neutralized by removal from their provincial strongholds. When Sheng returned to office again in the last years of the dynasty, his political power as well as his industrial enterprises were independent of the successive provincial machines to which in various degrees they previously had been subordinated.

4. *Sheng and the End of the Manchu Dynasty.* In the spring of 1907, with Yuan Shih-k'ai's power somewhat diminished as a result of his conflict with T'ieh-liang and Tsai-chen, president of the Ministry of Commerce, Sheng had been able to force his arch-enemy and Yuan's appointee, Hsü Jun, from the management of the China Merchants' Company.[122] Following his successful efforts to regain the direction of the shipping company, Sheng proceeded to consolidate his control of the Hanyang Ironworks and its mines by bringing them together to form one firm. With imperial approval, he registered the Han-Yeh-P'ing Coal and Iron Company with the Ministry of Agriculture, Industry, and Commerce as a private (*shang-pan*) enterprise on March 21, 1908.[123] Sheng's decision to end the company's *kuan-tu shang-pan* status coincided with, and was probably motivated by, Chang Chih-tung's departure from the post of Hu-Kuang governor-general in which capacity he had been its protector.

Soon after his appointment as commissioner for commercial treaty negotiations in March 1908, Sheng was granted a leave of absence to travel to Japan for medical care and to inspect Japanese industry and banking.[124] He reached Japan in September and in the next weeks talked with high government officials (including Itō Hirobumi, Matsukata Masayoshi, and Katsura Tarō) and leading financiers and industrialists (including the presidents of the Yokohama Specie Bank and the Bank of Japan, the head of the Mitsui Company, and the director of the Yawata Ironworks). Sheng was particularly impressed with the Japanese banking system and currency practices. His observations in that country were the basis of a lengthy and detailed plan for the unification of China's monetary system and the establishment of central banking which he presented in April 1909.[125] During his stay in Japan, Sheng also participated in talks with Nakamura Yujirō, head of the Imperial Ironworks at Yawata, regarding the purchase of ore and pig iron from Han-Yeh-P'ing by the Japanese. Apparently the ground was laid for further loans from the Yokohama Specie Bank and other Japanese sources to Sheng's coal and iron company.[126]

Sheng had been in Japan only two months when news of the death of the empress dowager and of the Kuang-hsü emperor in the middle of November sent him hurrying back to China. During the rest of 1909 he was primarily concerned with the affairs of the China Merchants' Company, which underwent a reorganization, and of Han-Yeh-P'ing. But he also gave considerable attention to the matter of monetary reform and prepared the lengthy memorial already referred to. At the beginning of 1910 there were reports that the Grand Council and the Ministry of Posts and Communications had jointly asked the regent, Prince Ch'un (Tsai-feng), to summon Sheng Hsuan-huai to Peking in order to take up his post as vice-president of that ministry.[127] Sheng was received in audience on August 14, 1910, and directed to assist the Ministry of Finance (now called *Tu-chih pu*) in planning monetary reforms in addition to resuming his office in the Ministry of Posts and Communications.[128]

The Ministry of Posts and Communications (*Yu-ch'uan pu*) had been established by imperial order in the ninth moon (October 18– November 15) of 1906. The administration of government railroads, which it took over from the Ministry of Commerce, formed one of its four principal sections, the others being concerned respectively with shipping, telegraphs, and the postal system. Sheng had been the most important single figure in the introduction of the modern means of communication which it directed or supervised. His appointment to the ministry, therefore, was a resumption of control over enterprises which he had personally developed in the past.

The president of the Yu-ch'uan pu in 1910 was T'ang Shao-yi, the very T'ang whom Yuan Shih-k'ai had pushed into Sheng's posts in 1905 and 1906. To Sheng, T'ang was an incompetent youngster, a mere overseas student in Hartford, Connecticut, at the time when Sheng had already been an important figure in Li Hung-chang's camp. The two men varied widely in personality, thinking, and policy. It was not to be expected that they could cooperate in one ministry, much less that Sheng would willingly remain subordinated to T'ang. In fact for months Sheng did not even put in an appearance at his office.[129]

Among the ministries only the Yu-ch'uan pu had a stable annual revenue; this consisted largely of profit from government railroads and at times had been used as security for small loans up to several hundred thousand taels. At this time, the Navy Ministry was seeking a Tls. 5,000,000 loan to finance naval construction and proposed to offer the income of the Railroad Bureau (*T'ieh-tao chü*) of the Ministry of Posts and Communications as security. The regent gave his approval and informed the Yu-ch'uan pu. But the head of the Railroad Bureau, Liang Shih-yi, who was a follower of Yuan Shih-k'ai, protested and he was joined in his refusal by T'ang. The regent was angered, while the Navy Ministry took advantage of the quarrel between T'ang and Sheng to push its proposal and attack T'ang. In the end, T'ang Shao-yi was dismissed, and on January 6, 1911, Sheng Hsuan-huai became president of the Ministry of Posts and Communications.[130] Liang Shih-yi did not last much longer; on February 22, 1911, Sheng memorialized raising questions about Liang's accounts and replaced him as head of the Railroad Bureau and the Bank of Communications, organized in 1908, with his own supporter Li Ching-fang, Li Hung-chang's nephew and adopted son.[131] This might be considered Sheng's final revenge on Yuan Shih-k'ai, who himself had been dismissed by the Regent in January 1909 and, shorn of his power, was biding his time at his villa in Honan. But Yuan and his followers had the last laugh, for when Sheng was cashiered at the end of 1911 and Yuan returned to the capital, T'ang was given the office of minister of the Yu-ch'uan pu and Liang was returned to the control of the Bank of Communications.

While the issue of a loan for naval construction was used as a pretext, the chief reason for T'ang Shao-yi's dismissal was his opposition to nationalization of the railroads which had been undertaken in the preceding decade by provincial gentry and merchants. Definite plans for a national railroad system had been under consideration at a policy level in Peking since at least 1907. The opposition in the provinces to this centralization policy represented a complex mixture of motives: the avarice of the local gentry who were well aware of the profits to be made from promoting railroad construction, however small the practical results might be; a growing anti-Manchu feeling aggravated by the economic and political concessions which the dynasty was making to the foreigner; and the revolutionary ideas of Sun Yat-sen and the T'ung-meng hui, which had won over many of the students who had flocked to Japan and returned to take their places among the lower gentry and lesser officialdom.

Not only was Sheng Hsuan-huai in the forefront of those who were attacked for selling out China's rights by borrowing from the foreigner, but he was also a leading exponent of railroad centralization and the author of the plan which was adopted to carry it into effect. In April 1911, Sheng and Minister of Finance Tsai-tse concluded a loan of £10,000,000 to be used for currency reform with the Four-Power Consortium; and in May Sheng, as minister of posts and communications, was the Chinese signatory to a loan agreement for £6,000,000 more from the Consortium, which was intended for the construction of the Canton-Hankow and Hankow-Szechwan railroads. During those negotiations Sheng was attacked in the provincial assemblies, in the press, and by members of the National Assembly (*Tzu-cheng yuan*), and accused of betraying China and pushing loans because of his personal economic interests in the Yangtze valley.[132]

Then in May 1911 Sheng presented a memorial proposing the nationalization of the railroads which provincial gentry-merchant capital had undertaken but had been unable to complete. The delays and corruption on the Canton-Hankow line and the Hankow-Szechwan railroad were pointed to in particular as injurious to the Manchu reform program and to national defense. These major trunk lines would be taken over and completed by the government, while branch lines might remain in private hands.[133] According to Sheng's plan, the Peking government would make a partial cash payment for the shares of the provincial railroad companies, with the balance being paid in non-interest-bearing bonds (in the case of the Kwangtung Railroad Company, for example, these parts would be 60 and 40 per cent respectively).[134]

The close association of the currency and railroad loans and the railroad nationalization policy of the Manchu government provoked provincial opposition to a new high pitch. Protest meetings, agitation, and riots increased through the summer of 1911. Extreme dissatisfaction with railroad policy joined with anti-Manchu feeling and led to serious outbreaks in Szechwan. Finally on October 10, 1911, the revolt of imperial troops at Wuchang set off independence movements throughout South China and brought about the collapse of the Manchu dynasty.

Sheng was impeached by the National Assembly and dismissed on October 27 as the Manchus were making the last vain efforts to preserve their rule. On the next day the assembly voted to execute him. He fled to the legation quarter, from which he was escorted secretly to Tientsin and then to Japan.[135] Sheng arrived in Japan in November and lived in Kobe for about a year before returning to Shanghai in October 1912 after the Republic had been established and Yuan Shih-k'ai had replaced Sun Yat-sen as provisional president.

Although his political power was ended and the revolution brought him considerable financial losses, Sheng retained his control of the China Merchants' Company and of Han-Yeh-P'ing (acting as chairman of the board of directors of each of them), and of his textile mills (which he had registered with the Hong Kong government in 1911 in order to protect them) and bank. To secure his property from confiscation, however, it is reported that he had to buy immunity with a contribution of Tls. 5,000,000 to the Republican treasury.[136]

From 1913 on, Sheng's activity was limited by sickness and old age, although he remained mentally active. After a long illness, he died in Shanghai on April 27, 1916, at the age of 71.

The narrative of Sheng's career has presented the main facts from which it is possible to proceed with an analysis of the influences determining his activities as an industrial entrepreneur. In particular, the following three sections are concerned with the ways in which Sheng's concurrent roles in his family, as a leading member of the gentry class, and as an official helped or hindered the performance of his entrepreneurial role.

II

Sheng Hsuan-huai and His Family

While overriding loyalty to family ties and obligations was an obstacle to entrepreneurial activity, it must also have been the early environment of Sheng's home which led him to depart as much as he did from traditional values and devote himself to commercial and industrial activities.

The son of the Hupei salt taotai, an important official in the administration of the rich Liang-Huai salt district, would have as much exposure to economic and fiscal matters, albeit of a traditional kind, as one would be likely to get in mid nineteenth-century China. In fact, Sheng's sons claim that at the age of nineteen their father was assisting their grandfather with his duties. They state that he drew up on his own an administrative plan to settle a conflict between the Szechwan and Liang-Huai salt districts which was accepted by higher authorities when it was presented by Sheng K'ang.[137]

Furthermore, as already noted, Sheng's father was for a number of years in the service of Hu Lin-i, a close associate of Tseng Kuo-fan and one of the initiators of the "self-strengthening" movement in the provinces. Sheng himself recalled that when he was young his father often spoke in praise of Hu Lin-i and his achievements in Hupei.[138] And Sheng's sons also report that he was greatly influenced by Hu.[139] Possibly this influence was in the direction of a more realistic appreciation of the strength of the West and the efficacy of its methods than was characteristic of the majority of his countrymen.

The father, Sheng K'ang, was remarkable in another way, as the compiler of the *Huang-ch'ao ching-shih wen hsü-pien* (A further collection of essays on statecraft of the Ch'ing dynasty), which was published in 1897.[140] This work was in effect an edition of the "reform" and "self-strengthening" memorials and essays which had been current in the preceding decades. The writings of K'ang Yu-wei, for example, form a conspicuous part of the contents. Sheng Hsuan-huai and his eldest son, Sheng Ch'ang-i (b. 1863), assisted Sheng K'ang in editing the collection.[141] The subject matter must thus have been current in the Sheng family, who apparently were part of the most progressive element on the Chinese scene at the time.

These were some of the favorable influences which had worked on Sheng when he joined Li Hung-chang's service in 1870 to begin his long career in the field of *yang-wu* or "foreign matters." Throughout this career the obligations which he bore to his family also had an adverse and limiting effect on his business role. The preeminence of the kinship orientation in traditional Chinese society exercised a formidable brake on Sheng's full participation in the behavior patterns which we have stated to be characteristic of the entrepreneur.

For more than forty years Sheng was associated with the China Merchants' Steam Navigation Company, the first example of and the model for later efforts to establish Western-type joint-stock enterprises in China. As has been noted already, he was one of the founders of the company; from 1885 to 1903 he controlled it completely; and in later years he headed its board of directors. At all times he was the largest shareholder, owning from 11,000 to 13,000 of the 40,000 shares outstanding.[142] It is a safe assumption that Sheng can be held accountable for the major policies and developments within the China Merchants' Company throughout this entire period.

Although it was a profit-making concern, the fact is that by the end of its first decade the company had just about reached its maximum size in regard to the number and tonnage of the steamers it operated and the routes it served. The contrast offered by the rapid and continuous growth of the Nippon Yūsen Kaisha, Japan's largest shipping company, is striking. The explanation of this discrepancy lies not merely in the huge official subsidies granted to the Japanese firm as part of a conscious government policy of developing shipping. Equally important was the contrast between the characteristic Japanese pattern of heavy reinvestment of profits in industry and the dissipation (in an economic sense) of the proceeds of China's pioneer modern industries. Iwasaki Yatarō, the founder of the Mitsubishi interests, mobilized all his financial resources to compete with and to effect an amalgamation with the rival Kyōdō Un'yu Kaisha and thereby form the Nippon Yūsen Kaisha.[143] Sheng, the director and the largest shareholder of the China Merchants' Company, invested the largest part of his returns from dividends and irregular looting of the company's surpluses in pawnshops, in real estate, and in land — that is, in the traditional way. His example was followed by his fellow shareholders.

Sheng owned real estate valued at 10 to 20 million taels in the Shanghai Foreign Concession in addition to land in Ch'ang-chou, Soochow, and Hangchow; and he had large amounts of capital in as many as ten pawnshops in Kiangsu province. This recourse to the safety and prestige of land and the profits of usury overshadowed even such large modern investments as Tls. 3,300,000 in the China Merchants' Company and $1,000,000 (Chinese) in the Han-Yeh-P'ing ironworks and mines.[144]

The motivation for making safe traditional investments rather than risking one's entire fortune on the uncertainties of industrial ventures is clear: Sheng's admittedly genuine concern for the development of commerce and industry in China had always to contend with an equally strong desire to develop and conserve his family wealth. One of his contemporaries wrote of him:

Sheng Hsuan-huai always secretly admired the ambition of the first emperor of the Ch'in dynasty [Shih Huang-ti, d. B.C. 210], who desired that his son and grandson and their descendants all be emperors. From the time that Sheng became wealthy, it was his deep wish that his descendants in later generations all be wealthy. Others tended to laugh at his stupidity in believing that a fortune could be maintained from generation to generation, not realizing that Sheng's behavior had this single underlying purpose which he pursued relentlessly.[145]

Sheng's principal method was to use his property during his lifetime to establish the Yü-chai *i-chuang,* a kind of family foundation in perpetuity. Sheng planned that 40 per cent of his wealth was to be used for philanthropic works and 60 per cent was to be shared by his sons and grandsons. Property added after the establishment of the *i-chuang* was to be divided in a like manner; and interest as it accumulated was added to the capital.[146]

The family fortune was dissipated in one generation after his death, despite Sheng's efforts, while the diversion of its accumulation to non-industrial uses was an impediment to his entrepreneurial activity. Family loyalties unqualified by higher loyalties to one's overlord and ultimately to the emperor, as in Japan, were not conducive to the establishment of a shared national goal of industrialization nor to the continued pursuit of innovating (and hence risky) economic activity. Other factors, of course, were also working to retard economic growth. That Sheng's enterprises did not expand to realize further economies of scale and greater profits was a product of his family loyalties, in combination with such considerations as the actual great risk involved in new ventures, and the fear of excessive size and notoriety which might lay the firm open to exactions of the kind discussed in the first two chapters.

Two other ways in which Sheng's ties to his family might have adversely affected the operation of his enterprises may be pointed to briefly. First, his undertakings could hardly have escaped the pervasive nepotism in public and private office. Unfortunately full information is not available. It is known that Sheng's uncle, the younger brother of Sheng K'ang, was a shareholder in the Hua-sheng Cotton Mill, and "for quite a number of years" he managed the China Merchants' Company and Imperial Telegraph Administration offices at Ningpo.[147] Also Sheng's third brother, Sheng Hsing-huai (d. 1903), had headed the Telegraph Administration office in Canton and at the time of his death was the manager of the Hua-sheng Cotton Mill.[148] Of course it cannot be inferred that these two men had been employed only because they were close relatives of Sheng Hsuan-huai and that therefore they were incompetent administrators. It is more than likely, however, that there were many more of Sheng Hsuan-huai's relatives employed in one or another of his enterprises whose only claim to employment was their kinship to the boss.

Second, the possibility that ritual mourning obligations for a close relative could provide the pretext for the removal of a key official from posts he had held for many years and which he was uniquely qualified to fill is again illustrative of the dominance of kinship values even at the possible expense of the rational pursuit of economic activity. The effect of the death of Sheng K'ang in 1902 has already been discussed. Sheng Hsuan-huai's dismissal from his several offices, and particularly from the direction of the China Merchants' Company and the Imperial Telegraph Administration, laid these enterprises open to the cupidity and intrigue of his enemies. The struggle for the control of these companies cannot but have had an untoward effect on their operation as business enterprises.

The admixture of the traditional and the new in Sheng Hsuan-huai's own immediate family, symbolic perhaps of its ambivalence towards business and commerce, is seen in his sons. The eldest, Sheng Ch'ang-i, won the *chü-jen* degree in 1891, accomplishing what his father had not been able to do in the traditional examination system.[149] On the other hand, the fourth son, Sheng En-i (b. 1892), was educated at the "Industrial High School" in Peking, at the University of London, and at Columbia University. He succeeded his father in his industrial enterprises, in the 1920's heading the Han-Yeh-P'ing Coal and Iron Company, the San-hsin (formerly Hua-sheng) Cotton Mill, and the Commercial (formerly Imperial) Bank of China.[150]

III

Sheng Hsuan-huai as a Member of the Kiangsu Gentry

Sheng's family held a prominent place among the gentry of Kiangsu province. His leadership in such gentry activities as raising funds for flood and famine relief, which has already been noted, attests to his position among his peers. What was the effect of Sheng's gentry role on his entrepreneurial activities?

Sheng's feelings about his native Ch'ang-chou are perhaps revealed by his compilation and publication in 1899 of a large collection of the writings of prominent persons of that district, the *Ch'ang-chou hsien-che i-shu* (Writings of eminent men of Ch'ang-chou) in 64 volumes. We may take this at once as evidence of the loyalty towards one's native place which is a prominent Chinese characteristic, and also of participation in the kind of scholarly compiling activity most typical of the educated gentry. Sheng's gentry role and his sharing of provincial loyalties, like his family ties, contributed to some extent to his success as an industrial entrepreneur. On balance, however, the absence of a national focus and direction in China's political life (which was a corollary of the fragmentation of China into conflicting provincial foci) was one of the most obvious obstacles to economic modernization.

On the positive side was Sheng's ability to enlist the support of the gentry of his province and the merchants of Shanghai to provide funds for his enterprises. He was the recognized leader of the Kiangsu and Chekiang shareholders of the China Merchants' Company in opposition to those from the Canton-Hong Kong area who were led by Sheng's arch-rival Hsü Jun. Thus in 1907, while Hsü Jun, whom Yuan Shih-k'ai had placed at the head of the company, was in Macao recuperating from an illness, Sheng called a meeting of the Kiangsu and Chekiang shareholders, who voted to attempt to register the company with the Ministry of Agriculture, Industry, and Commerce. Under the new Company Law this would have removed it from the control of Yuan Shih-k'ai and Hsü Jun. Hsü immediately gathered his supporters in Hong Kong in an attempt to head off the move by the northern shareholders. Sheng on his part sent his deputy Cheng Kuan-ying, a Cantonese with considerable influence in the south — he had been, for example, assistant director (*hsieh-li*) of the Canton Chinese Chamber of Commerce in 1905–1906 — to Hong Kong to try to win support from southern shareholders.[151] While Sheng was not fully successful this time, the incident does illustrate the importance of local groupings in the control of such modern-type enterprises as the China Merchants' Company.

The utility of provincial loyalties is very clear in the case of the establishment of the Imperial Bank of China (*Chung-kuo t'ung-shang yin-hang*). Yung Wing writes in his autobiography[152] that he had plans to organize a "National Bank of China" which were backed by the "Treasury Department" (*Hu-pu*). According to Yung Wing's account, Weng T'ung-ho, the president of the Hu-pu, was on the point of memorializing for imperial approval when he received a telegram from Sheng Hsuan-huai asking Weng to delay until Sheng arrived in Peking. Weng agreed because he and Sheng were friends and fellow provincials.[153] Yung Wing's statement that Sheng "came up to Peking with Tls. 300,000 as presents for two or three princes and other high and influential dignitaries, and got away with Tls. 10,000,000 of appropriations by setting up a bank to manipulate his projects" is inaccurate on the face of it in that the Hu-pu appropriated only Tls. 1,000,000 for

Sheng's bank. But Weng T'ung-ho did back his fellow provincial Sheng, who was given imperial sanction to organize the first Chinese modern bank.

On the negative side was Sheng's "habit in the days of his power — by no means a solitary instance in official circles — of keeping all lucrative posts within his gift for his relatives, protégés and fellow townsmen of Changchou." This is said to have antagonized "the most powerful officials in the North," [154] not the least of whom was Yuan Shih-k'ai. Several examples of men from Sheng's native *hsien*, Wu-chin, who were in his employ might be cited. There were Chang Ts'an-chen, an expectant taotai who was the manager of the P'ing-hsiang Coal Mines;[155] Ho Ssu-k'un, Sheng's Chinese secretary and director of the Nanyang school until his death in February 1901;[156] and T'ao Hsiang, an expectant taotai who was a high official on the Peking-Hankow railroad and a director of the China Merchants' Company.[157] As in the case of nepotism, the extent to which men were used primarily because they were the townsmen of the leader of a project is not known. This was, however, a widely accepted criterion for employment and must have undermined the more universalistic criteria of training and experience.

Although Sheng Hsuan-huai himself came to be able to look beyond purely provincial or local considerations in his public policy — even if not in his private enterprises — his efforts to establish the unified communications system necessary for industrial progress were frustrated by the strength of provincial interests. Sheng's support of a policy of railroad centralization was the result of his extensive experience as director-general of railroads, principal negotiator of China's railroad loans, and minister of posts and communications. But to the Kiangsu and Chekiang gentry, and to those in Szechwan and elsewhere who had organized provincial railroad companies, centralization carried with it the overtones of a Manchu resurgence and increased dependence on foreign creditors. In the end Sheng's railroad nationalization scheme precipitated the fall of the Ch'ing dynasty.

IV

Sheng Hsuan-huai in the Role of an Official

What effect did Sheng's lifetime official role have on his performance as an industrial promoter? There is no doubt that Sheng thought of himself primarily as an official. His sons relate that before his death, their father told them of three regrets he had about his life: first, that he had not passed in the provincial examinations for the *chü-jen* degree as his father and grandfather had done; second, that he had never held the post of *hsien* magistrate, but had passed his career in duties of a semitechnical nature related to "foreign matters"; and third, that while he had had many dealings with foreigners and many foreign friends, he had never traveled to Europe or America.¹⁵⁸ Although they may possibly be no more than the senescent sentiments of an old man reverting to youthful values, the first two of these three regrets seem to represent Sheng's underlying orientation to the traditional society in which the ideals of the gentry-official were dominant. The last regret might be taken to indicate that while he was perhaps two-thirds traditional, he had been able nevertheless to move a considerable distance towards accepting the value of Western techniques of industry and commerce and using his official station to promote their adoption in China.

Again, as we have seen with regard to his family and gentry roles, Sheng's official position was both beneficial and obstructive to his role as an industrialist. The more obvious influences stemming from his official role might be mentioned first.

On the positive side, in the period before Li Hung-chang's fall, Sheng headed the economic or industrial part of Li's regional "machine." In his direction of the China Merchants' Company, the telegraphs, and the Hua-sheng Cotton Mill, he stood halfway between the highest provincial officials and the shareholders and staff of the several firms. When necessary, Sheng was able to call on Li Hung-chang to obtain, for example, a monopoly franchise for the carriage of tribute rice, a subsidy for the telegraph lines, or a tax exemption for the textile plant.¹⁵⁹ Li acted as Sheng's protector against the many impeachments which were presented to the throne accusing him of extortion, self-seeking, bribery, and other malpractices.¹⁶⁰ While these indictments may often have had some basis, especially within the context of the *kuan-tu shang-pan* system in which the distinction between private and government property was a blurred one, Li invariably cleared his subordinate. In return Sheng's enterprises provided services, income, and sinecures for Li and his followers. After 1895, Governor-general Chang Chih-tung filled much the same role with respect to these enterprises. Sheng himself was able to play the intermediary role between local officialdom and the management of the several industrial undertakings which he headed. With the growth of his own political power after 1896 and his rise to prominence in metropolitan circles, of course Sheng's ability to obtain official support and protection for his projects was enhanced.

On the other hand, while the successful operation of new industries required government support, at least to the extent of tax concessions, Sheng's involvement in factional official strife both taxed his energies and hindered the operation of his industries. The seesaw battle for the control of the economic component of Li Hung-chang's Chihli satrapy has already been described. The principal modern economic institutions —

shipping, railroads, telegraphs — which were being fought over were considered by all parties more as sources of private revenue and power than in terms of their possible contribution to further economic development. As a result, the provision of an adequate communications network on which other enterprises might depend, particularly vital in a country of China's size, was retarded.

A further negative influence was the tendency to superimpose the practices of the official *yamen* — described in the pejorative phrase *kuan-ch'ang* — onto the operation of a modern-type business. While in office at Chefoo as a customs taotai, Sheng insisted on taking charge of even the smallest details of the operations of the China Merchants' Company in Shanghai.[161] His administration was no worse than that of the on-the-spot managers of these *kuan-tu shang-pan* enterprises who were often unable to run a purportedly modern firm as anything other than an old-fashioned government bureau.

Of equal importance with these direct consequences of Sheng's official role were the effects which might be attributed to the place occupied by his entrepreneurial activities within the general program which he sought to realize as an official. The defeat by Japan in 1894–1895 called forth many proposals to reform the inadequate Ch'ing finances. Lo Yü-tung, in his study of the fiscal situation in the Kuang-hsü period, notes a change of emphasis in these proposals away from exclusive concern with economy (*chieh-liu*, "reduce expenditure"). The new attention to means of developing revenue resulted from a frank acknowledgment that the domestic economy was in bad straits. This view was influenced by acquaintance with European fiscal methods. Lo points to Sheng Hsuan-huai as the best representative of the officials who were presenting the more realistic proposals of this period.[162] Chang Chih-tung's biographer, Hsü T'ung-hsin, also credits Sheng with opening the discussion of the measures which became the Manchu reform program of the post-Boxer years.[163] It should be profitable therefore to review his proposals which together constitute a plan of some substance.

In January 1901, soon after his appointment to negotiate revision of the commercial treaties, Sheng drafted a memorial to which Governors-general Chang Chih-tung and Liu K'un-i also added their signatures. A key sentence read, "After the return of peaceful conditions, if we are able to promulgate effective measures for the reform of our domestic institutions so that the powers shall know our determination to strengthen ourselves (*tzu-ch'iang*) and vigorously eliminate accumulated evils, our position during the treaty negotiations will be improved."[164] While the phrase had become a well-worn cliché, *tzu-ch'iang*, "self-strengthening" in order to cope with the West, was still a keynote of the program of reform which Sheng advocated. It was within this framework that he proceeded to offer more specific proposals.

His major project, which he entitled "A General Plan for Self-strengthening" (*Tzu-ch'iang ta-chi*), had been presented by Sheng in October 1896 when he was called to Peking to take charge of the newly established Imperial Railway Administration.[165] It was divided into three main sections: training troops (*lien-ping*), managing finances (*li-ts'ai*), and educating talent (*yü-ts'ai*). In the first section Sheng called for the establishment of a modern conscript army to replace the "Army of the Green Standard" (*Lü-ying*) whose faults and abuses he recounted. He had no qualms about admitting that Western military organization was superior. "At present the military system of all countries East and West is changing from the use of voluntary enlistments to a conscript army. This is the trend in the whole world, how can China alone be different?"

This first section, however, was subordinate to that on the management of China's finances which contained the most important of Sheng's proposals. Here his theme was "recovering [the wealth] which has flowed abroad" (*wan wai-i*). To achieve this end, Sheng suggested taking advantage of the foreigners' dislike of *likin* in order to abolish it in return for an increase in the import tariff. The larger proceeds from the tariff, plus a stamp tax (*yin-shui*) which should be initiated immediately, would together make up for the revenue lost by the end of internal transit taxes. A further good result would be an increase in the export of native products which now would be freed of most internal taxation, while foreign imports would gradually decrease in the face of a higher import duty. Secondly Sheng drew attention to the fact that foreigners marshaled the wealth of their lands for commercial purposes through the agency of banks. China should do likewise and not continue to depend on foreign banking facilities. The ultimate goal would be for Chinese banks, having established their soundness and won the trust of the merchants and people, to undertake domestic loans in place of foreign borrowing with its high interest rates and losses in exchange due to the falling value of silver in terms of gold. Sheng's third economic proposal was for monetary reform. He called for the establishment of a system of coinage based on the *ching-p'ing* or "Treasury" tael, 900 fine, whose dollars and subsidiary coins would replace the foreign dollars which were omnipresent in the treaty ports. A central mint would be established in Peking with branches at Canton, Hankow, Tientsin, and Shanghai; taxes were to be paid in this standard national coin and the use of bullion as currency prohibited except for treasury payments and receipts, in which case the exchange rate would be very favorable to the Ministry of Revenue. Finally, he proposed the appointment of a high official who would give his full attention to promoting commercial affairs.

In the third section, on training talented men, Sheng assigned the credit for the large number of competent men in the West to the schools and their utilitarian curricula. Education in China, on the contrary, while it once may have been in accord with current needs, had now become stultified. Therefore he urged the establishment of schools at the provincial level with Western-type curricula which would prepare Chinese in subjects appropriate to the modern world. However, the lesson of the T'ung-wen Kuan (established in 1861) and other early attempts to introduce Western-style education should be heeded.[166] Few first-class persons had been attracted because participation in the traditional examination system alone offered a secure future. The examination system could not be completely overthrown at the present (1896), but it was necessary to establish a parallel way to success through "new studies."

It may seem naïve for Sheng to have expected to accomplish the program he outlined in his "General Plan for Self-strengthening." He was himself, however, aware of the formidable difficulties. Sheng closed his memorial by expressing the fear that his three main points — which he described as no more than the ancient policy of "sufficient food and an adequate army" (tsu-shih tsu-ping) although it was also the way in which Europe and America had strengthened and enriched themselves — would not be adopted because of the resistance of the old order, in particular of the provincial officials and gentry. In that case year by year the foreigners, lured on by China's weakness, would make greater incursions.

Except for the proposal to establish an annual budget (i-nien k'uai-chi) of anticipated income and expenditure, which appeared in a memorial at the end of 1899,[167] the plan for chambers of commerce which has already been discussed, and the project for nationalization of the railroads, this "General Plan for Self-strengthening" contained in outline at least all the major items for fiscal reform and the promotion of commerce which Sheng proposed while he held high office between the years 1896 and 1911. Later memorials elaborated on most of these items; Sheng's efforts to achieve tariff revision and currency reform, for example, have been noted above. The opening of the Imperial Bank of China in 1897 represented the first step toward the realization of Sheng's schemes for central banking. The schools which he founded in Tientsin and Shanghai were intended to train the talent he called for in the "General Plan." Similarly the currency loan which he negotiated in 1911 was for the purpose of reorganizing the Ch'ing monetary system and establishing the Ta-Ch'ing Bank as a central government bank similar to the Bank of Japan as organized by Matsukata Masayoshi.

When they are held up for examination, it must be concluded that the measures which Sheng sought to achieve over a fifteen-year period that saw the "Hundred Days Reform" of 1898, the Boxer uprising and its repercussions, and the Manchu efforts to reform their tottering government, were essentially conservative ones. The "General Plan" included most of the major items later contained in the famous reform memorials of Chang Chih-tung and Liu K'un-i which were submitted in July 1901 and are generally taken to be the program of the post-Boxer Manchu reform movement.[168] More important, Sheng's proposals contained little that was not part of that conservative effort to shore up the dynasty. Even his economic proposals were limited to fiscal devices which only indirectly affected the underlying economy. Currency reform, central banking, the abolition of *likin*, the institution of an annual budget would all have contributed to ordering the muddled Ch'ing finances. But there were no sharp departures in Sheng's program comparable, for example, to the Japanese reform and centralization of the land tax, which more than anything else secured the financial stability of the Meiji regime. In this connection it is significant that political questions — above all, constitutionalism and central-local government relations which drew so much attention in the last years of the Ch'ing dynasty — were almost completely absent from his memorials. Moreover, he failed totally to come to grips with such issues as anti-Manchu nationalism, the decay of the official system, and the need for agricultural reform.

For all his attention to industrial and commercial affairs, Sheng was not a "merchant" as that term was employed in his own memorials and other contemporary writings. He was an official, and especially from 1896 an official very much concerned with fiscal matters in the empire. His industrial enterprises, next to their importance as a source of the family fortune, were essentially a basis for the power which he sought to wield in the Peking political arena. Recognition, fame, status, power were still accessible only through one major route, through winning and exercising a prominent place in the traditional governmental structure. This is clear in Sheng's biography, from which one gets the impression that he was much more disturbed about losing his political posts in 1902, 1903, 1905, and 1908 than he was about attacks directed against his several industrial enterprises.[169] Simply to be an industrial magnate, even to the extent of controlling a fortune of several tens of millions of taels, did not bring with it a status in Chinese society equal to that of a high official. This was a throwback, of course, to the lower status which had been assigned to the merchant in the traditional rank order of "gentry-official, farmer, artisan, merchant" (*shih, nung, kung, shang*). Sheng's concern about his failure to succeed in the examinations, his regret that he never had been a local magistrate ("the father and mother of the people," *fu-mu kuan*), are reflected in the reform program which he sought to carry out, a program oriented to bolstering the old political order by making it more efficient in economic matters.

The effect of Sheng's preoccupation with political status, parallel to the results of his concern to protect the family fortune, must have been that the operation of his industrial enterprises became, so to speak, a dependent variable. The efforts which he made to promote "commercial matters" (*shang-wu*), although they included specific proposals for commercial education, a commercial code, chambers of commerce, the promotion of exports, and the like, which were undoubtedly excellent and to the point, nevertheless were, I believe, accompanied by a sophisticated pessimism about the response to be expected from the Chinese merchants and people. His comment in 1889 on a proposal for industrial schools which would show success in ten years was, "People are flighty, ten years is rather soon." [170] On several occasions he characterized the Chinese merchant. For example, in connection with plans for financing the Peking-Hankow railroad Sheng wrote:

The Imperial Railway Administration originally intended to depend on raising private capital. But Chinese merchants will only come forward when the construction is completed and profits are visible. Your servant recalls his experience in managing the China Merchants' Company and the Telegraph Administration. When imperial proclamations and official exhortations are used in an effort to inspire confidence in a stock issue, those who respond are persons dependent on officials or those such as salt merchants and pawnshop operators whom the official power can reach. It is rarely heard that outside merchants and common people buy stock. They may be attracted by a completed enterprise, but it is impossible to depend on them for any new undertaking.[171]

And in a memorial on "commercial matters" presented in 1899, he remarked that

wealthy [merchants] are wont only to look after their private welfare or that of their families. Even those who are called "enlightened" at the best are no more than a handful of men combining their resources to open a shop. Joint-stock companies, as in the West, generally are not carried on in China. As for major projects to develop our economic potential, we have no recourse but to let foreigners handle them. This is much to be regretted.[172]

In these memorials Sheng knowingly attributed much of the blame for the hesitations of the Chinese merchant to "contributions" requested by the Peking government and exactions by *yamen* underlings. Yet from his own experience he must have been aware of the reality that economic development, and especially industrial growth, in China faced obstacles greater even than official exactions. With his knowledge that little improvement in this situation was to be expected immediately, the importance of Sheng's industrial ventures as purely business units operating in a competitive market economy was decreased in his eyes. Correspondingly their importance as enterprises which could furnish immediate revenue — at the expense perhaps of their future viability — was increased.

Sheng's role as an entrepreneur and manager will be shown in the following chapters, which consider the major *kuan-tu shang-pan* enterprises with which he was associated. In each case his activity was affected by his responsibilities in his concurrent roles — family, gentry, official. On balance they were powerful bonds tying him to traditional values and limiting his motivation and ability to do new things or to deal with old problems in a new way.

4

The China Merchants' Company: Merchant Management

First in time among the modern, Western-type enterprises which constituted Sheng Hsuan-huai's economic empire, and the prototype for all later *kuan-tu shang-pan* enterprises, was the China Merchants' Steam Navigation Company (*Lun-ch'uan chao-shang chü*), China's premier steamship line.[1] The importance of this company on the Chinese scene is indicated by the fact that in 1914, at the end of the period with which we are concerned, it owned 30 steamers aggregating 54,367 gross tons out of a total steam tonnage flying the Chinese flag estimated at 75 vessels and 89,237 tons. Its two nearest Chinese competitors could claim only five steamers and 4,808 tons and three steamers and 3,097 tons respectively. The company's preeminence among Chinese firms did not, however, extend to its position among the dozen shipping companies, mostly foreign, competing for the rich stake of the carrying trade in Chinese waters. No overseas commerce was carried in Chinese bottoms and only 13 per cent of the coastwise and riverine trade. In 1912 the average proportion of vessels under the Chinese flag entering the five major ports of Tientsin (15.2 per cent), Shanghai (16.26 per cent), Hankow (10.8 per cent), Swatow (1.8 per cent) and Canton (10.7 per cent) was only 10.9 per cent.[2] Thus while the China Merchants' Company may be studied as a leading example of Chinese efforts to introduce modern industry, it also stands witness to the limited results of these efforts.

The C.M.S.N. Co. was established as an effort to compete profitably with the foreign shipping, mainly British, which had come to dominate the carrying trade in Chinese waters. Its success must be measured by the extent to which this Chinese firm succeeded in replacing its foreign rivals, as well as by the size of the profits it returned to its promoters. The operations of the China Merchants' Company were not, however, an independent variable. Given the expansion of British (and later Japanese) commercial activity, and the existence of the treaty system as defined in 1858–1860, it must be admitted that the possibility of recovering for the Chinese flag the traffic controlled by foreign steamers was a limited one. The principal problem to which this and the next chapter are directed is, therefore, that of the performance of the Chinese company *within the margin* between the apparently irreducible minimum of foreign shipping and the gradually expanding coastal trade in which it participated. In what ways did its organization and operation as a *kuan-tu shang-pan* enterprise aid or hinder the success of the China Merchants' Company within this margin where profitable operation and growth were possible?

I

Origin of the China Merchants' Company

Yung Wing, one of the first Chinese to study in America and a graduate of Yale, records in his autobiography that in 1867 at the suggestion of his friend Ting Jih-ch'ang, governor of Kiangsu, he drew up a series of reform proposals. Prominent among them was a plan for the organization of a steamship company on a joint-stock basis. "No foreigner was to be allowed to be a stockholder in the company. It was to be a purely Chinese Company, managed and worked by Chinese exclusively." And, to insure its stability and success, the government was to grant to the company an annual subsidy in the form of a franchise to carry a specified percentage of the tribute rice from Shanghai to Tientsin.[3] Yung Wing's plan was submitted to the Tsungli Yamen, which gave its approval, but no action was taken to carry it out. However, as a result of this initiative and also in response to urging from the inspector-general of customs, Robert Hart, that Chinese traders be permitted to own and operate foreign-style vessels, provisional regulations for the operation of Chinese-owned steamers were drawn up and published in 1867.[4]

Suggestions for the establishment of a steamship company were also made by Feng Kuei-fen, at one time secretary to Li Hung-chang.[5] But the immediate occasion for the establishment of the China Merchants' Company was the vigorous response of Governor-general Li to pressure on the Tsungli Yamen by conservative officials seeking the end of steamship construction at the Foochow Arsenal and Shipyard. At the beginning of 1872, the grand secretary Sung Chin had memorialized indicting the Shipyard for failure to fulfill its original plan. Sung charged that sixteen warships in five years had been promised at a cost of Tls. 3,000,000, but only six had been completed, while expenditures already exceeded earlier estimates.[6] The matter was referred to Li, who came to the defense of steamship construction in his memorial of June 29, 1872. Li's principal argument was a plea for military self-strengthening; thus

> all other expenditures of our nation can be economized, but the expenses for supporting the army, establishing defenses, drilling in the use of guns and cannon, and building warships should never in any circumstances be economized. If we try to save funds, then we shall be obliged to neglect all these defense measures; the nation will never have anything to stand upon, and we shall never be strong.[7]

Simultaneously he urged that the Foochow Shipyard build merchant vessels, as Tseng Kuo-fan had planned to do at the Kiangnan (Shanghai) Arsenal, to compete with the foreign carriers who dominated China's coastal trade. But, Li continued,

> Tseng Kuo-fan and I have noted that none of the rich Chinese merchants are willing to enter into relations with officials; furthermore, if Chinese merchants receive government vessels, the foreigners who have monopolized the profits of the carrying trade will use all their resources to defeat the undertaking. It is therefore necessary that Chinese merchants themselves establish a joint-stock company, build their own godowns, and provide their own marine insurance.
>
> The capital needed will be large and the operations complex, and I fear that no profits can be expected in the beginning. . . . If there is not an upright and capable official who knows the merchant mind and is trusted by them to lead the merchants and take responsibility, the merchants will be too fearful to proceed. . . . And it will be necessary to permit them to carry tribute rice in order to provide a guaranteed income in the face of severe competition from foreign merchants.[8]

The essential ingredients of the C.M.S.N. Co. as a *kuan-tu shang-pan* enterprise were thus set forth in Li Hung-chang's memorial: Chinese merchants to organize and finance a shipping company, an official manager to direct them, and a concession for the carriage of tribute rice to ensure the company's profitable operation. All this was to be carried out under the supervision of Governor-general Li in his capacity as commissioner for the northern ports (*Pei-yang ta-ch'en*).[9] Though there were many modifications in detail, as will be shown below, this basic organization of the company remained unchanged until the Republican period.

Governor-general Li quickly discovered that Foochow ships were unsuitable for the carrying trade. Resort had to be made to the purchase of foreign-built steamers.[10] But the Foochow incident had served to direct his attention to the potentialities of a merchant-steamer project. In August 1872 he directed Chu Ch'i-ang, commissioner of sea transport for Chekiang province, and Sheng Hsuan-huai to draw up regulations for the projected company.[11] Chu and Sheng, after an investigation of shipping in coastal waters, reported to Li that while Chinese merchants in Shanghai had considerable capital invested in the coasting trade, it had all been put into foreign firms. As an example, they noted that Chinese funds accounted for more than half of the total investment in Russell and Company's Chin-li-yuan dock in Shanghai. It was a matter of concern that "in the event of financial irregularities, Chinese officials are unable to interfere." The situation would be rectified "by establishing an official bureau (*kuan-chü*) to solicit investments from Chinese merchants so as to enable those who have ties with foreign capital gradually to transfer their funds to the official bureau. This would both strengthen the empire and reassure the merchants." [12] Following a further positive report from the Shanghai and Tientsin customs taotais, Li ordered Chu to Shanghai, where with his brother, Chu Ch'i-chao, he established an office in October 1872.

Chu Ch'i-ang sought to raise funds in the Chinese mercantile community in Shanghai by approaching such prominent figures as Hu Kuang-yung, a customs banker and tea merchant later noted for his role in arranging China's first foreign loans; but his success was meager.[13] Only Tls. 10,000 in cash had been collected from merchants by April 1873; and that came entirely from one member of the Shanghai community, Yü Hsi-sheng, "probably a member of the famous junk-owning Yü family." [14] Although other merchants had subscribed for shares totaling more than Tls. 100,000, payments of these subscriptions were slow in materializing. To get the company under way, Li Hung-chang entrusted Chu with Tls. 50,000 of his personal funds. More important, he permitted the company to borrow Tls. 135,000 from Chihli military funds at 7 per cent interest.[15] With three steamers, godowns and docks at Shanghai and Tientsin, and a promise for the carriage of 200,000 piculs of tribute rice which Governor-general Li had obtained from Kiangsu and Chekiang provinces, the China Merchants' Steam Navigation Company formally began operations on January 4, 1873.[16]

II

The Company over Four Decades, 1873–1913

Between 1873 and 1913, the C.M.S.N. Co. was reorganized six times. These alterations consisted mainly of changes in its managerial personnel. For the most part the company's business operations continued uninterrupted. They could not, however, fail to be affected by the changes in the framework within which they were conducted.

The original manager of the company, Chu Ch'i-ang, was replaced in June 1873. From that time until 1885, the C.M.S.N. Co. was headed by the ex-compradores Tong King-sing (T'ang T'ing-shu) and Hsü Jun, who managed it as technically a merchant-operated or private enterprise (*shang-pan*). The firm, however, remained under the direct supervision of Li Hung-chang, Chihli governor-general and commissioner for the northern ports. From 1885 to 1902, the company was controlled by Sheng Hsuan-huai. This was the period *par excellence* of the C.M.S.N. Co. as a *kuan-tu shang-pan* enterprise. Li Hung-chang's fall in 1895 resulted temporarily in a marked attenuation of the control exercised by the commissioner for the northern ports. But in 1902, Yuan Shih-k'ai, who had become Chihli governor-general and commissioner in the previous year, was able to reassert the power of that office over the company and to replace its director-general, Sheng Hsuan-huai, with his own appointee. The *kuan-tu shang-pan* organization of the company, however, was retained largely unchanged. When Yuan's political position began to be undermined in 1907, Sheng was able to regain control of the firm from Yuan's followers. Then in 1909, jurisdiction over the China Merchants' Company, which since 1872 had been vested in the commissioner for the northern ports, was transferred to the Ministry of Posts and Communications as one phase of Peking's attempt to centralize control over communications. This move had the paradoxical effect of turning Sheng and his supporters into advocates of entirely private operation, and a long series of skirmishes ensued. With the collapse of the Manchu dynasty, the C.M.S.N. Co. was formally freed from any official control. While irregular interference by successive governments was by no means ended, until it was reorganized and taken over by the Kuomintang government (a lengthy process extending through the years 1927–1933), the company was operated as a private business firm.

These successive changes in the C.M.S.N. Co.'s directing personnel were in large part a by-product of the political context in which the firm operated. They can be correlated with the varying fortunes of Li Hung-chang, Sheng Hsuan-huai, and Yuan Shih-k'ai. In particular, they reflect one half of the dual nature enjoyed by every *kuan-tu shang-pan* enterprise. The China Merchants' Steam Navigation Company was an entrepreneurial venture, a joint-stock enterprise engaged in the steamship business. At the same time, it occupied the status of a political unit, a minor but by no means unnoticed fragment of the bureaucratic structure of late Ch'ing China. The existence and success of the company were affected both by happenings in the marketplace and within the walls of the official *yamen*.

Behind the changes just described, the company's structure remained remarkably stable. The kernel of the China Merchants' Steam Navigation Company was, of course, its existence as a business firm. It owned and operated ships, wharves, and warehouses which were employed in the carriage of passengers, general freight, and tribute rice. Its operations required a large number of seamen to command and sail its steamers, and workmen to repair them. Longshoremen to load and unload cargoes from ship or godown were hired through contractors. Numerous clerks were employed to keep the records of these activities in the company's branches, and at its Shanghai head office. This aspect of the C.M.S.N. Co. as an operating business unit, is shown in the diagram (at I) on page 102 in its relation to other facets of the company's structure.

The business of transporting and handling freight and passengers was superintended from the company's head office in Shanghai. Although the precise division of responsibilities and the names of the organs which carried them out naturally varied during the forty years under consideration, typically the managerial staff was divided into three sections. The shipping office supervised the procurement of cargoes and the operation of the company's steamers. The fiscal section kept the company's accounts and handled receipts and disbursements. It was headed by a chief accountant, and in a later period supervised by "auditors" selected at the annual shareholders' meeting. A third section handled the vast amount of paper work and general administration which the company's ramified operations made necessary. It was also responsible for the translation into Chinese or English, as the case might be, of the bills of lading, shipping papers, letters, and the like by means of which this business was carried out. The heads of these three sections, together with the managers of the company's branch offices in Shanghai and other ports, constituted the operating managerial staff, or business managers (at various times *shang-tung* or *tsung-tung* as will be explained below), of the C.M.S.N. Co. They are designated II, A in the diagram.

Policy matters were in the hands of the company's official managers (II, B). During most of the period under consideration they were usually three in number, a chief manager (at various times *tsung-pan* or *tu-pan*) and two assistants (*hui-pan*). An overlapping of personnel between the business management and the official management of the company was not uncommon, but its occurrence was usually limited to the assistant managers.

The company was owned by its shareholders (II, C). From 1909, when a board of directors elected by the shareholders was established, policy matters were also technically in the hands of that board. Prior to 1909 there had been only a minimal participation by the shareholders in the direction of the company's affairs, and even after that year their relation to the official managers was only partially defined. There was in fact, as might be expected, an overlapping of personnel between the company's managers (both the operating managerial staff and the official managers) and the owners of its stock. These three categories of

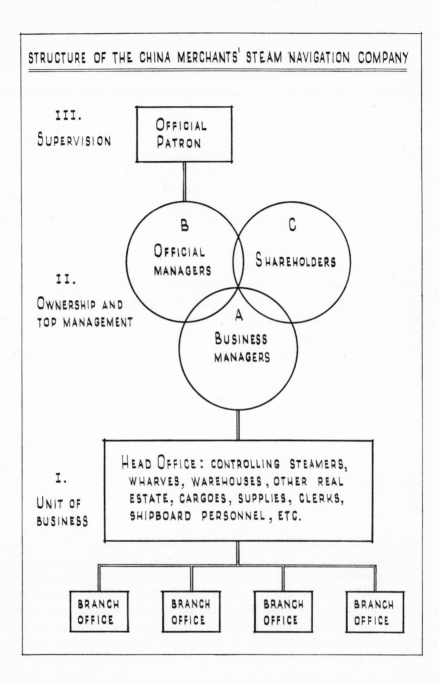

STRUCTURE OF THE CHINA MERCHANTS' STEAM NAVIGATION COMPANY

III.
SUPERVISION

OFFICIAL PATRON

B
OFFICIAL MANAGERS

C
SHAREHOLDERS

II.
OWNERSHIP AND TOP MANAGEMENT

A
BUSINESS MANAGERS

I.
UNIT OF BUSINESS

HEAD OFFICE: CONTROLLING STEAMERS, WHARVES, WAREHOUSES, OTHER REAL ESTATE, CARGOES, SUPPLIES, CLERKS, SHIPBOARD PERSONNEL, ETC.

BRANCH OFFICE

BRANCH OFFICE

BRANCH OFFICE

BRANCH OFFICE

persons are grouped together in the diagram as the owners and top management of the C.M.S.N. Co.

At the top of the company's structure were the successive high officials, from Li Hung-chang through Yuan Shih-k'ai, and after them the Ministry of Posts and Communications (*Yu-ch'uan pu*), who acted as its sponsors or patrons (III in the diagram). Liaison between the China Merchants' Company as a business firm and the governmental circles whose protection and assistance made the company a profitable venture was conducted by its official managers. In the eyes of its patrons, this *kuan-tu shang-pan* enterprise was looked upon as a variety of minor governmental bureau and treated accordingly.

The most ambiguous position was occupied by the official managers who stood between higher officialdom above and the company's shareholders and staff below. These men — in particular Chu Ch'i-ang, Tong King-sing, Hsü Jun, and Sheng Hsuan-huai — participated both in the "official supervision" and the "merchant management" of the enterprise. Their ambiguity of status was in proportion to the importance of the roles which they played. In other words, the history of the China Merchants' Company from 1873 to 1913 is largely a record of their activities. Since it is convenient to treat separately the mercantile and official sides of this history, Chapter 5 is concerned primarily with the relation of the C.M.S.N. Co. to the officials under whose aegis it existed. The remainder of the present chapter is devoted to a consideration of the company as a business enterprise and to the men who managed it.

III

The Company's Business

Examination of the company's accounts for any typical year will give a good indication of the nature and extent of its business operations. The following data for the most part are culled from the C.M.S.N. Co.'s 20th Annual Report for the year 1893, that is, during the height of Sheng Hsuan-huai's control of the enterprise.[17] Table 6 shows the company's operating account for 1893; the headings in this and the following tables are given as they have been translated in the sources I have relied upon. Table 7 shows the company's steamer working accounts for three years, 1884–1886; detailed data for 1893 are not available. In Table 8, I have expanded the entry "value of wharves, jetties, godowns, landed properties" in the company's 1893 balance sheet (not shown) in order to indicate how its real-estate holdings were distributed among the several ports.

In 1893, the C.M.S.N. Co. operated twenty-six steamers totaling 24,584 tons (net). These were roughly the number and tonnage of the

Table 6

C.M.S.N. Co. Profit and Loss Account, 1893 (in Shanghai taels)

Credit		
	1. Profit from working steamers	803,664
	2. Profit on tribute rice transport	37,765
	3. Cargo boat hire for rice transport	15,380
	4. Profit from northern godowns	49,245
	5. Godown rent from customers	55,018
	6. Rent received from all ports	57,141
	7. Sale of old stores	320
	8. Total	1,018,533

Debit		
	9. Rent of land at Shanghai	28,083
	10. Various repairs	32,723
	11. Sundry expenses	114,227
	12. Interest, various	23,763
	13. Interest to shareholders at 6 per cent	120,000
	14. Interest to shareholders at 4 per cent	80,000
	15. Depreciation on godowns and steamers	313,528
	16. Bonus to staff, 10 per cent on profit of Tls. 306,210	30,621
	17. Balance to reserve fund	275,589
	18. Total	1,018,533

Table 7

Steamer Working Accounts, 1884–1886 (in Shanghai taels)

	1884	1885	1886
Earnings	1,923,700[a]	1,773,978	1,868,833
Insurance	269,055	173,194	260,100
Current repairs	145,318	63,741	119,084
Coal	379,845	267,788	264,947
Salaries	405,418	321,208	345,353
Stevedores	165,034	482,803	186,974
Sundries	178,509		134,355
Expenses	1,543,082	1,308,736	1,310,615
Profits	380,617	465,235	558,017
Expenses as a percentage of earnings	80.2%	73.8%	70.1%
Permanent repairs (not included in expenses)	95,500	90,500	35,000

[a] All fractional taels have been omitted.

fleet it maintained during most of the period under consideration. Information regarding the routes followed by these vessels during 1893 is unfortunately not available, but it is unlikely that the schedule of a decade earlier, which is available, had been drastically altered. In 1880, the company had five steamers running on the Yangtze River between Shanghai and Hankow, and one steamer to Ichang further up the river. One vessel operated regularly in the inland waters between Canton and Macao. In the coastwise traffic the following lines were operated: Shanghai to Ningpo, one steamer; Shanghai to Wenchow, one steamer; Shanghai to Foochow, one steamer; Shanghai to Swatow, one steamer; and Shanghai to Canton, two steamers. Five vessels plied regularly between Shanghai and Tientsin, the route on which tribute rice was carried. Four others carried rice to Tientsin in the summer, but sailed to Hong Kong, Swatow, and Canton in the autumn and winter. One steamer followed a route connecting Hong Kong, Swatow, Amoy, and Taiwan; and at least four others were engaged in miscellaneous service.[18]

Reference to Table 8 will show to what extent the company's godowns and other real estate were concentrated in Shanghai. The total value of the wharves, jetties, godowns, and landed properties owned by the C.M.S.N. Co. in 1893 is given as Tls. 2,075,000. Judging from somewhat later data,[19] this total almost certainly represents a considerable undervaluation. In any case, nearly three quarters of the valuation is accounted for by Shanghai properties. The next largest totals are those for Hankow and Tientsin respectively. These figures accurately reflect the central position of the port of Shanghai for all of China's water-borne trade, as well as the importance of Hankow as the terminus of the company's Yangtze river line, and of Tientsin as the port of destination for tribute rice shipments.

The freight and passengers carried by the company's steamers to and from these several ports in 1893 brought in gross receipts of Tls. 2,161,354.[20] Shipboard personnel and the operating expenses of the vessels were paid from the gross receipts. After these sums were deducted, the net profit from general shipping operations came to Tls. 803,664 (Table 6, line 1). In this year the proportion of operating expenses to gross earnings was 62.9 per cent. An indication of the distribution of these costs among the major items such as salaries, insurance, coal, and the like may be obtained from Table 7. It appears from this table and from the figures just cited that the company's shipping operations showed a gain in efficiency in the decade 1884–1893; the drop from 80.2 per cent to 62.9 per cent in the proportion of gross receipts devoted to expenses is a considerable one.

Each spring the company's vessels transported tribute rice, which had been collected from the Yangtze provinces in the preceding months

Table 8

Value of C.M.S.N. Co. Wharves, Jetties, Godowns, Landed Properties, 1983

Location	Value (Shanghai taels)
Shanghai eastern godowns	20,000
Shanghai northern godowns	280,000
Shanghai central godowns	135,000
Shanghai southern godowns	800,000
Shanghai 16th ward landed property	14,000
Shanghai Chinese godowns	55,000
Shanghai Chinese landed property	100,000
Total Shanghai property	1,404,000
Tientsin	168,000
Tungchow	5,000
Chefoo	2,000
Ichang	4,000
Hankow	180,000
Kiukiang	70,000
Wuhu	20,000
Chinkiang	50,000
Ningpo	18,000
Wenchow	6,000
Foochow	24,000
Swatow	30,000
Macao	5,000
Hong Kong	84,000
Canton	5,000
Total all other properties	671,000
Grand total	2,075,000

and stored in Shanghai godowns, from Shanghai to Tientsin. The profits reported from the carriage of rice, a total of Tls. 53,145 (Table 6, lines 2–3), also appear to be net. Assuming that 500,000 piculs of rice were carried in 1893 at the going rate of Tls. 0.38 per picul, the gross receipts under this heading were probably slightly under Tls. 200,000.[21] It is not certain whether the figures reported as income from godowns and landed properties (lines 4–6) were actually net amounts. They totaled Tls. 161,404, but presumably would be subject to deduction of the item "rent of land at Shanghai, Tls. 28,083" (line 9). In this year the ratio of these three sources of income one to another was roughly 16:1:3. In an earlier period the role played by tribute rice carriage would have been many times greater; but long before 1893 the transport of general freight had become the company's principal source of revenue.

To obtain these cargoes, the company established a freight-brokerage system like that already in use by foreign shipping companies. Generous commissions and rebates were offered, enabling the C.M.S.N. Co. to secure the patronage of a large number of treaty-port merchants. In this matter the influence of Tong King-sing with the powerful "Canton Guild" was of great importance.[22] The company also undertook to operate vessels under charter from other owners in return for a commission of 5 per cent on the gross receipts.[23] However, it relied mainly on the efforts of the network of branches established in the principal ports to supply its steamers with cargoes.

Initially, branches were opened in Tientsin, Hankow, Hong Kong, and Swatow; and at Shanghai there was a shipping office distinct from the head office.[24] Later additional branches were established at Tungchow, Chefoo, Ichang, Kiukiang, Wuhu, Chinkiang, Ningpo, Wenchow, Foochow, Macao, and Canton. The deputy managers who headed these offices were usually shareholders in the C.M.S.N. Co., and many were former compradores. They were designated by the company's head and themselves hired their own staffs and warehouse employees.[25] Until 1878, 5 per cent of the annual gross receipts was set aside as "office expenses" (chü-nei ching-fei) to cover the salaries and operating costs of both the branches and the head office.[26] From 1879, although the operation of the head office was still charged to the gross receipts (Table 6, line 11), a new system was adopted for the branches. Each branch received a monthly expense allowance, and in addition it was allowed to retain 4 per cent of its receipts on outgoing cargo plus 1 per cent on incoming or transit cargo from other ports. Under this arrangement, the branch managers became essentially commission agents.[27] The abuses which developed in the operation of this system will be discussed below in connection with the problem of corruption in the C.M.S.N. Co.

IV

Management Personnel

The business operations of the company were controlled by its managers from the head office in Shanghai. These men, said the company's 8th Annual Report, "are the largest shareholders" and "the majority of the shareholders are friends and relations of the managers." [28] Moreover, the managerial personnel were linked together in owing their appointments to the officials who supervised the company. In the case of the successive official managers, Chu Ch'i-ang, Tong King-sing, Sheng Hsuan-huai, and Hsü Jun, for example, they were designated by the commissioner for the northern ports, that is, by Li Hung-chang and later by Yuan Shih-k'ai. The business managers who served under them held their offices on the recommendation of the official managers. As we shall see, these two categories in some instances overlapped. In the following pages, the careers of some of the most important of these individuals are examined; these careers may well be compared with that of Sheng Hsuan-huai which was described in Chapter 3. It seems most convenient to discuss successively the constitution of the C.M.S.N. Co.'s management in the six periods of its history which were outlined earlier in this chapter.

1. *1872–1873*. The first manager of the China Merchants' Company was Chu Ch'i-ang, whom Li Hung-chang despatched to Shanghai in October 1872 to establish an office and solicit merchant investment in the newly organized enterprise. Chu was a native of Shanghai, where he had been a local corps leader and a boat operator. Although he came from a merchant family and had no examination degree, he had acquired official rank through purchase and had held the substantive post of sub-prefect (*t'ung-chih*) in Chekiang. Chu was an expectant prefect (*chih-fu*) and commissioner for sea transport (*hai-yün wei-yuan*) — that is, in charge of the shipment of tribute rice by sea-going junk from Chekiang to Tientsin — when Governor-general Li selected him to head the C.M.S.N. Co. He was later guaranteed for the rank of taotai, and in addition to his duties with the China Merchants' Company is recorded as having played a large role in famine and flood relief in Chihli, Shansi, and Kiangsi.[29]

Chu's background represents a pattern which, with variations, is repeated in the lives of several others of the company's managers. He was a merchant; Li Hung-chang reported to Peking in 1872: "Chu himself owns *sha-ch'uan* [sea-going junks] and his relatives and friends have even more." [30] He had, however, acquired gentry status in the sense of holding office and possessing an official title. Perhaps he might be described as an official merchant, or as a merchant assimilated to official status. He was not, as were Tong King-sing, Hsü Jun, and others, a compradore; Chu's merchant occupation was of a traditional kind. In the face of the irreversible advent of the steamship in Chinese coastal waters, at least some of the junk carriers, as exemplified by Chu and his relatives, were willing to back a steamship line. It was their capital which Chu was to seek, as well as whatever other funds he could raise for the new enterprise from the merchants of Shanghai.

Because of his intimate connection with the junk business and with the shipment of tribute rice, Chu had seemed like the ideal person to manage a shipping company. But in his ignorance of steam vessels, he had paid prices totally out of line with their value for the steamers which he purchased. Moreover, Chu had little success in developing a commercial freighting service alongside the carriage of tribute rice.

Table 9

C.M.S.N. Co. Management Personnel, 1872–1911

Name	Years with Company	Position	Status
Chu Ch'i-ang	1872–1878	Mgr.; tribute rice mgr.	Local official; expectant taotai[a]
Chu Ch'i-chao	1872–1879	Tribute rice mgr.	Expectant and (1879) substantive official
Sheng Hsuan-huai	1873–1878; 1884–1902; 1907–1916	Asst. mgr.; mgr.; board chrmn.	Gentry background; substantive official
Tong King-sing (T'ang T'ing-shu)	1873–1884	Mgr.	Compradore; expectant taotai
Hsü Jun	1873–1884; 1903–1907	Asst. mgr.; acting mgr.	Compradore; expectant taotai
Chu Ch'i-shun	1873–[?]	Shanghai branch mgr.	Probably purchased official title
T'ang T'ing-keng	18[73?]–1884		
Yeh T'ing-chüan	1878–1879	Tribute rice mgr.	Expectant taotai
Cheng Kuan-ying	1882–1884; 1892–1902; 1907–[1921?]	Asst. mgr.; dir.	Compradore; expectant taotai
Chang Hung-lu	1882–1884	Asst. mgr.	
Ma Chien-chung	1884–1891	Asst. mgr.	Gentry background; taotai
Hsieh Chia-fu	1885–1891	Asst. mgr.	Gentry background; department magistrate
Shen Neng-hu	[1886?]–1897; 1902–1909	Asst. mgr.	Gentry background
T'ang Te-hsi	[before 1891]–1918	Asst. mgr.; dir.	
Ch'en Yu	[before 1891]–[?]	Asst. mgr.; dir.	
Yen Ying	[before 1891]–1903	Comptroller	
Ku Chao-hsi	1897–1903	Asst. mgr.	
Yang Shih-ch'i	1903–1906; 1912–[?]	Mgr.; dir.	Gentry background; substantive official
Hsü Chieh	1903–1906	Asst. mgr.	
Shih I-chüeh	1903–1914	Comptroller; dir.	
Chung Wen-yao	1906–[1911?]	Asst. mgr.; resident mgr.	Expectant taotai
Wang Ts'un-shan	1907–1916	Asst. mgr.; dir.	Expectant taotai
Ch'en Yu-sheng	1909–[1911?]	Asst. resident mgr.	

[a] "Expectant" taotai usually indicates a purchased official rank and title.

Sheng Hsuan-huai later claimed that it was on his suggestion that Li Hung-chang appointed Tong King-sing and Hsü Jun, "who were Cantonese and well versed in commercial matters," to take over the management from Chu.[31] It seems also that Sun Chu-t'ang, an official of the

Tsungli Yamen, was instrumental in persuading the governor-general that the Cantonese compradore-merchants in Shanghai, in particular Tong King-sing, were best qualified to head the steamship project. Chu Ch'i-ang agreed to transfer the fleet and wharves to Tong, but he was to continue to direct the collection and shipment of tribute rice within the reorganized company. For this he would receive 5 per cent of the total proceeds from rice carriage — enough, according to Hsü Jun, to yield an annual income in excess of Tls. 10,000.[32] In giving up his direction of the company's general shipping operations but retaining control of its tribute rice business, Chu was, so to speak, only returning to his former status as a semiofficial receiver of perquisites.

Under Chu's direction, the company had been technically a public enterprise with Chu as its official head. It had taken the name, in transliteration, *Lun-ch'uan chao-shang kung-chü* (literally, "a public — or government — bureau to invite merchant [investment] in steamships"). When the company was reorganized, the word *kung* (public) was dropped and the China Merchants' Company became simply *Lun-ch'uan chao-shang chü* ("bureau to invite merchant [investment] in steamships").[33] This change in nomenclature, however, did not alter the underlying structure of the company as a *kuan-tu shang-pan* enterprise. Under the management of Chu's successors as well as of Chu himself, the C.M.S.N. Co. was run as a business firm enjoying particularly close relations with its official patrons.

2. *1873–1884*. Tong King-sing assumed the direction of the China Merchants' Company in July 1873. The name used here is that by which he was usually known to his Western contemporaries. It is the Cantonese pronunciation of his surname (*hsing*) and "style" (*hao*), T'ang Ching-hsing. His proper name, in the northern pronunciation, was T'ang T'ing-shu. Tong was born in 1832 in Hsiang-shang-hsien, a district near Macao in Kwangtung. As a boy he studied in one of the earliest missionary schools in China, that of the Robert Morrison Society in Hong Kong. Among his classmates at the Morrison school was Yung Wing. Between 1851 and 1857, Tong was employed by the Hong Kong colonial government as an interpreter. From 1857 to 1861 he was with the Shanghai customs house as interpreter and chief secretary. During these years he began his career as a businessman by investing in native pawnshops. Tong resigned from his customs post in 1861 when he joined the leading English firm in Shanghai, Jardine, Matheson and Company, as a salesman of import goods at the Yangtze ports newly opened by the Treaty of Tientsin. In 1863 he succeeded his friend Acum (Lin Ch'in) as Jardine's compradore at Shanghai, holding this position until he assumed the management of the China Merchants' Company.[34] At Jardine's, in addition to his regular compradore duties, Tong assisted

the company in soliciting freight from Chinese shippers for its auxiliary steamship business. He also had funds invested in several steamship enterprises independent of Jardine's, and became "the spokesman and leader of a group of Cantonese shareholders" who nominated him to be a director on the boards of two of these firms (the Union Steam Navigation Company founded by Glover and Company in 1867, and the North-China Steamer Company founded by Trautmann and Company in 1868).[35] Before coming to the C.M.S.N. Co., then, Tong had had considerable experience with the functioning of a joint-stock steamship enterprise.

While manager of the C.M.S.N. Co., the desire to secure a profitable return cargo for the steamers carrying tribute rice to Tientsin, as well as an interest in developing a cheap domestic source of coking coal, led Tong to take a major part in the establishment of the K'ai-p'ing Coal Mines in 1877. From 1885 until his death in 1892, he gave his full time to the management of K'ai-p'ing.

As the head of the C.M.S.N. Co. from 1873 to 1884, Tong bore the designation *tsung-pan,* probably best translated as "commissioner." This was an indication of his status as official manager of the company.[36] Although he came from a merchant background, like Chu Ch'i-ang Tong had acquired an official title through purchase. He was an expectant sub-prefect (*t'ung-chih*) in 1873, and later rose to the rank of expectant taotai. Concurrently, he was described as the company's *shang-tsung,* "chief merchant" or "merchant manager." [37] This served to underline Tong's compradore origin and his influence among the Cantonese merchants in Shanghai and other ports whose support he obtained for the C.M.S.N. Co. But the company was no more a wholly private (*shang-pan*) enterprise during the period of his management than it was later under the regime of his gentry-official successor, Sheng Hsuan-huai. Tong did, however, play a more active personal part in the daily business operations of the company than Sheng did later. Moreover, he never reached Sheng's high rank, nor was he ever a substantive official. In these respects his administration may be said to have been more "mercantile." In addition to his roles as an official and as business manager, Tong was also a major shareholder in the company.

Li Hung-chang designated three other men to second Tong in the official management of the firm. Governor-general Li described his appointments as follows in a letter dated January 1, 1874, to Liu K'un-i, then governor of Kiangsi:

I have deputed four special officers (*wei-yuan*). The taotais Chu Ch'i-ang and Sheng Hsuan-huai are in charge of soliciting merchant investment (*chao-shang*) and the transport of tribute rice. The sub-prefect Tong King-sing and the department director Hsü Jun are in charge of all affairs relating to steamships and the freighting business. They are all capable and wealthy men whom I have appointed at various times.[38]

Chu, Sheng, and Hsü were each assistant managers (*hui-pan*). Chu remained in charge of tribute rice transport until his death in 1878. Sheng, who was appointed in September 1873, reduced his ties with the company in 1875 when he was sent to take charge of the development of coal and iron mines in Hupei; he left it entirely in 1878 when he became acting taotai in Tientsin. It was Hsü Jun who acted as Tong's chief deputy until they both left the China Merchants' Company in 1884.

Hsü Jun was born in 1838 in the same district, Hsiang-shan-hsien, Kwangtung, as his associate Tong King-sing. He came from a family of compradores and was a compradore himself. At the age of fifteen he had gone to Shanghai to join an uncle who was a compradore with Dent and Company, Jardine, Matheson's chief rival. Hsü eventually became an assistant to Mr. E. Webb, a partner in that firm, and on Webb's advice he bought up a large amount of Shanghai real estate in and near the foreign settlements. His real-estate holdings in Shanghai before his business failure in 1883–1884 were valued at Tls. 2,223,000. In addition, Hsü owned many tea firms in the Yangtze valley, two of which in particular did a large business exporting tea to Russia.

The China Merchants' Company was not the only industrial enterprise with which Hsü was associated. From 1881, he was also an assistant manager of the K'ai-p'ing Coal Mines, and in 1882 Li Hung-chang deputed him to take charge of the Kuei-ch'ih Coal Mines, Anhwei province, in which the C.M.S.N. Co. had invested some Tls. 200,000. Hsü subsequently played an important role in the management of silver mines in Kwangtung, the Chien-p'ing gold mine in Jehol, and the Yung-p'ing gold mine in Chihli. Further indications of the range of his industrial and commercial interests are Hsü's participation in the founding of the Hua-hsing Marine and Fire Insurance Company in Shanghai, and his term in 1904–1905 as assistant director (*hsieh-li*) of the Shanghai Chinese General Chamber of Commerce (*shang-wu tsung-hui*).

Hsü Jun was ousted from the C.M.S.N. Co. in 1884. He returned to the management in 1903 when Yuan Shih-k'ai acquired control of the company for a time, but Sheng Hsuan-huai secured Hsü's dismissal again in 1907. This phase of his career will be recounted below. Hsü died in 1911 at his home on Bubbling Well Road in the Shanghai International Settlement, the same street, by the way, on which his arch-rival Sheng Hsuan-huai lived. Several of Hsü's children and grandchildren were educated abroad — at Oxford and in the United States.[39]

In addition to his appointment as *hui-pan,* Hsü functioned as a business manager (*shang-tung*) in charge of the company's Shanghai branch office. He was assisted in this job by Chu Ch'i-shun, a younger brother of Chu Ch'i-ang and an expectant assistant department magistrate (*chou-t'ung*). (It is a measure of the potential for nepotism within the firm that a third Chu brother, Ch'i-chao, was also associated with the China Merchants' Company, in the tribute rice department, until he left to take an official post in 1879. Moreover, Tong King-sing's younger brother, T'ang T'ing-keng, acted as business manager of the company's Canton branch.[40]) Hsü Jun's participation in the C.M.S.N. Co. as manager and shareholder, like that of Tong, marked the entrance of compradore capital into this enterprise. But, also like Tong, Hsü had acquired official status by purchase. He bought his first title in 1862 when a young compradore aged 24; in 1873, he was an honorary department director (*lang-chung*) of the Ministry of War; he later rose to be an expectant taotai.[41] Thus in some degree his merchant outlook had been qualified by a long association with officialdom.

Three other men played important roles in the company's management under the direction of Tong King-sing. Cheng Kuan-ying is best discussed in connection with Sheng Hsuan-huai's administration of the C.M.S.N. Co. Yeh T'ing-chüan, from Kwangtung and an expectant taotai in Kiangsu province, was appointed to the company in 1878 to replace Chu Ch'i-ang. Yeh had formerly been assistant magistrate in Shanghai. Like his predecessor, he was in charge of the company's tribute rice transport, but he stayed with the C.M.S.N. Co. for one year only.[42] In the spring of 1882, Tong and Hsü requested Li Hung-chang to appoint Chang Hung-lu to assist them. Chang remained as a *hui-pan* until 1884, when he was dismissed, together with Hsü Jun, for misappropriating company funds. However, he continued as a shareholder at least until 1908, in which year his name, with thirty others, was signed to a telegram demanding that the Ministry of Posts and Communications permit the establishment of a board of directors for the C.M.S.N. Co.[43]

3. *1884–1903.* The sequence of events set in motion by the threat of hostilities with France over Annam in 1883 and 1884 led to the second reorganization of the company and the beginning of Sheng Hsuan-huai's long reign at its head. As a consequence of the ominous situation in Indo-China, in the summer and fall of 1883 some eighteen or nineteen Shanghai money shops (*ch'ien-chuang*) failed. Hsü Jun, it appears, had been borrowing C.M.S.N. Co. funds for use in his private business ventures. The failure of these money shops resulted in the default of Tls. 162,256 which he had "lent" to the Pao-yuan-hsiang Company, a

Shanghai real-estate firm. Hsü was able to repay Tls. 88,230 of the shortage in his accounts, and requested that the balance be canceled in view of his outstanding contributions to the company. But Sheng Hsuan-huai had already forwarded an indictment of Hsü's financial irregularities to the firm's patron, Li Hung-chang. Once the shortage was officially on record, Hsü was left no other course but to continue his efforts to make good the balance; to that end he deposited title deeds and other securities with the China Merchants' Company. When Tong King-sing, who had left for Europe in April 1883, returned to Shanghai in January 1884, he and Sheng proceeded to "put financial affairs in order" while Hsü Jun made the face-saving move of requesting to retire because of ill health.[44]

In Li Hung-chang's report to Peking regarding this incident, Hsü was named as the major culprit. But Tong, his younger brother T'ang T'ing-keng, and a third official of the company, Chang Hung-lu, were also charged with "the diversion of public means to private ends, followed gradually by audacious embezzlement of the Company's funds." The shares of the Tong brothers were confiscated and set off against their shortages, but the men retained their respective ranks and offices. Hsü and Chang, however, were cashiered by Li Hung-chang, allegedly because of their delay in repaying the funds which they had taken.[45] In April 1884 Tong King-sing left the company to devote himself full-time to the management of the K'ai-p'ing Coal Mines. As a consequence of his departure and Sheng's return to Tientsin, the direction of the C.M.S.N. Co. was left in the hands of Ma Chien-chung, whom Li had appointed a *hui-pan* early in 1884.

It was Ma who, in the summer of 1884, arranged the sale of the company's steamships to the American firm of Russell and Company — a fictitious transaction designed to protect the vessels from bombardment or capture by the French fleet (which sank the Chinese navy and shelled the Foochow Arsenal and Shipyard on August 23, 1884). The right of the China Merchants' Company to recover its property at the termination of hostilities was protected by a secret agreement, but this was not generally known to the Shanghai treaty-port community.[46] Retransfer of the steamers, however, was accomplished only after considerable wrangling over terms. Li Hung-chang entrusted these negotiations to Sheng Hsuan-huai, who from this time assumed control of the company with Ma Chien-chung as his assistant. On June 6, 1885, Sheng and Ma signed an agreement with C. V. Smith, a Russell and Company partner, providing for the recovery of the steamers "at the original [sale] price." The contract of sale (*shou-chieh*) and the secret agreement (*mi-yüeh*) were to be turned over to the C.M.S.N. Co. and destroyed on August 1. As for Smith, he was hired by the China Merchants' Company as a "supervisory director" (*tsung-ch'a tung-shih*) for a three-year period at an annual salary of Tls. 5,000.[47]

While Tong King-sing had been both official manager (*tsung-pan*) and chief merchant (*shang-tsung*), Sheng Hsuan-huai bore only the official title of *tu-pan*, director-general, of the C.M.S.N. Co. Unlike Tong, Sheng came from a gentry-official background and held high official posts himself; he was not a merchant. Nevertheless, the differences in the designation and background of its managers did not imply any fundamental variation in the character of the China Merchants' Company during their respective incumbencies. Tong and Sheng and the assistant managers who were associated with them performed — though not necessarily exclusively — the roles of officials through whose agency Li Hung-chang carried out the "official supervision" to be described in the next chapter. They were the links between the company and the metropolitan, provincial, and local bureaucracies; through them passed Governor-general Li's orders on the one hand and requests for assistance when the C.M.S.N. Co. was in need on the other. When the principal manager had substantive official duties elsewhere, as did Sheng Hsuan-huai, the chain of command would run from the governor-general's *yamen* at Tientsin[48] through Sheng at Chefoo to the assistant managers of the China Merchants' Company at the head office in Shanghai. The chief difference between the position of Tong at the head of the company and that of Sheng lay in the ability of the former to devote a good deal more personal attention to daily problems of administration and personnel. Tong could serve as the company's chief merchant as well as its official manager. Because of his background and the pressure of his other obligations, Sheng found it necessary to delegate the strictly business management to his assistants (although he did not forbear to insist that he be kept constantly informed of all major decisions). Only in this way could he function concurrently in his posts as customs taotai, as director-general of the Imperial Telegraph Administration, and as director of the Hua-sheng Cotton Mill. But from the point of view of Li Hung-chang and the Chihli authorities, the roles played with reference to the China Merchants' Company by both Sheng and Tong were nearly identical.

The major responsibility for the administration of the company during Sheng's tenure, from 1885 to 1902, lay with the assistant managers (*hui-pan*) and business managers (*shang-tung*) who served under him. In theory, the *hui-pan* were selected by the director-general for three-year terms on the recommendation of the company's shareholders.[49] In fact, they were designated by Sheng alone and invested with their office by Governor-general Li. At the company's head office, the administration was divided among eight sections: transport, shipping, tribute rice, finance, insurance, repairs, coal and supplies, translation, and the secretariat.[50] From 1891, these sections were headed by three *shang-tung*.

As evidence of continued compradore support for the China Merchants' Company after the departure of Tong and Hsü, the career of Cheng Kuan-ying may be cited.[51] Cheng had first joined the company in the spring of 1882 as one of the managers of its Shanghai branch. He served as a *hui-pan* until 1884 when he left the C.M.S.N. Co. to become an advisor to General P'eng Yü-lin, who headed the Chinese troops sent against the French in Annam. Sheng secured his reappointment as an assistant manager in 1892, and Cheng Kuan-ying continued in that post until Sheng lost control of the company in 1902. After Sheng had recovered his position in 1907, Cheng was elected to the first board of directors. His connection with the China Merchants' Company continued down to the early 1920's — the latest reference to him that I have found records his election as a director in May 1921. Throughout the long period of his association with the company, Cheng — despite his Cantonese origin — was a leading figure among the Kiangsu-Chekiang faction of the shareholders. This group was led by Sheng Hsuan-huai and was opposed by a Cantonese faction under the leadership of Hsü Jun.

Cheng, interestingly enough, was born in the same district, Hsiang-shan-hsien, in Kwangtung near Macao, as Tong King-sing and Hsü Jun. His origins are obscure. In his youth he had been a student of the classics, but after 1860 he gave this up to become a merchant. For some thirty years he was a compradore with Dent and Company and Butterfield and Swire, leading English firms in Shanghai. Cheng first came to the attention of Li Hung-chang in 1878–1879 as a result of his activity in raising funds for flood and famine relief in Shansi. Li arranged an audience for Cheng with the empress dowager, Tz'u-hsi, and dispatched him to take charge of the textile mill which Li was seeking to establish in Shanghai. From Cheng's role in inaugurating this first Chinese-owned cotton mill (see Chapter 6), it is possible to surmise that he may himself have been an importer of foreign-manufactured textiles.

In addition to his role in the C.M.S.N. Co. and the Shanghai Cotton Cloth Mill, Cheng played a part in the establishment and operation of a number of other *kuan-tu shang-pan* enterprises. He was one of the business managers of the Imperial Telegraph Administration while Sheng Hsuan-huai headed that enterprise. In 1896, he was the manager of the Hanyang Ironworks when it was taken over and reorganized by Sheng as a *kuan-tu shang-pan* company. Together with Sheng, Cheng arranged the amalgamation in 1908 of Hanyang with the Ta-yeh and P'ing-hsiang mines to form the Han-Yeh-P'ing Coal and Iron Corporation. At the end of 1904, he became general manager of the Kwangtung section of the Canton-Hankow railroad, and in 1906 was one of the five men elected by the Cantonese shareholders of that line to represent them on its board of directors.

All this is evidence of his very close relations with Sheng Hsuan-huai, and in fact Cheng was Sheng's principal adjutant in the management of the latter's industrial empire. It was through Cheng's southern connections that Sheng was able to obtain support for his projects from investors in Kwangtung. From July 1905 to November 1906, for example, and again from November 1907 to November 1908, Cheng held the position of assistant director of the Canton Chinese General Chamber of Commerce.

Cheng, the "scholarly compradore," was the author of an outspoken work, *Sheng-shih wei-yen* (Warnings to a seemingly prosperous age), which had considerable currency among "Westernizers" at the turn of the century. It first appeared in the 1860's and went through many editions. In it Cheng surveyed China's ills in a comprehensive manner and offered his suggestions for reform. Although his work was organized under traditional headings, its scope included everything from education for women to international commercial competition. With reference to the China Merchants' Company, for example, Cheng wrote:

> There are some who say that the China Merchants' Steam Navigation Company, this single enterprise, represents the true beginning of development along commercial lines (*shang-wu*) in China. It seems to me, however, that in all Western countries foreign steamers come only to the ocean ports; the river and coastwise traffic is reserved for the ships of the nationals of the country concerned. Foreigners are not permitted to intrude themselves. But in China today there is no place to which foreign steamers do not go; they gain large profits and successfully violate our sovereignty. The harm is beyond measure.[52]

Cheng's advice in this unfavorable situation was for increased support from the government, and the granting of official subsidies which would make it possible for the Chinese merchant to force the retirement of the foreigner because of the unprofitableness of his ventures.

Like his associates Tong and Hsü, Cheng acquired official rank by purchase. In 1869 he became a second-class secretary (*yuan-wai-lang*), in 1870 he rose to department director (*lang-chung*), and in 1878 he purchased the rank of expectant taotai.

Early in 1884, Li Hung-chang appointed his protégé Ma Chien-chung as an assistant manager of the C.M.S.N. Co. to fill the gap left by Hsü Jun's departure from the company. Ma was born in 1844 in Kiangsu, apparently into a gentry family. His experiences in Shanghai during the Taiping rebellion converted him into an advocate of *yang-wu*, "Westernization." Ma came to the attention of Li Hung-chang who was impressed enough with the young man to guarantee him for appointment as a taotai. For a number of years during the 1870's he studied in France where Li had sent him in order to acquire a closer knowledge of things Western. After the completion of his studies, Ma was a secretary in the Chinese legation in Paris. In 1881, he was sent as an "unofficial investigator carrying the Viceroy Li's letters of introduction and recommendation" to India. His mission was to approach the Indian government on the question of a gradual extinction of the opium trade. Li dispatched Ma to Korea in 1882, where he cooperated with Yuan Shih-k'ai and Admiral Ting Ju-ch'ang in the arrest of the father of the Korean king, the so-called Tai Wön Kun, who was leading a rebellion against the pro-Chinese party in power.

With the departure of Tong King-sing from the C.M.S.N. Co., as we have seen the affairs of the company were left in Ma's hands. He conducted the transfer of the company's property to Russell and Company for the duration of hostilities with France, and with Sheng Hsuan-huai, arranged for the return of the property in 1885. When Sheng was appointed director-general, Ma continued on as assistant manager, remaining with the China Merchants' Company until 1891. In 1896, he was part of Li Hung-chang's suite which traveled to Moscow for the coronation of Nicholas II.[53]

The years before his death in 1900 were spent in preparing a grammar of the classical Chinese language, the *Ma-shih wen-t'ung* (Mr. Ma's grammar), which was completed in 1898. Ma's reform writings appear in part in his *Shih-k'o-chai chi-yen* (Notes from the Shih-k'o-chai [studio]) and in several diaries which he left of his travels.[54]

Even this brief sketch of his life serves to show that in his background, career, and literary interests Ma Chien-chung differed considerably from the compradores Tong and Hsü, whom he succeeded in the management of the China Merchants' Company. Ma was rather of the same type as Sheng Hsuan-huai, under whom he served from 1885 to 1891, although he rose to neither the political power nor the affluence of Sheng.

There is unfortunately less information available about the other *hui-pan* who directed the China Merchants' Company between 1885 and 1902. Hsieh Chia-fu was an assistant manager from 1885 until 1891 when he left the company for reasons of health. A native of Kiangsu — as was his superior Sheng — he had passed the local examinations for the *hsiu-ts'ai* degree. For five years before coming to the C.M.S.N. Co., Hsieh had been an officer of the Telegraph Administration serving under Sheng, who apparently brought Hsieh with him when he replaced Tong at the head of the company. Hsieh was also connected with the Shanghai Cotton Cloth Mill, another of the *kuan-tu shang-pan* enterprises with which Li Hung-chang and Sheng were associated. In 1885 Li had memorialized recommending Hsieh for appointment as a *hsien* magistrate; he eventually held the rank of department magistrate (*chih-chou*). Hsieh was also widely known, in the years before his death in 1896, for his efforts to raise funds for flood and famine relief.[55]

Shen Neng-hu succeeded Hsieh as assistant manager in 1891, but apparently he had been with the company from a much earlier date as is evidenced by repeated references to him in letters written by H. B. Morse in 1886 and 1887 when Morse was with the C.M.S.N. Co. Aside from Morse's strong criticism of Shen, which will be discussed later, I have found no information about him except the dates of his service with the company. Shen remained as *hui-pan* until 1897; in 1902, when Sheng Hsuan-huai temporarily lost control of the company to Yuan Shih-k'ai, Yuan reappointed Shen in place of Sheng's supporter Cheng Kuan-ying. He left the company in 1909.[56]

Beyond the fact that Ku Chao-hsi replaced Shen Neng-hu as assistant manager in 1897 and himself was replaced in 1903, I have been able to discover no information about him.[57]

During most of the period of Sheng's administration and extending on into a later era, three men filled the posts of business managers in the C.M.S.N. Co.'s head office. They were T'ang Te-hsi, Ch'en Yu, and Yen Ying. Prior to 1891, the three had borne the designation *chu-chü pan-shih*, literally "resident managers." In 1891, in a move designed ostensibly to increase the representation of the company's shareholders in its management, they were given the title of *shang-tung*, literally "merchant director." Characteristically, it was Governor-general Li who appointed T'ang, Ch'en, and Yen as the shareholders' delegates.

T'ang Te-hsi remained with the company until 1918 when he retired because of illness. During this period he was in charge of the shipping office. For a time, in 1909 and 1910, he was also an assistant manager; and in 1913 T'ang was elected a director of the company.[58]

Ch'en Yu, a native of Kwangtung, headed the company's translation and office staff. Like T'ang Te-hsi, he was an assistant manager of the company in 1909 and 1910, and in 1913 he also was elected a director. In addition to his participation in the C.M.S.N. Co., Ch'en was a director of the *kuan-tu shang-pan* Imperial Bank of China which Sheng Hsuan-huai established in 1896. With Hsü Jun and Yen Hsin-hou he was a founder of the Hua-hsing Marine and Fire Insurance Company, which had offices in Shanghai.[59]

Yen Ying acted as the China Merchants' Company's comptroller or chief accountant until his death in 1903. He also played a role in several other *kuan-tu shang-pan* firms. Yen was a director of the Hua-sheng Cotton Mill when Sheng established it in 1894 after reorganizing

Li Hung-chang's Shanghai Cotton Cloth Mill, and in 1897 he was a member of the board of directors of Sheng's Imperial Bank of China.[60]

As an over-all comment on the character of the company's management during this period in comparison with the period of Tong King-sing's administration, it might be hazarded that among the *hui-pan* there was a larger proportion of persons with official backgrounds. Cheng Kuan-ying represented the continued participation of Shanghai treaty-port merchants in the management; on the other hand Hsieh Chia-fu and Ma Chien-chung were officials and of gentry origin. Still, the difference, if it was significant, represented more a shift of emphasis than a fundamental change in the company's composition. As we have noted, Hsü Jun and Tong King-sing themselves, compradores *par excellence,* were assimilated to official status.

4. *1903–1907.* The circumstances of the third reorganization of the C.M.S.N. Co. have already been described in Chapter 3 in connection with the repercussions following from the death of Sheng Hsuan-huai's father in 1902. Yuan Shih-k'ai was able to take advantage of the traditional twenty-seven months of mourning expected from Sheng for his deceased parent in order to acquire control of the C.M.S.N. Co. and the Imperial Telegraph Administration. The telegraphs were "nationalized," but the shipping company remained a *kuan-tu shang-pan* firm with Yuan assuming the role which Li Hung-chang had filled before 1895, and his appointees Yang Shih-ch'i and then Hsü Jun replacing Sheng at the head of the company.

As official manager of the China Merchants' Company, Yang Shih-ch'i bore the title *tsung-li,* general-manager. Yang, a native of Anhwei, came from a family of officials; his elder brother, Yang Shih-hsiang (1860–1909), for example, was governor-general of Chihli from 1907 to 1909. Yang himself was a *chü-jen.* He remained at the head of the C.M.S.N. Co., and concurrently of the Imperial Telegraph Administration, until 1906 when he resigned to become junior vice-president (*yu-shih-lang*) of the Ministry of Posts and Communications. In March 1912, Yang was elected a director of the China Merchants' Company and vice-chairman of the board of directors. He was chairman of the Sino-Japanese Industrial Company in 1914 when he resigned to become minister of communications under Yuan Shih-k'ai.[61] Like Sheng Hsuan-huai, Yang was primarily an official whose status and activities are to be sharply distinguished from those of such men as T'ang Te-hsi, Ch'en Yu, and Yen Ying, who continued to conduct the day-to-day affairs of the company.

Yang's chief assistant in the official management was Hsü Jun. Among the other personnel changes which Yuan Shih-k'ai carried out were the recall of Shen Neng-hu to the post of *hui-pan* and the replacement of Sheng Hsuan-huai's appointee, Ku Chao-hsi, by Hsü Chieh.[62] Hsü Chieh continued as an assistant manager until 1906 when he was succeeded by the expectant taotai Chung Wen-yao. Shen left the company finally in 1909.

The principal change among the business managers during the period of Yuan's domination of the C.M.S.N. Co. was the death of Yen Ying, the chief accountant, in 1903 and his replacement by Shih I-chüeh. Shih remained with the company until 1914 when he resigned because of ill health. In 1913 he was elected a member of the board of directors.[63] The business managers, who had been called by the title *shang-tung* since 1891, were known as *tsung-tung*, literally "chief directors," from 1904.

At the end of 1906, when the company's official manager, Yang Shih-ch'i, was appointed an official of the newly established Ministry of Posts and Communications, Yuan Shih-k'ai named Hsü Jun as acting (*tai-li*) manager.[64] A fourth reorganization of the company's management came in 1907 when Sheng Hsuan-huai was able to force Hsü out of his post for a second time in circumstances reminiscent of their clash some twenty years earlier.

5. *1907–1909.* Sheng's success was due to the beginning of a shift in the balance against Yuan Shih-k'ai in Peking, as has already been noted in Chapter 3. On November 20, 1906, Yuan was allowed "at his own request" to resign all his concurrent posts, although he remained as Chihli governor-general. This was a compromise in return for which he was able to retain direct control of four of the six divisions of the modern army which he had organized in Chihli.[65] It is clear that Yuan was in no position to oppose Sheng's efforts to oust Hsü Jun from the C.M.S.N. Co. and regain control for himself. Hsü himself later noted, "Sheng Hsuan-huai knew that Yuan Shih-k'ai's power had declined somewhat; and he intended to [take advantage of this in order to] attack me." [66]

The first attack on Hsü's position — an attempt to register the company with the Ministry of Agriculture, Industry, and Commerce as a private commercial firm and thus wrest it entirely from official control — ended indecisively.[67] But Yuan Shih-k'ai was forced to arrange a compromise with Sheng's powerful supporters in Peking whereby the latter might regain control of the C.M.S.N. Co. with as little loss of face as possible for Yuan.[68] Thus in June 1907, Governor-general Yuan was quick to seize upon a miscalculation in a report submitted by Hsü, which Yuan alleged would have resulted in a large loss to the shareholders, as a pretext for ordering him to vacate his post. In a typical fashion, Hsü's error was attributed to his recent illness: "That the taotai [Hsü] has in this instance been so careless was certainly a surprise;

most likely it can be attributed to the fact that after his illness his faculties have not yet recovered sufficiently for him to handle such matters." [69] While some face was preserved all around, Sheng Hsuan-huai again had *de facto* control of the China Merchants' Company.

Until April 1909 the company was headed by Sheng's supporter, the expectant taotai Wang Ts'un-shan. Wang, from Kwangtung, had earlier been the director of the statistical office of the Imperial Railway Administration where he had worked closely with Sheng. When the company came under the supervision of the Ministry of Posts and Communications in 1909, he became an assistant manager. In 1912, Wang was elected to the board of directors and held that office until his death in 1916.[70]

6. *1909–1916.* The China Merchants' Company underwent a fifth reorganization in April 1909 when an imperial order transferred it from the control of the commissioner for the northern ports and placed it under the jurisdiction of the Ministry of Posts and Communications.[71] From April 1909 to the fall of the dynasty at the end of 1911, the official management of the company was in the hands of officers (*tso-pan* and *hui-pan*) appointed by the ministry, while business affairs were under the control of managers (*tsung-tung*) who were technically representatives of the newly established board of directors. In practice, the official element dominated. The taotai Chung Wen-yao, whose entrance into the company in 1906 has already been noted, was appointed by the ministry as resident manager (*cheng-tso-pan*). His assistant (*fu-tso-pan*) was Ch'en Yu-sheng, who replaced Shen Neng-hu in the company. I have been unable to find additional information about these two men.

Immediately below these two representatives of the ministry, there were six other managerial posts to be filled: three official assistant managers (*hui-pan*) and three business managers (*tsung-tung*). T'ang Te-hsi and Ch'en Yu, who had been with the company for several decades as business managers, were now given official appointments as *hui-pan* as well. The third *hui-pan* post was filled by the company's manager from 1907 to 1909, the taotai Wang Ts'un-shan. Only one of the three business managers, Shih I-chüeh, the chief accountant, did not have concurrent official status. This was plainly an attempt on the part of the ministry to dominate the company; it was not well received by the shareholders. The course of the consequent struggle between the government and the company's board of directors will be outlined in the next chapter.

The upheaval brought on by the revolution of 1911 freed the C.M.S.N. Co. from the direction of the Ministry of Posts and Communications. Control over the management personnel of the company was assumed by its board of directors. The directors selected the chairman and vice-chairman of the firm from among their members; and they also designated from among themselves three business managers (called *k'o-chang*) to take charge of the principal operating departments. It should occasion no surprise that the old perennials, T'ang Te-hsi, Ch'en Yu, and Shih I-chüeh, now directors of the company, were also named the first *k'o-chang* under the new regime; nor is it unexpected that Sheng Hsuan-huai headed the company as chairman of the board (*hui-chang*) until his death in 1916.

This whole complex amalgam of merchant and official in the company's management was characteristic of the relation of these two elements in a *kuan-tu shang-pan* enterprise. The Chu brothers, Tong King-sing and his brother, Hsü Jun, Cheng Kuan-ying, and apparently at least Chang Hung-lu, T'ang Te-hsi, Ch'en Yu, Yen Ying, and Shih I-chüeh as well, were men with merchant backgrounds. Nevertheless it is a fact that their mercantile character was tinted with a generous dose of official coloring. More specifically, no less than a dozen of the men mentioned above are definitely recorded as having official titles, although only three aside from Sheng himself — Hsieh Chia-fu, Yang Shih-ch'i, and possibly Ma Chien-chung — were "regular" officials. Possession of at least an official title, in addition to the prestige it carried, was essential for carrying on the company's business. Contact with every level of the local bureaucracies — in regard to such matters as tribute rice cargoes and other official freights, tariffs and inland duties, and official passengers — was facilitated when the company's managers could proceed as equals or near equals to the incumbent officials. Undoubtedly this is the reason for the several instances in the above account in which Li Hung-chang secured appointments or promotions for the men whom he had designated to manage the China Merchants' Company.

It seems, however, that one consequence of this admixture was that the merchant management promised in the *kuan-tu shang-pan* formula tended to become bureaucratic management — in the pejorative sense. The habits of the "official arena" (*kuan-ch'ang*), as it were, often were dominant while those required for the rational pursuit of economic activity were recessive. This subject will be discussed further after the sources of the company's capital have been examined. Here too both the official and the merchant contribution to the enterprise must be taken into account.

V

Financing the C.M.S.N. Co.

The initial capital of the newly organized C.M.S.N. Co., as has already been mentioned, consisted of Tls. 110,000 which was raised from merchants in Shanghai, Tls. 50,000 invested by Li Hung-chang personally, and Tls. 135,000 more lent by Governor-general Li from Chihli military funds. By the end of the first year of operations, the paid-up share capital had increased to Tls. 476,000. The total grew slowly each year until in the eighth year, 1880, it at last reached Tls. 1,000,000, which was the amount of the company's authorized capital. In 1882 the authorized capital was increased to Tls. 2,000,000, a level at which it remained until 1897 when it was again raised, this time to Tls. 4,000,000. In 1914, after a financial reorganization which will be discussed below, the paid-up share capital stood at Tls. 8,400,000. Paralleling these increments in the share capital was a steady growth of borrowed funds from several sources as Li Hung-chang's original loan was quickly dwarfed. Table 10 shows the condition of the liabilities column of the China Merchants' Company's capital account during the company's first ten years and at intervals thereafter.[72] An analysis of the provenance of these funds will throw some light on the participation of merchants in the provision of capital for the company.

Paid-up Share Capital. So far as can be determined, all of the C.M.S.N. Co.'s share capital came from private, often mercantile, investors who may, however, have included officials acting in a private capacity. Li Hung-chang's initial investment may be taken as an example of this last case. No official organ held any of the company's shares.

The reorganization of the C.M.S.N. Co. in July 1873, whereby it passed out of the hands of the Chu brothers and under the management of Tong King-sing, also provided that the authorized capital should consist of 1,000 shares of Tls. 1,000 face value. (This was soon changed to 10,000 shares of Tls. 100 face value each.) Tls. 500 per share was to be called up immediately, and as 952 shares were subscribed for, the company ended its first year with a paid-up capital of Tls. 475,000.[73]

Who were these initial shareholders? The 1873 regulations of the company provided (Article 1) that large shareholders should be appointed as merchant directors or business managers (*shang-tung*) to assist the chief merchant (*shang-tsung*) at the major ports. Initially, there were to be two *shang-tung* at Shanghai and one each at Tientsin, Hankow, Hong Kong, and Swatow, "and their number should be added to from the large shareholders when the Company's operations are extended to other ports."[74] Hsü Jun and Chu Ch'i-shun, the brother of Chu Ch'i-ang, were designated at Shanghai. The shareholders Sung Chin, Liu Shao-tsung, Ch'en Shu-t'ang, and Fan Shih-yao were appointed *shang-tung* at Tientsin, Hankow, Hong Kong, and Swatow respectively.[75] Now since the company's by-laws provided (Article 3) "that for every 100 shares outstanding a *shang-tung* was to be elected, one of whom would be chosen as the chief merchant,"[76] these six men and the chief merchant, Tong King-sing, together must have accounted for at least 700 shares (or Tls. 350,000) of the company's paid-up capital.

Since Hsü and Tong were well-known compradores, the capital which they and their associates invested in the C.M.S.N. Co. in all probability had its origin in trading and commercial pursuits in the treaty ports. Of the other five men, two can definitely be identified as compradores: Liu Shao-tsung ("Seting") and Ch'en Shu-t'ang ("Asong").[77] The mercantile background of the Chu family, who were junk operators, has been noted earlier. As for the remaining two, the provision in the by-laws (Article 4) to the effect that the *shang-tung* were each to manage branches of the company gives credence to the assumption that they too were merchants. There is little question, then, that the bulk of the capital invested in the China Merchants' Company after its 1873 reorganization was subscribed by treaty-port merchants.

As reference to Table 10 will show, the growth of the company's paid-up capital in the next few years was extremely slow. In January 1877, when faced with the need to raise Tls. 2,200,000 in order to buy out Russell and Company's Shanghai Steam Navigation Company, the C.M.S.N. Co. had no course but to seek to borrow Tls. 1,000,000 from the government for the initial payments. It was necessary to turn for assistance to Shen Pao-chen, the Liang-Chiang governor-general.[78] Sheng Hsuan-huai, who conducted the negotiations with Shen which secured the loan of official funds to the C.M.S.N. Co., simultaneously outlined a scheme to the company's patron Li Hung-chang, whereby additional merchant capital would be sought with which to pay the balance owed to Russell and Company. Sheng suggested that, aside from some Tls. 200,000 which reputedly was invested in the S.S.N. Co. by Chinese merchants and which he expected would be transferred to the C.M.S.N. Co., the Liang-Huai district salt controller should be ordered to undertake the sale of China Merchants' Company shares to the salt transport merchants under his jurisdiction. If one tael were invested in the company for each outstanding salt transport license (*yin*), the yield would total Tls. 792,000. In addition, the provincial treasurers and customs taotais were to solicit the wealthy merchants of their localities seeking to sell them shares.[79] The China Merchants' Company planned to issue 15,000 additional shares at Tls. 100 in order to raise the necessary Tls. 1,220,000 as well as the Tls. 300,000 by which it was still short of its nominal capitalization of Tls. 1,000,000.[80]

Table 10

C.M.S.N. Co. Capital Account (Liabilities), 1873–1914 (in Shanghai taels)

Year	Paid-up share capital	"Borrowed" funds
1873–74	476,000	193,909
1874–75	602,400	747,623
1875–76	685,100	1,502,936
1876–77	730,200	4,032,401
1877–78	751,000	4,412,887
1878–79	800,600	3,514,627
1879–80	830,300	3,326,101
1880–81	1,000,000	2,755,278
1881–82	1,000,000	3,924,680
1882–83	2,000,000	3,664,627
1887	2,000,000	3,145,039
1892	2,000,000	2,972,331
1897	4,000,000	2,860,001
1902	4,000,000	5,008,930
1907	4,000,000	6,052,210
1912	4,000,000	6,065,812
1914	8,400,000	7,095,498

Only Tls. 45,100 of new merchant capital, however, was raised during the company's fourth year, bringing the total to Tls. 730,200.[81] Sheng's elaborate scheme to sell shares to the Liang-Huai salt merchants came to naught. As to "some few [Chinese merchants] who were interested in the old company" (that is, the American-owned S.S.N. Co.) and who had been "requested to join the new" (that is, the C.M.S.N. Co.), Sheng's expectation that they would bring Tls. 200,000 into the China Merchants' Company apparently was not realized.[82] While the precise amount of Chinese investment in the S.S.N. Co. is not known, K. C. Liu has given the names of nine Chinese who subscribed for shares of that company when it was first organized,[83] and six others are mentioned at one time or another in the minutes of the general meetings of the S.S.N. Co.[84] None of these fifteen appears to be included in a list which I have compiled of 83 persons who were associated with the C.M.S.N. Co. either as shareholders or managers from 1872 to 1911. Admittedly, the difficulty posed by the romanization of names pronounced in several different dialects leaves the matter somewhat uncertain.

During the fifth year, Tls. 21,000 in share capital was added, and Tls. 49,600 more in the sixth year, bringing the total to Tls. 800,600. While the notice of the latter increment describes it as a "further call" of capital, presumably from shareholders of record, the specific source is not stated. The company's annual report states with reference to the Tls. 29,783 added during the fiscal year 1879–1880 that "the chief holders of the new shares are Chinese merchants in Siam, Honolulu, and San Francisco," the only record that I have found of overseas Chinese as investors in the C.M.S.N. Co.[85] In all, then, only Tls. 145,000 of new merchant capital was invested in the company in the four years following the purchase of the Shanghai Steam Navigation Company in January 1877.

From about 1880, however, the reluctance of the Chinese mercantile community to put its capital into the C.M.S.N. Co. surprisingly gave way to a considerable demand for the company's shares. As the managers informed the shareholders in their Report for 1881–1882, "though our capital in the seventh year was Tls. 800,000 only, in the following spring not only had the full million been subscribed, but the number of applications that had to be refused was enormous." [86] The company's shares were at a premium of over 100 per cent on the market, and the managers planned to increase the capital to Tls. 2,000,000 (in order to purchase steamers) by offering a new stock issue. Priority would be given to the old shareholders who could purchase the new Tls. 100 shares by paying only Tls. 80 in cash, the discount representing a 10 per cent return on their old shares for the current year and 10 per cent additional on the newly purchased stock.[87] The additional shares were quickly taken up and from 1882 to 1883 the company's share capital stood at Tls. 2,000,000.

Two problems are raised by this development: to account for the change in the company's fortune in attracting merchant funds; and to identify more precisely the sources of the large capital increment that was realized between 1880 and 1885. The British-owned *North-China Herald* attested to the improved financial status of the C.M.S.N. Co. in a leader of October 4, 1881, which congratulated the company on the large increase in its capital in the preceding year and added this observation:

> We believe that this is due to the confidence which commercial Chinese have lately shown in the undertaking. That cautious class held aloof as long as the official element had control of the Company's affairs, but now that the Taotais and other officials have been bowed out, or ousted from its management, they have become shareholders.[88]

This explanation refers presumably to the acquisition of complete control by Tong King-sing and Hsü Jun as a result of the transfer of Sheng Hsuan-huai and others to official posts which prevented them from taking an active role in the company's affairs. Sheng's appointment at the end of 1878 as military administrative taotai for the Tientsin-Hochien district has been noted in Chapter 3. Chu Ch'i-ang died in 1878. Chu

Ch'i-chao left the company in 1879 to become acting Yung-ting taotai; and Yeh T'ing-chüan who had been designated by Li to succeed Chu Ch'i-ang remained with the company only briefly.[89] It may well be that the compradores Hsü and Tong were able to inspire more confidence in the Chinese mercantile community than these others, but this emphasis should not be pushed to the point of ignoring the fact that Tong and Hsü too were dependent on and had the closest relations with officialdom.

Clearly the China Merchants' Company's business success in the years after the addition of the Shanghai Steam Navigation Company's fleet and docks to its own must have been the decisive factor attracting new capital from the merchants of the treaty ports. As the managers stated in their 9th Annual Report,

The result of the sixth year's [1878–1879] working was so satisfactory that they had not only reduced the interest account by over Tls. 100,000, but after declaring a dividend of 10% wrote off Tls. 420,000 from steamer account for depreciation. The seventh and eighth years showed that the liabilities and interest account have undergone a steady annual diminution. Nor is this all; not only was Tls. 400,000 written off in each of those years, but during the two years specified the Company paid Tls. 700,000 to Government on account of Loan [sic]. This is sufficient to convince the shareholders that the Company has done splendidly.[90]

Despite the stepped-up competition from the steamship lines operated by Butterfield and Swire and Jardine, Matheson, the C.M.S.N. Co. with its augmented fleet and docking facilities and with official support was able to gain a larger portion of the coasting trade.[91] Thus, for example, the company's profit from running its steamers only (leaving aside rents and other income) increased from Tls. 137,000 in 1875–1876 to Tls. 425,000 in 1876–1877, and reached Tls. 618,377 in 1880–1881.[92]

It is impossible from the available sources to identify in detail the provenance of the Tls. 1,000,000 added to the company's capital in the years before the Sino-French war. Nevertheless a gross analysis may be attempted. The managers' annual reports on more than one occasion offered a rejoinder in this manner to the company's detractors:

They are utterly ignorant of the fact, however, that the Directors are the largest shareholders, and that the managers of the branch establishments are also shareholders; who therefore, among such officers, would not wish for the prosperity of the Company? . . . Why, the majority of the shareholders are friends and relations of the managers, and live so near together that detection could be inevitable. Who would let himself be cheated or hoodwinked? Therefore there is no necessity for official inspection; the mercantile public itself would never allow any dishonesty.[93]

With due allowance made for both the color of the translation and the exaggeration inherent in the managers' denial of malfeasance, their assertions are still worthy of some credence. The "directors" or "managers" in this instance are the four men who managed the company in the early 1880's, namely, Tong King-sing, Hsü Jun, Chang Hung-lu, and Cheng Kuan-ying. It was from the compradore background of these men and of their "friends and relations" that there came a good part of the new capital invested in the China Merchants' Company.

With regard to the amount of new capital each of these men brought into the steamship enterprise, we have detailed information only in the case of Hsü Jun. Of the company's paid-up capital of Tls. 2,000,000 in 1882, Hsü claimed to have subscribed 4,800 shares or Tls. 480,000 himself, and to have raised some Tls. 500,000 more from his relatives and friends.[94] That he did have large holdings is indicated by the fact that in 1884, in order to repay his indebtedness to the C.M.S.N. Co. resulting from the failure of other business undertakings in which he had used company funds, Hsü handed over 843 shares with a market value of Tls. 88,300.[95] One source states that on Hsü's departure from the company, funds were withdrawn by various (unidentified) other investors, with the result that Li Hung-chang was forced to appropriate Tls. 360,000 in order to keep the company on its feet.[96] Presumably the amount which Li provided was of the same order of magnitude as the funds withdrawn by these investors, who were Hsü's supporters and therefore probably merchants from the Hong Kong-Canton area. Shares held by Tong King-sing and by his younger brother, T'ang T'ing-keng, were also confiscated in 1884 and set off against the deficits in their accounts, but the number or value of the shares involved is not specified.[97] In the case of Chang Hung-lu, who was also implicated in these delinquencies, it is known that he surrendered shares to the value of Tls. 23,500 in partial payment of the amount in which he was in default.[98] Cheng Kuan-ying was also a shareholder, but the size of his holdings unfortunately is not recorded.

While these admittedly fragmentary figures account for a significant portion of the company's paid-up capital, unhappily they are too insubstantial for a precise quantitative conclusion to be based upon them. For example, were the funds withdrawn from the company by Hsü Jun's supporters actually share capital or, as is more likely from their easy recall, were they short-term loans? It can be concluded, however, that compradore capital as represented by the investments held by Tong, Hsü, Chang, and Cheng played an important role in financing the C.M.S.N. Co. at this time.

One other set of figures is of importance in determining the sources of the company's paid-up capital. These concern the holdings of Sheng Hsuan-huai. In 1897, for reasons to be stated in the discussion of official exactions in Chapter 5, the China Merchants' Company raised the amount of its paid-up capital to Tls. 4,000,000 and issued additional stock to its shareholders of record. This increase was financed by the transfer of the company's reserve and insurance reserve funds, which had been accumulated out of profits, to its capital account. After this new issue Sheng was described as holding at least 11,000 shares out of the 40,000 shares outstanding.[99] It is known that Sheng's purchase of China Merchants' Company shares on a large scale began in 1881. If he had held approximately the same proportion of shares before 1897 — that is, over one quarter of the total — his Tls. 500,000 or more added to the holdings already ascribed to Hsü Jun and others would account quite well for the Tls. 2,000,000 of paid-up capital which the company enjoyed between 1883 and 1897.[100]

Sheng's investment, in contrast to the others that have been discussed, cannot be described as "compradore capital." Sheng was never associated with a foreign firm, and in contrast to Tong and Hsü his claim to gentry status was based on his actual participation in the examination system and his occupation of substantive official positions. If Sheng had any extensive funds at all before his connection with the C.M.S.N. Co. and other *kuan-tu shang-pan* enterprises under Li Hung-chang's aegis, their origin is to be sought in the inherited wealth of his family, probably in land and pawnshops.[101] In a later period, as already noted, a considerable part of his large fortune was devoted to such traditional investments. As a prominent member of the Kiangsu gentry, Sheng was also able to secure funds for his enterprises from his friends and relatives. Thus the *North-China Herald* noted that Sheng Hsuan-huai "with the 13,000 shares that he owns himself and those that are owned by his family, is practically able to control the affairs of the [China Merchants'] company."[102] After his participation in the establishment and management of large-scale, Western-type industrial and commercial enterprises, the major sources of his wealth (and thus of the funds which he was able to invest in one or another of these undertakings) were the perquisites connected with his control of these companies as well as the normal yield of their shares. Sheng's participation in the China Merchants' Company, then, was that of a relatively enlightened member of the gentry who was attracted to "foreign matters" (*yang-wu*) as a new and challenging outlet for his energies and capital.

The Tls. 2,000,000 of paid-up capital which the C.M.S.N. Co. achieved by 1882–1883 was apparently the limit of the risk capital which merchant and gentry investors put into the company directly. Further capital increases in 1897 and 1913 were the results of the transfer to the capital account of accumulated profits which had been held in reserve, or of the capitalization of the company's extensive real-estate holdings which had not previously been reflected in its accounts.

The distribution of additional stock to shareholders in 1897 has already been mentioned. An abortive attempt to reorganize the company at the beginning of the Republican era brought out the fact that its assets, carried on its books at Tls. 9,500,000 (of which Tls. 4,000,000 represented the par value of its outstanding shares), had an actual value of more than Tls. 17,000,000. Of this total, approximately Tls. 13,670,000 was in ships, docks, warehouses, and landed properties in Shanghai and other ports. Tls. 3,800,000 represented real estate entirely unconnected with the shipping business. The large discrepancy between the book value of the company's assets and their market value was attributable in part to soaring real-estate prices in the treaty ports. But it was also the result of deliberate concealment.

There were rumors early in 1913 that Yuan Shih-k'ai, Sheng's ancient rival who had now returned to power as president of the Republic of China, had designs on the company's assets. The situation was similar to that following Li Hung-chang's fall, when the C.M.S.N. Co.'s assets were protected by issuing new shares to cover its accumulated reserves. In the present instance, in addition to issuing 44,000 new Tls. 100 shares in the China Merchants' Company to shareholders of record, the company's assets in nonshipping real estate were transferred to a newly established China Merchants' Holding Company (*Chi-yü kung-ssu*) which was capitalized at $4,400,000 (Chinese), the equivalent of approximately Tls. 3,188,406.[103] Shareholders in the C.M.S.N. Co. were given one $100 share in the new holding company for each share of C.M.S.N. Co. stock which they held prior to the stock issue.[104] Thus Sheng Hsuan-huai, for example, who had held 11,000 shares of the old stock of the China Merchants' Company, now held 22,000 shares of shipping stock and 11,000 shares of the holding company in addition.[105]

"Borrowed" Funds. A look at Table 10 shows immediately how important a position in the company's capital account was occupied by borrowed funds, the equivalent of the bonded debt plus short-term financing of a present-day firm. Especially in its first decade, before its paid-up capital had reached the authorized Tls. 1,000,000, the C.M.S.N. Co. was almost totally dependent on borrowed funds. To take an extreme example, in 1877–1878 these funds came to nearly six times the company's paid-up capital. Even in later years, when the share capital had increased first to Tls. 2,000,000 and then successively to Tls. 4,000,000 and Tls. 8,400,000, the company's indebtedness was almost always equal to or greater than its paid-up capital. The most general reason for these circumstances was the shortage of risk capital in the Chinese economy and the strong competition for available funds from traditional objects of investment such as land or usury. The three principal sources from which borrowed funds were obtained — the government, foreign lenders, and private depositors of several sorts — may be examined individually.

Government Loans. Borrowing from the government by the company was limited to the first decade of its existence. Four principal official loans were contracted. These consisted of Tls. 135,000 [106] which Li Hung-chang advanced from Chihli military training funds in 1872 to get the C.M.S.N. Co. under way; Tls. 450,000 which Li secured from Chihli, Kiangsu, and Chekiang and from the Tientsin customs in 1876 to aid the company in meeting the loss of business resulting from the murder of August Margary and the ensuing diplomatic crisis;[107] some Tls. 200,000 lent by Li Hung-chang in 1876 for the purchase of river steamers;[108] and Tls. 1,000,000 secured with the aid of Shen Pao-chen for the purchase of Russell and Company's Shanghai Steam Navigation Company in 1877.[109] By 1877 the China Merchants' Company's total indebtedness to the government stood at Tls. 1,928,000. After that year no further funds were obtained from official lenders; and by 1891 all of the Tls. 1,928,000 had been repaid.

It should be noted that neither Peking nor any provincial government ever held shares in the C.M.S.N. Co. Official funds were loaned to the company or, more strictly speaking, deposited at interest. These government deposits were to be repaid as quickly as possible, in theory from the steady flow of private investment which the promoters claimed would follow once the company was firmly established with official assistance. Meanwhile the funds on deposit would draw interest. Li Hung-chang's original Tls. 135,000 was guaranteed 7 per cent, and the first year's interest was deducted even before the funds were transferred to the C.M.S.N. Co. The Tls. 200,000 loan of 1876 was to receive 8 per cent, while the Tls. 450,000 loan of that year received the same return as merchant investments, namely, 10 per cent. The funds borrowed for the purchase of the S.S.N. Co. were also lent at 10 per cent interest. While 10 per cent or even 8 per cent may seem an unduly high rate for a loan intended primarily "to compensate for the inadequacy of merchant resources," these rates were actually considerably less than those demanded by the native banks (*ch'ien-chuang*) to which in any case the C.M.S.N. Co. was forced to have recourse in order to obtain operating capital. Thus the Tls. 450,000 loan of 1876 at 10 per cent was made to obviate the need for the company to borrow further from the *ch'ien-chuang* to which it already owed Tls. 613,200 on which Tls. 91,496, roughly 15 per cent, was paid in interest during the fiscal year 1875–1876.[110]

The use of the company's receipts from tribute rice carriage to repay its official indebtedness will be considered in Chapter 5. Repayment took a considerably longer time than Li Hung-chang confidently predicted in December 1877 when he proposed a three-year moratorium on the company's debt payments to be followed by liquidation of its Tls.

1,928,000 official debt in five annual installments of Tls. 385,600 each.[111] The delay may be attributed mainly to the fact that Li's proposal was founded on the unrealistic expectation of an annual yield of Tls. 350,000 from the carriage of 660,000 piculs of rice at a rate of Tls. 0.531 per picul. By the end of the moratorium, Tls. 127,820 had been returned to the several customs offices, leaving a balance of Tls. 1,800,180 when Li's scheme became operative in 1880.[112] Table 11 shows the progress of the gradual reduction of the China Merchants' Company's debt.[113] Two other unexpected circumstances account for the delay beyond the five-year limit proposed by Li. These were, first, the Sino-French War of 1884–1885, which occasioned the "sale" of the China Merchants' Company to the United States firm of Russell and Company, and then the necessity to borrow extensively from foreign lenders in order to get the company back on its feet after its recovery from Russell and Company at the end of the war. It was only with difficulty that Li Hung-chang was able to obtain an extension of time for the company in face of efforts by the Ministry of Revenue to obtain immediate repayment of the official funds still outstanding.[114] Li's request in 1886 that settlement of the official debt be deferred until after the C.M.S.N. Co. had liquidated its obligations to foreign lenders was turned down, but the company was permitted to repay the official funds in installments extending over five years.[115] By 1891 repayment had been completed.

Table 11

C.M.S.N. Co. Indebtedness to the Government, 1878–1891
(in Shanghai taels)

Year	Amount	Year	Amount
1878	1,928,000	1885	832,274
1879	1,928,000	1886	832,274
1880	1,800,180	1887	1,065,253[a]
1881	1,518,000	1888	793,714
1882	1,217,000	1889	688,240
1883	964,291	1890	90,240
1884	832,274	1891	none

[a] In 1887 an item appears in the company's accounts labeled "extra government loan." Since no new loan was obtained at this time, this item probably represents the interest on the previous debt which, at Li Hung-chang's request, had been deferred since 1877.

Foreign Loans. If we include the Tls. 1,200,000 still due to Russell and Company in 1877 after the initial payment for the purchase of the S.S.N. Co. had been made, the total value of the foreign loans contracted by the China Merchants' Company between 1872 and 1911 comes to approximately Tls. 4,623,328. These loans are shown in Table 12. The principal shortcoming connected with borrowing from foreign lenders in the treaty ports was the unstable exchange rate between gold and silver. Loans were usually made in gold pounds — a reflection of British commercial dominance — and repaid in silver taels. As is shown below, this sometimes resulted in considerable losses to the company.

Table 12

C.M.S.N. Co. Loans from Foreign Firms 1877–1911 (in Shanghai taels)

Year	Source	Amount
1877	Russell and Company	Tls. 1,200,000
1883	Adamson Bell and Company; Jardine, Matheson and Company	Tls. 743,000
1885	Hong Kong and Shanghai Banking Corporation	Tls. 1,180,328[a]
1911	Hong Kong and Shanghai Banking Corporation	Tls. 1,500,000
	Total	Tls. 4,623,328

[a] The loan was for £300,000; the equivalent in taels at the exchange rate of 1885 is shown here.

The balance owed to Russell and Company was paid by 1881. Owing to the small amount of new capital added in this period, the payments were made largely out of the company's current earnings.[116] In 1883, as a result of the uncertainty in relations with France because of the troubled situation in Annam, a number of Shanghai *ch'ien-chuang* which had left large deposits with the company withdrew their funds. To meet the need for operating capital, the C.M.S.N. Co. sought short-term advances from several foreign firms in Shanghai, borrowing Tls. 743,000 from Adamson Bell and Company and Jardine, Matheson on the security of its land and warehouses. These loans fell due in 1885 after the end of hostilities with France. Since there were no funds available with which to repay the loans — the company having realized no profits during the time that its fleet and other property were in the hands of Russell and Company — additional foreign loans were sought.

Sheng Hsuan-huai petitioned Li Huang-chang presenting a plan to borrow £300,000 from the Hong Kong and Shanghai Banking Corporation on the security of the company's property exclusive of its steamers. Rather than a short-term credit, the new loan was to run ten years at 7 per cent interest.[117] When the loan was being negotiated, the C.M.S.N. Co. had the option of accepting a silver loan at 9 per cent or a gold loan at 7 per cent. Apparently no one foresaw that the price of gold would rise as rapidly as it did (or alternatively that the value of silver would fall), for the management decided on a gold loan at the lower interest rate. At the time the loan was made, what appeared to be a fair exchange rate, 5s. 6d. per tael, was fixed. At this rate the total cost to the company would have been as follows:

Principal	£300,000	equal to	Tls. 1,180,328
Interest	£122,570	equal to	Tls. 482,243
Total	£422,570	equal to	Tls. 1,662,571

But by January 1886 the exchange value of silver had fallen to 4s. 8d. per tael, with a resultant loss to the C.M.S.N. Co. of Tls. 148,443. By August 1886 a further drop to 4s. 2½d. per tael had increased the loss to Tls. 345,683, and a higher total loss of Tls. 450,279 was predicted.[118] In addition, the C.M.S.N. Co. still owed Adamson Bell £50,000, or £56,250, if the interest is included. At 5s. 1d. per tael this came to Tls. 223,279; at 4s. to Tls. 283,753. The loss to the China Merchants' Company on the balance due to Adamson was thus Tls. 60,471 — but not merely Tls. 60,471, because the funds borrowed from the Hong Kong and Shanghai Bank in order to repay Adamson were themselves repaid at a greatly inflated value for the gold pound.

The China Merchants' Company was, however, able to repay these foreign loans with little difficulty — a further indication of its financial soundness, which will be contrasted below with its relative lack of expansion and growth as a business firm. In 1886, £25,000 was paid to Adamson Bell and Company, and by 1887 this debt had been repaid in full.[119] Two capital payments were made to the Hong Kong and Shanghai Bank in 1887, leaving a balance of Tls. 433,458 on the principal.[120] Despite a further payment in 1888, the balance still stood at Tls. 511,393 due to the depreciation of silver.[121] By 1892 the company owed only Tls. 321,111, and in the next year the balance was reduced to Tls. 237,455.[122] By 1895 the debt to the Hong Kong and Shanghai Bank, principal and interest, had been fully discharged.

One more foreign loan was arranged before the end of the dynasty. In September 1911, the China Merchants' Company secured Tls. 1,500,-000 from the Hong Kong and Shanghai Bank on the security of its land and buildings. The loan with interest of 6 per cent was to be repaid in fifteen annual installments. However, the company was forced to contribute one third of the sum received to the new revolutionary government at Nanking.[123]

It should be noted that the C.M.S.N. Co., in contrast to the Han-Yeh-P'ing Coal and Iron Corporation, did not fall into dependence on borrowed foreign capital for its financing. The foreign loans which it contracted were usually to meet emergency needs, and were repaid without serious detriment to the company's independence.

Deposited Funds. A third source of working capital for the China Merchants' Company was the funds deposited at interest with the firm for varying periods by individuals or borrowed on current account from native banks. One special case was that of the Jen-chi-ho Insurance Company, whose funds were entirely deposited with the C.M.S.N. Co., of which in fact it was a subsidiary.[124] Table 13 shows the condition of these deposited funds from 1875 to 1912.[125]

Table 13

Funds Deposited with the C.M.S.N. Co., 1875–1912 (in Shanghai taels)

Year	Jen-chi-ho Insurance Co.[a]	Native banks	Individuals	Total
1875–6	200,000	613,238	336,198	
1876–7	350,000	593,238	530,800	
1877–8	418,000	1,459,526[b]		
1878–9	582,632	624,087[b]		
1879–80	619,848	533,028[b]		
1880–1				1,101,662[c]
1881–2				2,319,545[c]
1882–3				2,370,345[c]
1884–6	600,000	338,682[b]		
1886–7	600,000	559,735[b]		
1887	500,000	488,057[b]		
1888	300,000	546,402[b]		
1889	300,000	492,491[b]		
1890	300,000	582,795[b]		
1891	200,000	707,202[b]		
1892	200,000	693,956[b]		
1893	?	569,882[b]		
1906				2,340,000[c]
1912	550,000	1,369,257[b]		

[a] Capital of Jen-chi-ho Co. on deposit with C.M.S.N. Co.
[b] Total of deposits by native banks and individuals.
[c] Total of all deposits; separate data not available.

The necessity to resort to short-term loans at excessively high and fluctuating interest rates was a product of the shortage of capital in China combined with the high returns available from investments of a traditional kind. Although earnings from the ownership of land, that is rent, might be no more than 7 per cent,[126] land-owning brought with it prestige as well as a lesser liability to official exactions than in the case of more liquid assets. Even more important than land as a competitor for capital with modern-type industrial enterprise were usury, which returned 30–50 per cent annually, and pawnshops and native banks, which paid 15–25 per cent.[127] There was therefore a tendency in gentry and official circles particularly — but also among the treaty-port compradores who were not unaffected by the dominant ideology — not to invest funds in a shipping company or cotton mill through the purchase of shares. In the absence of a developed financial structure for the buying and selling of securities, ownership of shares involved a sacrifice of liquidity which they were not willing to make. These investors, however, might be willing to put their funds into the C.M.S.N. Co. as long as they were earning as much as or more than what they could get from traditional investments. It was more convenient, therefore, to leave these funds in the form of deposits which could be withdrawn when profits fell or the political situation deteriorated. To complete the circle, the combination of a shortage of risk capital with the reluctance of the owners of the available funds to participate in joint-stock enterprises tended to make the company dependent on short-term, high interest advances from native banks for operating capital.

VI

Bureaucratic Management

From the letters of H. B. Morse, noted historian of China's foreign relations, who was "assistant to the Directors" of the China Merchants' Company from August 1885 to August 1887, it is possible to get a picture of the manner in which the firm was managed during the early years of Sheng Hsuan-huai's control.[128] Morse was an observer recognized for his objectivity, and it may be safely assumed that the shortcomings of "bureaucratic management" which he reports accurately reflect the situation both at the time of his writing and in later decades of the company's operation as a *kuan-tu shang-pan* enterprise. It should be remarked, however, that despite the reliability of his reporting, Morse does not escape entirely the typically superior tone of the treaty-port critic of mandarin behavior.

Morse had been granted leave by the Imperial Maritime Customs so that he might be deputed by Li Hung-chang to assist the China Merchants' Company with the retransfer of its assets from Russell and Company. This was completed in the spring of 1886, and thereafter Morse, on Li's orders, "remained temporarily attached to the Company for the purpose of assisting the Directors in the conduct of their relations with foreigners, both their own foreign employés and foreign houses with which the Company is brought in contact." [129] Apparently his duties were very broad — something like those of an "executive vice-president" — and in fact went beyond relations with foreigners. His immediate superior was Sheng Hsuan-huai, who at the time was customs taotai at Chefoo, while at the Shanghai head office Morse worked closely first with Ma Chien-chung and subsequently less happily, as we shall see, with Shen Neng-hu.

Morse was particularly critical of a situation in which the company's director-general was absent in an official post 500 miles away. He complained of Sheng's inaccessibility even when the latter came to Shanghai: "I can seldom get at Sheng, he is so surrounded by people, and move [?] for a long talk; my proposals have to be crystalized before opening on them." [130] This and other references to the difficulty of dealing with Sheng at a distance — a circumstance which required Morse to arrange to see Sheng at Chefoo every two or three months[131] — may be taken to indicate the extent to which Sheng's concurrent responsibilities as customs taotai and head of the Telegraph Administration limited the on-the-spot attention he could give to the affairs of the C.M.S.N. Co. Yet Sheng expected to be consulted even on matters of detail in regard to the company's operations, as the following list of some of the items, large and small, which Morse brought to his attention would indicate: dock improvement and the purchase of a floating crane, storage of tribute rice, Morse's salary, exchange of property at Hankow with Butterfield and Swire, an expedition to Chungking to survey the feasibility of inaugurating steamer service to that city, troubles over marine repairs, and Morse's resignation from the company.[132] Morse summed up this situation in a letter to Gustav Detring:

Sheng insists that he is to control, and impressed it on me; if he limits his control to very important matters, he can do it; but as he claims to control detail, he should be at Shanghai permanently; even if he promptly decided and promptly communicated his decision, his absence would cause delay and trouble; as he does neither the one nor the other, his absence will I predict breed confusion.[133]

What has been described here, although Morse fails to analyze it as such, is the traditional Chinese omnicompetent official. The principal axis around which the China Merchants' Company (and other comparable enterprises) was constructed was one of responsibility rather than achievement. Unremitting rational pursuit of political and economic goals — for instance, to compete effectively with foreign shippers in the coasting trade in order to assert China's sovereignty and to realize an adequate return on private investments — was subordinated to a conception of the enterprise as a personal holding for which its chief manager bore a responsibility to higher officialdom. The case is indeed similar to that of the *hsien* magistrate described in Chapter 1 who was theoretically omnicompetent in his district, the other side of the coin being that he bore total responsibility for events occurrring within his jurisdiction. Sheng, the type of the middle-rank official transformed in duty but not wholly in spirit, bore total responsibility to Li Hung-chang and indirectly to Peking for the operation and success of the enterprises he directed. His demand — as Morse tells it — to exercise complete control was a natural concomitant of that responsibility. Sheng's attitude was probably not simply a failure of judgment or an urge for personal aggrandizement; it was rather the accepted, institutionalized manner in late nineteenth-century China of administering the kind of enterprise that he headed. One further aspect of this institutional arrangement is that it did in fact present the opportunity for large personal gains to the officials who were all-powerful in their bailiwicks. Power, responsibility, and reward (though we might not consider this last entirely legitimized) all went together, as we should expect them to in an integrated social system.

Although Morse was critical of Sheng's insistence on controlling detail, he knew very well that the company could not operate without Sheng's intervention. He wrote to Detring:

Ma [Chien-chung] would make the best Managing Director for the head office. I doubt if his influence is great enough to enable him to *tu-pan* and conduct official business; but he is the only one who has any experience in business affairs, and really understands that a steamer company is not necessarily conducted on Chinese official lines.[134]

Sheng's responsibilities then were "to *tu-pan* and conduct official business"; and for these he had to possess sufficient influence with higher authorities, that is, with Li Hung-chang and in the appropriate places in Peking. The origin, nature, and development of Sheng's "influence" have been discussed in Chapter 3.

While Morse did not feel that Ma had sufficient authority to handle Sheng's post, he thought him more qualified that the other managers, Hsieh Chia-fu and especially Shen Neng-hu, to undertake the actual operation of the company's business at the head office in Shanghai. Throughout, Morse writes favorably of Ma, albeit sometimes with reservations as in the following:

As far as I can see there is little reason why Ma should not remain in the Directorate with a good colleague; he is not strong himself, and has too much tendency to allow things to drift; but he makes up for a good deal by his good will and good intentions.[135]

When Ma seemed about to resign because of conflicts with Shen Neng-hu, Morse wrote, "in that case I resign too."[136] Morse also thought well of the chief accountant Yen Ying, "who is a man of great ability and considerable influence." [137] But his *bête noire* was Shen Neng-hu:

the new Director Shen, without waiting to acquire knowledge which his past experience could not give him, has begun in every way to make changes which are inadvisable, and which will work great injury to the Company. If he is stopped in the present case [a conflict with J. P. Roberts, the foreign marine superintendent], that would not change him and he would proceed to work mischief in the future; and I desire to place on record my belief that his control of the Company's affairs, will do more to damage the Company, in credit, in working, and in money, than anything done in the past by former Directors.[138]

Morse was concerned in particular because Shen's first order was that all "Bills of lading and office shipping papers" should be prepared in Chinese as well as in English. To do this "the staff (about 30) would have to be doubled." And further, Shen had ordered that "*all* letters received should be translated into Chinese before a decision is taken and reply written, and that the reply be put into Chinese before being sent out. . . . To translate all this would require at least five good translators, probably ten." [139] While it is difficult to sympathize with Morse in the matter of Shen's desire to have the company's documents translated into Chinese — it was after all a Chinese firm — "the new Director" apparently was culpable in other matters:

A more important thing which Shen is ordering is that all bills paid shall henceforward be subject to 5 per cent discount. This is fatal. I have from the beginning struggled to have everything on the basis of net cash price. . . . If we cut 5 per cent we must allow them [the Company's creditors] to add 5 per cent, and they will certainly take the opportunity to add more. . . . I may say that if by an official discount they expect to cut off all chances of commissions, they will fail; commissions can be paid just the same, perhaps more readily.[140]

It is of interest to note that immediately after characterizing Shen as "a capable man who will not recognize that he has no experience," Morse proceeds to tell Detring that he had "always thought it a pity . . . that we could not connect Tong King Sing [T'ang T'ing-shu] with the Company, so as to have the advantage of his business capacity; he need not have had absolute control; meeting a board of Directors twice a week would have secured that. Ma will do as a pis aller." [141]

As a result of continued friction with Shen — the immediate issue was an order which Shen obtained reprimanding the marine superintendent, J. P. Roberts, after a disagreement on policy regarding the repair of steamers — Morse was on the point of resigning in December 1886. He went so far as to draft a formal letter to Li Hung-shang in which he set forth his grievances not only against Shen, but also with regard to Sheng Hsuan-huai. Morse brought three "dangers" to Li's attention: (1) "it is injudicious to have the Chief Director permanently absent from the Head Office in Shanghai." This resulted in error and delay in referring to Chefoo for decisions; (2) "having too many directors is a source of danger to the Company." Two were quite sufficient: "one Chief Director having the ultimate controlling voice in important matters, who should have special charge of the official business; and one Managing Director, who should attend to the working of the Head Office and have control of all matters of detail"; (3) with obvious reference to Shen Neng-hu, Morse cautioned against "the danger of appointing as Director anyone who has not had experience in the conduct of commercial affairs; the Director who manages the affairs of the Head Office must absolutely have this experience, and must also speak and read English, the foreign commercial language of the East." [142]

But Morse did not submit his letter of resignation at this time. He wrote Detring that although he had "got my resignation ready written, . . . things improved so much that I think Shen must have had a strong hint; since then I have been able to put right one or two false steps which he made in small matters, and to let him know that I did so." [143] As a second reason for not leaving, Morse indicated that there had been "a strong protest from Mr. Cameron of the [Hong Kong and Shanghai] Bank, who said he should carry the protest if necessary to the Viceroy; I did not wish to put Li Chung-tang [Li Hung-chang] in any troublesome position vis-a-vis the Bank, whether in the way of conceding to it or of withstanding it." [144]

This near resignation and the circumstances surrounding it are quite revealing in regard to the situation of the China Merchants' Company in these years. It is clear, first, that Li Hung-chang had the ultimate authority over the company. Morse's correspondence with Gustav Detring, the commissioner of customs at Tientsin and an intimate of Li,[145] was motivated by the desire to keep open a direct line of communication to the governor-general. If matters could not be settled through normal channels, they might be brought to Li's ear by a personal intermediary. Next, the administration of the company apparently suffered from the absence of Sheng at Chefoo, 500 miles from Shanghai; from the divided authority at Shanghai, where Ma Chien-chung, Shen Neng-hu and Hsieh Chia-fu each operated without any clearly defined division of responsibility and authority; and from the lack of the requisite knowledge and experience for the operation of a modern-type shipping firm on the part of some of the company's leading officers. The cumbersomeness and inertia characteristic of the traditional Confucian bureaucracy, which resulted from the check and balance of shared official duties combined with multiple office-holding, could not be entirely avoided in the C.M.S.N. Co. Third, Morse's reference to the remonstrances of a representative of the Hong Kong and Shanghai Bank describes the single instance that I have found of the company's actions being influenced by its foreign creditors.

In addition to describing the company's organization and the quality and ability of its managers, Morse's correspondence reveals something of the manner in which the daily business of the China Merchants' Company was carried on. Of great interest are the hints which appear in his letters of the strength of family and personal ties — so important in traditional economic activity in China — even in a modern-type enterprise. Without any special notice, Morse wrote Detring that "affairs progress smoothly in Ma's [Chien-chung] absence; his brother signs for him." [146] This brother, S. P. Ma,[147] was at the time involved in a scheme for the economic development of North Formosa and concurrently was promoting a plan for a steamer line on the Pearl River above Canton.[148] S. P. Ma was apparently able to act for his brother in the management of the C.M.S.N. Co. — although Chien-chung alone held the position of assistant manager — without occasioning any comment from Morse, who was usually quick to pick up any deviation from business practices. This is evidence, I believe, that particularistic considerations were too prevalent in the operation of the company for them to be called into question or even given special notice.

Another facet of the prevalence of traditional Chinese methods in the operation of the company is sharply illustrated by Morse's concern over the maladministration of the Kin Lee Yuen (Chin-li-yuan) wharves and warehouses. These three-story godowns were the best in Shanghai; one of Hsü Jun's principal claims when he laid before Li Hung-chang the list of his accomplishments for the C.M.S.N. Co. was to have undertaken their construction.[149] But Morse was of the opinion that although "the godowns there are very much the best in Shanghai; in fact a sinful waste of money was made by Chu Yu-chee [Hsü Jun] in making them such as they are . . . the third storey is and will be useless." [150] His description of the current situation in the godowns offers a striking example of the manner in which the details of the company's operations were handled:

Kin Lee Yuen requires no money spent on it, and only needs good management; and this I am sorry to say comes at once to having a foreign manager. . . . I will instance one thing: they complained of being filled up with tribute rice, and said they could take no more: I thought this strange as they had taken less than 300,000 bags into their spacious godowns, while the Hongkew wharves in their much smaller godowns had already 230,000 bags; so I asked Middleton to go there, look on it with his practical eye and tell me what the trouble was. He reported that they should have been able to put 80,000 bags more into the space occupied by the rice and that the trouble was that the rice was not stacked. Now the Head Coolie is paid so much a package for putting cargo into godown, taking it out, and putting on board steamers (or vice versa), while he employs his men by the day; if he can have the rice dumped down in a heap, he uses his men for more packages; a strict manager forces him to stack his cargo, while a lax manager allows him to throw it into a heap. This waste of godown room is a sufficient evil without the inevitable suspicion that the Manager gains personally by allowing loose piling of cargo.[151]

Apparently Morse's trouble with Shen Neng-hu came principally from his efforts to eliminate such practices as these. While "even those in the Shipping Office recognize that I always work for the Company even when I am opposing their views," [152] Morse was critical of Shen's lack of business experience and reliance on methods and policies which Morse felt would damage the company as a business enterprise.

One example, among many others, concerned the company's marine superintendent, J. P. Roberts, whose accomplishments Morse praised,[153] but whose policies with respect to repairing the company's fleet met opposition from Shen. Shen obtained an order from Sheng Hsuan-huai reprimanding Roberts;[154] and finally because "Ma [Chien-chung] would not avow that he had authorized the change in the 'Kiang-teen's' wheel and shoved the initial responsibility on Roberts who proposed it and upheld it by his authority," Shen was able to get Li Hung-chang to appoint a Chinese, Ch'en Yu, "to 'hui-tung' [act jointly] with Roberts!" This outraged Morse:

> A better way of getting nothing done I do not know. If the arrangement goes on, there will be trouble and we shall be back where the old Company was. Then Bolton looked after repairs, i.e. acted as Chief Foreman and in large questions exercised only a consultative voice; he pretended to control the staff, but as a man had only to go direct to Tong King Sing or Chu Yu Chee to get a decision given without reference to what had been the Marine Superintendent's opinion, the latter took care not to commit himself by decisions which might render him unpopular; and he did not pretend to check accounts rendered, with the result that many articles for which authority was refused, were still obtained and paid for. All this I hear from independent sources.[155]

Morse's description of "where the old Company was" is of interest as evidence that the administration of the China Merchants' Company under Tong King-sing and Hsü Jun was subject to as many nonrationalized, nonmodern practices as it was under Sheng Hsuan-huai and his associates.

The clash between Morse and the traditional elements in the company, as exemplified by Shen Neng-hu, led finally to Morse's resignation. The way in which this came about is a further illustration of the attitudes against which any desire to operate the China Merchants' Company as a modern business firm had to contend. In outline the affair was quite simple: Morse neglected to inform Shen of the appointment of one Captain R. Petersen to command the ship *Pautah* in place of its regular commander, a Captain Lancaster, who was ordered off the line by the company's doctor because of his poor health. The *Pautah* was subsequently wrecked. Paradoxically, it was Morse himself who had insisted that the designation of captains be referred to the managers for their consent:

> Of the 25 or so appointments of Captain made in the past two years, this is the only one made without the Director's approval; at first the Shipping Office tried to make changes, but I set my face against that and made it the affair of the Director. This one was made by me, and I must take the consequences.[156]

In the background, of course, was Morse's long-continuing feud with Shen Neng-hu. "The vital point is that the question is really part of the contest between Shen Neng-hoo and myself. Right (represented by me) prevailed six months ago; now he has found a weak spot in my armor, through my own carelessness."[157] That Morse's loss of face in this instance should be sufficient to make it necessary for him to resign from the C.M.S.N. Co., which thereby lost his valuable services, shows again the dominant part played by personal considerations, as opposed to more universalistic ones, in the operation of the company.

Morse wrote to Sheng Hsuan-huai informing Sheng of his resignation: "I would advise you not to make public my reasons for resigning, as it would make the Company a laughing-stock in the opinion of all foreigners, who cannot understand such responsibility."[158] The force of personal relations has been underlined in the present context, but it should be noted as well that the ubiquitous matter of vested interests, personal gains, and the like, as Morse clearly realized, was also at issue:

> Every month has made it more inevitable that sooner or later I should go. Reforms always touch the pocket of some-one; and many "some-ones" with their friends make up a crowd. My position might have been very easy, had I been content to draw my pay and execute orders; but the Viceroy's instructions given me at the outset forbade that, and I set to work to do what little I could in the way of reform. Every step alienated someone whose pocket was touched, and went to swell the volume of hostile criticism. Only yesterday I carried through a measure on which I had been working for some months, and thereby put (on the basis of last year's figures) Tls. 2600 a year in the pockets of the Company out of those of one, up to the present a supporter, now probably an opposer. I have comfort in thinking that I have done my duty, and am thankful to be quit of the whole concern.[159]

The Problem of Corruption

Consideration of "bureaucratic management" shades imperceptibly into the related problem of "corruption" in the China Merchants' Company. A difficulty arises for the student of this firm, and similarly of other *kuan-tu shang-pan* enterprises, in determining the dividing line between two kinds of actions. On the one hand are the traditional, institutionalized behavior patterns of Chinese merchants and officials. While these may not be modern, rationalized, or efficient by the standards of the present-day Western observer, they cannot be described as corrupt. It will not do, as one commentator wrote in the *North-China Herald* in 1877 about the managers of the China Merchants' Company, to condemn them "for their violation of the principles advocated by the most advanced school of Political Economy." [160] While Manchester "free trade" is no longer so regarded, the advice applies *a fortiori* to modern critics armed with Keynes or Taylor.

Such a practice as nepotism, for example, which appears to have been endemic in this and other enterprises, probably militated against the most rationalized operation of the company. Chu Ch'i-ang's cooptation of his brothers into the C.M.S.N. Co., the installation of the younger brother of Tong King-sing as manager of the Canton branch, the interchangeableness of the Ma brothers, the presence of Sheng Hsuan-huai's relatives in the company and those of Li Hung-chang as well, have already been mentioned or will be noted in Chapter 5. As one further example of nepotism, we may cite the case of the successive managers of the Hankow branch office whose malpractices will be considered below in detail. From 1893, when Sheng Hsuan-huai appointed Shih Tzu-ch'ing to head the Hankow office, five members of the Shih family in turn held that post, and usually there was a Shih serving as an assistant manager of the company as well.[161] But the introduction of one's relatives into a business or government office with which one was associated was accepted, even expected, behavior. Corruption, on the other hand, lay in yielding to the grosser temptations offered by a situation in which lines of authority and responsibility tended to be diffuse, in which the expectation of mutual support among relatives or fellow townsmen might be used to cover illicit activity.

Peculation of funds, if the embezzler were discovered, was in theory as serious a matter in China as it was elsewhere, and particularly so when public monies were involved. But in a situation, such as that to be described in Chapter 5, where exactions by a money-starved government were always an imminent threat to the company's accumulated reserves, one might naturally expect that the company's managers would prefer personally to divide the surpluses among themselves rather than leave the pickings to others. In the nature of the case, this drainage of the company's surpluses into the pockets of its chief officers can rarely be supported by documentary proof. It was current knowledge in the treaty ports that Sheng Hsuan-huai's fortune, for example, came in part from his share in such a division of the proceeds of his many enterprises. "Regularized squeeze" in the procurement and shipping of tribute rice has been documented by K. C. Liu for the early years of the company.[162] And we have already noted how the financial crisis in Shanghai in 1883–1884 revealed that Tong King-sing and Hsü Jun were employing company funds under their control in personal investments. Further direct evidence, however, is lacking.

It might be hazarded that the official connections of the company's officers made it possible for them to get away with a great deal. We may note, for example, a memorial submitted by the Tsungli Yamen in 1895 in reply to a censorial indictment of corruption in the China Merchants' Company. At the top, the reply conceded, these malpractices took the form of siphoning off a large part of the company's income into the private pockets of a few men. In view of the government's support of the company by providing tribute rice cargoes and granting partial exemption from tariffs, its reserves would have been much larger had it not been for this continual drainage. However, the Tsungli Yamen would not condemn the company too strongly or accede to the harsh measures of control which the censor Wang P'eng-yün proposed. After all, the C.M.S.N. Co. had repaid all the official funds it had borrowed, its vessels through the years had paid some Tls. 3,000,-000 in customs duties, and the profit from the millions in freights which it had collected might otherwise have gone to foreigners. "If there had been no China Merchants' Company, then all this profit would have gone exclusively to foreign merchants; thus the company has played a conspicuous role in recovering our economic rights (li-ch'üan)." [163]

While corruption at the top, in the Shanghai head office, is difficult to document, fortunately a detailed description of malpractices in the company's branch offices is available as a result of the investigations of a commission appointed by the Nationalist government in 1927 to draw up a plan for the reorganization of the C.M.S.N. Co.[164] The gross corruption and graft discovered in the Tientsin and Hankow branches of the company and in the associated China Merchants' Holding Company relate to the period after 1911, but we are doubtless correct in assuming that these conditions already existed in the pre-Republican period. The Tsungli Yamen memorial just cited, for example, raised questions about the honesty of the ships' compradores on the company's

Yangtze River route. And the Ministry of Posts and Communications reported similar malfeasances in 1910, including peculation of passenger receipts, pilferage of supplies, redundant employees, and excessive purchases of coal.[165]

The Regulations and By-laws of 1873 provided that deputy managers selected from among the major shareholders should be placed in charge of the company's branches at Tientsin, Hankow, Hong Kong, Swatow, and so on. These branch managers were to select their own staffs for whom they would stand guaranty. At regular intervals they were to send in reports to Shanghai of their income and expenditures, and of their cash balances.[166] As already noted (see Section III above), from 1879 on, in addition to receiving a monthly expense allowance, each branch was allowed to retain 4 per cent of its receipts on outgoing cargo and 1 per cent on incoming or transit cargo. We have here in embryo form a decentralized administrative organization in which the branch managers were more nearly like contractors or purveyors to the company than its employees. In Sheng Hsuan-huai's new Regulations of 1885, the injunction that the heads of branches be large shareholders was dispensed with. Only the requirement that they be men of ability and resources was stipulated. As before they were to choose and pay their own staffs. In theory the head office was to keep a close watch on the financial operations of the branches by means of a cumbersome system of records in quadruplicate which Sheng devised. In addition Sheng directed that the officers and employees of the company, including the branch managers, were to receive no emoluments other than their salaries and bonuses; that borrowing of the company's funds for private purposes was prohibited; and that no one could hold other employment during his tenure with the China Merchants' Company.[167] Despite the verbal safeguards of these and other regulations and orders, there developed a very considerable autonomy on the part of the branch managers, and with it a complex system of graft and falsification of records which obviously resulted in large losses of income every year for the shareholders. It is unlikely that, given the size of these peculations, all of the principal managers of the company should have been unaware of them and have failed to profit personally themselves.

To begin with, the investigation referred to above revealed that the Hankow branch office kept two sets of books: one on the basis of which reports were made to the head office, and a second set for the private use of the branch manager. Numerous devices were employed to defraud the head office of funds. For example, by taking advantage of the fact that between 1911 and 1925 the official exchange rate for the conversion of strings of cash into taels remained constant at 0.68 while the local Hankow rate fluctuated between 0.3585 and 0.55, the Hankow branch realized some Tls. 210,000 by reporting all its transactions to the head office on the basis of the official rate.[168] This juggling with exchange we recognize immediately as a member of ancient and honorable standing in the corpus of monetary practices occasioned by the absence of a unified currency in China.

The purchase of coal for the company's steamers was a major expense of the Hankow office. This coal was for the most part obtained from large mining companies on an annual basis: until the beginning of 1914, from the P'ing-hsiang mines (controlled by Sheng Hsuan-huai) in Kiangsi; to the middle of 1918, from the Pao-feng Mining Company and then to 1924 from the Hsieh-feng Mining Company. Small additional amounts were purchased from local Hankow dealers. On the books of the branch office the price paid for coal in the period 1918–1924 ranged three or four taels per ton higher than the average Hankow market price for this period. It is estimated that the branch manager profited to the extent of Tls. 489,641 in these seven years.[169] Not only was the price paid for coal in excess of the market price, but in addition the amount of coal purchased was carried on the Hankow branch's books at one tenth more than was actually the case. This brought the branch manager Tls. 332,541 between 1911 and 1926. A further Tls. 56,103 was netted by inflating the handling costs from Tls. 0.1 to Tls. 0.25 per ton of coal.[170]

In the period covered by the Nationalist government investigation, the basis for the commission allowed the company's branches had changed somewhat in detail, but the underlying system was still that established in 1879. The Hankow office, and each of the others as well, received a monthly allowance for operating expenses from the head office; and in addition the branch manager was allowed to retain 5 per cent of the freights collected above a stipulated minimum. This minimum, however, remained unchanged from 1912 to 1925 despite a steady increase in the amount of traffic handled. In 1925 it was at last raised from Tls. 375,000 to Tls. 500,000. Between 1913 and 1925 the Hankow manager realized more than Tls. 182,000 in commissions from this arrangement.[171]

A fourth major source of gain for the Hankow branch was the real property, for the most part godowns, which it managed. Half of the China Merchants' Company's real property at Hankow was used in its own business operations, while the other half was rented out. This second category represented an estimated value of Tls. 1,020,000. At the 10 per cent return usual in Hankow at this time, it should have brought in about Tls. 100,000 annually. However, the annual return reported by the Hankow office fluctuated between a low of Tls. 9,756 in 1913 and a high of Tls. 17,736 in 1925. The estimated loss to the C.M.S.N. Co. is estimated at more than Tls. 1,300,000 for the years 1913–1927, and at several million taels over three decades.[172]

Apparently these practices which were current at the company's leading Hankow branch were duplicated at Tientsin and elsewhere.[173] In the words of one member of the 1927 investigating commission: "We may be very definite that for corruption on so large a scale to have taken place without detection by the head office, cooperation between the branch manager and important executives in the head office must have occurred." [174] Here, it appears, we have one answer to the problem of how the "drainage" of the company's profits by its officers was carried out. An arrangement of the kind inferred between the men who sat in the company's head office and the branch managers through whose hands a large part of the company's funds passed seems only natural. Its probability is enhanced when the basis on which the branch heads were selected is recalled. In this instance, nepotism and particularistic loyalties may well have ripened into explicit corruption.

5

The China Merchants' Company: Official Supervision

I

Official Supervision of the China Merchants' Company, 1872–1895

Normally the establishment of a *kuan-tu shang-pan* enterprise was not the result of initiative taken by the imperial government. Peking did not provide material support or exercise direct supervision. On the contrary, such efforts as were made to introduce new industries resulted from the efforts of powerful provincial officials. In this connection, we may recall the activities of Li Hung-chang, the outstanding official promoter of "foreign matters," which have been discussed in Chapter 1. A unity is imposed on more than two decades of the history of the China Merchants' Company by Li's tenure in the post of commissioner for the northern ports. That office, held concurrently with the governor-generalship of Chihli since 1870, was the focus of official supervision over the C.M.S.N. Co. from its inception until the company passed under the purview of the Ministry of Posts and Communications in 1909.

Governor-general Li's role in founding the China Merchants' Company has already been narrated. Such matters as raising funds, securing a monopoly franchise for the carriage of tribute rice, obtaining tax exemptions, appointing managerial personnel, and protecting the company and its managers from attacks by competing sectors of officialdom bulked largest in Li's performance as the company's patron from 1872 to 1895. In return for these services, Li and his regional political organization were able to realize several substantial benefits from control of the C.M.S.N. Co. The range of his activities with regard to the company will illustrate the content of official supervision (*kuan-tu*) of a modern-type enterprise.

Li Hung-chang's Aid to the C.M.S.N. Co. The most direct means by which Li Hung-chang controlled the company was to retain in his own hands the right to appoint and dismiss its leading managerial personnel. Just as he had originally deputed Chu Ch'i-ang and Chu Ch'i-chao in 1872, so he appointed Sheng Hsuan-huai, Tong King-sing, and Hsü Jun in 1873, Yeh T'ing-chüan in 1878, Chang Hung-lu in 1881, Cheng Kuan-ying in 1882, Ma Chien-chung in 1884, and Sheng again in 1885. Even during the years when Sheng, Li's trusted deputy in industrial and commercial matters, headed the company, Sheng's associates (Ma Chien-chung, Hsieh Chia-fu, Shen Neng-hu, and Cheng Kuan-ying) were at least nominally designated by Li. And in 1891 it was Li himself who appointed Yen Ying, T'ang Te-hsi, and Ch'en Yu as "merchant directors" (*shang-tung*), ostensibly in order to give representation to merchant shareholders in the management of the company.[1] Undoubtedly Tong and Hsü and after them Sheng had some voice in the selection of their principal subordinates — Li's action might be in response to their petition. But the essential matter here is that these men, even those who were to represent the shareholders, had to be invested with their office by Li's authority. While Tong and Hsü might seek to maintain the fiction of their election by the shareholders,[2] it was in fact Li who installed and deposed.

This may be illustrated by the circumstance, already described, of Li's removal of both Tong and Hsü from the direction of the company in 1884 following accusations against them of "audacious embezzlement of the Company's funds."[3] The chief consequence of the nomination of its key personnel by a high provincial official was that the China Merchants' Company was irrefragably a semiofficial enterprise, regardless of the compradore origin of many of its managers or of the commercial provenance of much of its capital.

The assistance which Governor-general Li rendered the company in its efforts to secure adequate capital and operating funds represents the second main area into which his official supervision extended. In June 1874, at the end of the company's first year of operations under Tong's management and one and a half years after its establishment, the liability side of the ledger showed a paid-up capital of Tls. 476,000 plus Tls. 193,909 in borrowed funds.[4] The largest part of the company's borrowed funds in 1874 was accounted for by the proceeds of the 200,000 strings (Tls. 135,000) of Chihli military funds which Li Hung-chang had advanced at 7 per cent interest in 1872 in order to get the C.M.S.N. Co. under way.[5] While the size of the loans which Li himself provided the China Merchants' Company from the Chihli treasury was not in fact large, his aid came at crucial moments; and furthermore, he was able on several occasions to secure financial assistance for the company from other sources. For example, in the spring of 1876, Li came to the company's aid in the unsettled international situation resulting from the murder in Yunnan of Augustus R. Margary of the British consular service. Foreign shipping companies were taking the threat of hostilities as an occasion to reduce their rates sharply, seeking to win customers who might be hesitant about shipping in Chinese vessels. To compensate the C.M.S.N. Co. for its losses, Li arranged loans of Tls. 350,000 from Chihli coast defense and military training funds and Tls. 100,000 from the Tientsin customs; these funds were deposited with the company at 8 per cent and made possible the repayment of funds borrowed at usurious rates from native bankers.[6]

Li's influence was probably instrumental also in securing funds from Shen Pao-chen, the Liang-Chiang governor-general, for the purchase of the fleet and property of the Shanghai Steam Navigation Company in 1877. Shen had been the director-general of the Foochow Shipyard when the China Merchants' Company was founded and, together with Li, had favored the building of merchant vessels by the shipyard to be added to the C.M.S.N. Co. fleet. According to Hsü Jun's account, which could hardly err in the direction of giving too much credit to Sheng Hsuan-huai, it was Sheng who approached Shen on Li's behalf, seeking to borrow Tls. 1,000,000 in order to make the initial payment to the American firm of Russell and Company which operated the S.S.N. Co.[7] Shen at first refused, but "subsequently Sheng Hsuan-huai devised means to raise nearly Tls. 1,000,000. His arguments were sharp and he convinced His Excellency, but the funds were still inadequate. The next day Sheng together with the provincial treasurer petitioned Shen Pao-chen pointing out where there was Tls. 200,000 in gold that could be used. . . . Shen presented a memorial and the funds were appropriated. . . . Thus the China Merchants' Company was put on a firm foundation. In all this, Sheng's efforts were the greatest." [8]

Li Hung-chang's assistance was of crucial importance to the company in a third matter, closely related to the obtaining of funds. On several occasions he intervened to aid the company in the repayment of the large official debt which it had contracted. These official funds were deposited with the C.M.S.N. Co. at interest varying from 7 to 10 per cent. With the accumulated interest, the company's indebtedness to the government — in strict fact, to the several provincial treasuries — came to a total of Tls. 1,928,000 by mid-1877. At this time its paid-up share capital totaled only Tls. 730,200. In addition to the official debt, there were other liabilities totaling Tls. 2,104,401 and consisting of loans from native bankers, deposits by private persons, the assets of the Jen-ho Insurance Company which were on deposit, unpaid dividends, and current accounts. The company's total operating funds in 1877 thus came to Tls. 4,762,601, of which only Tls. 730,200, or one sixth, was paid-up share capital.[9]

Considering the heavy burden of the interest payments on this indebtedness and the very slow rate at which private merchant capital was coming into the company, Li Hung-chang approached the Tsungli Yamen on the company's behalf. His letter of November 4, 1877, concluded with the assertion that "this enterprise, as you have yourselves stated, is involved in the whole matter of commercial development. We cannot abandon it in mid-course and become the laughing-stock of the foreigners, while allowing them to gain control of China's economic rights (*li-ch'üan*). Officials and merchants must combine their strength to devise a way to bolster the company." [10] He then outlined a plan which provided for a delay in the repayment of government funds. Having obtained the acquiescence of the Yamen, Li presented his proposals to the throne in a slightly altered form in a memorial of December 19. The governor-general was very careful to point out that it had always been the intention of the China Merchants' Company to repay borrowed official funds as merchant investments were added to its capital. But private investment had not grown as quickly as had been anticipated. Therefore, Li suggested, payment of principal and interest due on the Tls. 1,928,000 in question should be deferred for three years. From 1880, while interest payments were still deferred, the company would repay the principal in five annual installments of Tls. 381,000. Thus in eight years the official loans would have been repaid; the deferred interest could then either be converted into official shares in the company or repaid in installments. [11]

In order to make possible the large annual installments of Tls. 381,000 which were to begin in 1880, Li found it necessary to assist the C.M.S.N. Co. in two additional ways: by securing for it an increased share of the transport of tribute rice, and by obtaining tariff concessions which favored the China Merchants' Company over other carriers. The importance of these measures and of other instances of monopoly and quasi-monopoly rights granted to the company by virtue of its status as a *kuan-tu shang-pan* enterprise will be considered in more detail later in this chapter. At present it is sufficient to record that Li Hung-chang requested that the provinces be ordered to ship 40 to 50 per cent of their tribute rice via the C.M.S.N. Co. and that the sea transport of all other official freight by the provinces be granted as a monopoly to the company. [12] In addition, Li proposed that the existing practice of exempting C.M.S.N. Co. vessels carrying tribute rice to Tientsin from 20 per cent of the customs duty be extended also to its vessels carrying copper from Canton to Tientsin. [13]

Apparently these measures received imperial approval, for in May 1880, at the end of the three-year period during which payment on the official debt was to be deferred, Li reported to the throne that the company had already repaid Tls. 126,500 which it owed to several customs offices and was ready to pay a first installment of Tls. 356,300 on the balance of Tls. 1,781,500. The income from tribute rice carriage for the next five years was to be allocated for this purpose.[14] Peking's sanction for the application of the company's receipts from tribute rice carriage to the repayment of its official debt is confirmed by a further memorial from Li, dated July 9, 1880, in which he stated that the funds scheduled to be repaid to the several provincial treasuries from these receipts were in most cases not urgently needed by the provinces concerned. He therefore requested and received imperial approval to divert the Tls. 1,000,000 due for the first three years to the purchase of warships in England for the Peiyang Navy.[15]

Li Hung-chang's exertions in such matters as those that have been described were usually, though by no means always, successful. But at least one major instance in which his efforts to assist the China Merchants' Company ran into effective opposition should be cited in order to indicate the limits of his power. At the same time it will illustrate a fourth role in which Li was active, namely as a protector of the company from attacks by hostile sectors of the metropolitan and provincial bureaucracy. In 1886, several months after Sheng Hsuan-huai had taken over the management of the China Merchants' Company, Li sought to assist the firm (which had suffered considerable losses during the recent hostilities with France when its vessels had been "sold" to Russell and Company) by requesting imperial approval for deferment of payments on the Tls. 770,000 debt which the C.M.S.N. Co. still owed to several provincial treasuries. Payments, to come as before from tribute rice carriage receipts, would be resumed when the company's foreign indebtedness (mainly a £300,000 loan from the Hong Kong and Shanghai Banking Corporation) had been repaid. The governor-general asked that the freight rate paid to the company for rice carriage be increased in order to expedite this repayment.[16] His memorial was referred to the Ministry of Revenue. The ministry immediately accepted two comparatively minor suggestions which were included in Li's proposals: a 20 per cent exemption from export duties on return trips for vessels coming with tribute rice to Tientsin, and reduced duties on coarse-quality teas carried by C.M.S.N. Co. steamers from Hupei to Tientsin. But it firmly opposed increasing the rate for rice carriage or deferring repayment of official funds. Moreover, the Hu-pu took advantage of this occasion to attack the company and indirectly Li Hung-chang himself. The ministry stated:

From the documents before them and from what people say, this Ministry sees that the so-called "profit and power" [evidently *li-ch'üan*] are neither in the hands of the state above, nor in those of the merchants below, but have entirely gone to the officials and gentry acting as middlemen. For instance, the impeachment of Tong King-sing and Chu K'i-ang in the first instance, and the shameful exposure of Sü Jun and Chang Hung-lu in the second, are clear evidence of the Ministry's statements.

In order to remedy alleged malpractices, the company was to be ordered to submit to the ministry annual reports of its property, income and expenditures, and personnel and their salaries.[17]

The final outcome of this exchange was that the freight rate was not increased, while the company's official debt was repaid according to a schedule established by the Ministry of Revenue.[18] Its significance lies primarily in illustrating one source from which attacks, often justified, on the operations of the C.M.S.N. Co. might come. Li Hung-chang was constantly occupied in defending his appointees, and in this manner he rendered a major service to the company and its management — if not to efficient and honest operation.

It is possible to cite a constant stream of impeachments directed against the China Merchants' Company. In the usual case these charges — emanating sometimes from such influential metropolitan censors as Wang Hsien-ch'ien[19] — were referred to Li Hung-chang with imperial instructions to conduct an investigation. Imperial action on the impeachments, if any, would generally follow Li's recommendations. The purchase by the C.M.S.N. Co. of the Shanghai Steam Navigation Company in 1877 was a particularly choice target for censorial denunciations. Thus in 1878 the censor Tung Chün-han charged that by its purchase of the S.S.N. Co. the China Merchants' Company had acquired too many ships for the available traffic, and in consequence was losing Tls. 50,000–60,000 a month due to unnecessarily high operating expenses. These losses, he continued, were aggravated by laxness in the employment of personnel and by inadequate financial records. As might be expected, this was a frequent complaint in censorial indictments. Li vigorously defended the company against the censor's charges, but agreed that thenceforth he would instruct the Shanghai and Tientsin customs taotais to inspect regularly the company's accounts in their respective jurisdictions.[20]

A much more inclusive denunciation of the China Merchants' Company, and of Sheng Hsuan-huai in particular, was made by the censor Wang Hsien-ch'ien at the end of 1880. The imperial instructions to Li Hung-chang directed him to conduct a strict investigation and to punish severely all instances of malfeasance and misappropriation of funds that he might discover. Li's conduct in this instance is typical of the manner in which he dealt with impeachments of his enterprises. He referred the matter to his subordinates, the Shanghai and Tientsin customs taotais, Li Jui-fen and Cheng Tsao-ju respectively, and they were joined by the taotai Li Hsing-jui, who had been sent by the governor-general at Nanking, Liu K'un-i. These officials investigated Wang's charges and reported back to Li Hung-chang. The petition he received from them was then the basis of the memorial which Li submitted to the emperor. In this case, as in others, he forcefully denied the censor's charges. The company's first steamers had not been purchased at an excessive price by Chu Ch'i-ang; Sheng and Tong King-sing definitely had not used company funds to purchase secretly shares in the Shanghai Steam Navigation Company and then arrange for its purchase by the C.M.S.N. Co. at an inflated price; Tong and Sheng had not pocketed the company's liquid assets which should have been applied to depreciation; and finally, contrary to Wang's assertions, official supervision was not so lax that Tong and the other merchants were able to use official funds for their private gain.[21]

To cite Governor-general Li's support of the China Merchants' Company (and of other enterprises under his wing) against such charges of corruption is not to conclude, however, that these accusations were without foundation. That the contrary was often the case is apparent even from this example. We have already noted that Chu did pay inflated prices for the company's first steamers. Tong, Hsü and others in fact were using official funds (more precisely the funds of the China Merchants' Company which included large official loans) in their private business ventures; it was because of these activities that they were later removed from the management. But Li's power and influence in Peking were usually enough to prevent action by the metropolitan authorities against any of the enterprises under his protection.

The C.M.S.N. Co., being situated in the middle of a system of institutionalized "squeeze," was undoubtedly a good target. In fending off accusations against it, Li was also protecting his own concentration of power in Chihli, one facet of which was his control of the shipping company. The attacks on Li came from two sources: from other provincial officials who were jealous of his power; and from adherents of a conservative clique known as the "pure-talk faction" (*ch'ing-i p'ai* or *ch'ing-liu p'ai*), who opposed even the relatively small attention which the court was directing to "foreign matters." [22] In his defense against censorial impeachments of his industrial undertakings Li utilized skillfully the ambiguous status of the *kuan-tu shang-pan* enterprises. When convenient to do so, he would fall back upon the half-fiction that "the gains and losses of the company are strictly the merchants' affairs, and are not a concern of the government." [23] And "as operating a commercial steamship company line involves relations with foreigners, it is even more apparent that officials should not be involved in it. Thus, this enterprise differs from others established with the appropriation of public funds." [24] Li could hardly concede, however, that the government had no responsibilities towards the company; he needed to justify his own obvious connection with it. Therefore he was quick to add, "But this enterprise is of great importance for the recovery of China's economic rights (*li-ch'üan*), and for that reason it must be aided by the government, even to the extent of lending official funds to compensate for the inadequacy of merchant resources." [25] As to specific charges of corruption, Li might deal with them in this manner:

> The stock of the company is managed by these two taotais [Tong King-sing and Hsü Jun in this instance] and each year the accounts are reviewed by the merchants themselves. Should these two managers attempt to misappropriate funds or make reckless expenditures, the merchants would act in their own interest without waiting for an official impeachment. Yet since the day that the company was established no merchant has ever come forward with such an indictment. [26]

In view of the services which Li Hung-chang rendered the China Merchants' Company, it is no surprise to find the managers of the company reporting to the shareholders that "the shareholders might be thankful for the position they are in now, for it is entirely due to Li that they are able to pay off the [government] loan and make a profit besides." [27]

Li Hung-chang's Gains from the C.M.S.N. Co. Li's efforts, of course, were not acts of philanthropy. The continued existence and success of the China Merchants' Company were directly beneficial to his political position in North China.

Of considerable consequence for Li Hung-chang's political power was the partial control of the sea transport of tribute rice to the capital which came into his hands through his authority over the China Merchants' Company. This tribute grain had an importance far out of proportion to its actual economic value by virtue of its consumption by the metropolitan garrison, the imperial household and court, and the nobles and officials in and near Peking. [28] While deliveries were originally made in kind, from the Chia-ch'ing period (1796–1820) on, the quotas due from all provinces except Shantung, Anhwei, Kiangsu, and Chekiang were commuted into payments in silver. By the end of the dynasty only Kiangsu and Chekiang were still remitting in kind. [29] In earlier days the largest part of these shipments had gone via the Grand Canal. But it has been estimated that by the years 1902–1905 the provinces of Kiangsu, Chekiang, Anhwei, and Shantung were shipping only 400,000 piculs annually by the canal, while an annual average of 1,626,-000 piculs went by sea from Shanghai to Tientsin. [30] The quotas in kind of 600,000 and 400,000 piculs respectively due from Kiangsu and Chekiang at the end of the dynasty were for the most part sent by the sea route. In the last years of Manchu rule not only was the Grand Canal displaced as a route for rice shipments, but steamers — foreign and Chinese — also steadily forced the sea-going junks (*sha-ch'uan*) out of the carrying business. Thus the Shanghai district gazetteer reported:

In 1873 the government permitted the tribute rice shipped by sea from Kiangsu and Chekiang to be carried by C.M.S.N. Co. steamers. They were allowed 20 per cent of the total while 80 per cent was allotted to the junks. Later the ratio was changed to 40 per cent and 60 per cent. Then, due to the daily decrease in the number of junks, in the winter of 1900 [Kuang-hsü 26] the entire tribute was given to the China Merchants' Company. At that time only 50 junks remained.[31]

To the extent that the capital, Peking, was still dependent on tribute rice shipments, control of the China Merchants' Company might be a useful club to wield in the arena of metropolitan politics.

Moreover, procurement and shipment of tribute rice could be a source of considerable personal gain for Li and his followers. It was the general practice before the China Merchants' Company entered the field that as high as 10 per cent of the government appropriation for rice "was regularly withheld as perquisites by officials supervising the hiring and dispatching of junks." [32] Undoubtedly Li and Chu Ch'i-ang — the latter being himself an official in charge of rice shipments as well as a junk owner — were fully aware of the lucrative potentialities of this trade when they organized the company.

The resources of the C.M.S.N. Co. were utilized in a more direct fashion in aid of Li Hung-chang's military power. In July 1880, for example, as we have already noted, the emperor approved Li's request to divert Tls. 1,000,000 of the company's expected earnings from tribute rice carriage to pay for warships which Li would purchase from England for his Peiyang Navy. The company's steamers provided services for Li's Huai Army in the form of transporting troops, for example, by carrying six "regiments" from T'ung-chou to Seoul in 1882, and by moving troops to Korea as the crisis with Japan deepened in 1894.[33] Furthermore, it was of considerable importance for the character of the company's management that places in it might go as rewards or sinecures to junior officials of Li's entourage; the case of Ma Chien-chung, whose career with the company has already been discussed, may be cited as an example.

On occasion the company's assets were used to furnish funds for others of Li Hung-chang's industrial or political undertakings — after the initial period, of course, in which it was itself dependent on the government for funds. Under a contract with the "Corean Foreign Office" dated October 1, 1882, the China Merchants' Company agreed to lend the Korean government Tls. 500,000 of which Tls. 200,000 was actually loaned.[34] This had been arranged by Li Hung-chang as part of his program for strengthening China's influence in Korea.[35] The loan was carried as an asset on the books of the company down to the Sino-Japanese War with a reduction to Tls. 123,000 recorded during 1891; there is no definite statement, however, that this indicated a partial repayment.[36]

In 1878, Li Hung-chang undertook to sponsor a modern coal mining enterprise in Chihli, the well-known K'ai-p'ing Mines, which later were merged into the Kailan Mining Administration.[37] The China Merchants' Company held some Tls. 210,000 in K'ai-p'ing shares in 1882, a natural concomitant of Li's sponsorship of both enterprises and of the fact that Tong King-sing, who headed the C.M.S.N. Co. from 1873 to 1884, was also the moving spirit behind the K'ai-p'ing Mines.[38] One consideration leading to the inauguration of K'ai-p'ing was the desire to obtain a regular and cheap supply of coal for C.M.S.N. Co. steamers. For the same reason Tls. 60,966 of the company's funds were invested in an attempt to develop coal mines in Anhwei sponsored jointly by Li Hung-chang and the governors-general at Nanking and Wuchang.[39]

In 1891 the company's funds were used to support Li's efforts to establish a modern cotton mill in Shanghai. "By the order of the officials a sum of Tls. 100,000 was taken out of the surplus fund and invested in the Shanghai Cotton Cloth Mill Company's shares," stated the managers of the C.M.S.N. Co. in their report to the shareholders for the year 1891.[40] Also to be noted for the period before 1895 is an initial investment of Tls. 15,000 in 1888 — increasing to Tls. 50,000 in 1892 — in a "Formosa shipping company" which had been founded by a brother of Ma Chien-chung.[41]

The use of China Merchants' Company funds to support other modern undertakings should not, however, be simply dismissed under the heading of benefits accruing to Li Hung-chang from his patronage to the company. Such enterprises as the K'ai-p'ing Coal Mines and the Shanghai Cotton Cloth Mill (and the same must be said of the China Merchants' Company itself) were genuine attempts to utilize Western techniques and technology in order to strengthen China against the feared incursion of the Occident. That these techniques were at the same time of greatest direct benefit to Li Hung-chang's regional power is only a corollary of the fact that he was one of the few persons who was in a position to employ them and who had some appreciation of the value of "foreign matters."

II

Official Supervision, 1895–1908

The post of commissioner for the northern ports, whose primary appointment was as governor-general of Chihli, was filled by five officials in succession between the removal of Li Hung-chang in 1895 and Yuan Shih-k'ai's promotion to the Grand Council in 1907: by Wang Wen-shao from August 1895 until June 1898, by Jung-lu between June and September 1898, by Yü-lu from September 1898 to July 1900, by Li Hung-chang again during the period of the Boxer negotiations, and then by Yuan Shih-k'ai from the time of Li's death in November 1901.[42]

Jung-lu's appointment, which was primarily a move by the empress dowager against the reformers, apparently had no effect on the China Merchants' Company. Nor is there any evidence that Yü-lu, the pro-Boxer official who committed suicide in August 1900 as the Allied armies advanced northward from Tientsin to relieve the siege of the Peking legations, showed any particular interest in the affairs of the company. Like his predecessor Wang Wen-shao, Yü-lu, together with the Hu-Kuang governor-general, Chang Chih-tung, had nominal control over the projects which Sheng Hsuan-huai was undertaking as director-general of railroads. But Yü-lu was an unregenerate Manchu reactionary and evinced little interest in these *yang-wu* projects, except possibly for the squeeze he could get from them.[43]

Wang Wen-shao presents a somewhat different case.[44] He was apparently a relatively progressive official, and during his tenure as Chihli governor-general gave his political backing to Sheng Hsuan-huai's economic activities. Together with Chang Chih-tung he proposed Sheng to the throne in 1896 for the position of director-general of railroads, and he approved Sheng's assumption of the control over the Hanyang Ironworks in the same year. But at no time does Wang seem to have interfered with regard to the C.M.S.N. Co.

The hands-off policy of Yü-lu and Wang Wen-shao, in contrast to the role played by Li Hung-chang, supports the impression that in the period following Li's fall the company was relatively independent of the provincial hierarchs who inherited his office. As has already been shown in Chapter 3, from 1895 the relations between Sheng and Chang Chih-tung became closer while, at the same time, Sheng's personal power was growing apace. With Chang's influence behind him and with his rise into the sphere of metropolitan politics, it was possible for Sheng himself to undertake many of the functions of "official supervision" which Li had performed for the company prior to 1895. Then too, the need for the financial backing which Li had provided had somewhat abated. By 1895, it will be remembered, the C.M.S.N. Co. had discharged in full its obligations to foreign creditors, while its debt to the provincial treasuries had been repaid as early as 1891.

But Yuan Shih-k'ai abruptly reversed this trend towards independence. Yuan's accession to the governor-generalship of Chihli was accompanied by an attempt to reassert the authority of that office over the C.M.S.N. Co., the telegraphs, and the other projects which had been launched under Li Hung-chang's auspices. Yuan as governor-general was undoubtedly a progressive official in regard to his attitude towards "foreign matters." [45] Nevertheless, his contest with Sheng for control of the C.M.S.N. Co. and the accompanying personnel shifts and divisions within the company were clearly less manifestations of his concern for the firm's success as a business operation than products of a desire to operate it through his own followers for the benefit of his political power in Chihli.

Paradoxically, as Sheng Hsuan-huai's own official power grew in the years after the Sino-Japanese War, Sheng, the official manager of the C.M.S.N. Co. from 1885–1902, became increasingly a supporter of private or mercantile management (*shang-pan*) for the company. Between 1902 and 1907 this attitude was a lever to be used against Yuan Shih-k'ai and his appointees. Sheng's attempt to register the China Merchants' Company with the Ministry of Agriculture, Industry, and Commerce as a *shang-pan* enterprise has already been mentioned in passing. Shortly after Yuan had appointed Hsü Jun as acting manager in February 1907, Hsü received a disconcerting telegram in Macao where he had gone for medical treatment. The company's head office in Shanghai was informing him that Sheng Hsuan-huai had held a meeting of the Kiangsu and Chekiang shareholders of the C.M.S.N. Co. on February 28, and the meeting had decided to petition the Ministry of Agriculture, Industry, and Commerce to register the company as a private commercial firm under the provisions of the new Company Law.[46] This was clearly an attempt on the part of the northern shareholders led by Sheng to wrest the company from official control, that is, from Yuan Shih-k'ai who as commissioner for the northern ports had ultimate jurisdiction over the *kuan-tu shang-pan* enterprise.

One hundred ninety-eight shareholders from the northern and central provinces — representing a little more than half of the total shares outstanding — had attended the meeting at Sheng Hsuan-huai's Bubbling Well Road residence in Shanghai. They selected a committee composed of men friendly to Sheng, which was directed to carry out the registration.[47] On receiving the report of Sheng's move, Hsü went immediately to Hong Kong where he met with leaders of the southern group of shareholders. On March 20, a general meeting of southern shareholders, outflanked by Sheng's actions, reluctantly agreed to participate in the attempt to register the company. But in response to Hsü Jun's warnings against Sheng's perfidy, they petitioned the ministry requesting that the registration be carried out by the incumbent management, that is, by Hsü; and they telegraphed Yuan Shih-k'ai urging him not to appoint other officers.[48] In the end, no action was taken to change the status of the C.M.S.N. Co., but as we have seen, the incident was a preface to Sheng's recovery of control over the enterprise. This control, exercised through the taotai Wang Ts'un-shan, was assured by Yuan's exit from the post of Chihli governor-general in September 1907.

It seems to have been the case that Sheng, as long as he was its official manager or could control the incumbent at that post, preferred to see the company organized on a *kuan-tu shang-pan* basis. This form of organization best suited the needs of the economic empire he was building and offered the greatest opportunity for financial gain. Probably this was why he did not proceed to register the firm as a *shang-pan* enterprise even after Hsü had been cashiered and Yuan had been "promoted" to the Grand Council. However, when he was unable to control the company directly through its management, Sheng, as in the above instance, would become a supporter of wholly private operation. He undoubtedly felt secure in the belief that as the company's largest shareholder he would have no difficulty dominating the board of directors, and through them the management, of a *shang-pan* firm.

From mid-1907 until the C.M.S.N. Co. was transferred to the control of the Ministry of Posts and Communications (*Yu-ch'uan pu*) in April 1909, Sheng, although he was not its official head, served as the intermediary between the enterprise and official circles. However, his position was weakened when political and personal enemies in Peking prevented him from taking active possession of the office of junior vice-president of the Ministry of Posts and Communications, to which he was appointed in March 1908. When an imperial edict transferred the C.M.S.N. Co. to the jurisdiction of that ministry, Sheng was in no position to continue the degree of control that he had maintained over the enterprise since 1907. It is not surprising, therefore, that despite his *de jure* post in the Yu-ch'uan pu, Sheng should assist his fellow shareholders in a concerted effort to minimize the official supervision which the ministry exercised.

III

The Directors vs. the Yu-ch'uan pu, 1909–1911

The firm's shareholders reacted immediately to the order placing the China Merchants' Company under the purview of the Ministry of Posts and Communications. Thirty-one leading shareholders, from both the northern and southern factions, joined in a telegram to the ministry which demanded the establishment of an elected board of directors. Meeting in Shanghai at the head office, the board would be in a position to operate the C.M.S.N. Co. in accordance with the stipulations of the Company Law which the Yu-ch'uan pu was expected to acknowledge.[49] The ministry was forced to agree, perhaps with Sheng's help from behind the scenes. A committee of shareholders headed by Cheng Kuan-ying and Yen I-pin, both Sheng's associates of long standing, proceeded to register the outstanding shares in preparation for a general meeting of shareholders. On August 15, 1909, 732 shareholders representing 31,164 shares elected a nine-man board of directors (tung-shih hui), composed overwhelmingly of men loyal to Sheng Hsuan-huai. Sheng himself led the list with 4,769 votes as compared to 1,686 for the second man and 983 for the ninth, and he was elected chairman of the board.[50]

The meeting also drafted new regulations (chang-ch'eng) for the company to replace those under which it had operated since 1885. In the form accepted by the ministry these were a considerable concession to "merchant operation" in that they provided for a board of directors chosen by the shareholders. But "official supervision" was continued by virtue of the rights reserved to the Yu-ch'uan pu in Chapter II of the regulations. Despite the general stipulation in Chapter I that the C.M.S.N. Co. was to be operated as a joint-stock limited liability company under the new Company Law, Chapter II defined the company as "merchant operated under the supervision of the Ministry [of Posts and Communications]" (shang-pan li-pu). The ministry reserved the authority to appoint officials to serve as manager and deputy manager (termed cheng tso-pan and fu tso-pan) and as assistant managers (hui-pan). In addition the company was directed to refer matters of importance to the ministry by petition (ping).[51]

In sum, the semiofficial status of the company had been only modified rather than ended by the government's acceptance of these regulations. Sheng, Cheng, et al. could no longer dominate the company's management by virtue of their official positions alone, as they had done from 1885 to 1902 and again from 1907 to 1909. They therefore attempted to utilize their roles as the leading shareholders in order to counter the authority of the official managers whom the Yu-ch'uan pu deputed to head the company. Their agent was a board of directors which they dominated. But the issue of whether the shareholders or the Ministry of Posts and Communications would have ultimate control over the operation of the C.M.S.N. Co. was not resolved at this time. It was fought out in a series of skirmishes which continued until the fall of the dynasty in 1911. The interest attached to these clashes lies first in the role played by Sheng Hsuan-huai, newly returned to office first as vice-president and then as president of the Ministry of Posts and Communications. Sheng utilized his official prerogatives in such a manner as to facilitate the transfer of effective control over the C.M.S.N. Co. to its shareholders and, in particular, to those interests to which he was himself closely tied. At least until the beginning of 1911 this paradoxical position can be explained by the continuing insecurity of Sheng's official position. After that time, the process was already far advanced, and Sheng's attention had shifted to other matters. Secondly, it was a sign of development within the Chinese mercantile community that the shareholders were able to assert themselves so effectively as to gain control of the company and thus, so to speak, put some starch into the limp phrase "merchant management."

The issue was drawn with the Yu-ch'uan pu at the first shareholders' meeting. Sheng Hsuan-huai headed the list of directors, as we have already noted, and the directors chose him to be chairman of the board. From March 1908 Sheng had been nominal junior vice-president of the Ministry of Posts and Communications; but he had never actively assumed that office. Assuredly, his dispatch to Shanghai three days after his appointment in order to participate in commercial negotiations in a subordinate capacity can be called a *de facto* dismissal. Despite the action of the shareholders, Sheng informed the meeting that he declined his election as a director and board chairman, giving as a reason the incompatibility of his holding of such posts in the company simultaneously with his office in the Yu-ch'uan pu.[52] It was certainly more than a coincidence that Cheng Kuan-ying and Yen I-pin, the two men who had taken the lead in bringing about the establishment of the board of directors, also at first declined their election to that body.[53] Could it have been that the Yu-ch'uan pu, unwilling to permit its strongest rivals for the control of the China Merchants' Company to head the company's board of directors, had applied pressure on Sheng and the others?

This seems to have been the case, for the reaction of the shareholders would indicate that there had indeed been something to protest against. Led by Shen Tun-ho, who had been associated with Sheng's railroad projects and was an official of the Imperial Bank of China,[54] 301 shareholders jointly signed a petition for Sheng's return to the company describing him as "a man to whom all others looked." They appealed to the Company Law of 1904 which stipulated that an official, of whatever rank, should be treated as any other shareholder with no distinctions (Article 44), and to the fact that Sheng's son, Sheng Ch'ang-i, who had also been elected a director and who might have succeeded his father, had died soon after his election. In the end, the Yu-ch'uan pu gave in to these remonstrances and telegraphed Sheng to accept his position at the head of the company.[55]

A second clash came over the matter of the officials who were designated by the Yu-ch'uan pu to supervise the C.M.S.N. Co.'s operations. Shortly before the August 15, 1909, meeting, Sheng had telegraphed Yang Shih-ch'i, vice-president of the Yu-ch'uan pu, with whom he obviously was on friendly terms, to inform him that there was considerable unrest among the shareholders because of the reported intention of the ministry to remove the incumbent official managers.[56] These were the taotais Wang Ts'un-shan and Chung Wen-yao, who had headed the company since Sheng had forced the dismissal of Hsü Jun in 1907. The shareholders were demanding that the matter be determined by them at the general meeting which would be held shortly. In effect, they were claiming the right to select the management of the company without the interference of the Yu-ch'uan pu and in accordance with the Company Law. While Yang was willing to maintain the fiction that the China Merchants' Company would in fact be governed by that law, he informed Sheng that "appointments made [by the Ministry of Posts and Communications] before the shareholders meeting certainly would not contravene the commercial code." [57] As it turned out, Sheng's intervention was adequate to secure the retention of Chung and Wang, but as the official appointees of the Yu-ch'uan pu and not as the delegates of the board of directors of the C.M.S.N. Co.

The second annual shareholders' meeting which was held in Shanghai on June 12, 1910, was highlighted by a third clash. The chief item of business was a proposal by the shareholder Shih Tse-ching, who was also one of the directors of Sheng's bank, that the meeting elect a general manager (*tsung-li*) and two deputy managers (*hsieh-li*) to assume the leadership of the company's affairs.[58] Shih's proposal was supported with an appeal to the *kuan-tu shang-pan* formula which the shareholders felt had been violated. In particular, it was alleged that in 1891 Li Hung-chang had stipulated that the company was to be managed jointly by "three officials and three merchants" (*san-yuan san-tung*); but this prescription had been ignored. Five of the six men filling the top posts in the company were official appointees, and five of the total of eight jobs which they filled were official positions. There was only one "merchant" in the management. The 500 shareholders attending the meeting overwhelmingly elected Sheng Hsuan-huai as *tsung-li,* and Yang Shih-ch'i, former head of the company and vice-president of the Yu-ch'uan pu, and Li Kuo-chieh, grandson of Li Hung-chang, as the two *hsieh-li.*[59] Sheng telegraphed Yang and Li that he felt it incumbent upon himself to accept the position offered him because the C.M.S.N. Co. was in need of strong leadership which the present managers could not give. But, Sheng concluded, it would be necessary to secure the agreement of the Yu-ch'uan pu; would Yang raise the matter in confidence? [60] The ministry, however, refused its sanction and charged the board of directors with violating the company's regulations by its actions. It stated flatly that the edict placing the C.M.S.N. Co. under the jurisdiction of the Yu-ch'uan pu had provided for no changes from the organization as it had been under the commissioner for the northern ports.[61] Faced with so strong a refusal, Sheng, Yang, and Li were forced to decline, with the result that the movement to circumvent the ministry's control over the company was temporarily blocked.

Despite the stern reply of the Yu-ch'uan pu to this action by the C.M.S.N. Co. shareholders, the ministry was apparently under considerable urgency to reach a compromise in the running battle for the control of the company. The uncertainty of its status was having an adverse effect on the firm's business operations.[62] In the background was the impending return of Sheng Hsuan-huai to active occupancy of the office of junior vice-president of the Yu-ch'uan pu, an event which took place on August 14, 1910. Thus when the C.M.S.N. Co.'s directors petitioned the ministry again in August 1910 complaining about the preponderance of official appointees in the company's management and the mismanagement allegedly resulting from this situation, their request for reorganization fell on more sympathetic ears.[63] The Yu-ch'uan pu's reply confirmed the "three officials and three merchants" formula and agreed to end the official status of two assistant managers "so as to comply with this ministry's approval of the board of directors' petition that no official (*yuan*) may be simultaneously a [merchant] manager (*tung*), nor any [merchant] manager be an official." [64]

The third annual shareholders' meeting, held in Shanghai on March 26, 1911, and attended by some 1,753 persons representing 28,917 shares, saw a further step in the process of reducing the authority of the Yu-ch'uan pu over the China Merchants' Company.[65] When the new board of directors was chosen, for the first time Sheng Hsuan-huai was not among them. On January 6, 1911, Sheng had been promoted to the presidency of the Yu-ch'uan pu, and he was now deeply involved in those negotiations for railroad loans and the centralization of provincial lines which were to provide the spark that set off the Republican Revolution of October 1911.

In a manner reminiscent of the traditional theory of "rectification of names" (*cheng-ming*), the shareholders proceeded to give new designations to the several groups of executives. The nine members of the board of directors were to be termed "policy-making directors" (*i-shih tung-shih*); the three heads of the shipping, translation, and finance sections of the company were to be called "managing directors" (*pan-shih tung-shih*); while the two comptrollers elected by the shareholders would be known as "inspecting directors" (*ch'a-cheng tung-shih*). These name changes were intended to demonstrate the dominance of the board of directors over the firm's official management. While, for the time being, the *tso-pan*, *fu tso-pan*, and *hui-pan* appointed by the Yu-ch'uan pu remained in charge of the company's operations, that they were clearly on the way out and with them control by the Yu-ch'uan pu is evident from the revised regulations which were promulgated shortly after the shareholders' meeting. Although Sheng did not otherwise play a major role in the C.M.S.N. Co.'s affairs in these last months of the Ch'ing dynasty, his support was undoubtedly important in obtaining the concessions formalized in these regulations.

The C.M.S.N. Co. was now to be registered with the Ministry of Agriculture, Industry, and Commerce as a private mercantile enterprise (Article 1).[66] While that ministry would appoint two officials (one "inspector" and another to oversee the transport of tribute rice), all the directors, managers, and staff were to be selected ultimately by the shareholders, and all decisions with regard to operating the company were to be made by the board of directors (Articles 3, 4, 19). If any manager (*pan-shih tung*) were found to be incompetent or dishonest by the Yu-ch'uan pu inspector (*chien-ch'a yuan*), the board of directors on notification would replace him. The directors, too, could remove an unsuitable manager, and could request the Yu-ch'uan pu to replace an inspector whom they found incompetent or dishonest (Article 24). The ships and routes of the company were to be registered with the ministry, to whom a financial report was to be submitted annually as in the past (Articles 6, 29).

It can be readily seen that the execution of these provisions would have removed the C.M.S.N. Co. from any but the most formal control by the Peking government. There was little opportunity, however, for them to have any effect and, as it turned out, they were hardly needed. Two months after their promulgation the regulations were rendered redundant by the outbreak of the Revolution and the fall of the dynasty. The officials appointed by the Ministry of Posts and Communications left the company in the wake of the October upheaval, and full control was assumed by the board of directors.

Full control fell to the board of directors, true, but the form of the company's organization in the early Republican period and the composition of its directing body remained to be settled. Sheng was forced to flee for his life to Japan in October 1911, impeached and dismissed for the policies of railroad centralization and foreign loans which had brought on the Revolution. He was still, however, the largest shareholder in the company, and his supporters remained in positions of influence. Wu T'ing-fang, from Kwangtung and nominally a leader of the southern shareholders, was chairman of the board from 1911 until June 1913 when Sheng Hsuan-huai, having returned from Japan, resumed active control of the company. On his return Sheng proposed that the administrative organization of the China Merchants' Company be reconstituted on the model of its Japanese competitor, the Nippon Yūsen Kaisha. The adoption of this scheme, whereby the board of directors elected by the shareholders assumed active charge of the management of the company by putting one of its members at the head of each of the three principal operational departments, effectively centralized the control of the company in the board and completed the evolution toward "merchant management." [67]

IV

The Tribute Rice Franchise and Tariff Concessions

One aspect of official supervision of the China Merchants' Company should be examined more closely for the light which it throws on the importance of official aid in the company's achievements. That is the role of the quasi-monopoly franchise to transport tribute rice which was granted to the enterprise from its inception. Of lesser importance, but also the result of official favor, were the tariff concessions which benefited the company at least from 1877 to 1899. Between 1880 and 1891 the C.M.S.N. Co. was able to liquidate a total of nearly Tls. 2,000,000 which it had borrowed from the various provincial treasuries by means of deductions from the freight charges owed by the government for the carriage of tribute rice. After 1885 this repayment of official funds took place simultaneously with the settlement of a large debt owed to foreign creditors. We must consider, therefore, that the ability of the company's official protectors to extract a noncompetitive price for tribute rice transport — as a cushion against the possibility of poor returns from ordinary freight and passenger traffic — was an indispensable factor in the company's success. In effect this was an official subsidy to the China Merchants' Company and it was so considered by its competitors.[68]

Complete figures for the carriage of tribute rice by the China Merchants' Company are unfortunately not available. The total number of piculs of rice shipped annually from Shanghai is easily determined from the Imperial Maritime Customs' annual *Returns of Trade*,[69] and Dr. Harold Hinton has compiled a useful table of "Tribute Grain Shipped by the China Merchants Company" between 1873–1893.[70] The *Returns of Trade*, however, do not indicate what proportions of the total were carried by steamer and junk respectively, nor what part of the steamer freight was assigned to the C.M.S.N. Co. As for Hinton's figures, which are based largely on translations of edicts and memorials appearing in the *North-China Herald*, they are admittedly incomplete. For the period before the Sino-Japanese War, however, a comparison of these two sets of data supports the conclusion that the company's steamers carried an average of at least 500,000 piculs of tribute rice annually.

The freight rate received for this carriage varied, usually in a downward direction, during the period we are considering. In its first years the China Merchants' Company had been paid as much as Tls. 0.562 per picul of tribute rice transported. This exceeded the rate for junk carriers by Tls. 0.031. In 1880 the two rates were uniformly set at Tls. 0.531. Under pressure from foreign shippers who tendered at rates as low as Tls. 0.35 per picul, by 1885 the freight paid to junks for rice transport had dropped to Tls. 0.431. This was in theory also paid to the C.M.S.N. Co., but in practice the net going rate after 1885 and until 1902 was Tls. 0.38 per picul (or Tls. 0.3881 if the allowance for wastage and repairs is included). At this last rate, 500,000 piculs of rice would produce roughly Tls. 195,000 in revenue annually.[71] For the twelve years, 1880 to 1891, during which the official debt was repaid, 500,000 piculs annually at Tls. 0.38 per picul would give a total income from rice carriage of approximately Tls. 2,340,000. This is a figure sufficiently large to provide for repayment of the official debt and yet leave the annual profit from tribute rice carriage which appears in Table 14.

Some quantitative indication of the importance of the tribute rice franchise for the company's general profitability aside from its debt repayment may be gained from Table 14. It shows that the C.M.S.N. Co.'s profit from rice carriage after deductions for repayment of government loans constituted a considerable portion of the surplus profit (*ching-yü*: gross income minus all operating expenses, wages and salaries, interest on loans, dividends on shares, bonuses and depreciation) which was added to the reserve fund each year. In some years, for example, in 1891 and 1892, the profit from rice carriage provided the margin between a rise or drop in the company's reserves.[72]

The importance of the ability of its patrons to influence the price paid for rice carriage during the C.M.S.N. Co.'s early years was dem-

Table 14

Profit from Tribute Rice Carriage, 1886–1893 (in Shanghai taels)

Year	Surplus profit after all deductions	Profit from tribute rice carriage after deductions for loan repayment[a]
1886	131,960	29,689
1887	194,617	59,948
1888	209,500	39,156
1889	167,916	33,226
1890	21,336	10,071
1891	17,395	79,765
1892	44,641	66,998
1893	275,589	53,145

[a] Includes Tls. 16–17,000 received annually as allowance for repairs and lighterage.

onstrated later, when they were no longer on the scene. In 1902, the hard-pressed Peking government was able to force the company to accept a lower freight rate as a condition for the continuation of its monopoly.[73] As a result of this reduction from Tls. 0.3881 to Tls. 0.3381 per picul in 1902, during the next thirteen years the company received nearly a million taels less from its rice franchise than if the old rate had been continued.[74]

Still it must be noted that tribute rice never, after the early years of the company's existence, seriously rivaled the shipment of general freight and the carriage of passengers as the main sources of the company's earnings. By the turn of the century it was still a welcome extra, but no longer the crucial necessity it had been during the period of debt repayment discussed above.

The benefit derived from the company's tariff concessions is more difficult to state quantitatively. In 1877, Li Hung-chang memorialized seeking a 20 per cent exemption from customs duty and *likin* for copper carried from Canton to Tientsin by steamer. This, he remarked, was an extension of the rule allowing such an exemption for C.M.S.N. Co. steamers coming with tribute rice from Shanghai to Tientsin.[75] Apparently the concession enjoyed by the China Merchants' Company was at first limited to the privilege of landing duty-free at Tientsin other cargo up to the value of 20 per cent of the market price of the tribute rice carried. A steamer bringing Tls. 10,000 worth of tribute rice, for example, would also be permitted to unload cottons valued at Tls. 2,000 without payment of duty. In February 1886 we find Li memorializing again, requesting an additional remission of 20 per cent of the export duty on return trips for tribute rice steamers. That is, if a vessel brought, say, 1,000 piculs of rice from Shanghai, it would be allowed the duty-free export from Tientsin of commodities such as soy beans up to the value of 200 piculs of rice.[76] The Hu-pu sanctioned this partial exemption from export duties; and it remained effective until September 1899 when Sheng Hsuan-huai explicitly agreed to relinquish both exemptions, very likely in return for the prestige of being placed in charge of impending negotiations with the powers for revision of the 1858 treaty tariff.[77] In 1886 Li also secured for the company a reduction of the duty on coarse-quality teas which its steamers carried to Tientsin for export to Manchuria and Mongolia. Since 1873, tea brought by Chinese steamers to Tientsin had already been exempt from *likin* duties when forwarded to Kalgan for the Mongolian and Russian markets. As a result of these two measures, the C.M.S.N. Co. came to carry the bulk of the export tea shipped to Tientsin.

It was estimated in 1886 that exemption from 20 per cent of the export duty at Tientsin for steamers which had brought rice, together with the reduction of the duty on tea, would save the company about Tls. 20,000 annually. However, the only reference that I have been able to find for the value of these concessions to the company makes no mention of the tea duties and places the tariff exemptions granted to C.M.S.N. Co. steamers at Tientsin for the period May 1886–April 1887 at Tls. 4,781, a figure which presumably includes exemptions on both imports and exports.[78]

While it is regrettable that the quantitative advantage accruing to the company from rice carriage and tariff concessions cannot be stated more exactly, it is as important to specify the qualitative significance of these measures. They were in effect monopoly or quasi-monopoly rights granted to the company by virtue of its being a *kuan-tu shang-pan* enterprise. The necessity for such rights was implicit in the context within which the China Merchants' Company and other *kuan-tu shang-pan* enterprises were inaugurated. These firms were undertaken first of all in order to challenge foreign domination of coastwise shipping, textile manufacture, and banking — that is, of those fields of economic endeavor which represented the beginning of the development of a modern sector within the Chinese economy. As Li Hung-chang wrote to the Tsungli Yamen: "The establishment of the China Merchants' Company was a carefully considered measure of self-strengthening the aim of which was the recovery of China's economic

rights." [79] None of these undertakings was an indigenous development which could look for support from a normal growth of the
domestic market. To begin with at least, the enterprises were grafts
whose existence in the face of severe competition from rival foreign
efforts (which themselves enjoyed the abnormal advantages of extraterritoriality and the "unequal treaties") depended on the extra nour-
ishment derived from such quasi-monopolies as the China Merchants'
Company's tribute rice concession.

A general prohibition against the use of foreign shipping by Chinese merchants was recognized as unfeasible if only because of the
affront which it would present to the foreign powers. Moreover, the
stronger financial position of the foreign steamship companies allowed
them to undercut the rates charged by the China Merchants' Company.[80] The Indo-China Steam Navigation Company, Ltd., and the
China Navigation Company, Ltd., for example, were operated by the
wealthy British firms of Jardine, Matheson and Company and Butterfield and Swire, respectively. It is hardly likely that Chinese merchants
would pass by any opportunity to send their goods at a lower cost.
Although he undoubtedly overstated the case, Li Hung-chang was on
solid ground when he complained to the Tsungli Yamen that foreign
steamship lines were willing to operate at a 4 per cent profit, which
he described as being customary in England, while the China Merchants' Company needed to realize at least 8 per cent annually in order
to attract capital and repay its large indebtedness.[81] Foreign shipping
could not be prevented from carrying commercial freight, but Li Hung-
chang was able to obtain an order that all official freight sent by the
provinces to Tientsin, as well as a large portion of the tribute rice
shipments, was to be carried in C.M.S.N. Co. bottoms.[82] Thus in 1886,
the governor of Hupei was obliged to memorialize explaining his error
in having loaded a shipment of copper destined for Peking from Yunnan upon a steamer owned by the German firm of Melchers and Company when "in accordance with the regulations it should have been
taken on by steamers of the China Merchants' Company." [83]

But the monopoly rights accorded the C.M.S.N. Co. can be seen as
having had a further purpose, in addition to assisting the company in
the face of severe foreign competition and an undeveloped domestic
market. The privileges enjoyed by the company were designed not only
to exclude foreign carriers from transporting certain classes of mer-
chandise, but also to prevent any potential Chinese competitor from
coming into the market. Thus "recovering China's economic rights" was
closely related to protecting the investment of the official and semiofficial
promoters of the *kuan-tu shang-pan* company.

V

Official Exactions

The official aid which the China Merchants' Company received must be balanced against the official exactions of funds to which the company was subject throughout its life. The aid, as we have shown, was largely a result of the efforts of the company's powerful provincial patrons, notably Li Hung-chang. In contrast, it was the Peking government's assertion of its own right to share in the abundant profits which was responsible for the exactions that plagued the enterprise. After Li's fall in 1895, the imperial court especially sought to "squeeze" the industrial projects that he had sponsored. But even while Governor-general Li's influence was yet undiminished, the C.M.S.N. Co. did not wholly escape the necessity of making "contributions" to the imperial coffers.

Several examples of these exactions while the C.M.S.N. Co. was still part of Li's regional political power may be cited. In 1891, for instance, the company's managers informed the shareholders that "through the intercession of H. E. Li Hung-chang, the interest on the Government loan in the reserve fund of the previous year was not collected, on condition that Tls. 100,000 be taken out of this fund and appropriated to Famine Relief." [84] How much of the Tls. 100,000 was in fact distributed as relief is, of course, open to debate. Another instance occurred in 1894, the sixtieth anniversary of the birth of Empress Dowager Tz'u-hsi. The "Imperial Celebration Fund" on this occasion was swelled by a contribution of Tls. 50,000 from the China Merchants' Company and Tls. 50,000 more from the "merchant directors" of the company.[85] Finally, during the Sino-Japanese War, the Ministry of Revenue "borrowed" Tls. 375,000 from the company at interest. In this case it is stated that interest of Tls. 41,000 was paid, but it is doubtful that the principal was ever returned.[86] These contributions were undoubtedly a burden on the modern sector in the Chinese economy as represented by the C.M.S.N. Co. and other *kuan-tu shang-pan* enterprises. But in the absence of a developed business ethic and a commercial code which would embody it, the shareholders had no legal appeal.

After the fall of Li Hung-chang these payments, which usually were recorded under the heading *pao-hsiao*, "efforts made to return [the imperial grace]," assumed larger proportions and were placed on a more regular basis. The financial troubles of the Ch'ing government which form the background for imperial demands for *pao-hsiao* payments have been recounted in Chapter 2. In addition to large foreign loans contracted in order to indemnify the victorious Japanese, in the five years before the Boxer uprising Peking concluded extensive loan agreements for railroad construction. To these burdens on the inelastic income of the central government must be added the funds needed in order to finance the new armies which Yuan Shih-k'ai was training. According to the estimate of the Ministry of Revenue, its deficit for 1900 was nearly Tls. 17,000,000, a figure which a leading modern student of Ch'ing finances would set at no less than Tls. 25,000,000.[87] This situation led to numerous and largely unsuccessful attempts to raise additional funds from the provinces, for the most part by seeking to increase Peking's share of traditional revenue sources exclusive of the land tax, namely, *likin,* salt, native opium, and various commercial taxes. Proposals to reorganize the fiscal system as a whole came to naught,[88] but some additional revenue was realized from such a *pis aller* as the junket of the grand secretary Kang-i into the southern provinces in 1899, as was described in Chapter 2.

The China Merchants' Company and other *kuan-tu shang-pan* enterprises were natural quarry for the imperial collectors. Something of Peking's attitude towards the company was contained in a memorial offered to the throne in July 1899 by the grand secretary Hsü T'ung and in the edict which it occasioned.[89] Hsü charged that while the C.M.S.N. Co., the Telegraph Administration, and the K'ai-p'ing Mines "go under the name of [enterprises which are] recovering China's economic rights, their operations in fact have not been of advantage to the government." The throne, therefore, should proceed to appropriate all the surpluses of these companies. The imperial response was an edict dated July 11, 1899, which ordered Sheng Hsuan-huai to draw up accounts of the financial status of the China Merchants' Company and the Telegraph Administration and submit them within three months, together with a plan for regular payment of the surplus profits of these enterprises to the Peking government. This order was followed closely by a second edict, which Kang-i brought to Sheng personally, reporting a denunciation of the C.M.S.N. Co. for "utilizing public authority to aid private interests" (*chia-kung chi-ssu*). It directed Kang-i to investigate the books of the company and the Telegraph Administration and, with Sheng, to present an accounting of the surplus funds. These were to be turned over to the public treasury.[90]

In the face of such concerted pressure from Peking, Sheng drew up the accounts as requested, although he claimed that "the surpluses which the two companies earned in the past were continuously used to expand their capital; thus there is no ready cash that can be transferred to the government." Nevertheless, he was willing to agree that thereafter the two companies should pay 20 per cent of their annual net surplus (*ying-yü:* net profit from operations minus dividends, interest, bonuses, depreciation) to the government as *pao-hsiao.* In concrete figures, which Kang-i demanded be stated rather than percentages, the China Merchants' Company would pay Tls. 60,000 annually and the Telegraph Administration Tls. 40,000 as *pao-hsiao.* In addition the contributions that the two *kuan-tu shang-pan* companies were already paying to support the schools in Tientsin and Shanghai which Sheng had founded were to be considered as *pao-hsiao.* However, if the gross surplus (*yü-li:* net profit from operations minus dividends and interest) of the C.M.S.N. Co. in any one year should exceed Tls. 700,000, or that of the Telegraph Administration exceed Tls. 470,000, an additional *pao-hsiao* payment would be made. Reciprocally, if in any year the companies' receipts were so low that the regular dividend could not be paid, the *pao-hsiao* due for that year was to be deferred and payment spread out over several later years. No other contributions of any kind were to be levied.[91]

Such were the demands of the Peking government, which, as will be shown below, could be met only at the expense of the C.M.S.N. Co.'s operation as a rationalized business enterprise.

With the exception of some minor items which are noted in Table 15, the agreement to limit *pao-hsiao* payments to the total amount set in 1899 seems to have been kept. When, in February 1900, a censor charged that the C.M.S.N. Co. and the Telegraph Administration were making excessive profits and should therefore pay increased contributions, Sheng was able to head off this threat. He memorialized in reply exposing in great detail the dependence of the Hanyang Ironworks and P'ing-hsiang Coal Mines on the profits realized by the shareholders of the China Merchants' Company and Telegraph Administration. Further demands for contributions would jeopardize the future of all four *kuan-tu shang-pan* companies. He also noted that, less than a year before, the throne had sanctioned his request that no additional payments be levied on his enterprises aside from the amount set in conjunction with Kang-i. Sheng's explanation was accepted and the *pao-hsiao* payments were not increased.[92]

The contributions paid by the China Merchants' Company to the Nan-yang kung-hsüeh, the school in Shanghai which Sheng founded in 1896, and the Pei-yang kung-hsüeh, which he had organized in Tientsin in 1895, cannot of course be termed exactions. But because Sheng considered them under the heading *pao-hsiao,* they are nevertheless included in the accompanying table.[93]

Where did the China Merchants' Company get the funds to meet its *pao-hsiao* obligations? From what little data we have, it appears that a large portion was taken from the company's depreciation ac-

Table 15

C.M.S.N. Co. *Pao-hsiao* Payments, 1891–1909 (in Shanghai taels)

Year	Schools	Nominal 20% of surplus	Other
1891			100,000 [a]
1894			100,000 [b]
1896	80,000 [c]		
1897	80,000		
1898	80,000		
1899	80,000	60,000	
1900	80,000	60,000	
1901	80,000	60,000	
1902	80,000	60,000	
1903	20,000 [d]	60,000	
1904	20,000	60,000	5,000 [e]
1905	20,000	60,000	5,500
1906	20,000	60,000	5,500
1907	20,000	60,000	5,500
1908	20,000	60,000	5,500
1909	20,000	[f]	5,400
Totals	700,000	600,000	232,400

[a] "Relief" contribution.

[b] Tz'u-hsi's birthday.

[c] *CTS-HCP*, 1.274 gives the annual contribution to the Pei-yang kung-hsüeh as Tls. 20,000 and that to the Nan-yang kung-hsüsh as Tls. 60,000; *YCTK*, 1.21a, puts the contribution to the Nan-yang school at Tls. 50–60,000; the higher figure is used here.

[d] Payments to the Nan-yang school were halted by Yuan Shih-k'ai.

[e] An annual payment to the Shang-pu (Ministry of Commerce) instituted by Yuan Shih-k'ai.

[f] C.M.S.N. Co. without funds; no payment.

count. For example, out of an approximate total of Tls. 640,000 for the five years 1899–1903, some Tls. 380,000 was paid from the depreciation account; and Tls. 210,000 out of the total *pao-hsiao* of Tls. 282,000 for the four years 1906–1909 came from the same source.[94] In fact, the reserve for depreciation was the only available source that could be "squeezed" to yield levies for the imperial government. Before the Sino-Japanese War and Li Hung-chang's disgrace the company had maintained a large insurance reserve and a regular reserve as well, each of about Tls. 1,000,000. So long as Li's protection could be depended on, there was apparently little concern that the Peking government would raid these funds. However, as already noted, in 1897 the company's share capital, which had stood at Tls. 2,000,000 since 1882, was doubled by transferring Tls. 2,000,000 from the insurance and regular reserves and issuing additional shares to the stockholders on record. While the reason for this impressive stock dividend was not explicitly stated at the time, it may be surmised from the above discussion of *pao-hsiao* contributions that the principal motive was a desire to protect the company's assets from his rivals and enemies who had been waiting for Li Hung-chang's downfall in order to have a go at the rich empire which Li had built for himself.

Thus when Hsü T'ung and Kang-i directed their attention to the C.M.S.N. Co. in order to fill the empress dowager's coffers, Sheng could deny the existence of any surpluses. It is only additional evidence of the folly of Tz'u-hsi and her advisers that neither of the two reserve funds in question would have been available in cash in any case. They would, of course, be balanced by items in the assets column of the company's financial statement. Undoubtedly because of the difficulty of explaining double-entry bookkeeping to a Confucian official, it was a matter of prudence to alter the accounts so that the invitingly large totals under "self-insurance fund" or "surplus" were transferred to "paid-up capital."

With other funds protected, *pao-hsiao* contributions, when they could not be met from the normal annual surplus, were paid from the depreciation account. The net effect of these exactions then was to establish an obstacle to the ability of the China Merchants' Company to replace its outworn ships, buildings, and docks as quickly as might be necessary in order to maintain its competitive position against foreign companies who were not subject to the same exactions.[95]

VI

Was the C.M.S.N. Co. a Success as a Business Operation?

It might be well, in conclusion, to bring together here the data bearing on the question of the success or failure of the China Merchants' Company. There are really two parts to this question, and the same answer need not be given to both. First, how did the company's promoters, managers, and shareholders fare through the years? Secondly, how successful was the company in recovering for China control of the shipping in her own coastal waters? [96]

Dividends. Undoubtedly, the holders of C.M.S.N. Co. stock did well for themselves (see Table 16).[97] In the early lean years, in order to attract capital, investors were guaranteed an annual official dividend (*kuan-li*) of 10 per cent on their investments. This was a fixed charge on the company, regardless of its profit or loss for the year. Only once, in 1875–1876, were the firm's profits inadequate to cover this 10 per cent dividend.[98] But the dividend was paid, nevertheless, from the working capital. In the next fiscal year, 1876–1877, the company's income from shipping was large enough to allow the deficit to be made up.[99] However, it was not uncommon in other firms, which operated at a loss more often than did the C.M.S.N. Co., for the *kuan-li* to be paid over long periods from capital or borrowed funds.[100] An extra dividend (*yü-li*) of 5 per cent was paid to the shareholders in 1874–1875 in addition to the guaranteed 10 per cent.[101] In sum, the first ten years of the China Merchants' Company were good ones for its shareholders. Its managers could report in 1882: "On a share of Tls. 100 the shareholders have during the last nine years received the whole back [in dividends] and their shares are today worth Tls. 200. Thus it will be seen that during nine years they have made over 20% average every year." [102]

The company paid no dividend during 1884 while its property was in the hands of Russell and Company and only 3 per cent in 1885. When Sheng Hsuan-huai assumed control in 1885, he issued new financial regulations which stipulated that the official dividend would thereafter be at least 6 per cent.[103] Down to the Sino-Japanese War, the C.M.S.N. Co. paid 6 per cent *kuan-li* on its paid-up capital each year, to which was added an extra dividend of 1 per cent in 1886 and 1887 and 4 per cent in each of the six years 1888 through 1893.[104] Because of the Sino-Japanese War, no dividend was paid in 1894. But in each of the three years 1895–1897 the company paid an extra dividend of 14 per cent in addition to the regular 6 per cent.[105] The average return for the years 1886–1897 on capital invested in the company was thus 12 per cent.

The large extra dividends during the period 1895–1897 should probably be considered as preliminary to the distribution of additional stock to the company's shareholders in 1897, which has already been discussed. Like it, the dividends were motivated by the fear of demands from the Peking government (or from Li Hung-chang's successor) on the tempting surpluses carried on the company's books. Such items as the following, for example, appeared in the 20th Annual Report for 1893: "Interest accrued on shares, Tls. 216,877," "Insurance risks on Company's own steamers, Tls. 1,186,716," and "Reserve fund, Tls. 876,588." [106] From the stock issue itself the shareholders received two Tls. 100 shares for each one they had held previously as a result of the transfer of the company's insurance fund and reserves to its capital account. Even compared with the amount realized from the 20 per cent rate which the company paid during 1895–1897, there was an increase in actual dividends after 1897. In 1898 the C.M.S.N. Co. paid a regular dividend of 6 per cent on the new shares (now totaling

Table 16

Dividends Paid by the C.M.S.N. Co., 1873–1913

	Official dividend (kuan-li)	Extra dividend (yü-li)
1873–74	10%	—
1874–75	10	5%
1875–76	10	—
1876–77	10	—
1877–78	10	—
1878–79	10	—
1879–80	10	—
1880–81	10[a]	—
1881–82	10[b]	—
1882–33	10	—
1883–84	—[c]	—
1885	3[d]	—
1886	6	—
1887	6	1
1888	6	4
1889	6	4
1890	6	4
1891	6	4
1892	6	4
1893	6	4
1894	—[e]	—
1895	6	14
1896	6	14
1897	6	14
1898	6[f]	6
1899	10	3.75
1900	10	3
1901	10	1.25
1902	10	—
1903	10	1.75
1904	10	4
1905	10	3.5
1906	10	2
1907	10	2.5
1908	10	2.5
1909	10	—
1910	15	—
1911	10	—
1912	10	—
1913	10	—

[a] Paid-up capital: Tls. 1,000,000.
[b] Paid-up capital: Tls. 2,000,000.
[c] No dividend, C.M.S.N. Co. "sold" to Russell and Co.

[d] Fiscal year changed to correspond to lunar year.
[e] No dividend, Sino-Japanese War.
[f] Paid-up capital: Tls. 4,000,000.

Tls. 4,000,000 as compared with the previous Tls. 2,000,000), and a 6 per cent extra dividend. This would be equivalent to 24 per cent on the old capital. From 1899 through 1913, it paid 10 per cent annually on its Tls. 4,000,000 paid-up capital, and through 1908 (with the exception of 1902) paid extra dividends ranging from 1¼ to 4 per cent.[107]

In 1910, 15 per cent *kuan-li* was paid, but only 5 per cent in cash, the other 10 per cent being distributed in shares of Sheng Hsuan-huai's Imperial Bank of China. And again in 1911, the 10 per cent regular dividend was paid in the shares of the bank which the China Merchants' Company had held since 1896. In these two years the company's total holdings of Tls. 800,000 in bank shares were liquidated and distributed to its individual shareholders. A similar distribution of the China Merchants' Company holdings of Han-Yeh-P'ing Coal and Iron Co. shares was made in 1912 and 1913. A dividend of 7½ per cent was paid in cash, and 3 or 4 per cent more in H.Y.P. shares.[108]

The company's second distribution of additional stock has also been noted already. In 1913 its capital was increased from Tls. 4,000,000 to Tls. 8,400,000, reflecting a more accurate appraisal of the value of the company's assets. Additional shares were issued to the shareholders, and a $100 (Chinese) share in the China Merchants' Holding Company, newly organized to manage the firm's extensive real-estate holdings, was distributed with every share of the new stock.

The foregoing account should leave it beyond question that the holder of China Merchants' Company shares profited richly. If an investor had purchased 100 shares (face value Tls. 10,000) in 1873, and had taken advantage of the option to buy 100 more in 1882, by 1914 without any additional outlay he would have had 800 shares (face value Tls. 80,000) in the C.M.S.N. Co., and 400 shares (face value $40,000 [Chinese]) more in the C. M. Holding Company. This is roughly the equivalent of a fivefold capital gain. In addition, he would have received a total in dividends of approximately Tls. 116,300, equivalent to an annual return of about 15 per cent on his actual investment of Tls. 20,000.

Bonuses. Moreover, for the men who served as the company's managers as well as being its leading shareholders, there were still other direct monetary benefits. According to regulations drawn up in the 1880's, a bonus was to be paid annually to the company's management in proportion to the firm's profits. Between 1887 and 1908, a total of Tls. 456,200 was so distributed.[109] While the precise manner in which these bonuses were paid is not known, it appears that the largest share went to the company's business managers.[110] The official managers were concerned with far bigger stakes.

Investments in Other Enterprises. For Sheng Hsuan-huai in particular, the accumulated profits of the C.M.S.N. Co. represented a ready source of capital for other *kuan-tu shang-pan* enterprises in which he was interested. Sheng's predecessor, Tong King-sing, too, had not hesitated to invest the China Merchants' Company's funds in the K'ai-p'ing Coal Mines, which he had organized under Li Hung-chang's patronage. Investments of this sort differ somewhat from the unauthorized diversion of the company's funds into real estate and exchange speculation such as led to the dismissal of Hsü Jun and Tong from the company's management in the early 1880's. But they are both instances illustrating how the general profitability of the China Merchants' Company directly benefited its official managers. It seems worthwhile to survey here the extent of the firm's investments in other enterprises with which its managers were also connected.[111]

Several years after the establishment of the C.M.S.N. Co., Governor-general Li and Tong King-sing founded a modern coal mining enterprise in Chihli, the K'ai-p'ing Mines. The 9th Annual Report of the China Merchants' Company, for 1881–1882, shows that it held some Tls. 210,000 of K'ai-p'ing shares. By 1889, the steamship company's holdings had increased to Tls. 252,000, but thereafter they declined rapidly until in 1892 the value of K'ai-p'ing shares held was given as only Tls. 16,000. They do not appear at all in the China Merchants' Company's 20th Annual Report for 1893.[112] Very likely, the decline may be attributed to Sheng's gradual elimination of Tong's influence in the shipping company.

The company's next major investment was the transfer in 1891 of a sum of Tls. 100,000 from its reserves to the Cotton Cloth Mill which Li Hung-chang was sponsoring in Shanghai. By the time that Sheng himself took over the direction of this enterprise in 1894 and reorganized it as the Hua-sheng Mill, the total investment by the C.M.S.N. Co. had increased to Tls. 300,000.[113]

Especially after Sheng's appointment as director-general of railroads in 1896, which marked the upswing of his independent political and economic power, we can seen an increased reliance on the China Merchants' Company as a source of funds for Sheng's other enterprises. Thus Tls. 800,000 of the initial capital of the Imperial Bank of China which Sheng founded in 1896 was taken from the reserve fund and the self-insurance fund of the C.M.S.N. Co. Furthermore, in 1898, the steamship firm invested Tls. 100,000 in the P'ing-hsiang Coal Mines in Kiangsi, which Sheng and Chang Chih-tung were seeking to develop as a source of coking coal for the Hanyang Ironworks. By 1901 the P'ing-hsiang shares held by the C.M.S.N. Co. had increased to Tls. 164,000, and there was a further increase to Tls. 381,400 in 1906.[114]

As for the ironworks themselves, the China Merchants' Company had invested Tls. 274,000 in its shares by 1901; and by 1907, this amount had grown to Tls. 460,000.[115] When the ironworks, the Ta-yeh Iron Mines, and the P'ing-hsiang Coal Mines were joined in 1908 to form the Han-Yeh-P'ing Coal and Iron Corporation, the steamship enterprise held Tls. 1,019,000 of the shares of the amalgamated firm out of an authorized capital of $20,000,000 (approximately Tls. 14,000,-000).[116]

The C.M.S.N. Co.'s holdings of shares in the Imperial Bank of China began to be liquidated in 1908; after the 1911 Revolution the same fate befell the H.Y.P. investment. But as late as 1914, the China Merchants' Holding Company still carried Tls. 516,000 of H.Y.P. shares on its books.[117]

Sheng Hsuan-huai employed the assets of the China Merchants' Company to help H.Y.P. in several other ways. In 1898, he offered the godowns and other shore property of the company situated on the "French Bund" in Shanghai as security for a loan of 4,000,000 marks from the German firm of Carlowitz and Company. The proceeds of this loan were to buy mining machinery and lay down a railroad to the P'ing-hsiang Coal Mines.[118] Moreover, on a number of occasions the C.M.S.N. Co. was able to extend short term credits to Han-Yeh-P'ing. In 1906, the ironworks owed Tls. 166,500 on this account, and the P'ing-hsiang Mines Tls. 250,000 more. By 1913 the total short term debt of H.Y.P. to the China Merchants' Company came to Tls. 292,000.[119]

While the above data are admittedly fragmentary, they do give an indication of the degree to which Sheng Hsuan-huai as official manager of the C.M.S.N. Co. was able to employ the profits of the shipping firm in the operation of his other *kuan-tu shang-pan* enterprises. The benefits to himself, what he realized from these other firms, were correspondingly great.

Regularized squeeze and the benefits of patronage have been mentioned in passing as among the perquisites which the managers of the C.M.S.N. Co. normally expected. The available information unfortunately does not lend itself to quantitative treatment. It is enough to say that all together, rich dividends, large bonuses, employment of the company's funds in other enterprises, squeeze, and patronage provided the company's promoters, managers, and shareholders with a most satisfactory return for their money and their efforts.

Relative Stagnation. When we turn to the second half of the question that heads this section, the record is less bright. There is a sharp contrast to be perceived between the rich dividends just described and the relative stagnation of the company in regard to the number and tonnage of its steamers and the amount of freight that they carried. The C.M.S.N. Co. operated only four ships (2,435 net tons) in 1874, but by 1876 its fleet had grown to 17 vessels (11,706 net tons).[120] In the next year the company purchased the assets of the Shanghai Steam Navigation Company and thereby increased its steamers to 33, totaling 23,967 net tons. By this doubling of its size, the firm became the largest operator in the steamship field in China. But this was to be the last significant growth of its fleet during the period we are considering. As of January 1, 1887, the China Merchants' Company operated only 28 steamers (24,039 net tons); and even in 1914, twenty-seven years later, the company had only 30 ships.[121]

For comparison, one might look at the experience of the Japanese steamship line, Nippon Yūsen Kaisha, whose early history in many ways paralleled that of the C.M.S.N. Co.[122] The N.Y.K. was an outgrowth of the steamship company which Iwasaki Yatarō (1834–1885) of Tosa had founded in 1870. Initially his Mitsubishi Shipping Company had only three steamers, but in 1875 it was entrusted with 13 additional vessels without compensation by the Japanese government. In 1882, the government sponsored the establishment of a rival Kyōdō Unyu Kaisha; and after a severe competitive struggle between the two companies, they amalgamated in 1885 to form the Nippon Yūsen Kaisha. The government, which had taken a leading role in effecting the merger, also guaranteed for fifteen years an 8 per cent annual return on the 11,000,-000 yen capital of the new firm, and "elected" as its first president Morioka Masazumi, a samurai of the Satsuma clan. The N.Y.K. "constitution," too, was drafted according to government order.

We may then consider the Nippon Yūsen Kaisha also to have been originally a type of *kuan-tu shang-pan* enterprise. Its constitution provided that for fifteen years after its establishment, the period during which profits were guaranteed, the government was to appoint its president, vice-president, and directors. The "accounts were scrupulously audited by the Ministry of Finance," and in general the company's business was subject to official supervision. However, in 1893 it became a wholly commercial firm, and was incorporated under the newly promulgated Commercial Code.

The contrast between the rapid growth of the Japanese shipping company (as shown in Table 17) and the relative stagnation of the Chinese company is remarkable.[123] Moreover, while the N.Y.K. in 1885 still operated exclusively in coastal waters in the same manner as the C.M.S.N. Co., the trial overseas ventures which it inaugurated between 1885 and 1891 developed into regular service to Europe, the United States, and Australia in the years following the Sino-Japanese War.[124] The C.M.S.N. Co. also experimented to the extent of sending two steamers to Honolulu and San Francisco in 1880 and 1881. One vessel, the *Meifoo,* was also dispatched to London with a cargo of tea in

Table 17

Number and Tonnage of N.Y.K. Steamships, 1886–1915

Year	No. of vessels	Net tons
1886	51	39,280
1890	46	42,675
1895	57	63,624
1900	67	127,340
1905	73	156,539
1910	69	175,102
1915	93	266,293

October 1881. But this was apparently the last effort.[125] The shareholders were told in the next annual report:

> The proposed scheme to send [steamers] to Honolulu and San Francisco has been suspended for the present, owing to the severe competition of foreign steamers. In September [sic] last the *Meifoo* was dispatched to England with tea, and returned last March; but through the jealousy of foreigners she made no profit out of the trip.[126]

Unable to recapture the traffic of China's coastal waters from foreign, chiefly British, competitors, the China Merchants' Company could hardly be expected to compete successfully for the overseas traffic.

One further contrast between the Japanese and Chinese shipping companies is of interest. Even in 1886, steamers of the N.Y.K. line were officered by a majority of Japanese personnel. Out of 63 captains, 37 were Japanese and 26 foreigners; there were 141 Japanese navigation officers as against 55 foreigners; and even among the engineering officers, the Japanese personnel outnumbered the foreigners 104 to 78.[127] But none — not one — of the 144 captains, mates, and engineers who are listed as officering the C.M.S.N. Co. fleet in 1885 was a Chinese. To judge from their names, they were overwhelmingly Englishmen or Americans.[128] Only as late as 1893 did Sheng produce a plan to train Chinese to fill the positions of "master mariner and marine engineer" on the C.M.S.N. Co.'s ships; but we unfortunately have no indication of what success Sheng's project attained.[129] This total dependence on foreign personnel for the operation of its steamers must be taken as one more symptom of the China Merchants' Company's failure to develop as an enterprise that seriously challenged foreign domination of the coasting trade.

Not only did the size of the company's fleet, the routes it followed, and its dependence on foreign officers remain almost constant; the freight receipts from the operation of these vessels also remained nearly unchanged between 1886 and 1911 (Table 18).[130]

Table 18

C.M.S.N. Co. Gross Income from Shipping, 1886–1911

Year	Income (in Shanghai taels)
1886	1,897,454
1887	2,057,485
1888	2,139,226
1889	2,182,445
1890	1,859,355
1891	1,984,560
1892	2,021,665
1893	2,161,354
1894	a
1895	a
1896	2,180,000
1897	2,612,000
1898	3,001,000
1899	3,117,900
1900	2,912,400
1901	2,783,800
1902	2,741,000
1903	3,168,000
1904	3,234,000
1905	3,171,000
1906	2,817,000
1907	2,478,000
1908	2,715,100
1909	2,727,200
1910	2,280,700
1911	2,100,000

a Data not available.

By way of comparison, the freight tonnage carried by the N.Y.K. line showed a steady upward trend (figures for gross income are not available):[131] 1886, 867,000 tons; 1891, 1,290,000 tons; 1896, 1,704,000 tons; 1901, 2,279,000 tons; 1906, 2,553,000 tons; 1911, 3,260,000 tons. What needs to be underlined here is that the China Merchants' Company failed to expand during a period in which the total foreign trade of China (as measured by Imperial Maritime Customs statistics) increased sixfold. In 1885 China's foreign trade was valued at Haikwan Tls. 153.2 million; by 1913 the total had risen to Haikwan Tls. 973.5

million.[132] Even if the coasting traffic did not increase at the same rate as China's international trade, it undoubtedly did expand. By merely holding on to the absolute position that it had won in the 1880's, the C.M.S.N. Co. in fact suffered a relative decline in importance as a steamship enterprise. Most of the new shipping business in the last decade of the Manchu dynasty was won by the British and, in particular, the Japanese firms whose steady growth has been noted above.

Other indices of relative stagnation might be consulted, but what has been recounted already is sufficient to allow the unhesitating conclusion that the C.M.S.N. Co., although it allowed rich returns to those who had an interest in the firm, was not successful in recovering control for China of the shipping in her coastal and riverine waters.

"*Mining.*" On the one hand, then, we find a steady increase in capital and reserves, and rich dividends and other perquisites to managers and shareholders; on the other, a relative stagnation in regard to the size of the company's fleet and of its gross shipping revenue. How is this paradox to be explained? A partial answer at least can be found in the fate of the company's earnings. It is clear that the C.M.S.N. Co. could produce profits at the size and scale of operations which it maintained after 1877. But instead of reinvesting these earnings in the expansion of the company's primary business, its managers were concerned with gaining large, immediate benefits for themselves and their fellow shareholders. For example, the distribution of the company's accumulated surpluses to its shareholders in 1897 and 1913 in the form of additional shares in the enterprise, combined with the maintenance of the high dividend rate that had been paid on the smaller capital, manifestly had the result of increasing the actual size of the dividends received by the promoters and investors. Doubling the company's paid-up capital on these two occasions was not in fact productive reinvestment of accumulated earnings; it was merely a paper transaction, not matched by any physical increment to the company's fleet.

This is to say, the manner in which the enterprise was operated may be compared with the process of mining, of working a vein of coal or copper. The miner is totally oriented to taking wealth out of the ground; he himself puts into the mine only the minimum amount of timber supports, pumping equipment, and the like that is absolutely necessary for the profitable working of the mine. When the vein is exhausted, the digging is abandoned. In the same manner, the men who operated the C.M.S.N. Co. thought first of securing early and sizable profits for themselves. But even to maintain these at a constant level, some capital replacement was necessary. Thus the company added 16 new ships between 1877 and 1893.[133] This was apparently sufficient to balance the 24 steamers lost through wrecks, dismantling, and sales during the same period, while maintaining the rate of return which the managers and shareholders expected. But as a consequence of inadequate allowance for depreciation, the company's "diggings" were brought very near the point of exhaustion. By 1896, the value of its fleet had dropped to Tls. 1,030,000. In the next period, a considerable replacement of obsolete vessels was necessary, and the value of the fleet climbed slowly to Tls. 3,385,000 in 1906, before entering a decline which again brought it down to Tls. 2,575,000 in 1911.[134] The conclusion to which one is impelled by these data is that the company's shipping assets were kept at the minimum size and level of maintenance consonant with the high profits which its managers sought. Given the dominant position within the firm accorded to its official managers by the *kuan-tu shang-pan* pattern, they were able to apportion its earnings in the manner they saw fit. As long as their political rear was protected either by a powerful official patron or by the influence of the director-general himself, and as long as a fair return was secured by the shareholders, no opposition to their policies would be forthcoming.

But even with the demonstrated draining off of its proceeds and the stagnation of its fleet, the record shows that the company's total assets increased steadily (see Table 10). In 1887, they stood at Tls. 5,145,039; by 1907, they had climbed to Tls. 10,052,210; in 1914, they were recorded at Tls. 15,495,498. The solution to this paradox will be found in the fact that while its fleet was comparatively negligible, the China Merchants' Company owned very extensive real estate (much of it unconnected with its shipping business) in Shanghai and other ports. Like its managers — Sheng Hsuan-huai, for instance, whose employment of a large part of his income in traditional ways was recounted in Chapter 3 — the C.M.S.N. Co. invested the largest share of its surpluses, when they were not tapped by its managers, in the traditional and safer way: in land, buildings, and other shore properties. Establishment of the China Merchants' Holding Company in 1914 to manage these properties underlined the phenomenon.

In fact, both the diversion of the company's earnings to large, short-term profits for its managers and the firm's own use of its reserves for the purchase of real estate were rooted in the same institutional patterns endemic to traditional Chinese society.

In the absence of legal security for property, the China Merchants' Company and other *kuan-tu shang-pan* enterprises were always subject to exactions of the kind discussed earlier. Undertakings of a more traditional nature, the salt merchants for example, were similarly liable. But industrial projects, because of their relative newness, tended to stand out and were particularly noticed by men, such as the grand secretary Hsü T'ung, who were anxious to fill the empress dowager's purse and their own as well. This situation reinforced what was already a natural tendency for Sheng Hsuan-huai and his associates. They were greatly concerned with the welfare of their families and clans; Sheng's establishment of a family foundation as a means to preserve his wealth may be taken as an example. In circumstances where their assets were invested in a modern-type enterprise which yielded good returns but was always open to demands from officialdom, they would naturally strive to pick the fruits of the enterprise as soon as they ripened and store them quickly in a safe place. Immediate profits invested in land, buildings, and pawnshops — which brought prestige as well as relative safety — seemed a surer bet than the long-range expansion and development of a firm whose very size and conspicuousness could only invite unwelcome attention. Even Sheng, who seems to have had a firm belief in the future of industry in China and did reinvest some of his earnings in new ventures, deemed it safer to diversify his investments rather than to expand any one enterprise exclusively.

This pattern of behavior, resulting from the anomalous position of a modern-type economic enterprise within the traditional political and economic structure, was reinforced by another factor, that is, the pressure of foreign competition which grew rather than decreased with each decade of the company's history. With the Ch'ing government unable to protect the domestic market for its own nationals, it was in truth a risky business to establish an enterprise in a line of endeavor in which the foreigner would possess advantages of capital and technology as well as the privileges of extraterritoriality. The *kuan-tu shang-pan* framework offered to the China Merchants' Company the grant of monopoly status — other Chinese firms would be excluded or limited in number — and government aid in order to permit successful competition with the foreigner. But this monopoly could also be turned into an institution functioning primarily to protect the merchant, gentry, and official investors who had already risked their funds in the firm. As the Peking government grew increasingly ineffective and as the competition of British and Japanese shippers became increasingly severe, this was exactly the evolution which the C.M.S.N. Co. underwent. What, in more favorable international circumstances, might have been a source of strength and an aid to expansion became instead an obstacle to further growth.

6

Three *Kuan-tu Shang-pan* Enterprises

I

Sheng Hsuan-huai's "Empire"

In the preceding chapter the operation of the China Merchants' Steam Navigation Company was characterized as "mining." Its managers — who were also the largest shareholders — "mined" the company's income and accumulated reserves for their private enrichment rather than reinvesting these funds in the expansion of the C.M.S.N. Co.'s business. In particular, the size of the fleet was not increased to take advantage of the opportunities offered by the growth of trade in China. Of course, not all of the proceeds of the company's relatively profitable operations were diverted to investments of a traditional kind in land or usury. My point is rather that this enterprise's failure to realize its full growth potentialities in some measure was due to the greater attraction of traditional objects of investment. It is of interest that the reinvestment of profits in Western-type joint-stock firms which did take place tended to be in other companies — not in the C.M.S.N. Co. itself. Perhaps, as we have already proposed, the fear of attracting too much attention (and official avarice) by excessive size (as compared to other firms in one's environment) was as important a deterrent to expansion as the admittedly severe competition presented by foreign-owned firms. In any case, the profitable operation of the shipping company within the limits set for its growth was the foundation upon which were established a succession of *kuan-tu shang-pan* enterprises — each a pioneer in its field.

The shareholders of the China Merchants' Company and the company itself supplied an impressive amount of the capital invested in the other *kuan-tu shang-pan* firms which Sheng Hsuan-huai controlled. In March 1900 Sheng reported to the throne: "The Shanghai textile mills, the Hanyang Ironworks, the P'ing-hsiang Coal Mines, and the Imperial Bank of China, which are managed by your servant, are all founded on investments by the Chinese shareholders in the China Merchants' Com-

pany and the Telegraph Administration out of their income from these
two enterprises." [1] There was a considerable overlapping of personnel
in the directorships of these undertakings; and, as has been shown, the
shipping company from time to time provided the other firms with
short-term financial assistance. After 1896, when Sheng Hsuan-huai
came into his own as a political figure in Peking, it is possible to speak
of an economic "empire" headed by this man and built on the foundation of his control of the China Merchants' Company, and, to a lesser
extent, of the Imperial Telegraph Administration.

This chapter will take up in turn three of the four *kuan-tu shang-
pan* projects which, together with the China Merchants' Company,
constituted Sheng's empire: the Imperial Telegraph Administration, the
Hua-sheng Textile Mill, and the Imperial Bank of China. I plan to
treat the history of the Han-Yeh-P'ing Coal and Iron Corporation in a
separate study. While each of these companies would merit treatment
in detail similar to that afforded to the C.M.S.N. Co. in Chapters 4 and
5, unfortunately the materials available — except for Han-Yeh-P'ing —
are inadequate. The object of the following sections is to illustrate
further the points raised in Chapter 1 and discussed at length in the
case of the China Merchants' Company

II

The Imperial Telegraph Administration

Potential ambiguity of status was as characteristic of the Telegraph
Administration as it was of the C.M.S.N. Co. Was the outsider, especially the denizen of the treaty ports, to look on it as an official or as
a private undertaking? One example will illustrate the fusion of merchant and bureaucratic attributes which were found in this *kuan-tu
shang-pan* enterprise.

In the aftermath of the "Hundred Days Reform" of 1898 and the
coup d'état which brought it to an end, Empress Dowager Tz'u-hsi
was anxious to insure that the Kuang-hsü emperor should not again
challenge her rule. A court conference decided in January 1900 to name
the son of Prince Tuan (Tsai-i), leader of the Manchu conservatives
and Tz'u-hsi's favorite, as heir apparent. But the plot to depose Kuang-
hsü was frustrated by the disapproval of both foreign diplomatic representatives in Peking and high provincial officials. [2] One striking
instance of provincial opposition was a telegram signed by Ching Yuan-
shan, manager of the Shanghai office of the Telegraph Administration,
and 1,230 others, "mandarins, gentry, and merchants from all the provinces residing in Shanghai," protesting against the naming of an heir
apparent to Kuang-hsü. [3] Ching was forced to flee for his life to Macao.

There he was arrested in March on charges, preferred by Li Hung-chang, of having absconded with $37,000 of Imperial Telegraph Administration funds — charges very likely fabricated in order to make Ching's extradition possible.[4]

Sheng Hsuan-huai — who was Ching's official superior as director-general (*tu-pan*) of the Telegraph Administration — was immediately accused by a censor of having let him escape. The imperial court itself threw the responsibility for apprehending and returning the fugitive onto Sheng.[5] Meanwhile the reactionaries in Peking were seething because the Telegraph Administration "as a commercial firm" had had to accept Ching's telegram; and they were "exceedingly anxious to get control of the Telegraphs."[6] In Macao, Ching's English lawyer, one J. J. Francis, Q. C., of Hong Kong, was quick to point to the anomaly of the Chinese government's efforts to extradite his client:

(1) In instituting proceedings against the defendent for alleged debts the Telegraph Administration, which is properly speaking a commercial undertaking, should have, in the first instance, appealed to the Shanghai Mixed Court, the defendent being a resident of Shanghai. (2) The plaintiffs were the Chinese Government, whereas being a commercial concern the charge should have been made out in the names of the shareholders in the said Telegraph Administration.[7]

Sheng was charged with apprehending Ching because as the official who headed the Telegraph Administration he bore responsibility for all that happened in that *kuan-tu shang-pan* company. As a commercial firm, the Telegraph Administration had to accept all messages so long as they were paid for. Yet it was not its merchant shareholders, but its official supervisors who lodged the complaint about the alleged malefactions of Ching Yuan-shan. This contradictory series of moves was possible only because of the ambiguous status of the company.

Establishment of the Telegraph Administration. Like the China Merchants' Company, the Imperial Telegraph Administration was organized under the aegis of Li Hung-chang during Li's long tenure as governor-general of Chihli. "People at home," wrote the *North-China Herald,* "who read of the Imperial armies, and Imperial navies, and of the Imperial Chinese Telegraph Administration, have a natural idea that these are government services as in the West. Really they are local institutions, the property of the various Viceroys, and the Imperial Telegraph Administration is a company controlled and directed by His Excellency Li Hung-chang."[8] "Imperial Telegraph Administration" was the usual treaty-port designation for the telegraph administration office which was first opened in Tientsin in December 1881 and which thereafter constructed and operated the principal trunk telegraph lines in China and Manchuria. The individual most responsible for the establishment of the administration and the spread of the telegraph in China was Sheng Hsuan-huai.[9]

After considerable pressure from the British minister, Sir Thomas Wade, permission had been granted in 1870 to the Eastern Extension Australasia and China Telegraph Company, Ltd. (*Ta-tung kung-ssu*), to lay a cable from Hong Kong northward along the coast to Shanghai where it was landed at a hulk anchored off Woosung. In 1871 the Danish Great Northern Telegraph Company (*Ta-pei kung-ssu*) opened a cable from Vladivostok to Shanghai and eastward to Japan. But the Chinese themselves were slow to inaugurate telegraphic communications. There had been earlier advocates of telegraph construction: for example, Shen Pao-chen at the time of Japan's Formosa expedition in 1874 had received imperial approval for a telegraph project which, however, never materialized. And a short line had been buit for military purposes in 1879 from Tientsin to Taku by Li Hung-chang, who employed government funds and Danish engineers.[10] However, only after the crisis over Ili in 1879–1880 had demonstrated the great inconvenience resulting from the absence of telegraphic communications between Peking and Shanghai were serious efforts made to establish telegraph lines linking China's principal cities.[11]

According to Sheng Hsuan-huai's biography, it was Sheng who in the spring of 1880 convinced Li Hung-chang of the necessity to build a telegraph line from Tientsin to Shanghai.[12] Li presented a memorial in September requesting imperial sanction for construction of that line and the expenditure of Chihli military funds to finance it. He envisaged that

after it is initially established, the telegraph company will follow the regulations of the China Merchants' Company with regard to selecting merchant directors (*shang-tung*), offering shares on the market, and raising capital in order that it may repay these initial [official] funds in annual installments. Then [the company] will become a *kuan-tu shang-pan* enterprise and raise its own funds to meet its expenditures.[13]

When the court approved Li's request, he sent Sheng to arrange with the Great Northern Telegraph Company for the purchase of equipment and the employment of Danish engineers. On December 24, 1881, the first telegram was sent from Tientsin to Shanghai over the newly opened line which had been completed at a cost of Tls. 178,700.[14] Sheng was appointed official manager of the Imperial Telegraph Administration (*Tien-pao tsung-chü*) which was established to operate the new line. He proceeded to solicit merchant investment, and on April 18, 1882, the Telegraph Administration was turned over to Sheng and his fellow shareholders to operate as a *kuan-tu shang-pan* enterprise in return for an initial installment of Tls. 60,000 towards repayment of the Tls. 178,700 in official funds which Li had expended.[15]

The regulations of the new company, which Sheng drew up and which were issued in 1882 after revision by Li, began with a hopeful picture of the relations that were to exist between the government and shareholders in this *kuan-tu shang-pan* firm.[16] They stated: "The first purpose of telegraph lines constructed in China is to transmit military messages; in addition they serve the convenience of the merchants and populace." As in the case of the steamship company, this is a clear indication that military self-strengthening was still the principal argument for Westernization. The regulations continued: "Without official aid and support this line could not be undertaken; and without merchant management it could not long survive." The *kuan-tu shang-pan* arrangement "allows the merchants to receive the profits (*li*), while the officials retain the authority (*ch'üan*)." Thus a very neat division indeed was made of the *li-ch'üan,* "economic interests," which the telegraphs (and other *kuan-tu shang-pan* firms) were to recover from the foreigners who had usurped them.[17]

The financial arrangements (Articles 1–3 of the regulations) whereby Sheng and his associates assumed the direction of the telegraphs were remarkably similar to those of the China Merchants' Company. After the initial payment of Tls. 60,000 which was made on April 23, 1882, the "merchants" were to benefit from a five-year moratorium while the company was getting on its feet. From 1887, they would repay Tls. 20,000 in four annual installments without interest. The remaining official funds, more than Tls. 90,000, would be refunded by deducting from the charges due for sending Class I official telegrams.[18] For the first five years, in addition, the government would assume responsibility for the cost of militia and supplies needed to protect the telegraph lines — about Tls. 11,000 annually.

Also like the C.M.S.N. Co., the Imperial Telegraph Administration was granted a monopoly of the operation of commercial telegraph lines. Additional lines built by raising merchant capital would be placed under the direction of this company; and no other telegraph company would be permitted. Some guarantee was given, too, that the lines would remain under merchant management. Sheng stated in the regulations:

Merchants have invested their funds and taken over the management [of the Imperial Telegraph Administration] because of their concern for the public welfare. This matter of inaugurating a Western-type enterprise requires many years — as much as several decades — to be carried out. We may hope that future profits will make up for today's losses. It is only right that the merchants who have invested their capital should be permitted to manage the company over a lengthy period and expand its operations. This is for the profit of the merchants, and for the welfare of the country as well.

This matter was later to be an issue when the government sought to nationalize the *kuan-tu shang-pan* telegraphs.

The obverse of monopoly privileges was the *pao-hsiao* payments which the government expected as its share in the company's success. Thus the Regulations of 1882 provided that even after the funds advanced by Li Hung-chang had been repaid, Class I official telegrams would continue to go free as *pao-hsiao* ("efforts to return [the imperial grace]").

Official Telegraph Lines. This was the situation as the company began operations in 1882. From the history of the next two decades under Sheng's control it is clear that there was a good deal more official interest in controlling — in contrast to merely profiting from — the Telegraph Administration than was true in the case of the C.M.S.N. Co. The obvious reason for this difference was the strategic importance of at least some sections of the telegraph network that was gradually constructed.[19] There were, for instance, both "official" and "commercial" stations under the supervision of the administration. In August 1889 these two divisions were described in the *North-China Herald* as follows:

> The commercial or private lines run from Peking through Tientsin to Shanghai, and down the east coast as far as Canton and thence to Hong Kong; from Chinkiang up the Yangtze to Chengtu; from Kaifong through Chining to Chefoo; and in Manchuria from Kirin to Hunchun. All the great extension west along the borders of Tongking and Burma and thence to Luchow near Chungking is a government undertaking, and so, with the exception noted above, are the Manchurian and Corean lines, and the Formosan cable and wires.[20]

One example of the relation of the administration to the official lines under its supervision may be cited. In 1884, in the face of a threat of hostilities with France, Li Hung-chang was anxious to connect Port Arthur and Shanhaikwan by telegraph, a route which would not be commercially profitable. "As this line will be primarily for military communications," he memorialized, "we cannot solicit merchant investment." The cost, estimated at Tls. 100,000, would have to be met from other sources. Li proposed and the court sanctioned the transfer of Tls. 23,100 which had been on deposit with pawnshops in Chekiang, together with the sum of Tls. 79,300 which remained from an earlier appropriation to purchase rice for shipment to Peking. Thus this strategic line was financed entirely with official funds. But Sheng, the manager of the *kuan-tu shang-pan* Telegraph Administration, was ordered to conduct a survey of the route, hire the required foreign technicians, purchase equipment, and supervise the construction.[21] It is probable, too, that the Telegraph Administration managed the completed line in this instance; it definitely did so in the case of the telegraph line to Korea which was built in 1885 with funds from the Shanghai customs.[22]

Not only the Tientsin-Shanghai telegraph, but other sections as well were begun as official lines and then acquired by the Telegraph Administration to be managed as commercial lines. For example, the Nanking-Chinkiang telegraph line which had been constructed with provincial funds was transferred to "the mercantile branch of the administration" from May 14, 1885. The official expenditure of Tls. 12,000 was to be set off against the annual subsidy of Tls. 3,000 which had been promised by the former governor-general, Tso Tsung-t'ang. Following the practice of the Tientsin-Shanghai lines, the sums expended annually for policing would be balanced against charges due from official use of the telegraphs. However, because of their importance for coastal defense, branch wires to the governor-general's *yamen* at Nanking and to Woosung remained in official hands.[23]

In another instance, the Honan provincial government undertook a telegraph line from Tsining to Kaifeng. When it was completed in 1888, the governor of Honan memorialized that although he had initiated the line as an official project ("the tract of land followed . . . contains no great trade centers . . . private messages are not likely to be numerous"), the Honan treasury would have great difficulty maintaining it as a government line because of extraordinary provincial expenditures for dike repair and relief. He had, therefore, entered into negotiations with Sheng Hsuan-huai, the director-general of telegraphs, with whom it had been arranged that the management of the entire enterprise "should be entrusted to merchants." The official outlay of Tls. 20,000 would be considered as a loan to the Telegraph Administration. But in accordance with the regulations in effect in other provinces, the company would have the use of the money for five years free of interest, after which time the sum would be repaid in annual installments. "The annual outlay in the future is entirely to be in the hands of the merchants, and the question of loss or gain is in no way to affect the Government." [24]

Li Hung-chang and the Telegraphs. Unlike the C.M.S.N. Co., the Imperial Telegraph Administration remained under one control, that of Sheng Hsuan-huai, during the entire period of its operation as a *kuan-tu shang-pan* enterprise. The administration and Sheng occupied the same position in relation to Li Hung-chang and his regional power in North China as did the China Merchants' Company — with the qualification already made of greater official interest in the construction and control of telegraph lines. It may be noted, for example, that it was through Li Hung-chang that the imperial court was informed of the situation of the telegraphs as a whole, regardless of the auspices under which individual lines were begun; and it was also through Li that Sheng Hsuan-huai forwarded requests for rewards from the court for those who had distinguished themselves in the establishment of the telegraph network.[25]

Even when the Telegraph Administration undertook to construct a line with funds raised entirely from merchant sources, Li's auspices and his memorials to secure Peking's sanction were *sine qua non*. The most important telegraph line to be undertaken after the completion of the initial Tientsin-Shanghai section was that along the southeast coast. It connected the bustling commercial centers of Kiangsu, Chekiang, Fukien, and Kwangtung and was opened in the summer of 1884. The construction costs (about Tls. 400,000) were raised by the sale of shares to private investors — there was little doubt about the profits to be expected from a line running through Soochow, Hangchow, Ningpo, Foochow, and Canton. But Li Hung-chang agreed to provide an annual subsidy of Tls. 20,000 for policing the line, and 200 troops were detailed for construction work. These official expenditures would be balanced against the fees due for transmitting Class I official telegrams which, however, would continue to pass free as token of the merchants' *pao-hsiao*, even after the official funds had been repaid. To aid the company further, Li secured for it exemptions from import tariffs and *likin* charges on the construction materials it used.[26]

When the governor-general of Yunnan and Kweichow, Ts'en Yü-ying, requested the construction of a telegraph connection to Yunnan, the court ordered Li to take charge of the project; and he turned the matter over to Sheng and the Telegraph Administration. Li arranged a loan of Tls. 150,000 from the provinces of Hupei and Szechwan to the Telegraph Administration, which would build and operate as a commercial line the section from Hupei through Szechwan to the Yunnan border. This advance was to be returned over a number of years in the same manner as the official funds loaned for the Tientsin-Shanghai line. For the section from the Yunnan border to Meng-tzu on the Indo-Chinese frontier, which would be operated as an official line, Li secured the appropriation of Tls. 160,000 from the Shanghai customs receipts. The line was built under Sheng's direction and completed at the beginning of 1887.[27]

The above examples illustrate Li Hung-chang's general responsibility to Peking for the telegraph lines operated by the Imperial Telegraph Administration, and his assistance to that company by securing official loans and granting subsidies for policing its lines. This last is of more than incidental interest in that it shows the existence of a good deal of local opposition in the areas through which the telegraph lines passed. In addition, Sheng and his subordinates in the management of the Administration were appointed by Li, who also delegated officers to manage the official sections of the telegraph network such as the line to Korea.[28] As in the case of the China Merchants' Company, the managers were themselves shareholders and intermediaries between the bulk of the investors and officialdom. Li's official supervision of the telegraphs included also the familiar task of protecting the administration and its managers. When, in the summer of 1884, Sheng was charged with misappropriating some Tls. 100,000 from the Chin-chou mines in southern Manchuria, Li (and the Liang-Chiang governor-general Tseng Kuoch'üan as well) came to Sheng's defense and praised his contributions to telegraph development. The funds in question, it was reported, had been temporarily transferred to the Telegraph Administration in order to help finance the Shanghai-Canton coastal line. As Sheng was in charge of both enterprises, the shareholders, it was claimed, had not opposed the move.[29] Finally, in addition to the financial assistance already noted, Li made a major contribution to the company's income when in 1887 he obtained Peking's sanction for a change in the status of Class I official telegrams. These were thereafter to pay 50 per cent of the charges rather than passing free.[30]

The advantages accruing to Li from his sponsorship of the Telegraph Administration were similar to those discussed in the case of the C.M.S.N. Co. He acknowledges in several places the military utility of telegraphic communications for his Huai Army units, for coast defense, as well as for the Chinese forces who fought the French in Annam.[31] The extension of the telegraph into the capital itself, to the offices of the Tsungli Yamen, in 1884 undoubtedly served to increase Li's influence in Peking.[32] And opportunities for dispensing patronage were extensive. But none of these considerations cancels out Li Hung-chang's belief in the value of limited Westernization (*yang-wu*), as exemplified in the construction of telegraphs, for "self-strengthening."

By the time the telegraphs were nationalized — a process extending over the years 1902–1908 — an extensive network connecting most of the commercial and strategic centers in China had been constructed. Some 41,417 *li* (about 14,000 miles) of telegraph lines — for the most part trunk lines — were operated by the *kuan-tu shang-pan* Imperial Telegraph Administration. In addition, 59,211 *li* (20,000 miles) of local lines, built with official funds, were operated by the various provincial governments.[33] Telegraph schools were established in Shanghai, Nanking, and numerous other places. Moreover, the Chinese trunk lines were connected with Danish and English cables at Shanghai, with the French at the Indo-Chinese border (1888),[34] and later with the Russian line at the Mongolian border (1892).[35]

After Li Hung-chang's disgrace in 1895, Sheng Hsuan-huai was more than ever the master of this array. On the foundation of his control of the China Merchants' Company and the Telegraph Administration he reached the industrial and political prominence described in Chapter 3. We can point to such direct benefits to Sheng's industrial empire as the branch telegraph lines that he had constructed to connect his mining properties with commercial centers (between his P'ing-hsiang Coal Mines and Changsha 100 miles away, and 130 miles from Kiukiang to his Ta-yeh Iron Mines and thence to Wuchang).[36] But equally valuable to him were the extensive negotiations which he conducted with foreign diplomats and businessmen on matters relating to shipping and telegraphs. These were a natural preparation for the more important railroad negotiations that he undertook from 1896.[37] But the death of his father at the end of 1902 led, as in the case of the C.M.S.N. Co., to the loss of Sheng's control over the Telegraph Administration. In this instance the change was irrevocable since the *kuan-tu shang-pan* telegraphs passed completely out of private hands and eventually into those of the Peking government.

Conflict over Nationalization of the Telegraphs. Yuan Shih-k'ai was primarily responsible for the nationalization of the telegraphs and their removal from Sheng's direction. At the time of Sheng K'ang's death, Yuan approached Chang Chih-tung, the Hu-Kuang governor-general, and won Chang's approval — most likely by pointing to the desirability of unifying the lines operated by the several provinces. Yuan then proceeded to Shanghai on a visit of condolence to Sheng and informed him of Chang's position. Although Sheng was reluctant to agree, he knew the strength of his opponents, and he therefore decided that he should direct his energies to keeping his post as director-general of railroads. However, Sheng still sought to put some obstacle in the way of Yuan's plans. In order to make nationalization more difficult, he set the value of the merchant investment in telegraphs at the high figure of Tls. 2,500,000. Yuan returned to the capital where he secured the issuance, on December 12, 1902, of an edict ordering himself and Chang Chih-tung to take charge of the transfer of the Imperial Telegraph Administration to official control. The two governors-general were directed to estimate the value of the property, and to devise means for raising funds with which to reimburse the investors.[38] On January 15, 1903, Yuan was appointed commissioner in charge of the telegraphs (*tu-pan ta-ch'en*) with Wu Chung-hsi, Chihli provincial treasurer, as his deputy in actual control of the head office in Shanghai.[39]

It was not until 1908, however, that the process of "officialization" — as the *North-China Herald* termed it — was completed. Funds were not immediately available to buy out the shareholders. Until the Ministry of Posts and Communications was established in 1906, the Telegraph Administration was in theory administered "directly under the control of the Government." [40] Actually it was Yuan's preserve as was the C.M.S.N. Co. during the same period.[41] Thus when Wu Chung-hsi was appointed to another official post in 1906, Yang Shih-ch'i, who as Yuan's appointee was then administering the China Merchants' Company, was also designated to succeed Wu at the head of the Telegraph Administration.[42]

There was a good deal of inquietude among the shareholders when the decree nationalizing the lines was issued. Because it had no funds with which to pay for them, Peking had provided that "should it so happen that merchants possessing shares [in the Telegraph Administration] . . . do not desire to sell them, they are permitted to retain their shares on the old basis." [43] But the shareholders' fear that their shares would suffer full or partial confiscation was not easily allayed. Approaches were made to foreigners in the treaty ports by Chinese investors anxious to transfer their holdings to foreign names.[44] But for the time being the merchant investors continued to receive the large dividends to which they had become accustomed, and the government took no definite action about redeeming the outstanding shares.

Then in November 1906, as has already been recounted, because of increasing friction with conservative Manchu officials, Yuan Shih-k'ai was forced to resign all his concurrent positions although he remained as Chihli governor-general. Control over the Telegraph Administration was transferred to the newly instituted Ministry of Posts and Communications which formally assumed direction in April 1907. The ministry appointed the taotai Yang Wen-chun, who had formerly been provincial judge of Fukien, to succeed Yang Shih-ch'i at the head of the telegraphs.[45] Sheng Hsuan-huai, who had been forced into the background by Yuan's advent onto the scene, now found his influence in Peking growing again. He was able, for instance, to head off a move by Yang Wen-chun and the Ministry of Posts and Communications seeking to reduce telegraph charges in the hope of increasing business.[46] But if Sheng had any plans about regaining his control over this company — as he was able to do successfully in the case of the C.M.S.N. Co. — they came to naught as the ministry proceeded to end the anomaly of the "nationalized" telegraph lines paying rich dividends to private shareholders. Unlike the C.M.S.N. Co., an effective board of directors elected by the investors, which made the government's control merely nominal, was not instituted. The Yu-ch'uan pu proposed rather to buy out all the shares owned by "merchants."

In the process of redemption of merchant shares which began in the spring of 1908, Sheng Hsuan-huai found himself in a difficult position between the shareholders (of whom he was one of the largest) and the government (on March 9, 1908, he was appointed junior vice-president of the Ministry of Posts and Communications).[47] Although he was prevented from active occupancy of his official post until 1910, Sheng was expected to aid the ministry in carrying out a policy which he opposed on the grounds that it "will destroy the faith of Chinese merchants and others, and thus put a check upon the establishment of industrial and commercial companies for the development of modern enterprise in China." [48] No doubt Sheng's personal position was also determined by the financial loss which he anticipated for himself and the other investors.[49] Opposition from the shareholders took the form of protest meetings held in Shanghai on June 4 and June 20, 1908 (at the latter more than 500 persons were present). However, in the end they had no course but to comply with the decision of the ministry.[50]

The issue resolved itself into the price to be paid for the outstanding shares and the method of payment. On an investment with a par value of $2,200,000 divided into 22,000 shares, the shareholders had been receiving as much as $20 per $100 share annually in regular and extra dividends. Because the market value of the shares fluctuated around $200, the shareholders were reluctant to accept the government's offer of $170, later raised to $180, per share. They were demanding at least $240.[51] The investors feared, too, that they might have some trouble getting hard cash for their shares because the $4,000,000 which the Yu-ch'uan pu had available was also earmarked for expansion and reorganization of the lines.[52]

Many telegrams passed back and forth between Sheng Hsuan-huai and the ministry. The ministry was anxious to have Sheng take the lead by selling his own shares at the offered price, and for him to secure the compliance of the others. For his part Sheng, who disliked the whole matter, tried ineffectually to have the ministry appoint some other official to deal with the shareholders.[53] On June 17, 1908, the president of the Yu-ch'uan pu, Ch'en Pi, presented his formal memorial setting forth the reasons and procedure for redeeming the shares and requesting imperial sanction.[54] When that was received, a deadline was established: shares turned in on or before August 26, 1908, would be redeemed at $180; after that date only $170 would be paid for each share. Despite their strong opposition, the overwhelming majority of the investors yielded, after all. Some 21,400 shares out of 22,000 were presented before the deadline. By the end of Kuang-hsü 34 (January 21, 1909), 21,567 had been redeemed at a total outlay of $3,862,060 (or approximately Tls. 2,884,741), excluding some Tls. 31,238 to cover the costs of carrying out the redemption.[55] The Imperial Telegraph Administration ceased to exist, and the *kuan-tu shang-pan* telegraphs became an entirely government-owned and operated enterprise.

Capital and Shareholders. When the Telegraph Administration was nationalized, its paid-up capital, as we have seen, totaled $2,200,000 divided into 22,000 shares with a par value of $100.[56] The available data are unfortunately inadequate to trace the growth of this capital in detail, but that progress may nevertheless be roughly inferred. The Tls. 60,000 of merchant capital which Sheng raised in 1882 at the time the telegraphs were turned over to merchant management, plus Tls. 20,000 of additional capital raised later, are equal to $110,000 in the accounting unit — the Mexican silver dollar — of the telegraph company.[57] Secondly, Sheng proposed to raise $800,000 from private investors to finance the Shanghai-Canton line. According to Li Hung-chang, $500,000 was actually raised; a second source gives the amount as Tls. 500,000 (= $675,000).[58] Let us assume that this last, which stands between the other two figures, is correct. Thirdly, Sheng informed the throne that between 1882 and 1899 $800,000 of accumulated surplus had been transferred to the capital account and stock issued to the shareholders.[59] He also stated that the company was still some Tls. 210,000 short in its efforts to raise the Tls. 500,000 required to finance a telegraph connection with the Russians at Kiakhta, implying that Tls. 290,000 (= $387,000) had already been invested by Chinese "merchants."[60] The total of these four items (see Table 19) is $1,972,000. While this total is still $228,000 short of the reported $2,200,000, it is not difficult to assume that the balance represents

Table 19

Telegraph Administration Paid-up Capital, 1902

Source	Amount (in Mexican dollars)
Merchant shares, Shanghai-Tientsin line	$ 110,000
Merchant shares, Shanghai-Canton line	675,000
Accumulated surplus transferred to capital account	800,000
Merchant shares, line to Russian border	387,000
Unaccounted for	228,000
Total reported, 1902	$2,200,000

a gradual increment of private investment over two decades. Shares in the Telegraph Administration were never held by the government before the process of nationalization described above.

The problem of identifying these shareholders is a difficult one. Judging from the report of the protest meeting held on June 20, 1908, at which over 500 investors were present, it seems that shares were widely held.[61] However, possibly twenty large shareholders had the dominant voice.[62] Among them was Sheng Hsuan-huai. He was "the original founder of the Imperial Telegraph Administration . . . and most of the present shareholders are his relatives or friends who purchased the shares chiefly through his advice." [63] Unfortunately, the number of shares owned by Sheng and his relatives or friends is not known. When, in June 1908, the Yu-ch'uan pu asked him to set an example for the other shareholders by selling his shares at the price of $180 which the ministry was offering, Sheng replied that he would. But, he continued, "last year [1907] when the Han-Yeh-P'ing company called for new capital, my relatives and associates sold their telegraph shares and invested in Han-Yeh-P'ing. Now we still have 900 shares unsold which we shall sell to the government at the price offered." [64] Undoubtedly Sheng, acting on inside information, had disposed of his telegraph shares before the redemption order was made public at a price at least $20 higher than the government offer. If he *still* had 900 shares left, the implication is that he had sold many more than the number remaining, but how many is not ascertainable. It is probable, to judge from the example of the China Merchants' Company, that the other large shareholders included many of the men who will be mentioned below as officers of the Telegraph Administration.

Government Loans and Subsidies. The Telegraph Administration benefited greatly from official loans and subsidies, although no shares were ever owned by the government. There are large discrepancies among the figures given in several places for the amount of these official loans. Sheng reported to the throne in 1899 that the company had repaid some Tls. 620,000 (= $827,000) of official and private loans since 1882. However, the accounts which he appends show only $448,656 under the heading "repayment of funds borrowed for the construction of telegraph lines." [65] Possibly the balance was repaid in the years 1898 and 1899 which are not included in the accounts, but this is not explicitly stated. And it is not clear in any case what proportion of the total he reported represented repayment of official funds. If we total the amount of the individual loans mentioned in other sources (Tls. 178,700 from Huai Army funds in 1882, Tls. 100,000 from Szechwan and Tls. 50,000 from Hupei in 1885, and Tls. 20,000 from Honan in 1888 [66]), we arrive at a sum of Tls. 348,700 (= $464,900) in contrast to Sheng's Tls. 620,000. It may be that the figure cited by Sheng included some part of the official subsidies received in the company's first five years of operations, which will be discussed presently. In any case, the amount of government aid was large, and it attests to the general profitability of the Telegraph Administration that it was all repaid without difficulty.

Although subsidies in the form of protection for the telegraph lines by militia units were granted by other provinces as well,[67] the greatest part of the official subsidies enjoyed by the Telegraph Administration was paid by Li Hung-chang. The 1882 Regulations provided that Li was to furnish Tls. 11,000 annually for five years to cover the cost of guarding the line from Tientsin to Shanghai; from the sixth year the company itself was to assume this expense. In addition, the commissioner for the northern ports would assume the major expense for opening and operating a telegraph school to train operators and clerks.[68] These funds were not to be repaid to the government by the company. In the case of the Shanghai-Canton line, Li agreed to appropriate Tls. 20,000 annually for five years for policing the line; this outlay, however, would be balanced against the charges due for transmitting Class I official telegrams. His *yamen* would also bear the cost of a telegraph school in Shanghai.[69] Under these several headings, the total amount appropriated by Li Hung-chang from Chihli military funds as subsidies for the Telegraph Administration for the years 1882–1888 was approximately Tls. 234,000 (= $312,000).[70] Of this sum, roughly Tls. 86,500 (= $115,333) was expended for protection of the Shanghai-Canton telegraph and in theory was to be repaid by deducting the cost of sending Li's telegrams. Some indication of the importance of Governor-general Li's aid may be gained from the fact that $312,000 represented approximately the average annual income of the Telegraph Administration from telegraph fees for the seven years 1882–1888.[71] This subsidy, equal to a whole year's gross income, was an advantage that the company gained by virtue of its being a *kuan-tu shang-pan* enterprise under Li Hung-chang's protection.

Official Exactions. But this advantage was more than offset by the contributions or exactions which other sectors of the official bureaucracy levied on the Telegraph Administration. These were generally classified under the heading *pao-hsiao* which we have already discussed; they may be looked upon as enforced royalties to the government in return for the privilege of operating as a monopoly enterprise (see Table 20). By the beginning of Kuang-hsü 10 (January 28, 1884), the Tls. 98,700 of Huai Army funds which the company was to repay by deducting from the charges due for Class I official telegrams had been returned in full. In accordance with the agreement made in 1882, however, Class I telegrams continued to go free "as evidence of the merchants' *pao-hsiao*" until the end of 1887.[71] At the lowest estimate, the *pao-hsiao* contributions during these four years totaled Tls. 52,000 (= $69,000); they may well have been as high as Tls. 200,000 (= $266,664).[73] From 1888 through 1902, Class I official telegrams paid one half the regular rate. In 1899, for example, the receipts from official telegrams at one half the regular fee were as follows:[74] from the Tsungli Yamen, Tls. 36,700; from the commissioner for the southern ports, Tls. 9,200; and from the commissioner for the northern ports, Tls. 2,000. The total of Tls. 47,900 would be equal to approximately $63,200. Assuming that 1899 was an average year, for the fifteen years 1888–1902, the company would have contributed approximately Tls. 718,500 (= $948,000) in the form of rebates on official telegrams.

Table 20

Telegraph Administration Estimated Pao-hsiao Payments, 1884–1902
(in Mexican dollars)

Year	Class I telegrams accepted free	Class I telegrams at half-rate	Pao-hsiao[a]
1884	$17,250– 66,666[b]		
1885	17,250– 66,666		
1886	17,250– 66,666		
1887	17,250– 66,666		
1888		$ 63,200	
1889		63,200	
1890		63,200	
1891		63,200	
1892		63,200	
1893		63,200	
1894		63,200	
1895		63,200	
1896		63,200	
1897		63,200	
1898		63,200	
1899		63,200	$ 53,333
1900		63,200	53,333
1901		63,200	53,333
1902		63,200	53,333
Total	$69,000–266,664	$948,000	$213,332

[a] As a result of Kang-i's trip; contributions to support Tientsin and Shanghai schools not included.

[b] The estimated minimum and maximum amounts are given.

A more direct form of contribution was the annual levy imposed on the Telegraph Administration as a consequence of the money-raising jaunt of the grand secretary Kang-i, which was discussed above in connection with the China Merchants' Company. The telegraph company was to pay Tls. 40,000 annually as pao-hsiao beginning in 1899.[75] Through 1902 the total pao-hsiao contribution would be Tls. 160,000 (= $213,332). The situation after that date is not clear, although there is some evidence that the payments continued until 1908.[76]

The grand total of official exactions for the years 1884–1902 would thus come to at least $1,240,000 and might have been as high as $1,438,-000.[77] As in the case of the China Merchants' Company, if funds of this magnitude had been invested in modernizing and expanding the company's physical plant and equipment, the telegraph lines would not have been in the state of disrepair in which the Ministry of Posts and Communications found them in 1908.

Management Personnel. The men who managed the Telegraph Administration were all chosen by Sheng Hsuan-huai with the approval of Li Hung-chang. Sheng himself owed his appointment as *tu-pan,* director-general, of the company to Li, who supervised it in his capacity as commissioner for the northern ports. While Sheng did not often take personal charge of the administration's head office (located first at Tientsin and from 1884 at Shanghai), he controlled it in the same manner and for the same reasons as he did the C.M.S.N. Co. Cheng Kuan-ying and Hsieh Chia-fu, whose careers have been discussed in Chapter 4, were also among Sheng's principal subordinates in the operation of the Telegraph Administration. Until 1900 the manager of the telegraph office in Shanghai was that Ching Yuan-shan with whose flight to Macao this section began. Ching held the official rank of expectant second-class secretary (*chu-shih*); earlier he had been associated with Cheng Kuan-ying in an attempt to establish a cotton mill in Shanghai.[78] Ching's successor was the taotai Chu Pao-k'uei. Chu had studied in the United States as part of the "Chinese Educational Mission." His association with Sheng extended over two decades, and included management of the Shanghai-Nanking railroad as well as of the telegraph office. Chu later served with the Foreign Office (*Wai-wu pu*) and in 1907 was made vice-president of the Ministry of Posts and Communications.[79]

An attempt to find a "merchant" among the early managers of the Telegraph Administration produces only one certain case. Wang Jung-ho, one of the *shang-tung,* merchant managers, of the newly established *kuan-tu shang-pan* company (along with Cheng Kuan-ying, Hsieh Chia-fu and others), is probably "Wong Su Ping," son of the Cantonese merchant "Wong Suen Hing" who had settled and prospered in Shanghai. Wong Su Ping was associated with the Telegraph Administration from 1881 to 1884 before entering the employ of Butterfield and Swire in Shanghai. His brother also was a compradore with that company.[80] For the rest, although they may have had mercantile backgrounds, in the available sources they are designated only as "expectant taotai" with little additional identifying information; for example, the expectant taotais Li Pi-ch'ang (who headed the Yunnan telegraph department and supervised the junction with the French lines),[81] Kuo Tao-chih,[82] Hsi Chao-yuan,[83] She Ch'ang-yü (superintendent of the northern section of the telegraph lines),[84] and the ex-Kiangsi magistrate Ho Ch'i-t'an (who built the line from Peking into Mongolia).[85] Sheng Hsuan-huai's uncle and brother were also connected with the Telegraph Administration for long periods. Sheng Keng (d. October 19, 1910), youngest brother of Sheng K'ang, was for many years manager of the Imperial Telegraph Administration and China Merchants' Company offices in Ningpo.[86] Sheng Hsing-huai (d. 1903), an expectant prefect (*chih-fu*), managed the Telegraph Administration branch in Canton.[87]

Even if the 500 and more shareholders recorded in 1908 included many merchants from the Shanghai area, still the management (as in the case of the China Merchants' Company) was dominated by men who were assimilated to officialdom whatever their backgrounds may have been. The Peking correspondent of the *North-China Herald* was probably correct when he predicted in 1908 that reorganization of the telegraphs would be difficult even if the Ministry of Posts and Communications suceeded in buying out the shareholders and gaining complete control. A major obstacle lay in the fact that all the managers and assistant managers "are officials of the ordinary type and know nothing about telegraphs." [88] Unfortunately we lack an intimate view into the operations of the Telegraph Administration — such as is afforded by H. B. Morse's letters concerning the China Merchants' Company which were quoted in Chapter 4 — on which to base an account of the "bureaucratic management" which must have prevailed in that company.

Relative Stagnation. The results of the operations of the Telegraph Administration, like the C.M.S.N. Co., show a sharp contrast between the profitable returns realized by its managers and shareholders on the one hand and the relative lack of success in providing China with a modern communications network on the other. If it was true, as Sheng Hsuan-huai claimed,[89] that in the early years it was difficult to attract merchant investment because the profits of the Telegraph Administration were small, this situation had been completely reversed by the turn of the century. By 1908 the market value of the par $100 shares was as high as $200. The annual dividend paid by the Telegraph Administration in the first years of the twentieth century was $400,000, a return equivalent to 20 per cent on the paid-up capital and at least 10 per cent on the market value of the company's shares.[90] This was indeed a rich yield for the investors, and all the more so when it is recalled that at least $800,000 of the $2,200,000 paid-up capital had originated in the transfer to the capital account of surpluses accumulated from the operation of the company. A theoretical shareholder who had invested $10,000 in 1882 would have held shares nominally valued at $16,666 in 1908, while their market value would have risen to $33,000. We may also assume, although again it cannot be proved, that for Sheng and his associates in the management there were large perquisites of a less public kind in addition to those just described.

This picture must be contrasted with the state of the telegraph lines at the time the merchant shares were redeemed in 1908. Ch'en Pi, the president of the Ministry of Posts and Communications, offered three principal reasons why it was important to go ahead with the redemption which would allow the ministry to take full control of the company's policies.[91] He outlined first the need for the construction of new lines in Manchuria, Mongolia, Tibet, and so on — that is, in areas which might not yield a high commercial profit. The *kuan-tu shang-pan* company had not been willing to undertake such expansion. Even more important was the need for extensive repairs on the present lines which the merchant-operated company had not carried out. It was estimated that at least $1,000,000 would be required to put the existing lines in good order.[92] Finally, the merchants had refused to agree to any rate reduction. This was sought by the ministry in the belief that the charges were unnecessarily high and that a cut would result in increased use of the telegraph and hence greater income.[93] A further consideration was the refusal of the International Telegraph Conference, which met in Lisbon in 1908, to take any heed of China's complaints of infringements of her sovereignty by the establishment of Japanese telegraph offices in Manchuria until the Chinese rates were lowered and the service improved.[94]

It is difficult not to conclude from this report of inadequate repairs, inflated charges, and unwillingness to expand the service that the *kuan-tu shang-pan* Telegraph Administration was, like the China Merchants' Company, being "mined" by its managers. There was a direct correlation between the extremely high profits cited above and the deficiencies described by Ch'en Pi. The *kuan-tu shang-pan* formula, designed to foster modern-style Chinese industrial and commercial undertakings in competition with foreign enterprises in the treaty ports, tended to be transformed into a system for protecting the investment and income of the company established under official aegis — to the neglect of the theoretical object of "recovering China's economic interests." Monopolistic profits for the investors, "squeeze" for the managers (who were also shareholders), *pao-hsiao* for the government — this was the way the pie was cut. But the development of the telegraph (and of the telephone, which came under Sheng's control in 1900,[95] as well), like shipping and railroads, after an initial period of inauguration and growth was characterized by a slowing down to a condition verging on stasis.

III

The Hua-sheng Spinning and Weaving Mill

The history of Sheng Hsuan-huai's textile interests illustrates the importance of monopoly status to a *kuan-tu shang-pan* enterprise. The troubled course of the Hua-sheng Mill and its predecessor is at the same time an edifying example of the difficulties that faced any effort to introduce modern industry into late nineteenth-century China.[96]

Establishment of the Shanghai Cotton Cloth Mill. No cotton yarn or cloth was produced in China by modern machine methods until 1890. But the first efforts to establish a Chinese-owned factory to manufacture cotton goods in competition with the huge and growing flood of imports from the mills of Lancashire and America go back at least to 1878. In October of that year an expectant taotai surnamed P'eng addressed a petition to Li Hung-chang, governor-general of Chihli, and Shen Pao-chen, Liang-Chiang governor-general, asking these two officials to memorialize the throne on his behalf for permission to establish "a spinning and weaving factory" in Shanghai.[97] P'eng declared that "Tls. 500,000 will be raised in shares in the same manner as the capital of the China Merchants' Steam Navigation Company was raised." But "without Imperial permission for the starting of such a factory, and the official nomination of Directors, there would be no sufficient guarantee of care or authority for the assumption of responsibility." It was necessary, therefore, that a memorial "be laid before the Throne, reporting the establishment of the factory, to give it an official status." Purchasers of shares were to be guaranteed an annual return of 9.6 per cent on their investment and a share of the surplus after all payments including this guaranteed dividend had been made. The company would use domestic cotton and pay taxes, on all cloth it produced, equal to the import duty on foreign cottons. Cloth sent into the interior, however, was to be exempt from *likin* charges.[98]

P'eng's petition did not actually employ the term "official supervision and merchant management," but it appears from the above that the organization of the projected textile mill was to be akin to *kuan-tu shang-pan*. Governor-general Li's reply to P'eng's petition expressed whole-hearted support for the project.[99] Even more than P'eng, he was of the opinion that official support and supervision were essential in order to guard against malpractices and to protect the company from the anticipated interference of other sectors of the bureaucracy.[100] "In starting all joint-stock companies, merchants and officials should be united," Li wrote. He added, however, an appropriate warning that "the company should not be imbued with the forms of officialdom." P'eng was to submit for Li's approval the names of the managers whom he had selected to operate the mill. And he was to inform the governor-general from what provinces the shareholders came so that it could be ascertained whether they had adequate funds.

After receiving Li's reply, P'eng proceeded to Tientsin where he submitted his proposals in person. Before returning to Shanghai he presented a further petition to Li Hung-chang which was his formal answer to the governor-general's prescriptions regarding official supervision and the raising of capital. P'eng agreed in effect to the establishment of the company on a *kuan-tu shang-pan* basis:

> I have now the honour to request Your Excellency to appoint an official to be a joint manager (with myself) and three assistant managers. Their names and birth-places I submit in a separate annex to this petition.[101]

Further appointments would be referred to Li as they became necessary.

The names of the three assistant managers selected by P'eng unfortunately are not known. But the official whom Li dispatched to share the management with P'eng was the expectant taotai Cheng Kuan-ying, who has appeared many times before in this study. Cheng, it will be remembered (see Chapter 4), was an ex-compradore who moved in bureaucratic circles, and as such was no doubt considered ideally suited for the job by Li Hung-chang. Li's instructions to P'eng were as follows:

> Cheng Kuan-ying and the other three gentlemen, whom you assert to be qualified for the duties of assistant managers, will in the course of time receive appointments. As he is a man in whom both foreign and Chinese merchants have long reposed confidence, you will do well to consult with him in everything, and future representations to me with regard to the Company's business should be made in your joint names. . . . When your machinery is bought and your buildings erected, then I and Shen [Pao-chen] will protect you from interference from any quarter.[102]

It seems not unfair to conclude that Governor-general Li Hung-chang, by appointing Cheng Kuan-ying, was seeking to insure his own control of the firm for which he had agreed to act as patron. As in the case of the other modern-type enterprises which he sponsored, Li was motivated both by the desire to reduce China's dependence on foreign sources for manufactured goods and by the expectation that the textile mill would benefit his regional bureaucratic machine in Chihli and North China. He had, after all, been told by the official whom he had sent to investigate the project that profits as high as 20 or 30 per cent were possible.[103]

But early in 1879, barely six months after P'eng had first approached Li Hung-chang, there were already rumors of a split among the promoters of the new company. The "Cantonese merchants and gentry interested in the concern" were reported "to have seceded, and to have bought the estate known as Dow's wharf, on the banks of the Hwangpoo, for Tls. 32,000, with a view to starting a cotton manufacturing mill on their own account." [104] The cause of the discord is not certain, but in addition to provincial rivalries it may have been the result of a conflict over the best method of financing the project. Cheng we know was Cantonese and probably led the southern investors mentioned in the report just quoted. P'eng's birth-place is not known, but in a petition to Li Hung-chang he stated that shares in the mill "have been taken up in

Hunan, Canton, Chihli and Shansi; some in Chekiang and Kiangsu, and a few in Anhwei and Hupei." [105] It is possible, therefore, that he himself came from Hunan, Chihli, or Shansi. As no further notice of the taotai P'eng appears in any source after this time,[106] it may be surmised that he led the other, non-Cantonese, faction and withdrew from the project after the split.

P'eng's financial proposals for the new enterprise in fact diverged sharply from the practices of the China Merchants' Company which he had stated he would follow. The Tls. 500,000 which he sought was to be loaned to the company by the shareholders rather than invested in shares on a joint-stock basis. This may be seen from P'eng's statement that "there is no difficulty in paying interest year by year, the difficulty lies in the repayment of the principal." His plan was to pay off subscribers for Tls. 10,000 or less in the first three years. Those who subscribed for Tls. 20,000–50,000 were to be repaid in three installments in the third, fourth, and fifth years. Subscribers for Tls. 50,000 and more would receive their funds back in five installments from the third through the seventh years.[107] This scheme proposed something less than a true joint-stock company and may well have led to a quarrel with Cheng. Certainly it was symptomatic of the difficulties connected with raising risk capital at that time.

Because of the slight progress which the original promoters had been able to achieve, Li Hung-chang now took a more active hand in the organization of the company. In the spring of 1882 he officially reported to the throne the establishment of the Shanghai Cotton Cloth Mill (*Shang-hai chi-ch'i chih-pu chü*) under his aegis. And to give assurance to prospective shareholders, Li secured for the mill a ten-year monopoly of the manufacture of cotton cloth and yarn. His memorial compared the steady growth of foreign textile imports with the decline of native exports. This he said was due to the superior quality and lower price of foreign machine-made goods. Li continued:

Among foreign imports, foreign cloth constitutes the largest item. In recent years some Tls. 22 or 23 millions worth has been marketed in the several ports. Foreign cloth is a necessity of daily living and its price is lower than native cloth. The people compete to buy it and use it. Thus the amount of Chinese money which has been diverted into foreign hands indeed is not small! Your servant therefore proposes to send gentry and merchants to Shanghai where they will purchase machinery and establish a bureau (*chü*) to imitate the manufacture of foreign cloth in the hope of decreasing somewhat the profit of foreign merchants.[108]

The governor-general then proceeded to outline the monopoly privileges which he sought for the company:

I note that according to Western practice, whenever anyone establishes a new industry which did not theretofore exist in his country, customarily it is conferred upon him as a monopoly for a given number of years. The employment of machinery to manufacture cloth by this company is such an unprecedented act. Therefore it should be stipulated that for the next ten years Chinese merchants will be permitted only to add their capital to this enterprise and will not be permitted to establish other companies.

As to the taxes for which it is liable, this company has just been established; it is still difficult to predict whether or not the market will be good. It is proper that its expenses be lightened in order to help it achieve great success and avoid being crushed by the foreign merchants. I propose that from the time it begins to produce cloth, that cloth shall be exempt from all duties if it is sold on the Shanghai market. If the cloth is transported inland from Shanghai or transported to another treaty port and then sent inland, it should pay the full import duty to the Imperial Maritime Customs at Shanghai, in the same manner as foreign cottons; but it shall be exempt from all *likin* charges in the interior as a manifestation of [imperial] concern [for the success of the company].

The ten-year monopoly and the tax exemptions were intended to give the mill an advantage over foreign cotton imports which paid a 5 per cent tariff when landed at Shanghai and 2.5 per cent more in lieu of *likin* when shipped into the interior. These inducements apparently were successful for it was reported at the end of 1881 that the capital had all been subscribed and commencement of operations was only a question of time.[109]

To head the firm Li designated the expectant taotais Cheng Kuan-ying, who had been with the project since its inception, and Kung Shou-t'u. Cheng, presumably because of his compradore background, took charge of the company's office (*chü*) in Shanghai and of all business matters (*shang-wu*). Kung was to handle all official matters (*kuan-wu*). Four other men, all with official titles, were also connected with the management. They were Tai Heng, who was a Hanlin compiler (*pien-hsiu*); Ts'ai Hung-i, a department director in one of the Six Ministries at Peking (*lang-chung*); Ching Yuan-shan, a second-class secretary in one of the ministries (*chu-shih*) who was also associated with the Imperial Telegraph Administration; and the taotai Li P'ei-sung.[110] These titles did not necessarily indicate that their holders, who were also the company's principal shareholders, held substantive official posts; in all likelihood the titles were purchased (as was definitely so in the case of Cheng Kuan-ying). But their possession was a *sine qua non* for the close contact with officialdom which any new enterprise needed in order to succeed.[111]

Cheng Kuan-ying and the Mill. Cheng Kuan-ying as the head of the company's business affairs was faced with two major tasks. He had first to raise sufficient capital. It was originally intended to sell shares to the amount of Tls. 400,000; later this was increased to Tls. 500,000. Five thousand Tls. 100 shares were offered to prospective buyers. By the end of 1881, Tls. 352,800 had actually been received from investors, representing a call of Tls. 70 on each Tls. 100 share.[112] Employment of the device of accepting partial payment from shareholders against the par value of the shares for which they had subscribed should be noted as one more indication of the great difficulties faced by an entrepreneur seeking capital for a modern-type enterprise. Secondly, Cheng had to proceed with the establishment of the company's physical plant, to purchase machinery, and to ensure an adequate source of raw cotton. He wrote to Yung Wing, then in the United States at the head of the Chinese Educational Mission,[113] asking Yung to engage an American technical expert to assist with these tasks. Some doubt was raised about the suitability of the shorter fibers of Chinese cotton for the machine manufacture of cloth. Therefore soon after the American, A. W. Danforth, had arrived in Shanghai, he returned to the United States taking with him samples of Chinese raw cotton. The cloth made in the United States with Danforth's samples fortunately was found to be comparable in quality with American cloth, so that Cheng decided to go ahead as planned.[114]

Danforth was engaged to superintend the construction of the factory and the selection and installation of the machinery.[115] A site, godowns, and spinning and weaving machinery were purchased with Tls. 209,000 out of the capital funds that had been collected. Cheng hired foreign technicians to install the machinery and to teach Chinese workers how to operate spindles and looms.[116] However, no progress beyond initial excavations was made towards erecting a factory, although the machinery which had been contracted for in England and the United States began to arrive in 1883. According to his associate Kung Shou-t'u, the failure of the company to begin production was due to the sweeping powers which Cheng Kuan-ying concentrated in his own hands.[117] Cheng, it was alleged, tended to treat the company's funds — he had been chiefly responsible for raising the capital stock of Tls. 352,800 — as his own. He had let out large sums in loans, or as investments in pawnshops and the like, pocketing the interest himself.[118] The precise details of Cheng's financial practices and of the presumed quarrel between himself and Kung Shou-t'u are not known.[119] But in the tenth moon (18 November–16 December) of 1884 Cheng left the company and returned to Kwangtung in response to an invitation to join the staff of the famous military leader P'eng Yü-lin. Kung petitioned Li Hung-chang indicting Cheng for his alleged malpractices, but the latter —

presumably with the backing of P'eng Yü-lin — did not return to Shanghai to present an accounting.[120]

Kung, who was left with responsibility for the enterprise, was unwilling (and unqualified, if we may judge from the fact that he had agreed to leave all business matters to the ex-compradore Cheng Kuan-ying) to undertake by himself the task of getting production under way. His immediate reaction after Cheng's departure was to approach Sheng Hsuan-huai, presumably in the belief that Sheng's business experience with the China Merchants' Company and the Telegraph Administration would qualify him to organize a textile mill as well. Sheng, however, declined because of the pressure of his other responsibilities. In the interim period Ching Yuan-shan, an assistant manager of the company, together with the Shanghai taotai, sought to collect additional funds from subscribers for shares who had not paid up their pledges. Some 449 shares were turned in by shareholders who would not support the enterprise further. After all debts were met, however, it is reported that only Tls. 800 in cash remained in the treasury. In 1887 the two men turned the cash and records of the company over to Kung I-t'u, younger brother of Kung Shou-t'u. The machinery had arrived and the foreign employees were still on the payroll, but the firm existed in name only and was without funds to meet its expenses.[121]

After almost ten years of endeavor, the enterprise had not yet progressed to the point where the production of yarn and cloth could be foreseen as an actual fact. An office had been opened in Shanghai. The compradore-official Cheng had raised Tls. 352,800 in share capital out of a hoped-for Tls. 500,000. A site had been selected, machinery contracted for, foreign experts engaged. And the project could look to the protection of the powerful Governor-general Li Hung-chang who had secured for it a ten-year guarantee against the existence of any competing company in the same line of business. Seemingly the elements necessary for a successful beginning were all present. But they could not be combined into an operating enterprise. When the reasons for this failure are sought, immediately one comes up against the ineptitude (not to mention the cupidity) of the promoters and managers of the project. Not only was the background of these men — even that of a compradore such as Cheng — bare of any experience in the operation of a large-scale manufacturing company, but provincial and personal rivalries prevented them from combining what little know-how they had. Moreover, even assuming experience and pristine honesty, it is doubtful that a mill for the spinning and weaving of cotton could be started with a capital as small as Tls. 352,800. Contemporary estimates set the minimum figure for the capital requirements of a weav-

ing plant at Tls. 400,000, and for a spinning mill at Tls. 300,000.[122]
By this standard the Shanghai Cotton Cloth Mill Company in the early
1880's could claim barely half of the required funds.

Reorganization of 1887. In order to begin production it was necessary that a considerably larger amount of capital be provided. Governor-general Li, the project's official sponsor, had not originally planned
to risk government funds in the company. The capital was to come
entirely from private (if possible, merchant) sources, while the official
role would be limited to supervision and garnering of the perquisites
connected with that function. But when it became clear that the semiofficial and compradore promoters could not provide the requisite capital, Li stepped in and took a more active part. In addition to such
considerations as the possible damage to his prestige from the mill's
failure, the governor-general was forced to this decision largely by the
increasing importunities of foreign firms seeking to establish textile
mills in the Shanghai area.[123]

Li Hung-chang's first move, in April 1887, was the appointment of
Sheng Hsuan-huai to accept and examine propositions to the Chinese
government from foreign or Chinese capitalists who might be willing to
loan funds for the establishment of cotton mills. Nothing, however, came
of this approach, primarily because of Li's refusal under any circumstances to give a concession to operate a mill to foreigners, or to permit
foreigners to be active members in any Chinese company.[124]

With no loans forthcoming from abroad, a further effort was made
to solicit funds from Chinese merchants. The company was reorganized
and new regulations (*chang-ch'eng*) were published in July 1887. Li
deputed Kung I-t'u — brother of Kung Shou-t'u and holder of the official title (probably purchased) of department director (*lang-chung*)
of one of the Six Ministries — to head the management. To raise funds
it was decided to make an additional call of Tls. 30 on the 2,900 old
shares still outstanding which would then be exchanged for Tls. 100
par value new shares. By July 9, 1888, some Tls. 48,000 had been paid
in by old shareholders; and the total paid-up share capital subscribed
by individual merchant and gentry investors, old and new, stood at Tls.
334,900 in 1893.[125] But the largest amount of new share capital did not
come from private investors. Once Sheng Hsuan-huai had become interested in the affairs of the Shanghai Cotton Cloth Mill — as we have
already noted, he was offered the management in 1884, and in 1887
Li had entrusted him with the matter of seeking foreign capital — it
was perhaps natural that the China Merchants' Company should be
looked to as a source of funds. By 1893, the C.M.S.N. Co. and its subsidiary Jen-chi-ho Insurance Company had invested Tls. 220,000 in the
shares of the Shanghai Cotton Cloth Mill.[126] In addition, the insurance

company had deposited Tls. 80,000 with the Cotton Cloth Mill at interest.[127] It seems clear that these funds were made available to the mill primarily because of the political and personal relations between Li Hung-chang and Sheng Hsuan-huai, the director-general of the shipping company. It was "by order of the officials," the Annual Report of the China Merchants' Company for 1891 stated, that monies "were taken out of the surplus fund and invested in the Shanghai Cotton Cloth Mill Co.'s shares." [128] Considering the poor record of the mill, which prior to 1891 had paid no interest on its capital,[129] it is doubtful that commercial advantages alone would have attracted the C.M.S.N. Co.'s investment.

But the total private investment (including that of the *kuan-tu shang-pan* shipping company), plus short-term advances from private and official sources amounting to Tls. 170,000, was still inadequate capitalization for a company on the scale projected by Li Hung-chang and the promoters. As he had done in the case of the China Merchants' Company and the Telegraph Administration, Governor-general Li now undertook to lend the mill a substantial sum from Chihli provincial funds. By 1893 official loans amounted to Tls. 265,390.[130] The sources of the capital of the Shanghai Cotton Cloth Mill — which totaled Tls. 1,090,290 in 1893 — are summarized in Table 21.

Table 21

Shanghai Cotton Cloth Mill Capital Account, 1893 (in Shanghai taels)

Liabilities		
Paid-up share capital subscribed by merchants and gentry	334,900	
Share capital held by C.M.S.N. Co.	220,000	
		554,900
Government loan, from Chihli funds	265,390	
		265,390
Deposited at interest by Jen-chi-ho Insurance Company	80,000	
Deposited by former Tientsin customs taotai Liu (Ju-i?)	20,000	
		100,000
Current indebtedness	170,000	
		170,000
Total		Tls. 1,090,290

With these funds in hand, work was begun on the main factory building which was designed to be three stories high, 500 feet long, and 80 feet wide. Construction was not completed until 1891, but already in 1890 part of the 35,000 spindles and 350 looms was in operation. Shortly after it opened the Cotton Cloth Mill was described as "the largest industrial enterprise in Shanghai" by a foreign observer who marveled somewhat that the Chinese should be able to operate such a plant.[131] In 1892 it produced 4,000,000 yards of cotton cloth "of various descriptions and excellent quality" and 1,000,000 pounds of yarn.[132] The company employed 4,000 workers under the direction of A. W. Danforth.[133] Once it had gone into production the Cotton Cloth Mill was an immediate business success, so much so that in 1893 it was able to declare a dividend of 25 per cent on its share capital.[134] Expansion of the plant was contemplated, and in July 1893 Li Hung-chang telegraphed the Chinese minister in London, Hsueh Fu-ch'eng, to place orders for additional machinery.[135]

Given the decline of handicraft production of cottons in the face of the importation of cheaper and better foreign cloth, and assured that it would be confronted with no Chinese competitors, the mill's success is small wonder.[136] The company's monopoly status, which made it impossible for others to enter what now appeared to be a lucrative field, aroused the ire of the Chinese-language Shanghai newspaper *Shen Pao*. In an editorial of December 7, 1892,[137] the *Shen Pao* deplored the "large and increasing business in the import of Indian yarn, which is shipped to all parts of the [Chinese] Empire, and concurrently with this . . . [the] large export of China cotton to Japan, for the use of Japanese mills."[138] "Here are we Chinese growing the best cotton of its kind in the world for the benefit of the Japanese, while we are importing inferior Indian cotton yarn to make into clothes for our population. . . . Why do we not spin our own cotton for our own use?" The indictment which follows of the policy of official sponsorship of one *kuan-tu shang-pan* enterprise to the exclusion of other companies is worth quoting *in extenso*. It should be noted, however, that while the editorial side of the *Shen Pao* was in Chinese hands, the newspaper was founded and owned by British interests.[139]

Why does all the money which goes into the pockets of the Japanese steamers which carry away the cotton, the insurance companies who insure it, the Japanese government who impose duty on it, why does all this profit not remain in China? Why does all the profit of Indian mills, the freight for bringing Indian yarn to China, the insurance, the merchants' profits, why do Chinese not have all these by spinning themselves? These questions are in every mouth, and strange as it may seem there is only one answer — that the mandarins will not allow mills to be built and worked by the people.

They cannot understand the details of business themselves, which require special training and supervision — why should they interfere? Probably we shall not be believed in saying that certain mandarins, knowing that large profits are to be made by Chinese using their own produce, treated by foreign methods, have resolved to create a monopoly of this industry, and that they have started a mill from which they hope to reap large profits, by keeping the industry in their own hands; that they are so short-sighted that they cannot see that by this policy they are preventing the trading classes from developing trade, and forcing them to pay immense sums yearly to foreigners.

As we shall see, however, Li Hung-chang and Sheng Hsuan-huai and their associates were not willing to forego the benefits of a monopoly position, and did not do so until the repercussions of the Sino-Japanese War changed the whole industrial picture in China's treaty ports.

Ruin and Reorganization. Before the new machinery which the company had sought could be purchased, the Shanghai Cotton Cloth Mill was totally destroyed by a fire that broke out on the morning of October 19, 1893. The blaze began among the scutching machines on the ground floor, and then spread very rapidly. According to an eye-witness report,

In a few minutes [after the fire began at about 9:20 A.M.] the flames ascended the tower which serves as a staircase at the corner of the building, and in five minutes the flames inside it at the top could be seen from the Yangtsepoo station.[140]

The loss suffered by the company as a result of this fire was at least Tls. 800,000 out of assets valued at over Tls. 1,000,000 (building, machinery, raw cotton, and cloth). As Sheng Hsuan-huai, who had been ordered by Li Hung-chang to survey the ruins, reported, "there now remains only the site of the mill, the houses of the master workmen, and machinery, boilers, and odds and ends of iron and steel damaged by the fire."[141] Unbelievably, the factory was not insured at the time of the blaze.[142] With the loss of its main building, the Shanghai Cloth Mill passed out of existence on October 19, 1893.

The domestic manufacture of cotton yarn and cloth had shown itself to be a potentially profitable venture. This was the case despite the fact that dividends the size of those declared in 1893 were obviously founded on reckless economies in other areas. Failure to insure the company's physical plant was the most egregious example; but, judging from the experience of other *kuan-tu shang-pan* enterprises, a doubt may also be raised as to whether adequate allowance was made for depreciation in the annual accounts. In view of its profitable operation, Li Hung-chang was anxious to reorganize the company and rebuild the plant without delay. Immediately after the fire, he dispatched Sheng Hsuan-huai — then the incumbent Tientsin customs taotai and Li's chief advisor in financial and industrial matters — to Shanghai where he was to "value the remnants of the machinery, *débris* of the mills, and the ground" and "to consult with the gentry and merchants who had an interest in the mills, and to get their assistance in clearing up matters and also to procure funds for the reconstruction [sic] of new mills, if possible on a larger scale than before." On this assignment, he was to act in conjunction with the Shanghai taotai Nieh Ch'i-kuei, son-in-law of Tseng Kuo-fan.[143]

Sheng Hsuan-huai's recommendation to Governor-general Li was that everything possible should be done to compensate the shareholders who had lost their funds in the razed mill. This was essential "in order to succeed in procuring the requisite funds" for a new plant and to "put a stop to rumours amongst merchants and the gentry, detrimental to the object in view." From Sheng's report it is clear that the shareholders feared that the government would try to recover immediately the Tls. 265,390 in official funds which Li had lent the Cotton Cloth Mill, thus wiping cut completely the remaining equity of the private investors. As Sheng stated, "According to immemorial custom in China, if anything fatal happens to a salt monopolist or pawnbroking concern, the first thing to be done is to pay the government deposits before any other debt." In this case at least, the decision taken by Li and Sheng was influenced by their consideration of the long-range potentialities of Chinese-owned textile mills. They agreed that "what may be styled the mercantile and gentry shares were subscribed in answer to calls from the government and cannot bear comparison with pawnbrokers, who borrow government money for their own advantage." Therefore the remaining assets of the Cotton Cloth Mill would be paid to the shareholders in proportion to the size of their investments, and in the form of shares in the new company which Sheng was organizing "so that the old shareholders may have the advantage arising from the money to be made by the new mills." As to repayment of the official loan, "the authorities should wait until the new mills are running, when the sum of one tael should be collected on each bale of yarn produced, and the money thus collected be paid to the government in gradual liquidation of the claims." [144] It was on this basis that Sheng proceeded to establish a new textile enterprise.

Early in February 1894, Sheng telegraphed Li Hung-chang that he had raised Tls. 1,000,000 and that a new *kuan-tu shang-pan* company had been organized.[145] The shareholders elected seven directors (*tung-shih*) headed by the expectant prefect (*chih-fu*) Sheng Hsing-huai, younger brother of Sheng Hsuan-huai.[146] Hsing-huai had earlier been manager of the Imperial Telegraph Administration office in Canton. Two of the remaining six directors were also associated with others of Sheng's enterprises. Yen Ying, whom we have already encountered as an officer of the China Merchants' Company, took charge of the procurement of raw cotton and the sale of cloth. The director Yang T'ing-

kao was later to be a member of the first board of directors of the
Imperial Bank of China which Sheng Hsuan-huai founded in 1896. The
other four directors of the textile mill were Yen Tso-lin, who became
comptroller; Ch'u Ch'eng-wei, the works manager; Shen T'ing-tung;
and Hsü Ch'un-ying.[147]

Yen Ying and Yang T'ing-kao were almost certainly Shanghai merchants, but the background of the other directors unfortunately is not
known. Their head, Sheng Hsing-huai — and also directing manager
(*tsung-kuan*) of the new mill until his death in 1903 [148] — was, of
course, a member of a prominent Kiangsu gentry family. It seems safe
from the foregoing to characterize the management of the mill as *shang-
pan,* in the sense that it was in private hands, merchant and gentry.
This is reflected also in the name which the new enterprise took. Sheng
Hsuan-huai reported from Shanghai to Governor-general Li that merchants in that city were hesitant about investing their capital: "The
merchant investors fear that when the mill is successfully under way,
there will be exactions by the officials." [149] To remedy this situation,
Sheng proposed and Li agreed that the name of the company should
express its character as a merchant managed enterprise. The word *chü*
(literally "bureau") with its official overtones would be dropped. In
its place the word *ch'ang* (literally "factory") would be used in order
to emphasize that the management was in private and not in official
hands. Thus the name of the company — which had been *Shang-hai
chi-ch'i chih-pu chü* — became *Hua-sheng fang-chih tsung-ch'ang* (Hua-
sheng Spinning and Weaving Mill).

Private management was formally guaranteed, but this did not imply that official supervision of the Hua-sheng Mill was appreciably
lessened at this time. Li Hung-chang described the company as a
kuan-tu shang-pan enterprise, and it is unlikely that others would dis-
agree with his formulation.[150] The official framework within which the
Hua-sheng Mill existed was in fact a complex one. As before, in the
last analysis the company was under the wing of Governor-general Li.
For all practical purposes, however, Sheng Hsuan-huai, whom Li had
invested with the title of *tu-pan,* director-general, controlled the company and handled its relations with officialdom.[151] Sheng's position in
this case paralleled exactly his status with respect to the China Merchants' Company and the Imperial Telegraph Administration. The
actual business operations of the mill were in private hands. But through
his brother, Sheng Hsing-huai, and because he was himself a large
shareholder, Sheng Hsuan-huai was able to exert his influence over
these matters as well as over the general policy of the company which
normally would have come within his purview as director-general.

Sheng and Li envisaged the Hua-sheng Mill as the central unit of a vast textile complex with factories in Ningpo and Chinkiang as well as in Shanghai. Their plan, which Li presented to the throne in May 1894, contemplated ten subsidiary mills (*fen-ch'ang*) of 20–40,000 spindles and 200–500 looms each in addition to the 70,000 spindles and 1,500 looms projected for the Hua-sheng main plant (*tsung-ch'ang*). This would give a total of some 320,000 spindles and 4,000 looms which would be increased to 400,000 and 5,000 respectively by the inclusion of the facilities of Chang Chih-tung's *kuan-pan* textile mill in Hupei. In one year these mills would be capable of producing yarn valued at Tls. 18,000,000 and cotton cloth with a value of Tls. 7,500,000. This, concluded Li, would be nearly sufficient to supplant imported foreign yarn and cloth whose value had totaled about Tls. 27,000,000 in recent years. Thereby the outward flow of Chinese funds would be halted and the livelihood of the people protected. "If we do not take this opportunity to raise funds quickly, purchase machinery, and operate spinning and weaving mills ourselves," he warned, "I fear that hereafter the harm to the wealth of the populace will not be limited to the foregoing figures." [152]

To control this complex Li and Sheng organized a Cotton Cloth and Yarn Administration (variously called *Fang-chih tu-hsiao kung-so* or *Fang-chih chi-ch'a kung-so*). In it was vested the ten-year monopoly which had previously been granted to the defunct Shanghai Cotton Cloth Mill. No additional mills — whether operated privately or by the government — were to be permitted outside of the eleven which Li projected. Until at least 1896 this administration served as the principal organ of official supervision over the textile industry. It performed such functions as levying a royalty of one tael per bale on the production of the several mills (as Sheng had proposed in 1893 in order to repay the official funds that had been loaned to the Shanghai Cotton Cloth Mill). It also "exercised more or less control over all of them, such as passing their materials through customs, and carrying on all negotiations with the Government or officials in connexion with their operations generally." [153] The Chinese and foreign heads of the administration were respectively Sheng Hsing-huai and A. W. Danforth, who were concurrently the managers of the Hua-sheng Spinning and Weaving Mill. It should be obvious from this fact that the new organ was primarily a device through which Sheng Hsuan-huai planned to dominate the Chinese textile industry.

Although the Hua-sheng Mill was partly in operation by 1894, the rest of the grandiose scheme of Sheng and Li was never realized in full. The problem of raising Chinese capital in an amount adequate for the establishment of the number of factories which they envisaged was not solved. And on the other hand, as we shall see, even before they had had the chance to make a maximum effort, the disastrous defeat by Japan and the provisions of the resulting Shimonoseki Treaty had totally changed the situation in China's treaty ports.

A. W. Danforth, who had been associated with the Shanghai Cotton Cloth Mill since its inception, was entrusted with the technical responsibility for erecting a plant, purchasing machinery, and organizing production for the new Hua-sheng Mill. Operations began on a limited scale in 1894. When completed, the plant was equipped with 64,556 spindles and 750 looms as compared with the 35,000 spindles and 530 looms of the old Shanghai Cotton Cloth Mill. In 1894 and 1895 four subsidiary textile companies came under the control of Sheng Hsuan-huai and the Hua-sheng Mill.[154] The first of these, the Hua-hsin Mill, was organized in 1891 by the Shanghai taotai T'ang Sung-yen as a joint official-merchant enterprise; among the principal shareholders was Nieh Ch'i-kuei. It appears to have been under Li Hung-chang's influence from the beginning and thus was easily amalgamated with Sheng's interests. In February 1894, Li ordered that the Yü-yuan Spinning Company (*Yü-yuan sha-ch'ang*), which had been organized by the (expectant?) taotai Chu Hung-tu and his son Chu Yu-hung, should become a subsidiary factory of Sheng's Hua-sheng Mill.[155] The two remaining plants, Yü-chin and Ta-ch'un, seem to have been organized by Sheng himself with funds raised from merchant and gentry investors in Shanghai.[156]

These five plants, together with Chang Chih-tung's Hupei mill, constituted the entire cotton textile industry (exclusive of handicraft production) in China before the Shimonoseki Treaty of April 1895. Table 22 shows the founding date, location, and the equipment of the factories in operation in 1895.[157] Their 174,564 spindles and 1,800 looms represented 43 per cent and 36 per cent respectively of the total capacity which Li Hung-chang had given as a goal in his 1894 memorial. Of this total, Sheng's five companies dominated the production of yarn with their 133,972 spindles. But they possessed only 800 out of the 1,800 looms.

The potential output of these 133,972 spindles may be estimated at 335 bales of yarn per day.[158] Assuming that the mills worked at least 300 days in a year, Shang's textile complex could then produce a minimum of 100,000 bales annually. At one tael per bale, this would mean a potential revenue of Tls. 100,000 per annum for the semiofficial Cotton Cloth and Yarn Administration. The size of the royalties actually paid by the five *kuan-tu shang-pan* firms unfortunately cannot be determined. But in any case, the long-range returns which Sheng anticipated were never to be realized. Two developments coming in the wake of the Sino-Japanese War undermined the basis of the monopoly which he and Li Hung-chang had established, led to the lapse of the Cotton Cloth and Yarn Administration, and were conducive to the failure of several of the subsidiary mills which had been established in 1894 and 1895.

Table 22

Cotton Spinning and Weaving Mills in China, 1895

Date opened	Location	Name	Spindles	Looms
1891	Shanghai	Hua-hsin Spinning and Weaving Company	9,024[a]	50[b]
1892	Wuchang	Hupei Cotton Cloth Mill	40,592[c]	1,000
1894	Shanghai	Hua-sheng Spinning and Weaving Company	64,556	750
1894	Shanghai	Yü-yuan Spinning Company	25,000	—
1895	Shanghai	Yü-chin Spinning Company	15,000	—
1895	Shanghai	Ta-ch'un Spinning Company	20,392	—
		Total	174,564	1,800

[a] 7,008 when opened; 2,016 added in 1892.

[b] 50 looms purchased in 1894.

[c] 30,440 when opened; 10,152 added in 1895.

The Decline of Sheng's Monopoly. First, the fall of Li Hung-chang made it easier for other Chinese-owned mills to be established outside of the control of Sheng and Li. Between 1896 and 1910, sixteen wholly Chinese cotton mills and three joint Sino-foreign firms began production with initial equipment which totaled 319,656 spindles and 516 looms.[159] The emphasis, it will be readily seen, was on spinning yarn — the field which Sheng Hsuan-huai's enterprises had previously dominated, and in which their position was now considerably dwarfed. Secondly, the Shimonoseki Treaty (Article VI, Section 4) for the first time sanctioned the establishment of foreign-owned manufacturing enterprises on Chinese soil. Lured by the profits which Sheng's mills had made despite the official royalty to which they were subject, "a precipitate influx of foreign capital" was attracted into the cotton textile industry after the signature of the treaty.[160] In 1897, there were 160,548 foreign-owned spindles in Shanghai; by 1913 the total had increased to 338,960, constituting 41.2 per cent of the total number of spindles — Chinese and foreign — in the entire country.[161]

The effect of these two developments on Sheng's enterprises was disastrous. When the foreign mills opened, they of course marketed their goods without paying the levy of one tael per bale of yarn which the Cotton Cloth and Yarn Administration had been collecting from Chinese mills. They did not in any way recognize its authority. Chinese-owned mills not under Sheng's control followed suit. The administration itself eventually "simply lapsed — became dormant." [162] Much more serious than the demise of that organization were the postwar difficulties facing the cotton mills which had supported it. They were unable to meet their needs for capital, the price of raw cotton rose precipitously and thus increased their costs, and the shortage of trained labor accompanied by severe competition for what there was both decreased their efficiency and raised their wages bill. Let us look first at the situation of the Hua-sheng Spinning and Weaving Mill.

In February 1894, Sheng Hsuan-huai had telegraphed Li Hung-chang to inform him that he had raised Tls. 1,000,000 in Shanghai and was proceeding with the organization of the Hua-sheng Mill. It seems, however, that Sheng had been overoptimistic at that time about the funds which would actually be realized from his efforts. For in September 1897, after the two processes which I have just described were well under way, he was in anxious communication with Li regarding the future of the mill, which was suffering losses of several thousand taels each month. Sheng attributed this to the inadequacy of the Hua-sheng company's merchant capital — which he now stated was only Tls. 800,000 — in the face of severe competition from foreign mills in Shanghai. [163] But his petition to lease the plant to foreigners for a three-year period and employ the rental to augment its insufficient capital was not granted at this time, [164] and Hua-sheng's difficulties continued unsolved. The initial plant and equipment had required an expenditure of Tls. 2,080,000. To meet the difference between this amount and the paid-up capital of Tls. 800,000, the management had borrowed large sums on which it paid interest of more than Tls. 160,000 in the seven years from 1894 through 1900. It had not, however, been able to raise further capital with which to repay the principal sum of these loans. As Sheng summed it up: "Foreign factories were established in droves, while Chinese investors acted as if they had bound feet." [165]

In addition to the burden resulting from undercapitalization "which led to disastrous overdrafts requiring large interest payments," [166] Sheng complained that "because of competition among the purchasers, the price of raw cotton has soared; and wages have gone up because of the competition for workers." [167] Between 1890 and 1895, the price of Chinese cotton in Shanghai varied between Tls. 12–14 per picul; by 1895 and 1896 it had jumped to Tls. 14–19 per picul, largely the result of increased demand from new Chinese and foreign mills. [168] At least in the first years after 1895 labor efficiency was a serious problem for the Hua-sheng and other firms. But after the turn of the century this shortcoming was to some degree overcome. Thus a report published in 1904 stated that "at present, the mills secure operators for from 22 or 23 to 30 cents a day who perform nearly a half more work than those paid 20 cents during the earlier days of the industry." [169]

Kuan-tu shang-pan Status Ended. The difficulties faced by the Hua-sheng Mill following the loss of its monopoly position provided the opportunity for Sheng Hsuan-huai, who had been directing the firm as its official manager, to take over full control of the company, convert it into a wholly private enterprise, and end its *kuan-tu shang-pan* status. In 1901, with the backing of Li Hung-chang and Liu K'un-i, Sheng arranged the sale of the mill to a new merchant corporation which was styled the Chi-ch'eng Company. His justification for this move was the unwillingness of Hua-sheng's merchant shareholders to furnish the additional capital which, as I have shown, was badly needed.[170] The new investors would agree to complete the transaction only if official supervision of the enterprise was terminated. In actuality, it now appears that the Chi-ch'eng Company was a dummy corporation which Sheng and his family and associates had established for the purpose of taking over the Hua-sheng Mill and removing it from official purview. They had been the largest shareholders in the old company and continued to be so in the new, which took the name Chi-ch'eng Spinning and Weaving Mill. From this time until 1931, when it was sold to the Hong Kong and Shanghai Banking Corporation and eventually became part of the Shen-hsin Spinning and Weaving Company, the mill continued as a private firm entirely in the control of the Sheng family.[171]

The four subsidiary plants fared no better than the main factory. The Hua-hsin Mill failed completely and was reorganized under new management in which Nieh Ch'i-kuei was a leading figure. The Yü-yuan Mill suffered heavy losses, eventually failed, and in 1918 passed into Japanese hands. In 1897 the Yü-chin Mill was reorganized as the Hsieh-lung Spinning and Weaving Company (usually known by the Shanghai pronunciation of its name: "Yah Loong Cotton Spinning Company"). It went bankrupt and was reorganized in 1901 before being sold to Mitsui interests in 1902. Finally, Japanese merchants leased the expiring Ta-ch'un Mill in 1905, and in the next year it was sold to them outright.[172]

It may seem an anomaly that the leading exponent of the *kuan-tu shang-pan* form of organization should have been the principal party to a ruse which removed one of his enterprises entirely from official supervision. The explanation is related to the basic characteristics of the system of official supervision and merchant management. On the one hand, the *kuan-tu shang-pan* pattern was intended as a device for the promotion of Chinese-owned and operated enterprises in what was a particularly unpromising environment. On the other hand, it was meant to guarantee the profits of the promoters who undertook to establish industrial firms in such circumstances. A principal component of the pattern was the establishment of a monopoly under the aegis of a powerful provincial official who might himself have a financial stake in the venture. Either a breakdown of the monopoly or the decline and fall of the official patron could weaken the position of the promoters. They would lose their advantages vis-à-vis their potential competitors or sections of the official bureaucracy who might seek to gain by exploiting the discomfiture of the fallen patron. In the case of the China Merchants' Company, the disgrace of Li Hung-chang followed by the rapid rise of Yuan Shih-k'ai was seen by Sheng as sufficient reason for seeking to guarantee that control over the shipping company would be in his own hands rather than in those of potentially hostile officials. In the present instance, the fall of Li had the same effect. And in addition, the end of the monopoly which the Hua-sheng Mill had previously enjoyed may well have made Sheng desirous of more freedom of action than was possible under official supervision. Consideration of his personal financial interests would have convinced him that there was little to be gained from government supervision without the monopoly. These private interests might even suggest to Sheng the advisability of disposing of the enterprise to foreign buyers — he made such a tentative move in 1897 when he sought to lease the Hua-sheng plant to Japanese interests.[173] And in 1911, Sheng took a further step in this direction when he registered the former Hua-sheng textile mill in Hong Kong as a British enterprise in order to protect it from possible confiscation by the Nanking revolutionary government and by that of Yuan Shih-k'ai which succeeded it.[174] This was something that a government officially committed to "recovering China's economic rights" through the promotion of industry could not easily condone. Because the requirements of Sheng's "empire" had outgrown the institutional framework within which it had been founded, he sought to transform the *kuan-tu shang-pan* Hua-sheng Mill into a private enterprise better able to meet his needs in the new circumstances.

IV

The Imperial Bank of China

The China Merchants' Steam Navigation Company had been the first Chinese-owned steamship company as well as the earliest example of a *kuan-tu shang-pan* enterprise. The Shanghai Cotton Cloth Mill (and its successor the Hua-sheng Spinning and Weaving Mill) was the first modern textile mill under Chinese control. Similarly, the *kuan-tu shang-pan* bank organized on Western lines which Sheng Hsuan-huai founded at the end of 1896 was the first Chinese firm of its kind. In its personnel and its capital, as well as in its conception, the Imperial Bank of China (*Chung-kuo t'ung-shang yin-hang*) was related closely to Sheng's other enterprises.[175]

Before 1897 the modern-style banks in China's treaty ports which dominated the foreign exchange business were all branches of foreign — especially British — institutions. From 1848, when the Oriental Banking Corporation (*Tung-fang yin-hang*) established its office in Shanghai, the British enjoyed for forty years a virtual monopoly of modern-style banking in China. Their dominant position was maintained largely by two firms, the Chartered Bank of India, Australia and China (*Mai-chia-li yin-hang*), whose first Chinese branch was opened in 1857, and the Hong Kong and Shanghai Banking Corporation (*Hui-feng yin-hang*), which began to do business in China in 1865.[176]

Chinese old-style banks were of several different kinds. The most well-known were the so-called Shansi banks which were engaged primarily in the transfer of funds from province to province by the issuance of drafts. In the major cities there were also local banks (called *yin-hao*, "silver banking shops," in Peking and Tientsin, and *ch'ien-chuang*, "money banking shops," in Shanghai and Hankow) independent of the nationwide network of Shansi banks. And in the latter part of the nineteenth century, a number of semiofficial customs banks (*hai-kuan kuan-yin-hao*) were established in the several treaty ports "to collect, hold in deposit, and forward" the payments due from local Chinese merchants to the Imperial Maritime Customs.[177] While the foreign-owned modern-style banks provided the model for its operations, some of the personnel and capital of Sheng's Imperial Bank of China originated in these semiofficial customs banks.

Founding of the Imperial Bank of China. It is certain that Sheng's proposal for the establishment of a modern-style bank was closely connected with his appointment in 1896 as director-general of railroads charged with the construction of the Peking-Hankow line. The "prospectus" (*shuo-t'ieh*) which he submitted to the Tsungli Yamen in Peking on September 22, 1896, outlined a plan for raising from private investors at least Tls. 7,000,000 of the estimated Tls. 40,000,000 total cost of the projected railroad.[178] This was to be handled, as in Western countries, through the instrumentality of a bank.[179] Sheng next raised the question of founding a modern-style bank in two memorials which were seen by the emperor on November 1, 1896. In the first of these — the "General Plan for Self-strengthening" which has been discussed in Chapter 3 — he described the way in which foreigners utilized banks to marshal the wealth of their countries for commerce. Sheng proposed that China do likewise, and at the same time end its dependence on foreign banks in the treaty ports. Once established, Chinese-owned modern banks would win the trust of the merchants and the populace in general. They would then be in a position to float domestic loans for the government at rates lower than those charged by foreign banks and without the additional burden resulting from the unfavorable exchange rate between silver and gold.[180]

In his second memorial Sheng outlined in greater detail his conception of how the proposed bank should be organized.[181] He opposed an institution that would be capitalized entirely with government funds provided by the Ministry of Revenue and run exclusively by high officials. "A government organization which handles business matters will run into numerous obstacles and accumulate evils," he stated. It was Sheng's opinion that

banking is a matter for merchants; if merchants do not trust the government, the financial power of the country cannot be concentrated; and if this power cannot be concentrated, a bank will not be successful. If we wish to begin carefully in order to get good results, we must accumulate small sums [from investors] to make a big fund. I venture to request that a high official be appointed to select honest and reliable gentry and merchants from all the provinces and recommend them for service as directors (*tsung-tung*) [of the bank]. They should raise Tls. 5,000,000 of capital from Chinese merchants and establish a Chinese bank, first in Peking and Shanghai and then with branches in other provincial capitals and trading ports. Following Western business practice, this bank should be managed by the merchants themselves.

Of course, the "high official" (*ta-ch'en*) whom Sheng had in mind to undertake this project was himself. And apparently his opposition to the establishment of a purely official bank was based on the belief that the *kuan-tu shang-pan* form of organization would be better able to raise private capital for the Peking-Hankow railroad, and could be more easily coordinated with his other commercial and industrial undertakings.[182] There were no immediate replies from the Grand Council, the Tsungli Yamen, or the Hu-pu to whom Sheng's proposals had been referred for their comments. But on November 12, 1896, an imperial edict was issued which directed Sheng to proceed with the selection of directors, to solicit merchant capital, and to establish the bank.[183] It should be underlined that the grant of imperial approval for a project of this scope before the opinions of the leading government organs were received — they were not seen by the emperor until December 6 [184] — was an unusual step. It seems likely that the edict of November 12 was obtained by the efforts of Sheng's backers, Wang Wen-shao and possibly Chang Chih-tung, who suspected that a delay in sanctioning the bank would provide an opportunity for its opponents to act. On May 27, 1897, premises were opened in Shanghai, and in the next months in Tientsin, Hankow, Canton, Swatow, Chefoo, and Chinkiang. Early in 1898 an office was opened in Peking.[185]

Before the Imperial Bank of China could begin operations, however, two considerable obstacles had to be overcome. First, Sheng found it necessary to negotiate at length with the Tsungli Yamen concerning the details of the bank's status, organization, and operations. Secondly, the whole matter of establishing a *kuan-tu shang-pan* bank was called into question by a censorial indictment which caused the throne to reconsider the approval it had given in November 1896. Closer examination of both of these developments will throw light on the nature of the Imperial Bank of China and on the environment in which it did business.

Conflict with the Tsungli Yamen. On February 2, 1897, Sheng Hsuan-huai telegraphed to the Tsungli Yamen in Peking the text of the regulations (*chang-ch'eng*) in twenty-two articles which he had drawn up for the bank.[186] In general, those of the Hong Kong and Shanghai Banking Corporation were taken as a model. The regulations stated explicitly that the bank was "established by special imperial edict" (*feng t'e-chih k'ai-she*) and that it was "under the special protection of the government" (*kuan wei hu-ch'ih*) (Article 1). And "the names of the chief officers will be memorialized to the throne" (Article 3). Certain exclusive privileges were granted to the bank: the right to issue notes, coinage of money, the deposit of Hu-pu funds, and the conveyance of taxes from the provinces to Peking. In return for its protection and the grant of these privileges, the government would receive from the bank annually 20 per cent of its surplus (*yü-li*) — after deductions for regular dividends on its shares, bonus payments to the managers and staff, and a stated apportionment to the bank's reserve fund — as *pao-hsiao*, that is, royalty payments to recompense the imperial grace (Article 9). On the other hand, despite its official ties, the bank was to be operated entirely as a commercial enterprise (Article 3); thus

all business methods pursued by the Bank will be entirely on the foreign plan, as has been the way with the Hong Kong and Shanghai Bank, which is to be made the model of this Bank in everything. In a word, the Bank is to be a commercial institution; hence there will be no official deputies (*weiyuans*) appointed and, in their stead, there will be Directors publicly chosen and appointed; there will be no Great Seal issued by the Peking Ministry of Works, but instead its seal will be the usual business "chop" of commercial institutions. All mandarinic etiquette and custom will be unhesitatingly tabooed and only such in vogue in commercial institutions, pure and simple, will be adhered to. "Integrity, Impartiality, and Strict Attention to Business" will be the motto of the Bank. No favouritism or nepotism will be permitted, as might be the case if the Bank were to be conducted otherwise. The power will be in the hands of the Directors while the profits will go to the shareholders.

Other articles dealt with the bank's capitalization, its management, and the conduct of its business. The head office, Sheng's regulations stated, would be located in Shanghai. The nominal capitalization of the bank was set at Tls. 5,000,000. However, Sheng intended to commence business with a paid-up capital of only Tls. 2,500,000. Of this amount, Tls. 1,000,000 would be subscribed by the China Merchants' Company and the Imperial Telegraph Administration. Sheng and the other directors of the bank would be personally responsible for Tls. 1,000,000 more; and the remaining Tls. 500,000 was to be offered on the open market to Chinese investors (Articles 6, 7). On these shares the investors would receive a guaranteed annual return of 8 per cent plus a share of the surplus after deductions for dividends, bonuses, and the reserve fund (Article 9). To provide the bank with adequate working capital, the Ministry of Revenue was to advance Tls. 1,000,000 which would be left on deposit (Article 8).

The board of directors was to consist of twelve men "of high reputation, business integrity, ability, and solid substance, possessing large interests in the Bank." Ultimate authority for the bank's operations would be vested in this board whose members had to be Chinese. Three of the directors (*tsung-tung*) would be selected to act as managing directors (*pan-shih tsung-tung*) and to take active charge at the bank's head office (Articles 10, 12). Under their direction, the Shanghai office was to be managed by an Englishman, A. M. Maitland, who had formerly been employed by the Hong Kong and Shanghai Banking Corporation, with the assistance of Ch'en Sheng-hsiao, who had been connected with native banks in Shanghai and was to be the company's compradore.[187] Maitland would select the foreign staff and Ch'en the Chinese staff of the bank (Article 15). At the several branch offices as well, there were to be foreign managers with the Chinese compradores acting as assistant managers. Both the foreign managers and the compradores would be hired by the board of directors (Articles 11, 14).

Articles 16–22 of Sheng's regulations were devoted to the bank's interest and discount rates, note issue, coinage, loans, and balance sheet. Several points should be noted. First, the matter of coinage was explicitly left entirely in Sheng's hands (Article 19). His "General Plan" of November 1896 had proposed the minting and circulation of silver dollars equivalent in weight to the *ching-p'ing* or "Treasury" tael and 900 fine. Imperial authorization was received in December 1896 to mint 100,000 one-tael dollars and circulate them as a trial in the southern provinces. (As we have already recounted, Sheng was to be concerned with the matter of monetary reform until the fall of the dynasty.) Article 17 discussed the issue of bank notes, that is, paper currency; the amount which the bank could issue was limited to the value of its capital.[188] Finally, in what seems to be a move to prevent demands on the bank from possibly hostile provincial authorities, it was provided that the consent of the Hu-pu would be required before a loan could be made to any province (Article 18).

On March 14, 1897, Sheng received a reply from the Tsungli Yamen which raised nine objections to these draft regulations.[189] Five of the Yamen's reservations represented substantive points directly affecting the nature of the bank as Sheng had conceived it. First the Tsungli Yamen opposed the location of the head office in Shanghai. It took the position that because the bank was to be a semiofficial organ charged with the receipt and disbursement of government funds, it was proper that both the Shanghai and Peking offices be head offices, while all the others would be branches. This can, I think, be interpreted primarily as an objection on the part of the Tsungli Yamen officials to letting the bank get outside of the range of their influence. Sheng had intended the bank as a means of raising funds for his projects from the mercantile community of Shanghai, and particularly from "compradore capital" whose origins were in international trade. To locate in Peking would mean closer ties with government fiscal policy (*ts'ai-cheng*) than he desired. Sheng's reply to the Yamen stressed the need to locate the bank in Shanghai because it was the center of foreign trade and because it was where the shareholders were. He concluded with the interesting argument that the headquarters of the Shansi banks were in Shansi and not in Peking; and that the Hong Kong and Shanghai Banking Corporation had its head office in Hong Kong, while it maintained only a branch office in London, the English capital.[190]

Secondly, the Yamen was not satisfied with Sheng's stipulation that 20 per cent of the surplus (after all regular payments, including dividends, bonuses, and the reserve fund) should go to the government as *pao-hsiao*. It demanded 50 per cent, and 50 per cent of the profits from coinage as well. Sheng rejected this demand by citing the example of Western banks which paid no levies to their governments themselves, although the individual recipients of bank dividends might be taxed. Merchant investors were reluctant enough to risk their funds as it was, he argued. Increased exactions would frighten them away entirely. Sheng would concede some share of the bank's profits from coinage, but the equity of the bank and its shareholders should not be open to official levies.

The question of the bank's note issue was also raised. The Yamen stated that the provision in Article 19 limiting the amount of bank notes issued to the value of the bank's paid-up capital was inadequate. It asked that a silver reserve covering a specified percentage of the value of the bank's notes should be deposited in Peking or in a provincial treasury. Sheng agreed to maintain a cash reserve equivalent to 33⅓ per cent of the note issue, but he held that this should remain on the premises of the Imperial Bank of China. His reluctance to entrust the bank's cash reserves to official hands other than his own was probably well founded.

It is evident too that the Yamen had doubts about the purposes for which Sheng intended to use the bank's funds. It asked that the regulations include a stipulation providing that

the bank's capital must not be transferred for the purpose of establishing sundry kinds of industries or engaging in other kinds of commercial activity for profit. Nor must it be used to purchase buildings or land. And the maximum which can be loaned to any one business or single merchant must not exceed 10 per cent of the capital.

As a protection against the employment of the bank's assets for such prohibited ends, the Yamen called for an immediate report of all transactions involving more than Tls. 100,000. This information would normally not be available even in the semiannual balance sheet. Assent to these two measures would have directly contravened Sheng's intention to utilize the bank as a means of raising capital for his other enterprises. He rejected both out of hand. The bank would follow its own rules with regard to the lending of its funds. As to reporting large transactions, in the first place there were too many transactions of this size. Even more important, the bank's customers were not willing to have the government know of their financial affairs; compliance with this demand would result in a loss of business.

Although he had accepted only a few minor items among the changes which the Tsungli Yamen proposed in his draft regulations, in the end Sheng received the Yamen's consent to proceed with the establishment of the bank — but with the reservation that "the discussion of unsettled matters would be continued at the appropriate time." [191] In essence, the above exchange is a demonstration of the increased difficulty of establishing a *kuan-tu shang-pan* enterprise on the lines of the China Merchants' Company or the Telegraph Administration in the absence of a powerful provincial patron such as Li Hung-chang had been. The demands of the Yamen had been primarily for measures which would ensure that Peking officialdom retained control over the bank. When Li was at the height of his power, before 1895, he had been largely successful in keeping official supervision of such enterprises in his own hands; other sectors of the bureaucracy, metropolitan and provincial, had played only secondary roles. After 1896, with his newly acquired political status in the capital, Sheng would have liked to take on Li's former role in addition to his own. But he soon had to fall back on the support of the influential provincial leaders, Governors-general Chang Chih-tung and Wang Wen-shao.

Censorial Indictment. It is likely, though not certain, that the attack on the idea of a *kuan-tu shang-pan* modern-style bank which took place in April 1897 was related to the "unsettled matters" which remained from the exchange between Sheng and the Tsungli Yamen. On April 30, an edict was issued which took note of a recent indictment of the bank's status and organization by the censor Kuan T'ing-hsien. While the throne still favored the establishment of a bank, it was now less certain as to whether its management should be put into merchant hands. Wang Wen-shao and Chang Chih-tung were ordered to discuss the censor's charges with Sheng and to memorialize their views on the organization of the bank.[192] Although the memorial in reply to this edict was submitted over the names of Chang and Wang, it was Sheng who actually drafted the text. Chang at first was not disposed to add his signature. He changed his mind only after considerable urging from Wang Wen-shao, who took the position that having proposed Sheng to head the Imperial Railway Administration, Chang and he were obliged to back Sheng in this related matter.[193] Their memorial, therefore, was a strong defense of the proposed *kuan-tu shang-pan* bank.[194]

Chang Chih-tung and Wang Wen-shao took up each of the main criticisms which the censor Kuan had leveled against the bank. In answer to his objection to the use of the term *Chung-kuo,* China, in its name, they replied that the *Chung-kuo t'ung-shang yin-hang* was distinguished from other banks in that it received treasury funds for deposit, and that it would represent China in relations with foreigners. Kuan feared that in the event it was forced to suspend payments, the bank would seek to obtain government funds on the grounds that it was, as its name implied, an official organ. This, the two governors-general stated, would never come to pass: there was no danger that the bank would default, and in any case it would not appeal to the government. In these two instances, the censor was in effect challenging the semiofficial status of the Imperial Bank of China. He described it as an "officially established bank" (*kuan-she yin-hang*) with the implication that the management, too, ought to be entrusted to officials.

Kuan was also suspicious of the bank's joint-stock form of organization. This was implied in his demand that the safe return of the Hupu's Tls. 1,000,000 deposit be guaranteed by individual wealthy merchants. That is, the bank's corporate guarantee was not considered adequate. To this Chang and Wang answered that the "directors are themselves all rich merchants" who had invested several million taels of their own capital. They could be entrusted to safeguard the official funds which, in any case, would be repaid as soon as additional merchant capital was forthcoming.

Each of the above points concerned matters — the name of the bank, the Hu-pu deposit — which were already, so to speak, *faits accomplis*. But the censor's ardor to ensure that official tax funds entrusted to the bank would be transferred to Peking in cash could not be so easily brushed aside. As we shall see, failure to reach satisfactory settlement of this point effectively canceled out one of the exclusive privileges on which the bank had counted most, namely, that of transmitting taxes from the provinces to Peking as provided in Article 9 of its regulations. The issue, of course, concerned the fate of the not inconsiderable profits which were to be made from translating the local currency into that of the capital, and from such extras as "meltage" fees and commissions.[195] The provincial holders of these perquisites would hardly yield them without adequate compensation. For the time being, the memorialists evaded the issue with a declaration that "the [bank's] regulations only state that commercial advances can be transferred by draft. If specie is not offered, then of course the Hu-pu treasury will not accept payment."

In conclusion, Chang and Wang came out strongly for a bank under official supervision and merchant management: "Like the China Merchants' Company, let it be *shang-pan*, while the government supports and protects it. . . . Profit and loss should be entirely an affair of the merchants." They were, however, willing to concede that the bank's note issue should be more strictly limited. The maximum issue was set at 90 per cent of the paid-up capital, and a cash reserve was to be maintained equivalent to 33⅓ per cent of the value of the notes in circulation. In the event, this turned out to be a meaningless concession, as the bank's notes never reached the maximum. Wang and Chang agreed also that, in their respective capacities as commissioners for the northern and southern ports, they would inspect the bank's accounts semiannually to ensure that the cash reserve was maintained and that the bank's other obligations were being observed.

Capital and Management. The intercession of these two powerful officials was enough to swing the balance in Sheng's favor, and the establishment of the Imperial Bank of China as a *kuan-tu shang-pan* enterprise proceeded apace. Sheng headed the twelve-man board of directors who were also the bank's leading shareholders. In addition to his personal investment, Tls. 1,000,000 of the bank's capital came from two other *kuan-tu shang-pan* enterprises which Sheng managed.

At the same time he was primarily responsible for the bank's official business and its relations with the government. Being a high official himself, he had the privilege of submitting memorials to the throne, and the possibility of social intercourse with influential members of the metropolitan and provincial bureaucracies. Through these means he endeavored to obtain increased government support for the bank. Sheng's efforts as the bank's official head will be considered further in the following discussion.

Two hundred thousand taels from the China Merchants' Company's surplus (*yü-li*) and Tls. 600,000 which had been carried on the company's books as "self-insurance fund" were invested in shares of the newly organized Imperial Bank of China at the end of 1896.[196] Sheng also had Tls. 200,000 transferred from the surplus of the Telegraph Administration, thus providing the Tls. 1,000,000 from these enterprises which he had promised in the bank regulations.[197] The twelve directors including Sheng Hsuan-huai — and probably their relatives and friends — took Tls. 1,000,000 more of the bank's shares. Fortunately the names of these men (and in some cases additional information) are known. It should occasion no surprise that overwhelmingly they were merchants doing business in Shanghai or other treaty ports. Five out of eleven, aside from Sheng Hsuan-huai himself, were at some time associated with one or more of Sheng's other enterprises.

The career of Yen Hsin-hou (Yen I-pin), an expectant taotai originally from Ningpo, has been discussed in Chapter 1. Yen was a customs banker who joined his treaty-port banks to the new project. He held shares in the C.M.S.N. Co. and in 1909 was elected to its board of directors. Under Sheng's direction, he organized the first Chinese Chamber of Commerce in Shanghai and served as its chairman. The latter part of his life was devoted to the numerous industrial and commercial firms in Ningpo and elsewhere in which he had substantial investments.[198]

Yen Ying we have encountered as an officer of the China Merchants' Company and of the Hua-sheng Spinning and Weaving Mill. The bank's director Yang T'ing-kao was also a director of the Hua-sheng Mill, and later, in 1904, he was an official of the Telegraph Administration.[199] Shih Tse-ching has already been mentioned as a director of the China Merchants' Company, and as the promoter of two insurance companies in Shanghai. The last of Sheng's five followers on the first board of directors of the Imperial Bank of China was Chang Chen-hsun. Chang was a Cantonese who had served as Chinese consul-general at Singapore in 1895 and 1896. In that post he had tried to sell Peking-Hankow railroad shares to the overseas Chinese community. He was later on Sheng's staff as the Canton general-manager of the projected Canton-

Hankow railroad. He speculated in agricultural products in Canton, and in 1905 organized a company in Chefoo, Shantung, to make wine using Western brewing methods. In 1907–1909 Chang was the director of the Canton Chamber of Commerce.[200]

Two of the remaining directors were well-known treaty-port merchants. I have already recounted the career of Yeh Ch'eng-chung in Chapter 1. The other, Chu P'ei-chen, of Chekiang, was an expectant taotai who was the promoter of many industrial enterprises. Among them were a pottery factory in Kiangsu (capital $400,000), an oil pressing plant in Kiangsu (capital Tls. 300,000), the Ssu-ming Commercial Bank (capital Tls. 1,500,000), and the Hua-hsing Fire and Marine Insurance Company in Shanghai (capital Tls. 500,000). His associates in these projects included Yen Hsin-hou and Chang Chien. Chu also established a silk mill in Shanghai (capital Tls. 400,000); and he was a founder — together with Shen Tun-ho and Shih Tse-ching — of the Hua-an Life Insurance Company, the first in China.[201] In 1905–1906, Chu served as assistant director of the Shanghai Chinese Chamber of Commerce.

One other director, the taotai Yang Wen-chun, has been mentioned earlier in this chapter as Yang Shih-ch'i's successor at the head of the Imperial Telegraph Administration in 1907. For three members of the bank's board of directors there is no information available other than their names: they were Wang Wei,[202] Liu Hsueh-hsün, and Ch'en Hsien.[203]

Two things might be pointed out about the make-up of this first board of directors. First, there is no doubt that Sheng Hsuan-huai dominated it, both because of his personal contribution to the establishment of the company and because at least five of the other members of the board were known to be his supporters. Secondly, it is well to note that, as in the cases of the China Merchants' Company, the Telegraph Administration, and the Hua-sheng Mill, the "merchant" directors and managers included a proportion of men who held official titles and a few who may have had actual official posts at some time. Thus, in addition to Sheng, at least Yen Hsin-hou and Chu P'ei-chen were expectant taotais. And Chang Chen-hsun (described as a "cashiered official") had held a diplomatic post prior to becoming a director of the bank.

Although the constitution of the bank's board for later years is not known in detail, the available data support the view that the two conditions just noted continued at least until the establishment of the Hu-pu Bank in 1905. The bank's regulations, it will be remembered, provided that three of the twelve directors were to serve as managing directors in actual charge of the bank's operations. And in addition, there would be an auditor to certify the accounts.[204] Three men signed the bank's report for the second half of Kuang-hsü 32 (August 20, 1906–February 13, 1907) as managing directors: Shen Tun-ho, Wang Ts'un-shan, and Ku Jun-chang. The signature of the auditor was Wang Ko-ch'en.[205] All four of these men were at some time associated with Sheng Hsuan-huai's other enterprises, and at least two of them held official titles.

Shen Tun-ho served as a managing director of the Imperial Bank of China at least from 1905. He may possibly have replaced Sheng Hsuan-huai whose·other commitments were too great to permit his continuing to give personal attention to the bank. Shen was born in Ningpo in 1857, the son of a tea merchant. He studied in England for a year and held many minor official positions after his return. In 1902–1903, he was co-director of the Bureau of Mines and Railways (*K'uang-wu t'ieh-lu tsung-chü*), and until 1905 he was on Sheng's staff as one of the two commissioners (*tsung-pan*) of the Shanghai-Nanking railroad. Shen held the rank of taotai. Together with Chu P'ei-chen and Shih Tse-ching, he founded the first life insurance company in China, the Hua-an Life Insurance Company.[206]

Wang Ts'un-shan, it will be remembered, was an expectant taotai who replaced Hsü Jun at the head of the China Merchants' Company in 1907 and managed that company in Sheng's interest until it came under the control of the Ministry of Posts and Communications.

In addition to serving as auditor of the China Merchants' Company, Ku Jun-chang was the founder of several industrial firms. These included a cigarette manufacturing company in Shanghai (capital Tls 100,000), and a machine shop, the Yangtze Machine Manufacturing Company (capital Tls. 175,000), in Hankow in which Sheng Hsuan-huai's Hanyang Ironworks also had an interest.[207] As for Wang Ko-ch'en, who is listed as the bank's auditor in 1906–1907, he is also known to have been an officer of the Hanyang Ironworks. Probably his designation of *shang-wu tsung-kuan* is best translated as "business manager" of the ironworks.[208]

The Imperial Bank of China thus was in the hands of men — merchants or businessmen for the most part, but also including a generous sprinkling of official titles — very similar in character to those who operated the other *kuan-tu shang-pan* enterprises that have been discussed. It is doubtful that, any more than in the China Merchants' Company, "all mandarinic etiquette and custom" were "unhesitatingly tabooed and only such in vogue in commercial institutions, pure and simple, . . . adhered to." There is, however, no direct evidence that the bank suffered serious harm from its bureaucratic administration.[209] Judging from the experience of the C.M.S.N. Co., it may be inferred that bureaucratic management was a handicap in the competition with foreign banks. But the main reasons for the failure of Sheng's project to realize the goals that he had set for it must be sought elsewhere.

Failure to Become a Central Bank. In 1896 Sheng had seen the bank as an organ for raising private Chinese capital for the construction of the Peking-Hankow railroad. But efforts to raise the Tls. 7,000,000 which Sheng had expected to obtain from private investors proved fruitless.[210] He (and Chang Chih-tung and Wang Wen-shao) soon realized that except for an initial outlay by Peking, completion of the line would depend on foreign loans. As Sheng informed the throne in 1898: "The Imperial Railway Administration originally intended to depend on raising private capital. But Chinese merchants will only come forward when the construction is completed and profits are visible. . . . It is rarely heard that private merchants and common people buy stock. They may be attracted by a completed enterprise, but it is impossible to depend on them for any new undertaking.[211] One of the principal roles which he had seen for the newly established bank was thus eliminated. To protect its business position, Sheng turned to Peking in an attempt to transform the Imperial Bank of China into what its name implied it already was — a central bank.

What Sheng specifically sought was to actualize the bank's theoretical privilege of acting as agent for the transfer of funds between the provinces and Peking. In the summer of 1898 he memorialized the throne expounding the key importance of the bank's success for China's commercial development in the face of foreign economic aggression.[212] The Imperial Bank of China was weaker than its foreign competitors in the treaty ports and needed government support. "Hereafter, in expanding China's commercial strength and recovering our economic rights, the controlling factor will be whether or not provincial receipts and payments are transferred through the Imperial Bank of China." If they were handled, as before, by native transfer banks and money shops,

then our commercial policy will suffer the scorn of the foreigners and the suspicion of the Chinese. . . . The effect on the general commercial situation can be great . . . as the bank brings both visible and invisible benefits to the country. If trade is flourishing, the merchants and people are better off — that is the invisible benefit. The greater the profits of the bank, the more income to the government [through *pao-hsiao* and other perquisites] — that is the visible benefit.

Sheng requested the throne to order the Ministry of Revenue to inform the provinces that thereafter all transfers of official funds should be undertaken through the Imperial Bank of China. It would not be too farfetched to compare this request and its purpose to similar demands by Li Hung-chang for the grant of a monopoly of tribute rice carriage to the China Merchants' Company. In each instance the transfer of tax receipts was involved: taxes in kind in the case of the tribute rice, money taxes in the present case. Just as the tribute rice monopoly had been the equivalent of a handsome subsidy for the C.M.S.N. Co., Sheng hoped that the bank would benefit from the transfer of provincial specie payments to the capital.

Sheng's memorial was referred to the Ministry of Revenue which gave its general assent on the grounds that "the bank was established by the government. If the government in the first instance does not put trust in it, how can it be expected that the merchants and people will put their trust in it?" However, the matter was one that should be dealt with according to the merits of each specific case. Provincial officials should be ordered to use the facilities of the bank for transfers and deposits whenever the bank's charges were lower and dividends higher than those of the Shansi banks and money shops.[213] An edict issued on July 13, 1898, confirmed this position and ordered the Hu-pu to "inform provincial officials that in all places where there are branches of the Imperial Bank of China, if the transfer of government funds and aids (*hsieh-hsiang*) is found to be conducted at lower cost, that function shall be turned over to the Imperial Bank of China to undertake with care, in order to favor commercial development." [214]

But somewhat more than a year later, in November 1899, Sheng was still complaining to the throne that the edict was not being observed. The accounts of the bank's ten branches showed that only rarely were official funds transferred through their facilities. And the provincial officials had refused to negotiate agreements with Sheng as the edict of July 13 had ordered. He was much distressed, he said, that the Chinese were not supporting this Chinese bank, while foreign governments all deal with the banks of their respective countries.[215] It is clear that provincial resistance to giving up the perquisites connected with the transfer of funds was too great for Sheng to overcome. The interests involved were considerably more influential than the *sha-ch'uan* operators and their official supervisors who had been replaced by the steamers of the C.M.S.N. Co. Not only was Sheng not able to transform his Imperial Bank of China into a real central bank handling all government receipts and disbursements, but the establishment by the government of a national bank was, as we shall see, already in the offing.

The failure of the *kuan-tu shang-pan* Imperial Bank of China to obtain the monopoly grant which it sought did not, however, mean the financial collapse of the bank. No doubt its attraction as an investment — without the informal but lucrative perquisites which control of the transfer of provincial tax funds would have brought — was reduced for men like Sheng. For some time the bank was unable to pay its guaranteed dividend of 8 per cent. But it never paid less than 6 per cent, and the volume of its commercial business increased steadily although very slowly. The net profit and dividend paid in four semiannual periods for which data are available are shown in Table 23 below.[214] The bank's balance sheet for the same periods is given in Table 24. It should be noted that the Tls. 1,000,000 deposited by the Ministry of Revenue in 1897 was gradually repaid. By the end of 1906, the balance had been reduced to Tls. 200,000. On the other hand, commercial deposits showed a considerable increase in the same period, and an even larger jump between 1906 and 1913. These two developments, in conjunction with several others to be discussed presently, may be taken to mark a significant change in the bank's status.

Table 23

Imperial Bank of China, Net Profit and Dividend Paid, 1898–1913
(in Shanghai taels)

	Net profit	Rate (per cent)	Dividend
KH 24/1–6 (January 22–August 16, 1898)	130,370	8	100,000
KH 24/7–12 (August 17, 1898–February 9, 1899)	111,048	8	100,000
KH 32/7–12 (August 20, 1906–February 12, 1907)	108,009	6	75,000
July 1–December 31, 1913	121,289	8[a]	100,000

[a] This is stated to be the first time in many years that 8 per cent was paid.

As early as the autumn of 1903, Sheng Hsuan-huai learned that the Ministry of Revenue was discussing plans for the organization of a national bank. Among the shareholders of the Imperial Bank of China, this news brought forth proposals to transfer their capital to other uses. But Sheng, although he had failed to obtain the important concession for the transfer of provincial funds, apparently was not yet ready to give up the bank. He saw an important role for his firm in circulating the new, unified currency which presumably would result from the establishment of a national bank.[217] However, financial ties with the government were reduced as the Hu-pu's deposit with the Imperial Bank of China was refunded; and Sheng himself was out of office for a long period after 1905. Moreover, the establishment of the Hu-pu Bank in 1905 did not produce the unified national currency which Sheng had hoped for. The official status of the Imperial Bank of China, in a word, withered away. This process was helped by the opening of a second government bank, the Bank of Communications (*Chiao-t'ung yin-hang*), in 1908, and by the reorganization of the Hu-pu Bank into the Ta-Ch'ing Bank with a capital of Tls. 10,000,000 in the same year.[218] While the Imperial Bank of China (*Chung-kuo t'ung-shang yin-hang*) continued to exist as a private commercial bank, Sheng's interest ended with the decline of its *kuan-tu shang-pan* status. In 1910 the China

Table 24

Imperial Bank of China Balance Sheet, 1898–1913 (in Shanghai taels[a])

Liabilities	KH 24/1–6	KH 24/7–12	KH 32/7–12	Second half 1913
1. Paid-up capital	2,500,000	2,500,000	2,500,000	2,500,000
2. Hu-pu deposit	1,000,000	1,000,000	200,000	—
3. Other deposits	974,867	1,671,032	1,742,788	3,898,031
4. Bills payabie	76,686	172,077	402,447	217,101
5. Notes in circulation	—	287,306	1,705,238	1,250,650
6. Reserve	181,071	192,119	401,293	1,057,889
7. Balance between head office and branches	38,179	—	—	—
Totals	4,743,804[b]	5,822,536	6,951,767	8,923,672
Assets				
1. Cash	53,316	387,630	286,505	2,128,001
2. Loans outstanding	4,486,288	3,953,373	5,990,778	5,388,903
3. Bills receivable	156,297	1,255,881	123,626	396,942
4. Bank premises	28,621	42,467	13,798	10,748
5. Furniture and stationery	14,280	40,550	24,965	3,000
6. Balance between head office and branches	—	142,631	512,093	996,076
Totals	4,743,804[b]	5,822,536	6,951,767	8,923,672

[a] Fractional taels have been omitted; therefore addition of the columns of figures may show minor variations from the totals given in the table.

[b] The figures for KH 24/1–6 (which I give here exactly as they were printed in NCH, March 6, 1899, 392) are obviously garbled. Liabilities in fact add up to 4,770,803; assets to 4,738,803. Surely item 7 under Liabilities should be placed under assets as was done in other years.

Merchants' Company liquidated one half of its Tls. 800,000 holdings in the bank by distributing its shares in lieu of dividends. The remaining Tls. 400,000 was liquidated in the same manner in 1911. Presumably Sheng too sold his personal shares at about the same time.[219]

The Chung-kuo t'ung-shang yin-hang, now known as the Commercial Bank of China, was still in existence in the early 1930's. In 1933 its capital was recorded as Tls. 2,500,000. The head office was located, as before, in Shanghai; and there were branches in Ningpo, Nanking, Hankow, and Tinghai. But no member of the Sheng family was listed among its chief officers. The first modern Chinese bank, which Sheng Hsuan-huai had seen as the cornerstone of a vast commercial and industrial empire, and had hoped to make into China's first central bank, was reduced to a second-rate private firm, dwarfed by the official quartet which dominated banking in Kuomintang China.[220]

The histories of these three enterprises are remarkably similar. They were, first, all parts of Sheng Hsuan-huai's economic empire. Moreover, their careers illustrate the same basic features of the *kuan-tu shang-pan* system. For each of them the part played by a powerful official patron was decisive in its early years. They were all dependent on treaty-port or compradore capital and secondarily on funds from gentry investors; financial assistance from official sources was limited to short-term loans. In each case, the management of the firm was in the hands of officials or compradore-officials. They were all in different degrees burdened with official exactions. And finally, each of these three *kuan-tu shang-pan* companies sought to obtain a monopoly of its field of enterprise. As long as their monopolies were maintained, their promoters and investors profited handsomely. Invariably, the ending of their monopoly status saw a movement away from the *kuan-tu shang-pan* pattern on which they had been established.

7

Conclusion: Toward "Bureaucratic Capitalism"

Despite their importance to the historian as indices of China's response to the West in the last part of the nineteenth century, the *kuan-tu shang-pan* industries remained marginal undertakings within their own environment. Their establishment and operation did not represent a fundamental break with the traditional agrarian economy and the conservative economic outlook which reflected it. China would have to go through three revolutions, foreign invasion, and civil war before a concerted and relentless effort to industrialize would be begun.

The *kuan-tu shang-pan* system was in fact a compromise with traditional institutions and patterns of behavior. It provided a vehicle whereby the overwhelming inertia of an imperial political system and Confucian ideology, the basis of which was a society founded on prescientific intensive agriculture, could be adjusted to the compelling need for modern industry and means of communication. But the modern-type enterprises started in China in the latter part of the Ch'ing dynasty failed to develop into a genuine "industrial revolution." Perhaps the most important lesson to be drawn from this checkmate is the following: one institutional breakthrough is worth a dozen textile mills or shipping companies established within the framework of the traditional society and its system of values.

Three examples will serve to suggest the whole. In terms of its ultimate contribution to economic change, to overturn the low status accorded to the merchant in traditional Chinese society would be a greater achievement than developing a coal mine. Similarly, replacement of the negative or passive attitude of the government towards economic activity (other than the preservation of the time-honored agricultural economy) would have far greater consequences than erecting two or three more plants like the Hanyang Ironworks. To put this point in another way, what was needed was the replacement of the traditional Chinese preoccupation with dividing a static economic pie — the agrarian surplus — among landlords, merchants, and officials, with a recognition of the need for and possibility of increasing the size of the pie. And, one more example, the substitution of universal and specific criteria of managerial ability and business success for such diffuse and particularistic considerations as kinship ties and overriding obligation to family and clan would have greater influence on China's economic development than the completion of a railroad trunkline.

It may be argued that this dichotomy is a false one, that institutional breakthrough and the establishment of modern enterprises are in fact interdependent processes. From a long-range historical perspective this objection may be well-founded. The industries organized by Sheng Hsuan-huai represented a chipping away at institutional barriers and thereby contributed to establishing the preconditions for a later breakthrough. This study has perforce attempted to stay within the boundaries of economic and social history, but never with the presumption that the whole story of China's response to the West could be told from that vantage point alone. Certainly recent efforts to assess modern China's intellectual history, in particular the work of J. R. Levenson,[1] have demonstrated the extent to which once deep-rooted beliefs and traditional attitudes that had been an integral part of the old society were being undermined. And to this corruption of the traditional Confucian order the industrialization effort here described contributed its considerable share. Nevertheless, from the shorter perspective of an evaluation of China's pre-1911 industrialization effort, the *kuan-tu shang-pan* compromise did not materially undermine these institutional barriers. It came to terms with them, to all appearances because only by so doing could any progress at all be made in introducing enterprises of the type discussed in this study. After longer or shorter periods of initial success, these firms in the end were overwhelmed by the weight of traditional practices, bureaucratic motivation, and official exactions.

In the expression *kuan-tu shang-pan* itself, we see reflected a dichotomy between official (*kuan*) and merchant (*shang*) which reveals the underlying negative attitude towards commercial enterprise in a saturated agricultural society. The official (or government) was suspicious of the merchant who was a competitor with the landlord and bureaucrat for the surpluses of peasant production. Although he too, in the last analysis, lived on the proceeds of the traditional economy, the presence of the merchant might upset the equilibrium that had been reached among three interests: (1) the minimum return to the peasantry consonant with further production (and reproduction!); (2) rents and interest on usury for the landlord-gentry; and (3) the bureaucrat's perquisites in the form of taxation or less legitimate "squeeze." Therefore the activities of the merchant were regulated in the interest of the *status quo* by the official, whose existence was most directly dependent on the continued operation of the equilibrium. Government monopolies of commerce in such essential commodities as salt and iron, which extend back at least to the beginning of the imperial epoch in the Han dynasty, are to be seen in this light. Through them the merchant was licensed and his activities kept within safe limits, while he and the government together shared in the profits of commerce.

The late nineteenth-century *kuan-tu shang-pan* industries continued this same pattern of relations between official and merchant. In most general terms, merchant management was to be guided by official supervision. There were two specific ways, moreover, in which the dominant role of the bureaucrat was maintained and the merchant pure and simple constrained. First, the treaty-port merchant who had made good tended to be assimilated to the official bureaucracy. He could and did use his money to purchase official titles, thereby acquiring not only the title but inevitably some of the outlook of officialdom as well. The compradore, whatever the extent of his contacts with Occidentals and with Western ways, thus identified himself with the traditional order and supported it with his contributions. Secondly, the position of the treaty-port merchant was never allowed to be secure. Like the salt merchants, who also depended on government favor and support, he was always liable to official exactions on his personal wealth or the assets of his enterprises.

But at the same time that the official sought to regulate mercantile activity and keep it within safe dimensions in regard to its scope and size, he was not averse to profiting personally from commerce. It was taxed and "squeezed" for the benefit of government coffers and private purses. Beyond this, and despite legislation forbidding it, the Confucian official would himself engage clandestinely in commercial activity under the cover of some merchant accomplice. This means of seeking after personal gain, however, was not equivalent to the legitimization of commercial endeavor or the acceptance of equal status for merchants as a class.

New motives for official involvement in commercial affairs appeared in the latter half of the nineteenth century. Out of the suppression of the great Taiping Rebellion, there came into existence a number of regional foci of political and military power headed by the gentry-officials whose armies had defeated the Heavenly Kingdom of Great Peace. While they did not openly contest with Peking for hegemony, Li Hung-chang and Chang Chih-tung in particular became the effective governors of north and central China respectively. The exertions of these regional leaders from the 1870's until the end of the century provided a sharp contrast to the passivity and weakness of the imperial government. It was Li and Chang who, proceeding on the basis of the "self-strengthening" ideology which they helped to fashion, sought to meet the challenge, or threat, of the Occident. As part of their program of self-strengthening these officials sponsored the foundation of arsenals and then of commercial manufacturing enterprises within the regions that they dominated. But the *kuan-tu shang-pan* enterprises thus established did not represent to their patrons an effort to remake the fundamental bases of traditional society. These mines, textile mills, and so on, were at once to bolster Li's and Chang's regional power, and simultaneously to hold the line against the West while an effort was made to strengthen China's traditional bases. In the oft-quoted dichotomy, they were the "instruments" (*yung*) by means of which the "essence" (*t'i*) of traditional, Confucian, agrarian China was to be preserved.

While the industrialization effort of the late Ch'ing period was thus not designed to subvert the old order, the *kuan-tu shang-pan* firms which it begot did have to cope somehow with the principal obstacles standing in the way of the development of modern industry on even a limited scale. These impediments (which have had to be faced in more recent decades as well) may be conveniently summarized under five headings: foreign competition, governmental weakness, inadequate capital, technical backwardness, and deficient motivation.

This study has looked only in a cursory way at the problem of foreign economic pressure on China. A comprehensive picture of the impact of European manufactured imports, financial institutions, and shipping on China's nineteenth-century economy still waits to be produced. Undoubtedly, the handicraft textile industry, which had been an important supplement to peasant income, was undermined by imported Lancashire cottons. In the coastal carrying trade, native junks could not compete with steamers. And, from 1895, foreign manufacturing establishments in Shanghai and other treaty ports contended with Chinese firms for the domestic market. Given an artificially low tariff and the privileges of extraterritoriality, and able to depend on highly developed industrial economies in their home countries, foreign merchants and manufacturers operated at an advantage. Furthermore, the large indemnity and loan payments to foreign creditors after 1895 represented a siphoning off of a significant portion of China's all too small capital surplus. The sum of these developments was imperialist domination of the modern sector of China's economy, and the effect, on balance and when the political side of imperialism is taken into account, was probably to handicap economic growth within China.

The *kuan-tu shang-pan* system attempted to cope with foreign economic domination by the grant of monopoly rights to industries established under official auspices. This in effect was to guarantee to Chinese firms at least that portion of the market which the government was able to influence. The China Merchants' Company's tribute rice franchise, or

Han-Yeh-P'ing's concession to supply rails for the Peking-Hankow railroad may be cited as examples. In addition to its monopoly status, the *kuan-tu shang-pan* firm in its early years might sometimes secure short-term government loans to tide it over until it had raised adequate capital from private investors. But neither the imperial government nor the regional patrons of these enterprises were in a position to alter the basic facts which secured the position of Western commerce and industry in China. Li Hung-chang, despite much pressure on him, was able to keep foreign textile mills out of Shanghai until 1895; but after the disastrous defeat by the Japanese, even this last defense was breached. Only in 1928 did the Nationalist government recover tariff autonomy; and only under the present Maoist regime have the provisions of the Shimonoseki Treaty been effectively repealed.

The growing impotence of the imperial government in the last decades of the Ch'ing dynasty has been noted by many students. In part this development can be ascribed to its increasing financial embarrassment, in part to the ignominy of successive defeat in three wars and the effects of an almost successful peasant revolution, certainly in part to aggravation of Sino-Manchu differences as the dynasty weakened. Peking was unable to assume the direction of even a limited program of self-strengthening and modernization. Possibly the situation would have changed radically if the "Hundred Days Reform" of 1898 had had a more happy outcome. But the "Manchu Reform Movement" which followed was at best designed only to maintain the dynasty. In these circumstances, the *kuan-tu shang-pan* pattern permitted some degree of leadership in "foreign matters" to be given by powerful regional figures such as Governor-general Li, and by those gentry-officials who, like Sheng Hsuan-huai, saw the importance of economic self-strengthening. Sheng's shortcomings as an industrial entrepreneur resulting from his family, local, and class loyalties set limits to what he could achieve. In like manner, the type of regional power which Li Hung-chang held could not take the place of a vigorous, national directing authority comparable, for example, to the Meiji oligarchy which governed Japan.

The political weakness and disunity of China continued on into the Republican era as major obstacles to economic development. Even the period of Kuomintang hegemony was never so free of internal dissension or external aggression that the government, had it so willed, could have undertaken and supported a program of all-out industrialization. For the Communist regime, the transformation of China into an industrial power has become the first goal of a powerful state apparatus able to subordinate all else to its achievement.

Inadequate capital accumulation was, of course, endemic to China's circular flow economy. Furthermore, such savings as were realized were normally, for reasons of security and prestige, put back into agriculture, either by the purchase of additional land or in the form of loans, often at usurious rates, to the peasantry. To secure capital for their projects, Li Hung-chang and Sheng Hsuan-huai turned to the treaty-port compradore who, since the "opening" of China, had been making his fortune in Shanghai and elsewhere from the profits of trade with the foreigner. Compradore capital, however, was strictly limited in quantity. The profits of China's foreign trade, and of banking in the treaty ports and shipping between them, even if they had gone entirely into Chinese purses, were not a broad enough foundation on which to base a large scale industrialization effort. Moreover, there were strong pressures to invest these funds not in modern industry but in real estate and pawnshops. The fact of Sheng's own investment in the *kuan-tu shang-pan* enterprises which he managed suggests that, to some degree, these firms could also attract capital from the gentry-landlord class, especially as a handsome guaranteed return on the investment was an essential ingredient of the *kuan-tu shang-pan* formula. Utilization of the proceeds of taxation on agriculture, as in Meiji Japan, to start certain key industrial projects on their way was interdicted by the political circumstances of China in the nineteenth century. At best, Sheng's firms could sometimes secure short-term government loans through the intervention of their provincial patrons. In short, the savings potential of the agricultural sector of the economy was hardly touched at all as a possible source of industrial capital.

China's government in the Republican era remained as completely divorced from control of the land tax revenue as its Ch'ing predecessor had been. The present regime, by means of forced savings in agriculture and the employment of the labor surplus in the countryside on capital construction projects — both policies made possible by the degree of its political control — is making a relentless attempt to overcome the shortage of capital.

The fourth problem to which the *kuan-tu shang-pan* system had to adjust was one of an environment characterized by a profound technical backwardness. There were neither trained personnel experienced in the management of industrial projects nor facilities for training them. This situation was met in a partial way by the employment of those same compradores whose capital was sought for the new enterprises. Some, like Tong King-sing, had acquired considerable familiarity with the operation of the foreign firms who employed them or in which they had invested. They were thus better qualified than the usual run of lower rank officials to handle the business end of the China Merchants' Company and other firms. But the number of such qualified persons was never large, and in any case the treaty-port merchant suffered from certain severe disabilities. Despite his business experience he was not technically trained; the more technical aspects of the companies' affairs had to be put in charge of foreign employees. Thus the Telegraph Administration employed Danish technicians, the China Merchants' Company had the services of Morse and the marine superintendent Roberts, Danforth supervised the Hua-sheng Cotton Mill, and Maitland the Imperial Bank of China. Sheng Hsuan-huai's establishment and support of modern schools in Tientsin and Shanghai were limited efforts to solve the problem of providing Chinese technical personnel to staff his enterprises.

Moreover, the compradore, even if he had purchased official rank, did not have sufficient influence to manage the complex official transactions in which the *kuan-tu shang-pan* firms were continuously involved. This responsibility was assumed by the official managers, such as Sheng Hsuan-huai, for the enterprises in which they had an interest, and by such men as Chang Chien for other companies. By specializing in the direction of the affairs of modern-type industrial enterprises these men were departing somewhat from the pattern of the theoretically omnicompetent Confucian official. Much of Sheng's official career was devoted to the administration of such projects and to the conduct of negotiations with foreigners. He acquired thereby a competence as an executive which was acknowledged by his Western peers. Notwithstanding their specialization, the official managers of *kuan-tu shang-pan* undertakings remained officials; it was their place in the Confucian bureaucracy which provided the leverage indispensable for conducting the official business of the firms they headed.

In the Republican period, a greater number of Chinese studied abroad, and the development of a modern educational system in China itself was furthered. But in terms of the potential need — if radical economic changes were to be undertaken — the number of trained personnel supplied was minute. And these people for the most part were absorbed into the government bureaucracy. The supply of competent technicians and executives has continued to be a major problem for the industrialization program of the Communist regime. Even with the aid of Russian experts and an expansion of the educational system, the matter is still a long way from solution.

The problem of motivation has come up several times throughout this study. Within its terms is encompassed a psycho-ideological block which played its part in obstructing a solution in each of the areas just discussed. "Self-strengthening," which underlay the establishment of the *kuan-tu shang-pan* firms of the late Ch'ing period, proved too shallow a font of inspiration. Its failure can be attributed to the fact that it was not accompanied by the institutional changes which might have marshaled the support of wider circles of the populace behind it. Only such a transformation could have overcome, at least in strategic areas, the weight of family and local ties, the low valuation of mercantile and industrial activity, and the shortcomings of the traditional relations between official and merchant. These remained a drag on the outlook and response even of those men most directly connected with trade and industry. Apparently nationalism, unaided, was not a much better motor than self-strengthening, although this judgment may need to be modified by a consideration of the totally unfavorable international circumstances in which the Kuomintang government existed after 1931. The present regime has sought to combine nationalism with Marxism-Leninism as a generator of change — with what success in the long run remains to be seen.

The *kuan-tu shang-pan* enterprises which faced these obstacles were all pioneering ventures. Their promoters were undertaking industrial projects for which there were no precedents on the Chinese scene. That they operated at all in the unpromising circumstances that have just been described, weighs somewhat in the balance against their failure to develop into a more extensive industrial revolution. One outstanding feature of the record of these firms, as presented in the preceding chapters, is the appearance over and over again of the same names, of the same small group of men whose funds and enterprise made possible the initiation of the China Merchants' Company, the Telegraph Administration, the Hua-sheng Mill, Han-Yeh-P'ing, the Imperial Bank of China, and other like undertakings. The corollary to this phenomenon was the passing back and forth among these firms of the same limited supply of venture capital. These circumstances are of course a reflection of the shortages of capital and trained personnel which have already been recounted. They also highlight the pioneering aspect of the *kuan-tu shang-pan* companies: a few men operating on the margin of the traditional society to establish institutions which in the long run would contribute to the disintegration of the old order.

Despite their pioneering character and the fact that they were only a handful, the *kuan-tu shang-pan* companies controlled by Sheng Hsuan-huai showed a range and diversity which are altogether remarkable. Heavy industry (coal and iron mines, a steel plant), light manufacturing (textile mills), communications (a steamship company, telegraph lines, and railroads), and finance (a modern-style bank) were all represented. It is undeniably a considerable achievement for one man to have pioneered in all these fields, especially in the unpropitious environment of late Ch'ing China. It is all the more notable that Sheng should have undertaken and managed these enterprises while following an active political career in Peking. While due credence must be given to the well-founded belief of his contemporaries that more than a little of Sheng's fortune was founded on corruption and sharp dealing, and that a substantial part of his political influence was purchased, there nevertheless remains a residue of achievement which establishes him as an exceptional personage.

Sheng and his associates realized good returns from the enterprises they directed. When even their legitimate profit averaged 8–10 per cent on their investment, these men, who also had access to large unrecorded perquisites, would certainly have acknowledged that their venture was being amply rewarded. The rich fruits enjoyed by the promoters and shareholders were not, however, reflected in the growth of their projects. So long as the barriers described above were not shattered, there were definite limits to the growth potential of these enterprises. Since they were unable to break out of the framework of the old order, an accommodation had to be found to the traditional society and its values. In the enterprises which have been described, this accommodation invariably took the form of accenting the monopoly patents which the firms in question had received. The possibility of expansion was circumscribed by foreign economic pressure, official indifference if not outright rapacity, capital and personnel shortages, and by the total framework of values in which the *kuan-tu shang-pan* enterprises existed. Their monopoly position, however, could be relied on to sustain the profits and perquisites and protect the capital investment of the promoters. In a word, after an initial period of growth and expansion, the modern-type enterprises which Sheng Hsuan-huai founded tended to be transformed into institutions for the protection of bureaucratic capital.

While the *kuan-tu shang-pan* industries did not eventuate into a basic transformation of the Chinese economy, they unhappily foreshadowed a pattern of industrial organization which would be continued in China until the middle of the twentieth century. Sheng may be seen as standing halfway between the "self-strengtheners" and such successors in more recent times as Liang Shih-yi and Yeh Kung-cho of the so-called "Communications Clique," and T. V. Soong and H. H. Kung of the Kuomintang. While Li Hung-chang did not hesitate to profit personally from the enterprises that he sponsored, his support of modern-type industry was clearly part of a larger concern with diplomacy and national defense and with the development of his regional power. For Sheng, the acquisition of a large fortune from his modern industrial and commercial firms was still in large part a means to acquire political power and office, the highest goals of traditional Chinese society. In the cases of Liang, Yeh, Soong, and Kung, men originally of only moderate personal means, what stands out is the direct utilization of their high places in the governing bureaucracy in order to benefit their private economic interests or buttress those of their political group. Here we may see a link between the *kuan-tu shang-pan* system, which conditioned efforts at industrialization in the late nineteenth century, and the "bureaucratic capitalism" of more recent decades, which stood in the way of efforts to modernize China within a democratic framework.

NOTES

INDEX

ABBREVIATIONS USED IN THE NOTES

(See bibliographies for full citation and characters)

CTS-HCP: Chiao-t'ung shih (History of communications [in China]). *Hang-cheng pien* (section on shipping).

CTS-LCP: Chiao-t'ung shih, Lu-cheng pien (section on railroads and motor roads).

CTS-TCP: Chiao-t'ung shih, Tien-cheng pien (section on telegraphs, telephone, and radio).

CWHK-Memorials: Memorials (*tsou-i*) by Chang Chih-tung in *Chang Wen-hsiang-kung ch'üan-chi* (Complete papers).

Hummel: Arthur W. Hummel, ed., *Eminent Chinese of the Ch'ing Period.*

Letterbooks: "Letterbooks of H. B. Morse," ms., Houghton Library, Harvard University.

LWCK-Letters: Letters (*p'eng-liao han-kao*) by Li Hung-chang in *Li Wen-chung-kung ch'üan-chi* (Complete papers).

LWCK-Memorials: Memorials (*tsou-kao*) by Li, *ibid.*

LWCK-Telegrams: Telegrams (*tien-kao*) by Li, *ibid.*

LWCK-TLYM Correspondence: Communications to the Tsungli Yamen (*I-shu han-kao*), *ibid.*

NCH: North-China Herald.

NKSPTCP: Nung-kung-shang pu t'ung-chi piao (Statistical tables of the Ministry of Agriculture, Industry, and Commerce).

THHL-KH: Tung-hua hsü-lu, Kuang-hsü-ch'ao (Continuation of the Tung-hua records, Kuang-hsü reign).

YCTK: Sheng shang-shu Yü-chai ts'un-kao ch'u-k'an (Collected drafts of Board President Sheng Hsuan-huai).

TC: the T'ung-chih reign, 1862–1874.
KH: the Kuang-hsü reign, 1875–1908.
HT: the Hsuan-t'ung reign, 1909–1911.

Notes

Only the author and title of works cited are given in these notes; see the bibliographies for fuller data. Unless otherwise indicated, all translations in the text and notes are my own. Where the translated title of a Chinese work appears in quotation marks in the notes, I have merely copied the translation given as a subtitle in the work itself; I am responsible for the translation of all other titles.

CHAPTER 1

Official Supervision and Merchant Management

1. For general accounts see Kung Chün, *Chung-kuo hsin-kung-yeh fa-chan-shih ta-kang* (An outline history of the development of modern industry in China), and Ssu-yü Teng and John K. Fairbank, *China's Response to the West: A Documentary Survey, 1839–1923*, 61–131.

2. The data here are compiled from the *Nung-kung-shang-pu t'ung-chi piao* (Statistical tables of the Ministry of Agriculture, Industry, and Commerce), *Ti-i-tz'u* (First collection, 1908) and *Ti-erh-tz'u* (Second collection, 1909), cited respectively as *NKSPTCP-I* and *NKSPTCP-II*, followed by the *chüan* and page number, as, for example, *NKSPTCP-I*, 3.6b.

The data in the following secondary studies correspond in varying degrees with those presented in this section and are probably ultimately derived from the publications of the ministry through a complicated process of filiation: Tezuka Masao, *Shina jūkōgyō hattatsu shi* (History of the development of Chinese heavy industry), 98, Table 35; Kung Chün, *op. cit.*, 69–71, Table 6; Yang Ch'üan, "Wu-shih-nien-lai Chung-kuo chih kung-yeh" ("China's Industrial Enterprises for the Past 50 Years"), 5–6, Table 2; Asobe Kyuzō, "Chūgoku kindai kōgyō no hatten" (Development of modern industry in China), 178–179, Table 2.

3. The text of the "Company Law" appears in *Ta-Ch'ing Kuang-hsü hsin-fa-ling* (New laws and ordinances of the Kuang-hsü reign), 16.2a–11b; it has been translated by E. T. Williams in *Recent Chinese Legislation Relating to Commercial, Railway, and Mining Enterprises*, 10–45.

4. *NKSPTCP-I*, 5.4b–6a and *passim*. On Chang Chien (1853–1926), see Teng and Fairbank, *op. cit.*, 215, 216, 219. The word "tael" (a Portuguese modification of the Malay *tahil*, "weight") is the usual translation of the Chinese word *liang*, "ounce," when the latter is employed in a monetary sense. Unless otherwise indicated, tael (Tl.) as used in this study refers to the standard unit of account current in Shanghai, the "Shanghai tael" of 524.93 grains of fine silver. In the late nineteenth century, there were three taels of currency which had a more or less national range, in addition to a number of local taels such as that current in Shanghai. The value in United

States dollars of the "Haikwan" or "Customs" tael (which differed only slightly from the Shanghai tael) stood at $1.60 in 1872, and thereafter steadily fell to a low of $0.63 in 1902. At five year intervals the equivalents were as follows: 1877, $1.47; 1882, $1.38; 1887, $1.20; 1892, $1.07; and 1897, $0.72 (H. B. Morse, *The Trade and Administration of the Chinese Empire*, 119–169; C. F. Remer, *The Foreign Trade of China*, 250).

5. *List of the Principal Foreign and Chinese Industrial Enterprises in China and Hong Kong* (*Revised to December 31st, 1917*), 22.

6. See William W. Lockwood, *The Economic Development of Japan: Growth and Structural Change, 1868–1938*, 499–549.

7. D. K. Lieu, *China's Industries and Finance*, 91, Tables VI, VII.

8. Franklin L. Ho and Hsien Ding Fong, *Extent and Effects of Industrialization in China*, 12, Table XII.

9. *Ibid.*, 11, Table XI.

10. See the *List of the Principal Foreign and Chinese Industrial Enterprises, passim.*

11. Yen Chung-p'ing, *Chung-kuo mien-yeh chih fa-chan* (The development of China's cotton industry), 111, 129.

12. C. F. Remer, *Foreign Investments in China*, 359–360.

13. *Ibid.*, 69.

14. *Ibid.*, 429–431.

15. Chang Hsin-ch'eng, *Chung-kuo hsien-tai chiao-t'ung shih* (A history of modern communications in China), 436–441.

16. Wang Chin-yü, "Chin-pai-nien-lai Chung-kuo t'ieh-lu shih-yeh" (Chinese railroads during the past hundred years), 73–78.

17. The estimate of Tls. 55,000 per mile is derived from Sheng Hsuan-huai's presentation of the finances of the Peking-Hankow railroad in *YCTK*, 11.29a–33a, memorial endorsed KH 31/7/13 (August 13, 1905).

18. See Tokunaga Kiyoyuki, *Shina chūō ginkō ron* (Central banking in China), 14–50.

19. For sources of Table 3, see note 2 above.

20. D. K. Lieu in *The Growth and Industrialization of Shanghai*, 17–19, presents a tabular view of seven different opinions with regard to the proper periodization of China's modern industrial development, followed by his own 7-period classification.

21. Kung Chün, *op. cit.*, 13–14, 49–50, 65–69.

22. *THHL-KH*, 139.6b–7b, Tsungli Yamen memorial of KH 23/2/23 (March 25, 1897).

23. Ellsworth Carlson has studied the K'ai-p'ing mines in his *The Kai-ping Mines (1877–1912)*. On the Han-Yeh-P'ing complex, see Ch'üan Han-sheng, "Ch'ing-mo Han-yang t'ieh-ch'ang" ("The Han-yang Iron and Steel Works, 1890-1908"). For the early history of the China Merchants' Company, see K. C. Liu, "Two Steamship Companies in China, 1862–1877," Chapter 3. The Mo-ho Gold Mining Company was formally established in 1887 with a capitalization of Tls. 200,000 in 2,000 shares. But only Tls. 60–70,000 had been actually raised by 1888 when Li Hung-chang took an active hand and procured Tls. 100,000 from Tientsin merchants. Another Tls. 15,000 was raised by the Manchu military governor of the Amur River region. Operations were begun at the end of 1888. By 1891, 62,000 ounces of gold dust had been processed, thus permitting the repayment of the company's debts as well as the distribution of dividends. Later the Mo-ho mine fell into Russian

hands. In 1910 it was repurchased by the Chinese government, but operations thereafter were none too successful. At its peak the company employed some 1,000–1,500 workers (Kung Chün, *op. cit.*, 36; China, Imperial Maritime Customs, *Decennial Reports*, 1882–1891, 21).

24. See *Ch'ing-shih kao* (Draft history of the Ch'ing dynasty), *Shih-huo chih* (Monograph on economic conditions), 4.1b, 19b, 20a and *passim*.

25. Some idea of the complexity of the salt gabelle may be obtained from the Imperial Maritime Customs publication, *Salt: Production and Taxation*, Shanghai, 1906.

26. In Hunan, for example, the salt district was administered by a *tu-pan* appointed by the Nanking governor-general for a tenure of one year, possibly extended to two or three. This was apparently judged long enough for that official to make his fortune before the office was sold to another bidder (*ibid.*, 65).

27. *LWCK-TLYM Correspondence*, 1.39b–40a, TC 11/11/23 (December 23, 1872). The Tsungli Yamen (full name, *Tsung-li ko-kuo shih-wu ya-men;* literally, "office in general charge of foreign affairs") was established in 1861 as a special subcommittee under the Grand Council. Until the creation of the Ministry of Foreign Affairs (*Wai-wu pu*) in 1901, it was to be concerned with all aspects of relations between China and the Western powers, including the efforts made to initiate Western-type industrial enterprises.

28. For Li Hung-chang (1823–1901) see Hummel, 1.464–471. In the nineteenth century the administration of the eighteen provinces of China proper was organized in the following manner. Each of the provinces with the exception of Chihli and Szechwan had its governor (*hsün-fu*) who had general responsibility for provincial affairs. The administration of the metropolitan province of Chihli and of the province of Szechwan, because of their special importance, was in each case headed by a governor-general (*tsung-tu*). With the exception of the three provinces of Shantung, Honan, and Shansi, the remaining provinces were grouped under governors-general as shown in the following table (in which the Wade-Giles romanization is employed for the titles of the governors-general, but the standard post-office forms for the names of the provinces):

Kiangsu ⎫ Anhwei ⎬ Kiangsi ⎭	Liang-Chiang governor-general
Shensi ⎫ Kansu ⎭	Shen-Kan governor-general
Fukien ⎫ Chekiang ⎭	Min-Che governor-general
Hupei ⎫ Hunan ⎭	Hu-Kuang governor-general
Kwangsi ⎫ Kwangtung ⎭	Liang-Kuang governor-general
Yunnan ⎫ Kweichow ⎭	Yun-Kuei governor-general

The governors-general had over-all authority over the provinces and the provincial governors under their juisdiction. But the two officials were obviously placed so as to check each other, for they were expected to take action and memorialize jointly on important matters.

29. On Chang Chih-tung (1837–1909) see Hummel, 1.27–32.

30. *THHL-KH*, 131.11a–13a, KH 21/12/24 (February 7, 1896); 139.6b–7a, KH 23/1/23 (March 25, 1897); 145.23a–25a, KH 24/5/23 (July 11, 1898); 181.14ab, KH 29/7/16 (September 7, 1903); 185.1ab, KH 29/12/5 (January 21, 1904); 200.1ab, KH 32/4/2 (April 25, 1906); 202.9b–10a, KH 32/8/20 (October 7, 1906); 208.12b–13a, KH 33/7/23 (August 31, 1907).

31. *NCH*, August 28, 1896, 368; *THHL-KH*, 134.10b–12a, KH 22/6/5 (July 15, 1896).

32. On Ting Jih-ch'ang (1823–1882) see Hummel, 2.721–723. After being in charge of the Kiangnan Arsenal, Ting was promoted to be salt controller of the Liang-Huai region in September 1865, and in early 1866 he was made financial commissioner of Kiangsu. Then in 1867 he became governor of Kiangsu, owing his rapid promotions in large part to the support of Li Hung-chang.

33. See Stanley Spector, "Li Hung-chang and the Huai-chün," a detailed study of the military basis of Li's regional power.

34. The first successful railroad in China was the 13-mile line from T'ang-shan to Hsü-ke-chuang built in 1882 to carry coal from the K'ai-p'ing mines to the nearest water transportation (Tseng K'un-hua, *Chung-kuo t'ieh-lu shih* [History of Chinese railroads], 31–33). An earlier unauthorized line from Shanghai to Woosung completed by Jardine, Matheson and Company in 1876 had been purchased and scrapped by the Chinese government in the same year (*ibid.*, 26–31).

35. See Wu To, "Chin-t'ung t'ieh-lu ti cheng-i" ("Controversy concerning the proposed railway line between Tientsin and T'ung-chow [1888–1889]").

36. On Liu K'un-i (1830–1902) see Hummel, 1.523–524.

37. *CWHK-Memorials*, 42.11b–13a, KH 21/12/28 (February 11, 1896).

38. Whether these investors were treaty-port merchants or gentry or both is not explicitly stated. See Chang Hsiao-jo, *Nan-t'ung Chang Chi-chih hsien-sheng chuan-chi* (Biography of Chang Chien), 69. If we judge from the situation of the three men who backed Chang's second mill, it is likely that gentry interests played a dominant role. See Yen Chung-p'ing, *op. cit.*, 122.

39. Chang Hsiao-jo, *op. cit.*, 68–75; Yen Chung-p'ing, *op. cit.*, 82–85; and see Liu K'un-i's memorial of KH 26/2 (March 1900) about the Nantung mill in *Kuang-hsü cheng-yao* (Important documents of the Kuang-hsü period), 26.5a–6a.

40. See Negishi Tadashi, *Baiban seido no kenkyū* (A study of the compradore system), 34–75, for a brief outline of the history of the compradore in China.

41. In the 8-*chüan* edition of 1900, *chüan* 4 deals with fiscal matters, *chüan* 5 with commercial affairs, and *chüan* 8 with industry. A copy of this edition is in the East Asiatic Library, Columbia University.

42. China, Imperial Maritime Customs, *Decennial Reports*, 1892–1901, 1.513.

43. Yen Chung-p'ing, *op. cit.*, 123.

44. *Ibid.*, 120–130; this is a general discussion of the problem of invest-

ment in the cotton textile industry on which the present account is based in part.

45. *NCH*, January 8, 1902, 10.

46. *Decennial Reports*, 1892–1901, 1.515; *YCTK*, 5.41b–42a, memorial endorsed KH 28/8/21 (September 22, 1902). The correct date is certainly KH 27/8/21 (October 3, 1901), since the preceding and following memorials in *chüan* 5 are both dated KH 27.

47. Yen Chung-p'ing, *op. cit.*, 79.

48. *Ibid.*, 124.

49. Wu Ching-ch'ao, "Han-Yeh-P'ing kung-ssu ti fu-ch'e" (The lesson of the Han-Yeh-P'ing Company), 28, quoting a government representative who was present at a meeting of the company in 1918.

50. See Marius B. Jansen, "Yawata, Hanyehping and the Twenty-one Demands."

51. H. B. Morse to G. Detring, Letterbooks, October 19, 1886. The career of Tong King-sing (1832–1892) will be considered in more detail in Chapter 4 in connection with the China Merchants' Company.

52. Morse to Detring, Letterbooks, April 16, 1886. Note, however, that in general Hsü Jun (1838–1911) was no mean businessman. His career is discussed in Chapter 4.

53. *YCTK*, 4.22a, memorial endorsed KH 26/2/? (March 1900); *ibid.*, 4.25b, memorial endorsed KH 26/2/19 (March 19, 1900) in which Sheng states, "Those who have invested in the ironworks are the shareholders of the China Merchants' Company and the Telegraph Administration. We depend on the slight surpluses of these two companies to make up the deficits of the ironworks."

54. *Ibid.*, 3.10b, memorial endorsed KH 25/7/27 (September 1, 1899).

55. Many other names which might profitably be followed up can be found in the lists of joint-stock companies registered with the Ministry of Agriculture, Industry, and Commerce in *NKSPTCP-I* and *NKSPTCP-II*.

56. On Yeh Ch'eng-chung (1840–1899) see *NCH*, January 3, 1900, 22; and Ku Hung-ming, "Yeh-chün chuan" (A biography of Yeh Ch'eng-chung).

57. On Yü Ho-te (1867–1946) see Fang T'eng, "Yü Ch'ia-ch'ing lun" (On Yü Ho-te); Negishi Tadashi, *Chūgoku shakai ni okeru shidōsō: kirō shinshi no kenkyū* (Leading classes in Chinese society: a study of elders and gentry), 156–164; and Negishi Tadashi, *Baiban seido no kenkyū*, 303–306. Yü is also remembered as an early patron of Chiang Kai-shek.

58. On the early career of Jung Tsung-ching see "Wu-hsi Jung-shih ch'i-yeh chia-tsu chi ch'i ch'i-chia ti mien-fen-yeh" ("The Yung's [*sic*] Family and their Flour Industry"), 19–21; and *Mao-hsin Fu-hsin Shen-hsin tsung-kung-ssu sa-chou-nien chi-nien-ts'e* ("The Thirtieth Anniversary Memorial Book, 1898–1928, Mow Sing & Foh Sing Flour Mills and Sung Sing Cotton Mills").

59. Yen Chung-p'ing, *op. cit.*, 121–122; for 1916–1922, Yen finds 21 merchants or industrialists among the operators of 32 cotton mills established during this period about which he was able to find information (157–159).

60. Arnold Wright, ed., *Twentieth Century Impressions of Hongkong, Shanghai, and other Treaty Ports of China*, 540–544.

61. *NCH*, March 12, 1897, 460–461; *YCTK*, 5.4b, memorial endorsed KH 26/9/15 (November 6, 1900); 1.14b–15a, endorsed KH 22/9/26 (November 1, 1896); *NKSPTCP-II*, 5.11a, 5.6b; *NKSPTCP-I*, 5.28, 2.27a, 5.9a, 5.18a.

62. On Chou Chin-piao (b. 1855[?]) see *Gendai Shina jimmei kan* (Biographical dictionary of contemporary Chinese), 1928 ed., 887; for his enterprises see *NKSPTCP-I*, 5.3a, 5.19a, 5.28a; *NKSPTCP-II*, 4.22a.

63. *YCTK*, 7.35a–37b, memorial endorsed KH 28/9/? (October 2–31, 1902).

64. *LWCK-Memorials*, 20.32b–33a, TC 11/11/23 (December 23, 1872).

65. *Ibid.*, 44.22a–24a, KH 8/8/16 (September 27, 1882).

66. *YCTK*, 5.7a, memorial endorsed KH 26/9/15 (November 6, 1900).

67. *CWHK-Memorials*, 44.4ab, KH 22/5/16 (June 26, 1896).

68. See Thomas C. Smith, *Political Change and Industrial Development in Japan: Government Enterprise, 1868–1880.*

69. See Derk Bodde, "Authority and Law in Ancient China," 49–50, especially 50, n. 8, which translates a penitential edict of the T'ung-chih Emperor in 1862.

70. Morse to G. Detring, Letterbooks, October 19, 1886.

71. Quoted in Yen Chung-p'ing, *op. cit.*, 96, n. 118.

72. See Yen Chung-p'ing, *op. cit.*, 88–89.

73. *NCH*, June 4, 1902, 1120; July 9, 1902, 84; September 10, 1892, 535; November 19, 1902, 1074. These mills which began operations in 1898 should be distinguished from the Hupei Government Textile Mill which Chang had established several years before and which was referred to on p. 18 above.

74. Ch'üan Han-sheng, *op. cit.*, 19–20.

75. Wu Ch'eng-lo, *Chin-shih Chung-kuo shih-yeh t'ung-chih* (Handbook of modern Chinese industry), 1.155.

76. *Decennial Reports*, 1892–1901, 1.514.

77. *NCH*, March 12, 1902, 488–489.

78. *Ibid.*, July 15, 1910, 149.

79. *Decennial Reports*, 1892–1901, 1.513–514.

80. Wu Ching-ch'ao, *op. cit.*, 30–31.

81. Statement by Tong King-sing in China Merchants' Steam Navigation Company 9th Annual Report, *NCH*, October 18, 1882, 419.

82. *LWCK-Memorials*, 36.35a, KH 6/3/27 (May 5, 1880); 20.33a, TC 11/11/23 (December 23, 1872).

83. *THHL-KH*, 134.10b–12a, KH 22/6/5 (July 15, 1896), memorial from the Tsungli Yamen endorsed, "Let it be carried out as proposed"; and see *NCH*, August 28, 1896, 368.

84. *NCH*, September 3, 1902, 461–462.

85. Foreign goods paid a nominal 5 per cent import tariff (actually much less, since the tariff schedule did not reflect the rise in the price of gold in terms of silver which occurred in the last quarter of the nineteenth century) and a nominal 2.5 per cent more in lieu of transit taxes if they were shipped into the interior. The Treaty of Shimonoseki provided that goods manufactured in the treaty ports by foreigners would be considered on the same basis as imports with regard to the privilege of commuting transit duties by the payment of one half of the regular import tariff (the so-called *tzu-k'ou shui*). Although provincial officials were often wont to collect *likin* from foreign goods despite their having taken advantage of the commutation privilege, this concession obtained in the Treaty of Tientsin of 1858 definitely gave foreign goods a competitive advantage over Chinese products.

86. See, for example, *LWCK-Memorials*, 43.44ab, KH 8/3/6 (April 23, 1882), where Li Hung-chang requests that Chinese cotton manufactures

pay no duty if sold in the treaty ports, 5 per cent if shipped into the interior, and no other levies.

87. *CWHK-Memorials*, 44.29a–31b, KH 22/9/23 (October 29, 1896).

88. *YCTK*, 25.18b–19a, KH 22/10/25 (November 29, 1896), telegram from Sheng to Weng T'ung-ho (1830–1904), president of the Ministry of Revenue.

89. *Ibid.*, 5.44a–46a, memorial endorsed KH 27/9/30 (November 10, 1901).

90. *Ibid.*, 13.3a–6b, memorial endorsed KH 32/8/14 (October 1, 1906).

91. See above, pp. 97–98.

92. *LWCK-Memorials*, 43.44a, KH 8/3/6 (April 23, 1882).

93. Chang Hsin-ch'eng, *op. cit.*, 443–447.

94. *CWHK-Memorials*, 44.5b–6a, 9b–10b, KH 22/5/16 (June 26, 1896); Mai Chung-hua, compiler, *Huang-ch'ao ching-shih-wen hsin-pien* (New collection of essays on statecraft of the Ch'ing dynasty), 13A.3a, Tsungli Yamen memorial; *YCTK*, 2.13a, memorial endorsed KH 24/3/26 (April 16, 1898).

CHAPTER 2

Economic Conditions in the Late Ch'ing Period

1. Chao Feng-t'ien, *Wan-Ch'ing wu-shih-nien ching-chi ssu-hsiang shih*. See also Hsia Yen-te, *Chung-kuo chin-pai-nien ching-chi ssu-hsiang* (Chinese economic thought in the last hundred years), 13–100; and So Kwan-wai, "Western Influence and the Chinese Reform Movement of 1898," 183–191.

2. Chao Feng-t'ien, *op. cit.*, 305–314; T'ang Ch'ing-tseng, "Ch'ing-tai T'ai-hsi shu-ju wo-kuo chih ching-chi ssu-hsiang" (The introduction of Western economic thought into China during the Ch'ing dynasty).

3. Chang Yen-chü, "Wu-hsü pien-fa shih-ch'i wan-ku-p'ai chih ching-chi ssu-hsiang" (Economic thought of the conservative party in 1898) is slight and not comparable in quality to Ch'en Ch'iu, "Wu-hsü pien-fa shih fan-pien-fa jen-wu chih cheng-chih ssu-hsiang" (The political thought of the anti-reformers during the Reform Movement of 1898). The several collections of *Ching-shih-wen pien* (Essays on statecraft) published toward the end of the Ch'ing dynasty and including extensive materials on economic questions are essentially compilations of reform writings. See Momose Hiromu, "Shimmatsu no Keiseibumpen ni tsuite" (On the *Ching-shih-wen pien* of the late Ch'ing dynasty).

4. The use of the word "reformers" in this context is not meant to be limited to the partisans of K'ang Yu-wei and Liang Ch'i-ch'ao. The men whose works are excerpted by Chao Feng-t'ien are a good cross-section of the group to whom I refer. Only one (Chang Chih-tung [1837–1909]) was a high official with any influence on government policy. Hsueh Fu-ch'eng (1838–1894) was a middle-range official and diplomat. At least three (Chang Chien [1853–1926], Ma Chien-chung [1844–1900], Cheng Kuan-ying [fl. 1880–1910]) were at some time active in the management of modern-type industries. K'ang Yu-wei (1858–1927) and Liang Ch'i-ch'ao (1873–1929) were leaders of the 1898 Reform Movement. Four (Feng Kuei-fen [1809–1874], Huang Tsun-hsien [1848–1905], Yen Fu [1853–1921], Wang K'ang-nien [1860–1911]) were minor officials, scholars, or writers with no effective political or economic power. One (T'ang Shou-ch'ien [fl. 1905–1916]) was a leader of the Chekiang

gentry, and later a member of Yuan Shih-k'ai's cabinet. Ch'en Chih (fl. 1898), Ho Ch'i (fl. 1898), and Hu Li-yuan (fl. 1898) were each the compilers of widely circulated compendia of reform writings.

5. T'ang Ch'ing-tseng's relatively sophisticated *Chung-kuo ching-chi ssu-hsiang shih* (A history of Chinese economic thought) was never finished, the first volume which appeared in 1936 carrying the account only through the Warring States period. The well-known study of traditional economic thought by Ch'en Huan-chang, *The Economic Principles of Confucius and his School,* is the work of a self-acknowledged disciple of K'ang Yu-wei and reflects K'ang's reformist interpretations.

6. On Hsueh, see Ssu-yü Teng and John K. Fairbank, *China's Response to the West: A Documentary Survey, 1839–1923,* 117–118, 140–146; and Hummel, 1.331–332.

7. Hsueh Fu-ch'eng, *Hai-wai wen-pien* (Collection of essays written while abroad), 1897 ed., 3.38a–39b (in Chao Feng-t'ien, *op. cit.,* 93–94).

8. William W. Lockwood, *The Economic Development of Japan: Growth and Structural Change, 1868–1938,* 574, 575.

9. On Cheng, see Teng and Fairbank. *op. cit.,* 113–115; and Chapter 4 below.

10. Cheng Kuan–ying, *Sheng-shih wei-yen* (Warnings to a seemingly prosperous age), 1900 ed., 8 *chüan,* 5. 11ab (Chao Feng-t'ien, *op. cit.,* 99–100, cites the 1895 ed., 14 *chüan,* "Shang-wu san" [Commerce, Part III], 3.3ab).

11. Lockwood, *op. cit.,* 25.

12. On Liang see Teng and Fairbank, *op. cit.,* 153–154 and *passim;* and Joseph R. Levenson, *Liang Ch'i-ch'ao and the Mind of Modern China.*

13. Liang Ch'i-ch'ao, *Yin-p'ing-shih ho-chi* (Collected works and essays of the Ice-Drinker's Studio), "Wen-chi" (Collected essays), 1.129, 130–131 (in Chao Feng-t'ien, *op. cit.,* 29–31).

14. See Chao Feng-t'ien, *op. cit.,* 19–41.

15. *THHL-KH,* 135.24b–26b, KH 22/8/30 (October 6, 1896).

16. Chang Chien, *Chang Chi-tzu chiu-lu* (Collected writings of Chang Chien), "Shih-yeh lu" (Industry), 3.17b (in Chao Feng-t'ien, *op. cit.,* 40).

17. Ch'en Chih, *Hsü fu-kuo ts'e* (A further plan to enrich the country), 1897, 3.10ab (in Chao Feng-t'ien, *op. cit.,* 69).

18. Lockwood, *op. cit.,* 325.

19. Hsueh Fu-ch'eng, *op. cit.,* 3.21a–22b (in Chao Feng-t'ien, *op. cit.,* 59–61).

20. Ch'en Chih, *op. cit.,* 3.15a (in Chao Feng-t'ien, *op. cit.,* 72).

21. On K'ang, see Teng and Fairbank, *op. cit.,* 147–149, and *passim.*

22. K'ang Yu-wei, *Jih-pen shu-mu chih* (A catalog of Japanese books), 1897, 2.11a (in Chao Feng-t'ien, *op. cit.,* 55).

23. Shao Tso-ch'uan, *Shao-shih wei-yen* (Bold words from Mr. Shao), 1898, "Hsi-i" (Industrial arts), B.7a–9a (in Chao Feng-t'ien, *op. cit.,* 63).

24. Lockwood, *op. cit.,* 330, 331.

25. See Chao Feng-t'ien, *op. cit.,* 57, 64, quoting Huang Tsun-hsien and Ch'en Chih.

26. Cheng's point is that the Shanghai Cotton Cloth Mill was essentially a mercantile undertaking. See Chapter 6 below, and Yen Chung-p'ing, *Chung-kuo mien-yeh chih fa-chan* (The development of China's cotton industry), 73–76.

27. Chang Chih-tung undertook the Hupei textile mill in 1889 as an

entirely official enterprise. Operations did not begin until the end of 1892, and its profits were dissipated in Chang's concern to provide capital for the Hanyang Ironworks. Yen Chung-p'ing, *op. cit.*, 77–79; Kung Chün, *Chung-kuo hsin-kung-yeh fa-chan-shih ta-kang* (An outline history of the development of modern industry in China), 33–34.

28. Cheng Kuan-ying, *op. cit.* (in Chao Feng-t'ien, *op. cit.*, 102).

29. *Ibid.* (in Chao Feng-t'ien, *op. cit.*, 102, n. 24).

30. *Ibid.* (in Chao Feng-t'ien, *op. cit.*, 106–108).

31. On Chang Chien, see Teng and Fairbank, *op. cit.*, 215, 216, 219.

32. Chang Chien, *op. cit.* (in Chao Feng-t'ien, *op. cit.*, 35–40).

33. Ho Ch'i and Hu Li-yuan, *Hsin-cheng chen-ch'üan* (A true exposition of reforms), 1901, 2.29b–32a (in Chao Feng-t'ien, *op. cit.*, 53). See Wan Kuo-ting, "Pei-ch'ao Sui T'ang chih chün-t'ien chih-tu" (The equal land allotment systems of the Northern, Sui, and T'ang dynasties).

34. See T. C. Smith, *Political Change and Industrial Development in Japan: Government Enterprise, 1868–1880;* and E. Herbert Norman, *Japan's Emergence as a Modern State,* 104–135.

35. T. C. Smith, *op. cit.,* 69ff.

36. Lockwood, *op. cit.,* 326.

37. See Lo Yü-tung, "Kuang-hsü-ch'ao pu-chiu ts'ai-cheng chih fang-ts'e" ("The government policies of meeting the financial crisis during the Kuang-hsü period [1875–1908]"), 189, 215.

38. T'ang Hsiang-lung, "Min-kuo i-ch'ien ti p'ei-k'uan shih ju-ho ch'ang-fu ti" ("A study of the indemnity payments before 1911"), 281.

39. Lo Yü-tung, *op. cit.,* 189–215.

40. From these annual reports Liu Yo-yün, a secretary in the Hu-pu, has compiled detailed tables of central and provincial income and expenditure for 1885–1894 (Kuang-hsü 11–Kuang-hsü 20), under the title *Kuang-hsü K'uai-chi piao* (Kuang-hsü fiscal tables). A similar work comparing the data for 1893 (Kuang-hsü 19) with those for the preceding year is Li Hsi-sheng, *Kuang-hsü k'uai-chi lu* (Fiscal statistics of the Kuang-hsü period), by a secretary of the Ministry of Punishments (*Hsing-pu*). Both compilations are quite detailed, but their categories are vague and protean, and their figures are only rough indices of the actual order of magnitude. E. H. Parker's comment on Chinese official accounts is apt:

Notwithstanding this universal corruption [in the collection and remission of taxes], accounts are kept in scrupulous good order, and fractions are often worked out to the hundred-millionth part of a tael. . . . In 1886 I came across the accounts of the "Grand Almoner of Peking," who calculated his fractions down to the ten-billionth part of a tael for each item ["The Financial Capacity of the Chinese," 88].

41. See Charles J. Stanley, "Hu Kuang-yung and China's Early Foreign Loans."

42. Lo Yü-tung, *op. cit.,* 212, 213, Table V; T'ang Hsiang-lung, "Min-kuo i-ch'ien kuan-shui tan-pao chih wai-chai" ("The foreign loans secured on the customs revenue before 1911"), 35–36, Table I.

43. Liu Yo-yün, *op. cit.,* 1.3a–5b.

44. See Franz Michael, "Military Organization and the Power Structure of China During the Taiping Rebellion"; and Shen Nai-cheng, "Ch'ing-mo

chih tu-fu chi-ch'üan" ("On the powers of the viceroy and the governor of the provinces in the last years of the Tsing dynasty").

45. See Stanley Spector, "Li Hung-chang and the Huai-chün."

46. See P'eng Yü-hsin, "Ch'ing-mo chung-yang yü ko-sheng ts'ai-cheng kuan-hsi" ("The financial relations between central and local government in Tsing dynasty [*sic*]"); James T. K. Wu, "The Impact of the Taiping Rebellion upon the Manchu Fiscal System"; C. J. Stanley, "Chinese Finance from 1852 to 1908."

47. Lo Yü-tung, *Chung-kuo li-chin shih* (A history of *likin* in China), 1.22, Table V; 1.224–225 and *passim*.

48. These figures are adapted from George Jamieson, *Report on the Revenue and Expenditure of the Chinese Empire*, 33, and from A. Forke, "Das chinesische Finanz- und Steuerwesen," Part II, 54; they are based on item-by-item surveys of Chinese taxation. Among other estimates, note the following which in general do not diverge greatly from that of Forke: E. H. Parker (1897 expenditure), Tls. 81,030,000 (*China Past and Present*, 33–36); Sir Robert Hart (1901 income), Tls. 90,400,000 (S. R. Wagel, *Finance in China*, 338–339).

49. Lo Yü-tung, "Government policies," 198–202, 219, 236–239, 244–245, 251–252.

50. H. B. Morse, *The Trade and Administration of the Chinese Empire*, 118; Morse's chapter "Revenue and Expenditure" in this volume is still the most illuminating that has been written on the subject.

51. Lo Yü-tung, "Government policies," 260; on the *Ts'ai-cheng shuo-ming-shu*, see John K. Fairbank and Kwang-ching Liu, *Modern China: A Bibliographical Guide to Chinese Works, 1898–1937*, 333–337.

52. For *likin* see note 47 above; Morse estimates that only Tls. 26,000,000 of "the almost provable actual collection, Tls. 102,000,000" was reported by the provinces (*op. cit.*, 94). A good description of the ways in which land tax above the legal quota due in Peking was collected is given by Wang Yü-ch'üan, "Ch'ing-mo t'ien-fu yü nung-min" (Land tax and peasantry in the late Ch'ing dynasty); this article also appeared in an English version, which is listed below in the bibliography of Western works.

53. E. H. Norman, *op. cit.*, 138–144; Lockwood, *op. cit.*, 98.

54. E. H. Norman, *op. cit.*, 140, 142.

55. Lo Yü-tung, "Government policies," 241; T'ang Hsiang-lung, "A study of indemnity payments," 271.

56. H. B. Morse, *The International Relations of the Chinese Empire*, 3.53–54; T'ang Hsiang-lung, "The foreign loans secured on the customs," 29, lists seven *likin* collectorates in this connection and makes no mention of salt.

57. C. F. Remer, *The Foreign Trade of China*, 76, 125.

58. See Wu Ch'eng-hsi, "Pai-nien-lai yin-chia pien-tung chih hui-ku" ("The price of silver, a review of its fluctuations 1833–1931").

59. Lo Yü-tung, "Government policies," 215–241.

60. *THHL-KH*, 142.13b–15a, edict of KH 24/1/14 (February 4, 1898).

61. *Translations of the Peking Gazette*, January 11, 1899, 3–4.

62. *Kuang-hsü cheng-yao* (Important documents of the Kuang-hsü period), 24.40b, Hu-pu memorial of KH 24/7 (August 17–September 15, 1898).

63. T'ang Hsiang-lung, "A study of indemnity payments," 280, Table XI.

64. *Ibid.*, 277.

65. Lo Yü-tung, "Government policies," 243–244.

66. *Kuang-hsü cheng-yao*, 27.71a–73a, telegram of KH 27/11 (December 11, 1901–January 9, 1902).

67. Lo Yü-tung, "Government policies," 245–246.

68. *Ibid.*, 243.

69. T'ang Hsiang-lung, "A study of indemnity payments," 278–279, Table X.

70. *Ibid.*, 283–284: a summary of the sources of the provincial payments.

71. Lo Yü-tung, "Government policies," 246–248, feels that there was a considerable additional tax burden on the populace in order to meet the high indemnity payments.

72. *NCH*, June 19, 1899, 1103–1104; and see June 5, 1899, 1012–1013; June 12, 1899, 1060.

73. *THHL-KH*, 154.23a–24b, KH 25/6/23 (July 30, 1899). *NCH*, August 7, 1899, 287, gives a rough breakdown of Kang-i's exactions in Kiangsu.

74. Lo Yü-tung, "Government policies," 229–230.

75. See the leader entitled "Financial Reform in China" in *NCH*, August 14, 1899, 309–310.

76. *YCTK*, 3.5a–11a, memorial endorsed KH 25/7/27 (September 1, 1899).

77. *Ibid.*, 3.5ab.

78. See, for example, Marion J. Levy, "Contrasting Factors in the Modernization of China and Japan."

79. See Honjō Eijirō, *The Social and Economic History of Japan*, 125–222.

80. Thomas C. Smith, "Landlords and Rural Capitalists in the Modernization of Japan," contains much interesting material on the extent of capitalist economic development in the countryside in the Tokugawa period. Scholars on mainland China are at present devoting considerable attention to the *Urgeschichte* of Chinese capitalism. The general line is that a transformation from the "feudal" to the "capitalist" stage, which might have been expected in the late eighteenth and early nineteenth centuries, was impeded by the advent of European imperialism. See, for example, *Chung-kuo tzu-pen chu-i meng-ya wen-t'i t'ao-lun chi* (Collected papers on the problem of the incipiency of capitalism in China); and Albert Feuerwerker, "From 'Feudalism' to 'Capitalism' in Recent Historical Writing from Mainland China."

81. See Ch'üan Han-sheng, "Sung-tai kuan-li chih ssu-ying shang-yeh" (Clandestine commercial enterprises of Sung officials).

82. See Kōsaka Torizō, *Chūgoku kōeki kikō no kenkyū* (A study of commercial institutions in China), 205–280.

83. On the Liang-Huai salt merchants see Ho Ping-ti, "The Salt Merchants of Yang-chou: A Study of Commercial Capitalism in Eighteenth-Century China."

84. *Ibid.*, 154–168: detailed examples of the "dilution of the wealth and capital" of the Liang-Huai salt merchants.

85. Lockwood, *op. cit.*, 306.

86. Hsü Jun, *Hsü Yü-chai tzu-hsü nien-p'u* (Chronological autobiography), 39b; *Translations of the Peking Gazette*, October 24, 1885, 155–156, memorial of Li Hung-chang.

In the late Ch'ing administration, the taotai or "circuit intendant" occupied an intermediary position between the provincial governor and the district magistrates of a province. His circuit might encompass several *hsien* or "districts." In some cases (as, for example, those of the Tientsin and Shanghai customs taotai) the office of intendant carried with it specific functional responsibilities rather than a vague territorial jurisdiction. See above, pp. 64–66, for an account of Sheng Hsuan-huai as Tientsin customs taotai.

87. *Translations of the Peking Gazette*, March 11, 1890, 34, memorial of Li Hung-chang.

88. Hsü Jun, *op. cit.*, 34a–36a, 36b–40a and *passim*.

89. On the customs banks see Lien-shang Yang, *Money and Credit in China, A Short History*, 87–88.

90. *YCTK*, 1.14b–15a, memorial endorsed KH 22/9/26 (November 1, 1896).

91. See Lien-sheng Yang, *op. cit.*, 84–85, on the *ch'ien-chuang*.

92. Miyashita Tadao, "Hōgaki Shina ginkōgyō no bokkō" (The rise of modern Chinese banking), 81.

93. See Stanley, "Hu Kuang-yung and China's Early Foreign Loans," especially 65–84.

94. *LWCK-Letters*, 13.2a–3a, TC 12/2/18 (March 16, 1873); 13.12b–14a, TC 12/intercalary 6/6 (July 29, 1873).

95. For example, *YCTK*, 4.24b, memorial KH 26/2/19 (March 19, 1900). On the tendency for the Chinese compradore to fuse with the gentry and officialdom, see Negishi Tadashi, *Baiban seido no kenkyū* (A study of the compradore system), 272–284.

96. *YCTK*, 7.35a–37b, memorial endorsed KH 28/9/? (October ?, 1902).

97. The estimate of 20–50 per cent is that of Chang Chien, cited by Yen Chung-p'ing, *op. cit.*, 123. Lien-sheng Yang, *op. cit.*, 98–103, estimates 30–50 per cent annually from usury, and 15–25 per cent from pawnshops and native banks.

98. Lockwood, *op. cit.*, 325.

99. Tezuka Masao, *Shina jūkōgyō hattatsu shi* (History of the development of Chinese heavy industry), 85, Table 34.

100. See G. C. Allen and Audrey G. Donnithorne, *Western Enterprise in Far Eastern Economic Development*, 13–81.

101. *Report of the Mission to China of the Blackburn Chamber of Commerce, 1896–7*, H. Neville and H. Bell's Section, 229.

102. *CWHK-Memorials*, 44.3a, KH 22/5/16 (June 26, 1896); *YCTK*, 4.24a, memorial endorsed KH 26/2/19 (March 19, 1900).

103. *Japan Year Book, 1933*, 391.

104. Lockwood, *op. cit.*, 319.

105. *Report* (see note 101), H. Neville and H. Bell's Section, 195–196.

106. C. F. Remer, *op. cit.*, 46, 81.

107. *Japan Year Book, 1933*, 394, 395.

108. C. F. Remer, *op. cit.*, 141.

109. Allen and Donnithorne, *op. cit.*, 60–68, 202, 242–243.

110. Nathan Pelcovits, *Old China Hands and the Foreign Office*, has shown that while the belief that China was a boundless market was strong among British merchants in the treaty ports, the Foreign Office, on the basis of a Board of Trade decision that the Chinese market was not worth the effort, reluctantly declined to back the merchants fully in an active policy that would have made China a second India.

111. *Report*, H. Neville and H. Bell's Section, 357. Also of interest in this

connection is the report by the Lyons Chamber of Commerce, *La mission lyonnaise d'exploration commerciale en Chine, 1895–97,* which is concerned largely with the commercial possibilities of Yunnan and Szechwan. Belgian interest in the China market is shown in *La Chine en 1899, rapport de la mission commerciale de Jules Duckerts, Consul Général, Chargé d'affaires de Belgique.* For the United States, see U. S. Bureau of Statistics (Treasury Department), *Commercial China in 1899.*

CHAPTER 3

Sheng Hsuan-huai (1844–1916): Official and Industrialist

1. See especially Joseph A. Schumpeter, "The Creative Response in Economic History," and *Business Cycles: A Theoretical, Historical and Statistical Analysis of the Capitalist Process.*

2. Schumpeter, "The Creative Response in Economic History."

3. See Henri Pirenne, *Les périodes de l'histoire sociale du capitalisme.*

4. See William W. Lockwood, *The Economic Development of Japan, 1868–1938,* 574, 575 and *passim.*

5. See T. C. Smith, *Political Change and Industrial Development in Japan: Government Enterprise, 1868–1880.*

6. Sheng T'ung-i et al., *Hsing-shu* (Biography [of Sheng Hsuan-huai]), in the prefatory volume *(chüan-shou)* of *Sheng shang-shu Yü-chai ts'un-kao ch'u-k'an* (Collected drafts of Board President Sheng Yü-chai [Hsuan-huai], first issue). This collection in 51 volumes *(ts'e),* intended as the first part of Sheng's complete works, was edited by a former advisor *(mu-liao),* Lü Ching-tuan, and published in 1939 in a very limited edition for distribution to Sheng's family and close friends. It was reprinted in Peking in 1942 by the Hsiu-keng-t'ang Book Company. Included are Sheng's memorials (20 *chüan*), telegraphic memorials (3 *chüan*), and telegraphic correspondence (77 *chüan*). The first 23 *chüan* of memorials were compiled while Sheng was still alive and are nearly complete; but even the 6,053 telegrams included represent only 30–40 per cent of the available drafts. The second issue of Sheng's works, which was to have included his official correspondence and letters, has never appeared. All the documents printed in the first issue were written between 1896 and 1911; documentation on Sheng's activities before the Sino-Japanese War, when he had not yet risen high enough in the bureaucracy to be in a position to memorialize the throne, would have been included in the second issue. See the review of the 1939 edition of *YCTK* by Gideon Ch'en (Ch'en Ch'i-t'ien) in *The Yenching Journal of Social Studies,* 3.2 (August 1941), 242–247; and notices of the 1942 reprint in *T'u-shu chi-k'an* ("Quarterly Bulletin of Chinese Bibliography"), Chungking, 4.3–4 (1943), 105, and in *Kuo-li Hua-pei pien-i-kuan kuan-k'an* (Bulletin of the National North China Compilation and Translation Bureau), Peking, 1.3 (December 1, 1942). The Seminar on Modern China (Kindai Chūgoku kenkyū iin kai) has published a table of contents to the memorials of Sheng and of Yuan Shih-k'ai: *Sei Senkai En Seigai sōgi mokuroku* ("List of memorials presented to the Emperor by Sheng Hsuan-huai and Yuan Shih-k'ai").

Biographical notices of Sheng Hsuan-huai include the following: *Tōyō rekishi daijiten* (Encyclopedia of Oriental history), 5.145 and *passim;* Ts'ai Kuan-lo, compiler, *Ch'ing-tai ch'i-pai ming-jen chuan* (Seven hundred Ch'ing dynasty biographies), 3.1522–1524; Hashikawa Tokio, compiler, *Chūgoku bunkakai jimbutsu sōkan* (Comprehensive dictionary of personalities in Chinese cultural circles), 512; Sonoda Kazuki, compiler, Huang Hui-ch'üan and Tiao Ying-hua, translators from the Japanese, *Fen-sheng hsin Chung-kuo jen-wu-chih* (Personalities of the new China arranged by provinces), 150–151, 153; Japan, Foreign Office Intelligence Section (*Gaimushō jōhōbu*), *Gendai Shina jimmei kan* (Biographies of contemporary Chinese), 1928 edition, 934; Herbert A. Giles, *A Chinese Biographical Dictionary*, 1703; *Who's Who in the Far East*, 1906–07, 289; *Ch'ing-shih kao* (Draft history of the Ch'ing dynasty), 477.1a–3a; and Albert Feuerwerker, "A Draft Biography of Sheng Hsuan-huai, Official and Industrialist (1844–1916)."

In general, the *Hsing-shu* will not be cited when it is the source of information in the following account; other sources will be noted as they are used.

7. *Li Wen-chung-kung ch'üan-chi* (Complete papers of Li Hung-chang), 100 *ts'e,* Nanking, 1905; reprinted in a photolithographed edition by the Commercial Press, Shanghai, 1921.

8. *Chang Wen-hsiang-kung ch'üan-chi* (Complete papers of Chang Chih-tung), 120 *ts'e,* Peiping, 1928.

9. *Wu-chin Yang-hu hsien chih* (Gazetteer of Wu-chin and Yang-hu districts), 1879 edition, 19.20b.

10. *Ibid.,* 19.37b.

11. The following account of Sheng K'ang is based for the most part on a biography by his sons: Sheng Hsuan-huai and Sheng Shan-huai, *Sheng K'ang hsing-shu* (Biography of Sheng K'ang). This is a rare volume, of which a copy is included as *ts'e* 200 in a collection carrying the bookseller's title *Chuan-chi hsing-shu hui-chi* (Biographical collectanea) in the East Asiatic Library, Columbia University.

12. For Hsiang Jung (d. 1856), see Hummel, 1.292–294.

13. See William James Hail, *Tseng Kuo-fan and the Taiping Rebellion, with a Short Sketch of his Later Career.*

14. On Hu Lin-i (1812–1861), see Hummel, 1.333–335.

15. On Yen Shu-shen (d. 1876), see *ibid.,* 1.335.

16. See China, Imperial Maritime Customs, *Salt: Production and Taxation,* 1906, on the Hupei salt administration.

17. Literally, *chin-hsien pu-yung tao,* "[expectant] taotai to be employed at the first opportunity," which had chiefly an honorific value in this case and did not imply that Sheng K'ang was actually being considered for a substantive appointment.

18. A brief sketch of Sheng's career in Marion J. Levy, Jr., and Shih Kuo-heng, *The Rise of the Modern Chinese Business Class,* 30–34 and *passim,* contains, among many other factual errors, the statement that Sheng received the *chü-jen* degree. These errors have been repeated in derivative studies, for example, in Charles D. Sheldon, "Some Economic Reasons for the Marked Contrast in Japanese and Chinese Modernization as Seen in Examples from 'Premodern' Shipping and Trading by Water."

19. *Hsing-shu,* 4a.

20. In 1874 Sheng Hsuan-huai was made a brevet provincial treasurer in recognition of his relief work in Chihli. He played an active part in raising

funds for famine and flood victims in Chihli and Shantung in 1878. Timothy Richard, for example, mentions his association with Sheng in distributing famine relief in Shantung in 1878 (*Forty-five Years in China*, 142). In later years, Sheng was constantly occupied with relief activities. See, for example, *YCTK* 8.23a–30b, 15.8a–16b, 16.28a–37b, 17.20a–25a, 18.1a–18a, 21.26b–28a and *passim*.

21. See Arthur W. Hummel, Jr., "Yuan Shih-k'ai as an Official Under the Manchus."

22. On Shen Pao-chen (1820–1879), see Hummel, 2.642–644.

23. *LWCK-Memorials*, 19.44a–50b, TC 11/5/15 (June 20, 1872).

24. *Hsing-shu*, 5ab, quoting the petition in question.

25. *LWCK-Memorials*, 20.32b, TC 11/11/23 (December 23, 1872).

26. *Ibid.*, 25.4a–5a, KH 1/2/27 (May 3, 1875).

27. Kwang-ching Liu, "Two Steamship Companies in China, 1862–1877," Chapter 3.

28. *LWCK-Memorials*, 29.9ab, KH 3/2/24 (April 7, 1877). On the Shanghai-Woosung railroad, the first to be built in China, see Cheng Lin, *The Chinese Railways, An Historical Survey*, 1935 ed., 2–8. After the line was recovered by the Chinese, it was torn up and shipped to Formosa where for the most part the rails were simply allowed to rust away. According to the *Hsing-shu* (6b), Sheng secretly regretted the tearing up of the railroad.

29. *LWCK-Memorials*, 49.45a, KH 10/4/16 (May 10, 1884); *ibid.*, 43.37a, KH 8/3/6 (April 23, 1882).

30. See Chapter 6 for the *kuan-tu shang-pan* telegraph lines.

31. H. B. Morse, *The International Relations of the Chinese Empire*, 3.336–337.

32. *Hsing-shu*, 9a.

33. *LWCK-Memorials*, 38.16a–17a, KH 6/8/12 (September 16, 1880).

34. *Ibid.*, 44.22a–24a, KH 8/8/16 (September 27, 1882).

35. Most of the documentation with regard to these negotiations, which have little intrinsic interest today, can be located through the index to the *Ch'ing-chi wai-chiao shih-liao*: Wang Liang, ed., *Ch'ing-chi wai-chiao shih-liao so-yin* (Index to historical materials on foreign relations in the latter part of the Ch'ing dynasty), Peiping, 1933, 12 *ts'e*. In addition to contacts with foreigners in talks on telegraph matters, Sheng was on Li Hung-chang's staff during the negotiations which Li conducted in 1882 and 1883 with regard to China's troubled tributary states, Korea and Annam. And in the winter of 1883 he was deputed to negotiate an indemnity with the British for the burning of foreign buildings on Shameen Island by rioters (*Hsing-shu*, 10b, 11a, 11b, 12a).

36. *Translations of the Peking Gazette*, July 23, 1891, 100, memorial by Chang Yao (1832–1891).

37. J. O. P. Bland, *Li Hung-chang*, 121.

38. J. O. P. Bland, *Recent Events and Present Policies in China*, 248. Paul King, who was in the Maritime Customs at Chefoo in 1889, reports favorably of Sheng (*In the Chinese Customs Service*, 94).

39. *LWCK-Memorials*, 74.30a–31a, KH 18/5/24 (June 18, 1892).

40. Stanley Spector, "Li Hung-chang and the Huai-chün," 310–320.

41. See Chapter 6.

42. The estimate of Tls. 200,000 was made by United States Consul Read at Tientsin; see Spector, *op. cit.*, 602–604.

43. Ch'üan Han-sheng, "Ch'ing-mo Han-yang t'ieh-ch'ang" ("The Han-yang Iron and Steel Works, 1890–1908"), 5.

44. Spector, *op. cit.*, 602–604, citing Tientsin Consular Despatches (National Archives), September 17, 1894, and July 21, 1895.

45. William L. Langer sums up his account of the origins of the war with the statement that "it is almost impossible to evade the conclusion, which was widely held at the time, that Japan precipitated the war because of domestic considerations" (*The Diplomacy of Imperialism*, 1951 ed., 173).

46. *Hsing-shu*, 21ab.

47. No biography of Wang Wen-shao (1825?–1908) is included in Hummel's *Eminent Chinese of the Ch'ing Period;* for summaries of his career, see NCH, July 19, 1907, 143–144; December 19, 1908, 721; and *Ch'ing-shih kao*, 443.2a–3a.

48. But Jung-lu (1836–1903) in particular had considerable military power; see Hummel, 1.405–409.

49. *CWHK-Memorials*, 50.3a–8b, KH 25/6/17 (July 24, 1899). The loan was made to finance the P'ing-hsiang Coal Mine.

50. Sheng as *t'ieh-lu tu-pan* ("director-general of railroads") assumed charge of all official railway projects with the exception of the Imperial Railways of North China, that is, the Peking-Mukden line and its feeders. The latter were under the direction of Hu Yü-fen (d. 1906), who also had the title of *tu-pan* or director-general. Hu was a native of Anhwei, a *chin-shih* of 1874, a considerable rival of Sheng Hsuan-huai, and from January 1902 a close associate of Yuan Shih-k'ai, the Chihli governor-general (*NCH*, December 7, 1906, 550, obituary of Hu Yü-fen).

57. Li Chien-nung, *Chung-kuo chin-pai-nien cheng-chih shih* (Political history of China in the last hundred years), 1.296, quoting an unidentified contemporary account. Hsü T'ung-hsin's generally reliable chronology of the life of Chang Chih-tung does not support the story of Chang's unloading the Hanyang white elephant onto Sheng's unwilling shoulders. But this work does note Sheng's hesitancy about taking over the ironworks unless a market for its output were guaranteed in the form of purchases by the railroads, and his reluctance to assume responsibility for the Lu-Han line unless the potentially more lucrative Canton-Hankow railroad were also placed under his charge (Hsü T'ung-hsin, *Chang Wen-hsiang-kung nien-p'u* [A chronology of the life of Chang Chih-tung], 103, 105).

52. *CWHK-Memorials*, 44.19b–27b, KH 22/7/25 (September 2, 1896), and appended imperial edict.

53. YCTK, 21.12a–13a, telegraphic memorial sent KH 24/5/11 (June 29, 1898) reporting the expenditure of railroad funds.

54. See Chapter 1, note 94.

55. See Tseng K'un-hua, *Chung-kuo t'ieh-lu shih* (A history of Chinese railroads), 72–78; and CTS-LCP 1.74–84.

56. See William R. Braisted, "The United States and the American China Development Company."

57. See J.-M. Frochisse, *La Belgique et la Chine: relations diplomatiques et économiques (1839–1909)*, 255–347.

58. See E-tu Zen Sun, *Chinese Railways and British Interests, 1898–1911, passim.*

59. YCTK, 1.14a–15b, memorial endorsed KH 22/9/26 (November 1, 1896).

60. The Imperial Bank of China is discussed further in Chapter 6.

61. The text of Sheng's plans for the Tientsin school is printed in Shu Hsin-ch'eng, compiler, *Chin-tai Chung-kuo chiao-yü shih-liao* (Historical materials relating to education in modern China), 1.23–35.

62. *THHL-KH*, 129.4b–6a, KH 21/8/12 (September 30, 1895).

63. See John C. Ferguson, "Dr. Charles D. Tenney," 5–6.

64. *YCTK*, 1.11a–13a, memorial endorsed KH 22/9/? (October 1896); 2.18a–26b, memorial endorsed KH 24/5/19 (July 7, 1898), giving much detail about the organization, curriculum, and finances.

65. Ferguson, the noted Sinologue, was closely associated with Sheng until the latter's death in 1916, as president of the Nanyang College, 1897–1902; chief secretary to the Imperial Chinese Railway Administration, 1903–1905; member of the Commission for Treaty Revision, 1903–1904; foreign secretary to the Ministry of Communications, 1911; and as a personal friend and adviser. See his account of his first meeting with Sheng, and the establishment of the Nanyang College in the preface volume (*chüan-shou*) of *Yü-chai ts'un-kao*, Sheng's posthumous collected writings. Also see the following: R. H. van Gulik, "Dr. John C. Ferguson's 75th Anniversary"; *The China Who's Who 1927 (Foreign)*, A Biographical Dictionary Compiled and Published by Carrol Lunt, 77–78. Ferguson's personal papers, which are reported by his daughter to be still intact but inaccessible in his house in Peking, should be a mine of inside information on China in the first decades of the twentieth century.

66. On the later history of Nanyang, see these memorials by Sheng among others: *YCTK*, 1.21a–22a, endorsed KH 22/12/12 (January 14, 1897), about the *Ta-ch'eng kuan*, or special class for adult students of which Ts'ai Yuan-p'ei (1867–1940) was the Head Teacher; 6.20a–22b, endorsed KH 27/12/27 (February 5, 1902), and 9.5a–8b, endorsed KH 29/8/20 (October 10, 1903), about commercial education at Nanyang; 8.31a–34b, endorsed KH 28/9/29 (October 30, 1902), about the problems of securing official recognition and employment for the graduates; and 11.1a–3b, endorsed KH 31/3/7 (April 11, 1905), about the transfer of the school to the control of the Ministry of Commerce. See also *Shang-hai-hsien hsü-chih* (Supplementary gazetteer of the Shanghai district), 11.4b–5a; and Morisawa Rakugoro, "Shanhai ni okeru kyōiku" (Education in Shanghai), 320.

67. *YCTK*, 2.27a–28a, memorial endorsed KH 24/5/19 (June 7, 1899); 5.33a–35b, 5.36a–37a, 5.38a–39a, memorials endorsed KH 27/7/12 (August 25, 1901); and 6.15a–19b, memorial endorsed KH 27/12/27 (February 5, 1902).

68. *Ibid.*, 8.35a–36b, memorial endorsed KH 28/9/29 (October 30, 1902).

69. Ssu-yü Teng and John K. Fairbank, *China's Response to the West*, 213.

70. *NCH*, December 18, 1899, 1211; but the source of the quotation is not given. The *North-China Herald* remarked with regard to Sheng's educational projects:

It is refreshing to see that astute official Sheng Taotai finding so harmless an outlet for his energies and wealth as the liberal foundation of a great school. We heartily hope his Excellency will increasingly direct his zeal and attention to such work. Philanthropy may now well claim his attention for a while; commerce and statecraft, or perhaps we may omit the word state, have richly endowed him with the sinews of war for a long campaign of educational benevolence. He has our best wishes and congratulations in his new activity (November 1, 1895, 724).

71. See notes 61 and 64 above.
72. *YCTK*, 7.35a–37b, memorial endorsed KH 28/9/? (October 2–31, 1902).
73. *Ibid.*
74. *NKSPTCP-I*, 4.1a–46b.
75. *YCTK*, 1.16a–17a, memorial endorsed KH 22/11/1 (December 5, 1896).
76. *Ibid.*, 2.1a–2a, memorial endorsed KH 24/1/7 (January 28, 1898).
77. *Ibid.*, 5.19ab, memorial endorsed KH 26/12/2 (January 21, 1901).
78. *Ibid.*, 5.20a–21b, memorial endorsed KH 26/12/13 (February 1, 1901).
79. *Ibid.*, 6.13a–14b, memorial endorsed KH 27/12/1 (January 10, 1902).
80. *Ibid.*, 6.24a–25a, memorial endorsed KH 28/2/? (March 10–April 7, 1902).
81. *Ibid.*, 4.27a–36a, memorial endorsed KH 26/2/24 (March 24, 1900); and 4.37a–44b.
82. The documentation on the agreement to pacify South China during the Boxer uprising, including considerable material about Sheng's role, has been collected in Chien Po-tsan *et al.*, eds., *I-ho-t'uan* ([Source materials on] the Boxer uprising), 3.321–362, 517–539. Fully 16 *chüan* among the 77 *chüan* of telegrams in Sheng's collected works are concerned with the Boxer year, and many memorials as well. See Chester C. Tan, *The Boxer Catastrophe*, 77, 80–81, 85 and *passim*; also Great Britain, *Parliamentary Papers, China. No. 3 (1900)*, Nos. 128 ff.

The *Hsing-shu* states [37b–38a] that although Sheng's role in concluding an agreement with the foreign consuls in Shanghai is known, it is not generally known that during the siege of Peking he had secretly telegraphed Jung-lu and convinced him to allow the besieged diplomats to communicate by telegraph with the outside world. There followed Minister Conger's telegram to Washington which let the world know that the legation quarter was safe. G. N. Steiger (*China and the Occident*, 234) attributed the resumption of communications to the efforts of Wu T'ing-fang.

83. A detailed account of these negotiations, which is quite fair to the Chinese side, appears in Stanley F. Wright, *China's Struggle for Tariff Autonomy, 1843–1938*, 353–391. See also *YCTK*, *chüan* 6–9, *passim*.
84. On Lü Hai-huan (1840–1927), see *Gendai Shina jimmei kan*, 1928 edition, 14.
85. *YCTK*, 7.21a–23b, memorial endorsed KH 28/7/17 (August 20, 1902).
86. *NCH*, November 6, 1901, 874.
87. *Ibid.*, January 14, 1903, 73.
88. *Ibid.*, November 5, 1902, 962.
89. *THHL-KH*, 176.9a, KH 28/9/25 (October 26, 1902).
90. *NCH*, November 5, 1902, 963.
91. *Ibid.*
92. *THHL-KH*, 177.15a, KH 28/12/17 (January 15, 1903).

93. *YCTK,* 59.28a–29b, telegram of Chang Chih-tung to the Grand Council, KH 28/12/28 (January 26, 1903).

94. On the development of Yuan Shih-k'ai's military power see Ralph L. Powell, *The Rise of Chinese Military Power, 1895–1912,* 129 *et seq.*

95. The long rivalry between Sheng and Yuan, going back to the time when they were both subordinates of Li Hung-chang, is described by Matsushima Shūe, for over a decade the Tokyo *Nichi-nichi shimbun* correspondent in Peking, in an anecdotal work, *Shinchō matsuro hishi* (Secret history of the end of the Ch'ing dynasty), 211–217.

96. See *Hsing-shu,* 31b; and Li Chien-nung, *op. cit.,* 1.182–187.

97. *NCH,* March 26, 1903, 600; Shou Tsu-hsien and Wu K'ai-sheng, *Jung-an ti-tzu chi* (An account of Yuan Shih-k'ai by his disciples), 4.5ab.

98. Li Chien-nung, *op. cit.,* 1.257–261; L. F. Lawton and H. Hobden, "The Fall of Yuan Shih-k'ai," 420–434.

99. See these decrees citing memorials among others: *THHL-KH,* 188.15b–16a, KH 30/8/27 (October 6, 1904); 190.20a, KH 30/12/18 (January 23, 1905); 193.5a, KH 31/4/11 (May 14, 1905); 200.10b–11b, KH 32/4/28 (May 21, 1906); 200.18a–19a, KH 32/intercalary 4/13 (June 14, 1906).

100. *NCH,* March 26, 1903, 600.

101. *Ibid.,* April 23, 1903, 786.

102. *Ibid.,* May 28, 1903, 1047.

103. *THHL-KH,* 179.4b–5a, KH 29/3/20 (April 17, 1903).

104. *Hsing-shu,* 41a; *THHL-KH,* 179.4a, KH 29/3/10 (April 7, 1903).

105. Hsü T'ung-hsin, *op. cit.,* 172–173; *NCH,* May 21, 1903, 1019.

106. *CWHK-Memorials,* 60.15b–22b, KH 29/2/19 (March 17, 1903).

107. See E-tu Zen Sun, *op. cit.,* 74–80, which examines the disagreement between Sheng and Chang.

108. *Hsing-shu,* 43a; *YCTK,* 12.18a, memorial endorsed KH 32/2/27 (March 21, 1906).

109. *YCTK,* 12.1a–3a, and 12.7ab, memorials endorsed KH 31/8/9 (September 7, 1905).

110. *NCH,* October 6, 1905, 24.

111. *YCTK,* memorial endorsed KH 31/6/26 (July 28, 1905).

112. *NCH,* November 17, 1905, 371; November 24, 1905, 428.

113. *Ibid.,* November 24, 1905. P. H. Kent, *Railway Enterprise in China,* 134, prints a report that Sheng's son had been engaged in land speculation along the Shanghai-Nanking right of way, buying up land on the basis of prior knowledge of the route and reselling it to the government at a big profit.

114. *YCTK,* 12.17a–19b, memorial endorsed KH 32/2/27 (March 21, 1906).

115. *Ibid.,* 13.7a–12a, memorial endorsed KH 32/9/7 (October 24, 1906).

116. *NCH,* October 5, 1906, 55.

117. See note 20 above.

118. E-tu Zen Sun, *op. cit.,* 62 *et seq.*

119. *YCTK,* 14.9a–10a, memorial endorsed KH 34/2/8 (March 10, 1908).

120. *Ibid.,* 14.11a, memorial endorsed KH 34/2/11 (March 13, 1908); *THHL-KH,* 214.14a, KH 34/2/9 (March 11, 1908).

121. Hummel, 2.951–952.

122. Hsü Jun, *Hsü Yü-chai tzu-hsü nien-p'u* (Chronological autobiography), 125a–132b; and see Chapter 4.

123. *YCTK*, 14.13a–17b, memorial endorsed KH 34/2/11 (March 13, 1908); *NKSPTCP-II*, 5.4b.

124. Sheng's diary of his trip to Japan, entitled *K'ao-ch'a Jih-pen pao-kao* (Report of my observations in Japan), is appended as a final volume to his collected works, the *Yü-chai ts'un-kao*. The statement in Teng and Fairbank, *op. cit.*, 213, that "to avoid sharp criticism in China he traveled to Japan in 1908 on the pretext of seeking treatment for tuberculosis" is unfounded. Sheng's illness, probably acute asthma, was a legitimate one, and he did in fact spend considerable time with doctors in Japan. Severe attacks in 1902, for example, had necessitated a delay in the commercial treaty negotiations at that time (see Wright, *op. cit.*, 362).

125. *YCTK*, 14.31a–76b, memorial endorsed HT 1/intercalary 2/12 (April 2, 1909); this proposal was translated by John C. Ferguson as *China's National Bank and Currency Reform, A Memorial by Sheng Hsuan-huai, Junior Vice-President of the Board of Posts and Communications*, Shanghai, 1909, 24 pp.

126. See Marius B. Jansen, "Yawata, Hanyehping, and the Twenty-one Demands," 37.

127. *NCH*, January 14, 1910, 84.

128. *YCTK*, 15.17a–18a, memorial endorsed HT 2/7/14 (August 18, 1910).

129. Matsushima Shūe, *op. cit.*, 214–215.

130. *Ibid.*, 216; *YCTK*, 16.11a–12a, memorial endorsed HT 2/12/7 (January 7, 1911).

131. *YCTK*, 16.22a–24a, memorial endorsed HT 3/1/? (February 1911); see Liang's biography: Feng-kang, *Liang Yen-sun hsien-sheng nien-p'u* (Chronological biography of Mr. Liang Yen-sun [Shih-yi]), 1.91–92, 100, 120. This work has its own view of Sheng's contribution to railroad development:

> China's first railroads were undertaken by Li Hung-chang and Liu Ming-ch'uan, and the managers were Tong King-sing, Wu T'ing-fang, et al. Sheng came onto the scene later. After getting Li's favor, he built up his power by claiming the accomplishments of others as his own. He acquired great wealth by devious means. From the time of the establishment of the T'ieh-lu tsung-kung-ssu, the details of his affairs are obscure (p. 54).

See also Teng Chih-ch'eng's review of Liang Shih-yi's biography, 297–298, for a statement of the relations between Sheng and Liang.

132. See Sun, *op. cit.*, 112–119; Tseng K'un-hua, *op. cit.*, 107–121; and John Gilbert Reid, *The Manchu Abdication and the Powers, 1908–1912*, *passim*.

133. *YCTK*, 17.1a–3b, memorial endorsed HT 3/4/11 (May 9, 1911).

134. *Ibid.*, 17.31a–33a, memorial endorsed HT 3/5/21 (June 17, 1911).

135. Great Britain, *Parliamentary Papers, China. No. 1 (1912)*, No. 59, gives the text of the memorial impeaching Sheng and Minister Jordan's comments on Sheng's policy and behavior; P. H. Kent, *The Passing of the Manchus*, 110 *et seq.*

136. Kent, *The Passing of the Manchus*, 292–293.

137. *Hsing-shu*, 3a.

138. *Sheng K'ang hsing-shu*, 10ab.

139. *Hsing-shu*, 3b.

140. Sheng K'ang's work in 120 *chüan* was one of three with the same title (the others appearing in 1882 and 1888 respectively) published as

continuations of the *Huang-ch'ao ching-shih-wen pien* (Ch'ing dynasty essays on statecraft) of Ho Ch'ang-ling (1785–1848), which appeared in 1827. At least five other continuations or supplements, containing reform memorials, essays, and translations from Western works appeared in the first years of the twentieth century. See Momose Hiromu, "Shimmatsu no Keiseibumpen ni tsuite" (On the *Ching-shih-wen pien* of the late Ch'ing).

141. *Sheng K'ang hsing-shu*, 21ab.

142. Eleven thousand, according to Liu Sheng-mu, *Ch'ang-ch'u chai sui-pi*, 5.9b-10b; 13,000, according to *NCH*, March 28, 1914, 897, which states that Sheng Hsuan-huai "with the 13,000 shares that he owns himself and those that are owned by his family, is practically able to control the affairs of the company."

143. *Golden Jubilee History of Nippon Yusen Kaisha, 1885–1935*, 9–11, 41–42.

144. Liu Sheng-mu, *op. cit.*, 5.9b–10a, gives the following account of Sheng's fortune:

The actual final amount of his wealth cannot be definitely known from information available in 1929, but since 60–70 per cent is accounted for, I shall note it here.

The capital left for the support of the board president's second wife, the lady Chuang, amounted to Tls. 700,000, not including the increase in value due to the accumulation of interest nor the value of the many books in his library. There was also a residence in the city of Ch'ang-chou on Chou-hsien street, a fifteen-court house with more than 240 rooms; more than 3,000 mou of land in the Cho-yuan i-chuang; shares in the Chi-feng pawnshop; the four yards of the Ch'ien-feng Lumber Company; three pawnshops each in Wu-hsi-hsien and Chiang-yin-hsien, and one pawnshop in I-cheng-hsien [all in Kiangsu], but no accurate figures are known for the capital of the pawnshops; land in the two cities Soochow and Hangchow; and the Chi-p'ing pawnshop in Chia-ting-hsien and the Ta-cheng pawnshop in Ch'ang-shu-hsien [both in Kiangsu].

Also $700,000 in Finance Ministry treasury bonds secured on the cigarette tax; 11,000 shares of the old stock of the China Merchants' Steam Navigation Company, each valued at Tls. 200 which is equal to 22,000 shares of the new stock; 11,000 shares of stock in the China Merchants' Holding Company each valued at [$100 (Chinese)].

And 20,267 shares of Han-Yeh-P'ing Coal and Iron Company stock, each share worth $50 [Chinese]; 4,800 shares in the Jen-chi-ho Insurance Company each valued at [no figure given, probably $100 (Chinese)]; real estate in the Shanghai Foreign Concession worth ten to twenty million taels, accurate figures not being available.

In all Mr. Sheng's wealth came to several tens of millions of taels.

145. *Ibid.*

146. *Ibid.* Reputedly the Sung statesman Fan Chung-yen (989–1052) established the first *i-chuang*. Fan purchased land the income of which was used to aid members of his clan who were in need of funds in order to marry, bury their dead, or prepare for the civil service examinations. Apparently this land was considered to be held in common by the clan. The practice was copied by others in later years. The Yü-chai *i-chuang*, however, seems to have been intended first as a method of preserving the Sheng family

fortune and only secondarily, if at all, as common property for the benefit of the needy members of the Sheng clan.

147. *NCH,* November 14, 1900, 1045.

148. *Ibid.,* August 14, 1903, 340.

149. *Sheng K'ang hsing-shu,* 29b.

150. *Who's Who in China,* 3rd edition, 1926, 661.

151. Hsü Jun, *op. cit.,* 125a–132b; *NCH,* March 28, 1907, 679.

152. Yung Wing (Jung Hung [1828–1912]; Hummel, 1.402–405), *My Life in China and America,* 234–236; see Chapter 6, note 182.

153. Excerpts from Weng T'ung-ho's diary in Chin Liang, *Chin-shih jen-wu chih* (A gazetteer of modern personages), 233–234, would indicate that he was on intimate terms with the Sheng family; on Weng (1830–1904) see Hummel, 2.860–861.

154. *NCH,* March 13, 1908, 620–621.

155. *YCTK,* 14.24a–28a, memorial endorsed KH 34/4/19 (May 18, 1908).

156. *Ibid.,* 6.1a–5a, memorial endorsed KH 27/11/? (December 1901).

157. *Gendai Shina jimmei kan,* 1928 edition, 95–96; *YCTK,* 10.36a–37b, memorial endorsed KH 31/1/6 (February 9, 1905).

158. *Hsing-shu,* 60b.

159. *LWCK-Memorials,* 30.33ab, KH 3/11/25 (December 29, 1877); 59.28a–29b, KH 13/2/9 (March 3, 1887); 78.11b, KH 20/3/28 (May 3, 1894).

160. *Ibid.,* 40.20a–26b, KH 7/2/11 (March 10, 1881), a good example; see also Weng T'ung-ho's reference to Li Hung-chang's replying to impeachments of Sheng Hsuan-huai in Chin Liang, *op. cit.,* 233.

161. Morse to Detring, Letterbooks, October 19, 1886.

162. Lo Yü-tung, "Kuang-hsü-ch'ao pu-chiu ts'ai-cheng chih fa-ts'e" ("The governmental policies of meeting the financial crisis during the Kuang-hsü period [1875–1908]"), 222.

163. Hsü T'ung-hsin, *op. cit.,* 143.

164. *YCTK,* 21.28b–29a, telegraphic memorial of KH 26/11/28 (January 18, 1901).

165. *Ibid.,* 1.3a–10a, memorial endorsed KH 22/9/26 (November 1, 1896).

166. On the T'ung-wen Kuan, see Teng and Fairbank, *op. cit.,* 73–79.

167. *YCTK,* 2.49a–50b, memorial endorsed KH 25/10/16 (November 18, 1899).

168. These memorials are admirably summarized and translated in Teng and Fairbank, *op. cit.,* 195 *et seq.*

169. *Hsing-shu,* 41a, 43b.

170. *NCH,* November 15, 1889, 594–595.

171. *YCTK,* 2.34b–35a, memorial endorsed KH 24/6/10 (July 28, 1898).

172. *Ibid.,* 2.63b, memorial endorsed KH 25/10/16 (November 18, 1899).

CHAPTER 4

The China Merchants' Company: Merchant Management

1. So far as I am aware, there is no substantial published material on the China Merchants' Company in Western languages or in Japanese. Kwang-

ching Liu's ms. Ph.D. thesis, "Two Steamship Companies in China, 1862–1877" (now being expanded for publication) is of great value for the early years of the firm. In Chinese, brief accounts may be found in Wang Kuang, *Chung-kuo hang-yeh lun* (On the Chinese shipping business), 35–56; and Chang Hsin-ch'eng, *Chung-kuo hsien-tai chiao-t'ung shih* (A history of modern communications in China), 265–271. A major source, reprinting many documents, is *Chiao-t'ung shih* (History of communications [in China]), *Hang-cheng pien* (section on shipping), 1.139–319; this will be cited hereafter as *CTS-HCP.* The translation of the company's name as it appears in this study, China Merchants' Steam Navigation Company, follows exactly an example of its letterhead bound in *Chinese Bills, Notes, etc. Collected by Hosea Ballou Morse,* Harvard University Library.

2. *NCH,* May 2, 1914, 349–351.

3. Yung Wing [Jung Hung], *My Life in China and America,* 171–172.

4. *LWCK-TLYM Correspondence,* 1.38b, TC 11/11/23 (December 23, 1872); Stanley Wright, *China's Struggle for Tariff Autonomy,* 336–337. For the text of the 1867 regulations see *NCH,* September 14, 1867, 253; see also "Regulations for the purchase of foreign steamers, sailing ships and other vessels by Chinese from Foreigners," *NCH,* August 23, 1873, 158–159.

5. Feng Kuei-fen, *Hsien-chih-t'ang kao* (Literary works), 10.14a–15a, suggested Chinese operated steamships in an essay titled "On the Manufacture of Foreign Warships"; a partial translation appears in S. Y. Teng and J. K. Fairbank, *China's Response to the West,* 52–54.

6. *LWCK-Memorials,* 19.44a, TC 11/5/15 (June 29, 1872); *LWCK-Letters,* 12.1b–3a, TC 11/1/21 (February 29, 1872). For Sung Chin (*chin-shih,* 1844; d. 1873) see his biography in *Ch'ing-shih kao* (Draft history of the Ch'ing dynasty), 428.4a–5b; on the Foochow Shipyard see Gideon Ch'en (Ch'en Ch'i-t'ien), *Tso Tsung-t'ang,* 14–46.

7. *LWCK-Memorials,* 19.45b, TC 11/5/15 (June 29, 1872); Teng and Fairbank, *op. cit.,* 108–110, translate this memorial in part, and their wording is used here with slight modifications.

8. *Ibid.,* 19.49a.

9. Li also described the organization of the company to the Tsungli Yamen as follows (*LWCK-TLYM Correspondence,* 1.40a, TC 11/11/23 [December 23, 1872]):

The enterprise will be under official supervision and merchant management. While the government will lay down the general principles and keep its eye on the company's merits and demerits, the merchant directors will be permitted to propose their own regulations so that the shareholders will be satisfied.

10. K. C. Liu, *op. cit.,* 147–148, notes that

in 1874, one of the Foochow ships, the Haiching *(409 tons), was attached to Li's project on a consignment basis, but she drew too much water and "could not enter the Taku estuary"; she was returned to the government around October, 1874.*

11. *LWCK-Memorials,* 20.32b, TC 11/11/23 (December 23, 1872), mentions only Chu Ch'i-ang by name. Sheng's biography claims that he and Chu drew up the provisional regulations; see Sheng T'ung-i et al., [*Sheng Hsuan-huai*] *Hsing-shu* (Biography of [Sheng Hsuan-huai]), 5b; see Chapter 3, pp. 61–62.

12. Translated from the text of the petition as given in *Hsing-shu*, 5ab, which, however, ascribes it to Sheng alone and places it in time before Li's appointment of "Chu Ch'i-ang and others." The version cited by Li (*LWCK-Memorials*, 20.32b, TC 11/11/23 [December 23, 1872]) is apparently a condensation of the fuller text in the *Hsing-shu;* but because it was contemporaneous to the events described, the story as told in Li's memorial has been followed here in preference to the *Hsing-shu*.

13. See Charles J. Stanley, "Hu Kuang-yung and China's Early Foreign Loans."

14. K. C. Liu, *op. cit.*, 110.

15. *CTS-HCP*, 1.140.

16. A "picul" (*tan*) equals 133⅓ lbs.

17. The source of Tables 6 and 8 is the 20th Annual Report of the C.M.S.N. Co., *NCH*, April 13, 1894, 569–570. Table 7 is adapted from a chart prepared by H. B. Morse and enclosed in Morse to Detring, Letterbooks, July 13, 1887.

Until 1885, the C.M.S.N. Co.'s fiscal year commenced on the first day of the seventh moon of the Chinese lunar calendar and ended on the 30th day of the sixth moon in the following year. From 1886, the fiscal year was adjusted to begin on the first day of the first moon and end on the 30th day of the twelfth moon, thus bringing it into rough correspondence with the Western calendar year. Thus, for example, in this study in connection with the company's accounts "1879" indicates the fiscal year between August 18, 1879, and August 5, 1880; and "1893" the fiscal year between February 17, 1893, and February 5, 1894.

18. 7th Annual Report, *NCH*, September 30, 1880, 301–302.

19. *CTS-HCP*, 1.218–220.

20. *YCTK*, 3.20a–30b, C.M.S.N. Co. accounts appended to memorial endorsed KH 25/7/27 (September 1, 1899).

21. See the section on tribute rice in Chapter 5.

22. Kwang-ching Liu, "The Steamship Business in Nineteenth-Century China, An Essay on Some Problems of Entrepreneurship," 20.

23. C.M.S.N. Co. 1873 By-laws (*chü-kuei*), *CTS-HCP*, 1.143–144, Article 10; a rough translation was printed in *NCH*, April 21, 1877, 400–401.

24. C.M.S.N. Co. 1873 Regulations (*chang-ch'eng*), *CTS-HCP*, 1.145–146, Article 1; translation as in note 23.

25. C.M.S.N. Co. 1885 Regulations, *CTS-HCP*, 1.165, Articles 4,5,6.

26. 1873 Regulations, Article 3.

27. 6th Annual Report, *NCH*, October 3, 1879, 331; 7th Annual Report, *NCH*, September 30, 1880, 301–302; *CTS-HCP*, 1.182.

28. 8th Annual Report, *NCH*, September 21, 1881, 320–322.

29. *LWCK-Memorials*, 31.38b, KH 4/5/14 (June 14, 1878); 25.4a–5a, KH 1/2/27 (May 3, 1875); *Ch'ing-shih kao, lieh-chuan* (biographies), 239.3ab.

30. *LWCK-Letters*, 12.29b, TC 11/10/10 (November 10, 1872).

31. *YCTK*, 3.8a, memorial endorsed KH 25/7/27 (September 1, 1899). This statement is repeated in Sheng's biography (*Hsing-shu*, 6a), but K. C. Liu ("Two Steamship Companies," 111–112) attributes the major role to Sun Chu-t'ang.

32. Hsü Jun, *Hsü Yü-chai tzu-hsü nien-p'u* (Chronological autobiography), 36b.

33. Chang Hsin-ch'eng, *op. cit.*, 265–267; Wang Kuang, *op. cit.*, 41–42, also discusses the C.M.S.N. Co. under the headings "*shang-pan* period" (1873–1884) and "*kuan-tu shang-pan* period" (1885–1907).

34. Ellsworth Carlson, *The Kaiping Mines (1877–1912)*, 4–7, reviews most of the known biographical data about T'ang. There is a sketch of T'ang's life translated from an unidentified Western source in Hsü Jun, *op. cit.*, 57a–58b; and see *LWCK-Memorials*, 41.20a, KH 7/6/9 (July 4, 1881), 42.27a, KH 7/10/26 (December 17, 1881); "Death of Mr. Tong King-sing," *NCH*, October 14, 1892, 568; K. C. Liu, "Two Steamship Companies," 113–117, 159–160.

35. K. C. Liu, "Two Steamship Companies," 114–115.

36. Hsü Jun, *op. cit.*, 18a.

37. 1873 By-laws, Article 3; Regulations, Article 1. *LWCK-Memorials*, 30.29a, KH 3/11/25 (December 29, 1877); 36.32a, KH 6/3/27 (May 5, 1880); and *LWCK-Letters*, 13.13b, TC 12/intercalary 6/6 (July 29, 1873) refer to Tong as the *shang-tsung* of the company.

38. *LWCK-Letters*, 13.24b, TC 12/11/13 (January 1, 1874).

39. On Hsü Jun, see his autobiography, *Hsü Yü-chai tsu-hsü nien-p'u*, especially 8a, 14a, 16b, 18a–19b, 34a–37a, 53a, 55b, 58b–73a, 75a–77a, 86a–89b, 113b–114b. Also *NCH*, October 24, 1883, 471; Arnold Wright, ed., *Twentieth Century Impressions of Hong Kong, Shanghai, and other Treaty Ports of China*, 566; NKSPTCP-I, 4.3b, NKSPTCP-II, 5.28a.

40. *CTS-HCP*, 1.142, 170.

41. Hsü Jun, *op. cit.*, 9b, 16b.

42. *LWCK-Memorials*, 30.20a, KH 4/7/23 (August 21, 1878).

43. *CTS-HCP*, 1.185, 201.

44. Hsü Jun, *op. cit.*, 36a–40a, 86a–89a; *CTS-HCP*, 1.153, 185. For Sino-French relations in this period, see H. B. Morse, *International Relations of the Chinese Empire*, 2.340–367.

45. *Translations of the Peking Gazette*, October 24, 1885, 155–156; this memorial by Li does not appear in Li's printed papers edited by Wu Ju-lun. In his autobiography, Hsü Jun admits that he was impeached and dismissed, but he denies that his financial dealings in any way damaged the China Merchants' Company. In support of his claim, he offers a very questionable financial statement showing a "balance" of more than Tls. 1,000,000 after ten years of his administration (Hsü Jun, *op. cit.*, 39b–40a, 33ab).

46. See the lengthy exchange of telegrams between Ma and Li in *LWCK-Telegrams*, 3.4 *et seq.*

47. *LWCK-Memorials*, 54.1a–2b, KH 11/6/8 (July 19, 1885).

48. Although Pao-ting-fu, about 100 miles inland from Tientsin, was the official capital of the province of Chihli, Li made Tientsin his home and principal place of business as commissioner for the northern ports. When purely provincial business required it, he traveled to Pao-ting-fu. This concentration in Tientsin, which as a major treaty port was a kind of "window" to the Occident, perhaps symbolizes the degree to which Li's efforts were devoted to defense and "foreign matters." See James Harrison Wilson, *China: Travels and Investigations in the "Middle Kingdom,"* 105–106.

49. 1885 Regulations, Article 2.

50. 1885 Regulations, Article 3.

51. There is a brief summary of Cheng's career in Teng and Fairbank, *op. cit.*, 112–113. Also see *CTS-HCP*, 1.187, 198, and *passim;* Hsü Jun,

op. cit., 132a; Yen Chung-p'ing, *Chung-kuo mien-yeh chih fa-chan* (The development of China's cotton industry), 73–76; Yen Chung-p'ing, *Chung-kuo mien-fang-chih shih kao* (A draft history of Chinese cotton spinning and weaving), 101; *LWCK-Memorials*, 45.32a, KH 8/12/8 (January 16, 1883); *YCTK*, 25.1b–2a, telegram dated KH 22/5/13 (June 23, 1896), 16.36a–37b, memorial endorsed KH 31/1/6 (February 9, 1905); *NCH*, May 4, 1906, 252; *NKSPTCP-I*, 4.9b, 10a; *NKSPTCP-II*, 4.4b; P'eng Yu-lin's preface, dated 1884, to 8 *chüan* edition of *Sheng-shih wei-yen*, 1900 (East Asiatic Library, Columbia University).

52. *Sheng-shih wei-yen*, 1898 T'u-shu chi'ch'eng 16 *chüan* edition, as excerpted in Chien Po-tsan *et al.*, eds., *Wu-hsü pien-fa* ([Source material on] the reform movement of 1898), 1.82.

53. *Ch'ing-shih kao, lieh-chuan*, 233.6b–7a; Teng and Fairbank, *op. cit.*, 88, 95–97; Hummel, 2.950; Hsia Yen-te, *Chung-kuo chin-pai-nien ching-chi ssu-hsiang* (Chinese economic thought in the last hundred years), 48–52; Stanley F. Wright, *Hart and the Chinese Customs*, 561; H. B. Morse, *International Relations of the Chinese Empire*, 2.102.

54. *Shih-k'o-chai chi-yen, ts'e* 27 in *Hsi-cheng ts'ung-shu*, preface dated 1897.

55. Min Erh-ch'ang, ed., *Pei-chuan-chi pu* (Supplementary collection of memorial inscriptions), 55.19b–23a; *LWCK-Memorials*, 45.32a, KH 8/12/8 (January 16, 1883); *Translations of the Peking Gazette*, October 15, 1882, 152.

56. *CTS-HCP*, 1.186.

57. *Ibid.*

58. *Ibid.*, 1.186, 187, 191.

59. *Ibid.*; *NKSPTCP-II*, 5.28a; *NCH*, March 12, 1897, 460–461.

60. *NCH*, March 12, 1897, 460–461; Yen Chung-p'ing, *Chung-kuo mien-yeh chih fa-chan* (The development of the Chinese cotton industry), 76.

61. *Gendai Shina jimmei kan* (Biographies of contemporary Chinese), 497; Hummel, 2.872; *YCTK*, 69.29ab, KH 32/10/20 (December 5, 1906); *NCH*, February 12, 1904, 290; April 12, 1906, 82; September 14, 1906, 634; November 30, 1906, 491.

62. *CTS-HCP*, 1.186.

63. *Ibid.*

64. Hsü Jun, *op. cit.*, 118ab, prints the text of Yuan's order of KH 32/12/26 (February 8, 1907).

65. *Ta-Ch'ing li-ch'ao shih-lu, Kuang-hsü* (Veritable records of the Ch'ing dynasty, Kuang-hsü reign), 565.5a, KH 32/10/5 (November 20, 1906); Ralph L. Powell, *The Rise of Chinese Military Power, 1895–1912;* 215–219; *NCH*, January 18, 1907, 107–108.

66. Hsü Jun, *op. cit.*, 117b.

67. *Ibid.*, 125a–132a; *NCH*, March 1, 1907, 473.

68. This was reflected in a dispatch from the Peking correspondent of the *North-China Herald* (March 28, 1907, 679):

We understand that due to representations brought to Peking recently from quarters hostile to the present management of the China Merchants' Company, drastic measures are now being considered amongst those now holding the reins of the Company, as the measures of reorganization that were expected during the past six months or so have not, so far, been realized.

69. Texts of Hsü's proposals and Yuan's reply in Hsü Jun, *op. cit.*, 128a–130a and 130b–131a respectively.

70. *YCTK*, 10.36a–37b, memorial endorsed KH 31/1/6 (February 9, 1905); *CTS-HCP*, 1.187.

71. For the C.M.S.N. Co.'s management 1909–1916, see *CTS-HCP*, 1.187–196, 201–205.

72. Table 10 is compiled from *CTS-HCP*, 1.287–290, 292–294.

73. Minor discrepancies in these figures, as that between Tls. 476,000 and Tls. 475,000, are due to the rounding of totals in some sources but not in others.

74. *CTS-HCP*, 1.145–146.

75. *Ibid.*, 1.145.

76. *Ibid.*, 1.143–144.

77. See K. C. Liu, "Two Steamship Companies," 123.

78. On Shen Pao-chen (1820–1879), see Hummel, 1.642–644.

79. Sheng's petition to Li, quoted in *LWCK-Memorials*, 40.23a, KH 7/2/11 (March 10, 1881).

80. 3rd Annual Report, *NCH*, April 12, 1877, 373.

81. 4th Annual Report, *NCH*, November 1, 1877, 400; *LWCK-TLYM Correspondence*, 7.28a, KH 3/9/29 (November 4, 1877).

82. The *North-China Herald* explained the lack of support in this way (April 5, 1877, 344–345):

Its [C.M.S.N. Co.] official position in a country so mandarin-rid as China, enables pressure of all kinds to be brought to force native merchants to support it. . . . It seemed very desirable to keep up the colourable mercantile character of the organisation after the arrangement for the purchase of the S.S.N. Co. had been completed, but Chinese merchants have not shown any great alacrity to come forward. Accordingly some few who were interested in the old company have been requested to join the new. . . . Fortunately the relief of the Shantung sufferers was exercising the residents of Shanghai; so the honour of joining the China Merchants' Company was declined, but the refusal was accompanied by various drafts of corresponding amounts in favour of the sufferers by famine. Even a mandarin could not refuse to acknowledge such a gift.

83. Kwang-ching Liu, "Financing a Steam-Navigation Company in China, 1861–1862," 169–170. Four men on Liu's list had been compradores for Russell and Co. He estimates that Tls. 300,000–400,000 of the Tls. 1,000,000 capital of the S.S.N. Co. was subscribed by the foreign community in Shanghai exclusive of the members of Russell and Company; and that members of Russell and Company, together with Chinese investors, owned a majority of the shares, probably 600,000–700,000. There is also evidence that the number of shares held by Chinese was greater than that held by the American members of Russell and Company itself.

84. Shanghai Steam Navigation Company, *Minutes of a General Meeting of the Shareholders* and *Report of the Board of Directors to the General Meeting*, February 21, 1868; March 5, 1870; March 4, 1871; January 15, 1877.

85. 6th Annual Report, *NCH*, October 3, 1879, 331–332; 7th Annual Report, *NCH*, September 30, 1880, 301–302.

86. 9th Annual Report, *NCH*, October 18, 1882, 417–420.

87. *Ibid.*

88. *NCH*, October 4, 1881, 346.

89. *CTS-HCP*, 1.170.

90. 9th Annual Report, *NCH*, October 18, 1882, 419.

91. A severe rate war with Butterfield and Swire's China Navigation Company (*T'ai-ku lun-ch'uan kung-ssu*) and Jardine, Matheson's Indo-China Steam Navigation Company (*I-ho lun-ch'uan kung-ssu*) followed upon the acquisition of the S.S.N. Co. This was settled in the winter of 1877–1878 by the signature of uniform rate agreements (*CTS-HCP*, 1.151).

92. 3rd Annual Report, *NCH*, April 12, 1877, 374; 4th Annual Report, *NCH*, November 1, 1877, 400; 8th Annual Report, *NCH*, September 27, 1881, 322.

93. 8th Annual Report, 322.

94. Hsü Jun, *op. cit.*, 86ab.

95. *Ibid.*, 37b; *Translations of the Peking Gazette*, March 11, 1890, 34 — a memorial by Li Hung-chang which I have not found in his collected works.

96. *CTS-HCP*, 1.153.

97. *Translations of the Peking Gazette*, October 24, 1885, 155–156 — a memorial by Li Hung-chang not found in his collected works.

98. *Ibid.*

99. *CTS-HCP*, 1.158; Liu Sheng-mu, *Ch'ang-ch'u chai sui-pi*, 5.9b–10b; *NCH*, March 28, 1914, 897.

100. Miyazaki Ichisada, "Shōshōkyoku no ryakushi, Chūgoku no doku-senteki kisen kaisha" (A short history of the C.M.S.N. Co., China's monopolistic steamship company), 63–69.

101. By the definition offered in the most recent study of the gentry in China (Chang Chung-li, *The Chinese Gentry*, 3), Sheng was a member of the "regular" gentry, that is he acquired his status through the examination system and by appointment to substantive official posts (see Chapter 3 above). Tong King-sing and Hsü Jun, who also had official rank, were "irregular gentry" in that their rank and their status as expectant officials were purchased or acquired through Li Hung-chang's favor. While this distinction clarifies the difference between the status of Sheng and that of his early associates in the C.M.S.N. Co., Dr. Chang's exclusive reliance on examination status or official rank in defining the Chinese gentry is open to question. It leads to the postulation of extensive sources of gentry income not derived from land, usury, or mercantile pursuits and the "hypothesis that gentry status itself provided the possibility of income" (*ibid.*, 216–219). Might not the contrast between the large number of gentry biographies which Chang notes as giving only a general "indication of wealth" and "the small number of cases in which there is information on private sources of income such as land or merchant enterprises" be more simply explained by the fact that landholding and other traditional sources of wealth were too much of a commonplace to be especially recorded by the biographer?

102. *NCH*, March 28, 1914, 897.

103. In 1913 the following approximate equivalents prevailed: Tls. 1 = $1.38 (Chinese) = U. S. $0.73.

104. Li Ku-fan, *Chao-shang-chü san-ta-an* (Three major cases relating to the C.M.S.N. Co.), 151–155; *CTS–HCP*, 1.218–220.

105. Liu Sheng-mu, *Ch'ang-ch'u chai sui-pi*, 5.9b–10b.

106. *LWCK-Letters*, 12.29a, TC 11/10/10 (November 10, 1872); *LWCK-*

Memorials, 20.33a, TC 11/11/23 (December 23, 1872); *CTS-HCP.* 1.140.

107. *LWCK-TLYM Correspondence,* 7.21b–22b, KH 2/9/29 (November 4, 1877).

108. *Ibid.,* 7.26b.

109. Hsü Jun, *op. cit.,* 18a–19b; *CTS-HCP,* 1.148–149.

110. 3rd Annual Report, *NCH,* April 12, 1877, 374; *LWCK-TYLM Correspondence,* 7.22a, KH 3/9/29 (November 4, 1877).

111. *LWCK-Memorials,* 30.31ab, KH 3/11/15 (December 19, 1877).

112. *Ibid.,* 36.33a, KH 6/3/27 (May 5, 1880).

113. Table 11 compiled from C.M.S.N. Co. annual reports as printed in the *North-China Herald.*

114. H. B. Morse wrote to Gustav Detring, "I suppose you know of the attempt of the Hu-pu to force the Company to repay its debt at once; that would cripple the Comp'y completely." Letterbooks, June 19, 1886.

115. *LWCK-Memorials,* 56.3ab, KH 12/1/21 (February 24, 1886); *NCH,* March 9, 1887, 269–271, translation of Hu-pu memorial.

116. 4th Annual Report, *NCH,* November 1, 1887, 399–400; 5th Annual Report, *NCH,* October 17, 1878, 376; 6th Annual Report, *NCH,* October 3, 1879, 331–332; 7th Annual Report, *NCH,* September 30, 1880, 301–302.

117. *CTS-HCP,* 1.157, 271–273.

118. "Memo on Exchange as affecting the China Merchants S.N. Co.", enclosure in Morse to G. Detring, Letterbooks, August 3, 1886. Morse wrote:

To show the constant drain on the Company's resources we may take the figures for one year. In 1888 the Co. must pay to the Bank, in principal and interest the sum of £ 47,889; at 5/1 per Tael, this would require Tls. 188,415 of silver; at 4/– per Tael, it would require Tls. 239,444; a loss to the Co. of Tls. 51,029 in one year.

119. 13th Annual Report, *NCH,* March 30, 1887, 360–361; 14th Annual Report, *NCH,* April 13, 1888, 421.

120. 14th Annual Report.

121. 15th Annual Report, *NCH,* April 5, 1889, 405–406.

122. 19th Annual Report, *NCH,* April 28, 1893, 605–606; 20th Annual Report, *NCH,* April 13, 1894, 569–570.

123. *NCH,* February 3, 1912, 306–307.

124. Hsü Jun and Tong King-sing were responsible for the establishment of the Jen-ho Maritime Insurance Company in 1875; it was originally capitalized at Tls. 250,000. "The first year of operations returned a handsome profit," wrote Hsü, "and we added Tls. 250,000 to the capital raising it to a total of Tls. 500,000." These funds were deposited with the C.M.S.N. Co. at interest. In 1878 Hsü and Tong inaugurated the Chi-ho Maritime and Fire Insurance Company, whose capital was also deposited with the China Merchants' Company. Both were in effect subsidiaries of the shipping company. In 1888 the two were combined to form the Jen-chi-ho Insurance Company, and 10,000 shares of Tls. 50 each were issued. See Hsü Jun, *op. cit.,* 18a–19b; *CTS-HCP,* 1.217; Shen Lei-ch'un ed., *Chung-kuo pao-hsien nien-chien* (Chinese insurance annual), 1937 edition, B-53.

125. Table 13 is compiled from the annual reports of the C.M.S.N. Co.; Hsü Jun, *op. cit.,* 119ab; *CTS-HCP,* 1.292–294.

126. Lien-sheng Yang, *Money and Credit in China,* 102.

127. *Ibid.,* 98–101.

128. Morse's ms. Letterbooks, consisting of copies of his semiofficial correspondence as an officer of the Imperial Maritime Customs, are deposited in the Houghton Library, Harvard University. All references to Morse's correspondence in the following notes are to these Letterbooks.

129. Morse to Li Hung-chang, December 1, 1886; marked "cancelled, not sent" in red pencil on the face of the letter.

130. Morse to G. Detring, April 16, 1886.

131. Morse to Detring, October 19, 1886.

132. Morse to Detring, April 16, 1886; July 1, 1886; October 19, 1886; November 3, 1886, and January 6, 1887; Morse to Sheng Hsuan-huai, August 3, 1887.

133. Morse to Detring, October 19, 1886.

134. *Ibid.*

135. Morse to Detring, May 8, 1886.

136. Morse to Detring, November 3, 1886.

137. Morse to Detring, May 8, 1886.

138. Morse to Detring, November 3, 1886.

139. Morse to Detring, October 19, 1886.

140. *Ibid.*

141. *Ibid.*

142. Morse to Li Hung-chang, December 1, 1886; marked "cancelled, not sent." See also Morse to Detring, November 3, 1886.

143. Morse to Detring, December 2, 1886.

144. Morse to Robert Hart, December 2, 1886.

145. Gustav Detring, commissioner of customs at Tientsin, is described by Sir Robert Hart's biographer as "the *fidus Achates* of the powerful Li Hung-chang, . . . the instigator of the Li-Fournier convention, and . . . the promoter at Tientsin of numerous official undertakings" who was Li's candidate as successor to Hart (Stanley Wright, *Hart and the Chinese Customs*, 537); see also Paul King, *In the Chinese Customs Service, A Personal Record of Forty-seven Years*, 73–75, 190–191.

146. Morse to Detring, August 16, 1886.

147. Morse to Detring, May 20, 1886; I have not found his full name.

148. *Ibid.*; Morse to A. E. Hippisley, June 15, 1886.

149. Hsü Jun, *op. cit.*, 87b–88a.

150. Morse to Detring, April 16, 1886.

151. *Ibid.*

152. Morse to Detring, May 8, 1886.

153. Morse to Li Hung-chang, December 1, 1886; marked "cancelled, not sent."

154. Morse to Detring, November 13, 1886.

155. Morse to Detring, January 6, 1887; November 3, 1886.

156. Morse to Detring, August 2, 1887; Morse to Li Hung-chang, August 2, 1887.

157. Morse to Detring, August 3, 1887.

158. Morse to Sheng Hsuan-huai, August 3, 1887.

159. Morse to [William?] Cartwright [chief secretary, Imperial Maritime Customs?], August 25, 1887.

160. *NCH*, August 4, 1887, 113.

161. Li Ku-fan, *op. cit.*, 52–53.

162. K. C. Liu, "Two Steamship Companies," 132–137, 143–145, 182–183.

163. *Ch'ing-ch'ao hsü wen-hsien t'ung-k'ao* (Encyclopedia of the historical records of the Ch'ing dynasty), 11046–11047.

164. Li Ku-fan, the author of *Chao-shang-chü san-ta-an* (Three major cases relating to the C.M.S.N. Co.), was a member of the investigating commission, and his book is based on its findings.

165. *CTS-HCP*, 1.190.

166. *Ibid.*, 1.143–146 prints the texts.

167. *Ibid.*, 1.156–157.

168. Li Ku-fan, *op. cit.*, 7–12.

169. *Ibid.*, 17–18.

170. *Ibid.*, 13–19.

171. *Ibid.*, 20–22.

172. *Ibid.*, 45–51.

173. *Ibid.*, 83–149.

174. *Ibid.*, 17–18.

CHAPTER 5

The China Merchants' Company: Official Supervision

1. *LWCK-Memorials*, 20.32–33b, TC 11/11/23 (December 23, 1872), 31.38a–39a, KH 4/5/14 (June 14, 1878), 32.20ab, KH 4/7/23 (August 21, 1878); *LWCK-TLYM Correspondence*, 7.25b, KH 3/9/29 (November 4, 1877); *YCTK*, 3.7b–8b, memorial endorsed KH 25/7/27 (September 1, 1899); Hsü Jun, *Hsü Yü-chai tzu-hsü nien-p'u* (Chronological autobiography), 18a–19b; *CTS-HCP*, 1.185–186.

2. In 1882, they offered to resign from the company because of adverse criticism of their administration, stating that "should the shareholders recognise the grounds which they claim for their release, they will please elect members to fill their places. And when they have done so, the undersigned [Tong King-sing, Hsü Jun, Cheng Kuan-ying, and Chang Hung-lu] will send in their official resignations to the Viceroy" (9th Annual Report of the C.M.S.N. Co., *NCH*, October 18, 1882, 420).

3. *Translations of the Peking Gazette*, October 24, 1885, 155–156.

4. *NCH*, September 19, 1874, 293; *CTS-HCP*, 1.287–290.

5. *LWCK-Memorials*, 20.33a, TC 11/11/23 (December 23, 1872): "I propose that the government follow the regulations of the Ministry of Revenue which provide for the loan at interest of *lien-chün* (military training) funds to Kiangsu and Chekiang pawnbrokers. The said company should be permitted to borrow the sum of 200,000 strings to be part of its capital as an indication of the government's good faith. We should, however, require that the merchants pay interest in advance toward relief work." Two hundred thousand strings of cash equaled roughly Tls. 135,000.

6. *LWCK-TLYM Correspondence*, 7.21b–22a, 27ab, KH 3/9/29 (November 4, 1877).

7. S. Y. Teng and J. K. Fairbank, *China's Response to the West*, 112, state that "Sheng on behalf of Li Hung-chang asked the governor-general of Liang-chiang to contribute one million taels from official funds."

8. Hsü Jun, *op. cit.*, 18a–19b; *CTS-HCP*, 1.148–149.

9. 4th Annual Report, *NCH*, November 1, 1877, 399–400.

10. *LWCK-TLYM Correspondence,* 7.22b, KH 3/9/29 (November 4, 1877).

11. *LWCK-Memorials,* 30.31ab, KH 3/11/15 (December 19, 1877).

12. *Ibid.,* 30.33a, KH 3/11/25 (December 29, 1877); *LWCK-TLYM Correspondence,* 7.23b, KH 3/9/29 (November 4, 1877).

13. *Translations of the Peking Gazette,* September 1, 1877, 122–123.

14. *LWCK-Memorials,* 36.32a–34a, KH 6/3/27 (May 5, 1880).

15. *Ibid.,* 37.33b, KH 6/6/3 (July 9, 1880); 40.56b, KH 7/4/27 (May 24, 1881).

16. *Ibid.,* 56.1a–4a, KH 12/1/21 (February 24, 1886).

17. Hu-pu memorial translated from the newspaper *Shen Pao* in *NCH,* March 9, 1887, 269–271; minor changes of wording by the author.

18. The rate per picul in 1885 stood at Tls. 0.38; it remained at about this level until 1902 when it was reduced to Tls. 0.3381 (*YCTK,* 7.32a–33a, memorial endorsed KH 28/9/? [October 2–31, 1902]). After 1890 no government funds are listed in the company's annual report, thus fulfilling the Hu-pu's directions that the funds be repaid in five annual installments (15th, 16th, 17th, 18th, 19th, and 20th Annual Reports, *NCH,* April 5, 1889, 405–406; May 16, 1890, 609–610; April 24, 1891, 506; April 14, 1892, 502–503; April 28, 1893, 605–606; April 13, 1894, 569–570).

19. Wang Hsien-ch'ien (1842–1918) is noted as the compiler of part of the *Tung-hua lu,* selected edicts, condensed, for the reigns of the Ch'ing dynasty.

20. *LWCK-Memorials,* 30.29a–31b, KH 3/11/15 (December 19, 1877); *CTS-HCP,* 1.149.

21. *LWCK-Memorials,* 40.20a–26b, KH 7/2/11 (March 10, 1881).

22. See Huang Ta-shou, *Chung-kuo chin-tai shih* (History of modern China), 2.448–449; Fan Wen-lan, *Chung-kuo chin-tai shih* (History of modern China), 1.257; Ch'en Kung-lu, *Chung-kuo chin-tai shih* (History of modern China), ch. 6–7; Hummel, 2.611 (under Pao-t'ing).

23. *LWCK-Memorials,* 36.35a, KH 6/3/27 (May 5, 1880).

24. *Ibid.*

25. *Ibid.*

26. *Ibid.,* 36.35b.

27. 9th Annual Report, *NCH,* October 18, 1882, 419.

28. See Harold Hinton, "The Grain Transport System of the Ch'ing Dynasty."

29. Wu Chao-hsin, *Chung-kuo shui-chih shih* (History of taxation in China), 2.36–37.

30. H. B. Morse, *Trade and Administration of the Chinese Empire,* 95.

31. *Shang-hai-hsien hsü-chih* (Supplementary gazetteer of the Shanghai district), 7.15a.

32. K. C. Liu, "Two Steamship Companies in China, 1862–1877," 104, 149.

33. 9th Annual Report, *NCH,* October 18, 1882, 417.

34. H. B. Morse, Letterbooks, "Memo on Korean Loan," March 26, 1887.

35. See H. B. Morse, *International Relations of the Chinese Empire,* 3.10 ff.

36. 18th Annual Report, *NCH,* April 14, 1892, 502–503. Even as late as 1906, when Korea had long been lost to China, Hsü Jun included an item "Korean loan, principal and interest, Tls. 209,000" in his version of the company's accounts (Hsü Jun, *op. cit.,* 119ab).

37. On the K'ai-p'ing Mines see Ellsworth Carlson, *The Kaiping Mines* (1877–1912).

38. 9th Annual Report, *NCH*, October 18, 1882, 420.

39. *Ibid.*, 417–420.

40. 18th Annual Report, *NCH*, April 14, 1892, 502–503.

41. Morse to G. Detring. Letterbooks, May 20, 1886; 15th Annual Report of the C.M.S.N. Co., *NCH*, April 15, 1889, 405–406; 19th Annual Report, *NCH*, April 28, 1893, 605–606.

42. *Ch'ing-shih kao* (Draft history of the Ch'ing dynasty), 206.30b–35b (Tables of provincial officials).

43. On Jung-lu (1836–1903), see Hummel, 1.405–409; on Yu-lü (d. 1900), *ibid.*, 1.407.

44. See *Ch'ing-shih kao*, 443.2a–3a; *NCH*, July 19, 1907, 143–144.

45. See Ralph L. Powell, *The Rise of Chinese Military Power, 1895–1912,* 139 and *passim*.

46. Hsü Jun, *op. cit.*, 125a.

47. *NCH*, March 1, 1907.

48. Hsü Jun, *op. cit.*, 125a–132b.

49. *NCH*, May 15, 1909, 410; see the "Kung-ssu lü" (Company Law), promulgated January 21, 1904, in *Nung-kung-shang-pu hsien-hsing chang-ch'eng* (Current regulations of the Ministry of Agriculture, Industry, and Commerce).

50. *CTS-HCP*, 1.187, 201.

51. For the 1909 regulations, see *CTS-HCP*, 1.159–160 which gives a summary of the text. The Company Law provided that any commercial enterprise whether operated by merchants or by officials, or by both jointly, could come under its provisions (Article 30). It was specifically set forth that in every company coming under the Law, the board of directors was to be the leading organ of the enterprise and the managers (*tsung-pan* or *tsung ssu-li jen*) were to submit to it all matters of importance (Articles 67, 79, 95). And, most important, the managers and other executives were to be selected and removed only by the board of directors (Article 78). Needless to say, the Yu-ch'uan pu was not willing to allow these provisions to become operative for the C.M.S.N. Co.

52. Sheng T'ung-i *et al.*, [*Sheng Hsuan-huai*] *Hsing-shu* (Biography of [Sheng Hsuan-huai]), 51b; in a telegram to Wang Tzu-chan, Sheng repeats this reason, but he is obviously very reluctant to yield and proud to have received 4,769 votes while the others elected to the board had only 1500–1600 (*YCTK*, 74.29b–30a, HT 1/6/30 [August 15, 1909]).

53. *CTS-HCP*, 1.201.

54. For Shen Tun-ho (1857–?) see above, p. 236.

55. *CTS-HCP*, 1.187; the exchange of telegrams between Sheng and the Yu-ch'uan pu on this matter is highly formal: see *YCTK*, 74.30a, 32b–33b, telegrams dated HT 1/7/3, 18, 19, 20 (August 18, September 2, 3, 4, 1909).

56. *YCTK*, 74.26b–27b, Sheng to Yang Shih-ch'i, HT 1/6/6 (July 22, 1909).

57. *Ibid.*, 74.29ab, Yang Shih-ch'i to Sheng, HT 1/6/29 (August 14, 1909).

58. *CTS-HCP*, 1.202, 188. In addition to being a director of the Chung-kuo t'ung-shang yin-hang, Shih was associated with Yen Hsin-hou and Hsü Jun in founding the Hua-hsing Fire and Marine Insurance Company (capi-

talized at Tls. 1,000,000) in 1907 (*NCH,* March 12, 1897, 460–461; *NKSPTCP,* I, 5.28a).

59. *CTS-HCP,* 1.188 states Yang and Li Ching-hsi, a nephew of Li Hung-chang, were elected as *hsieh-li.* Sheng's telegrams in *YCTK,* however, are addressed to Yang and Li Kuo-chieh (1881–1939), Li Hung-chang's grandson. I have assumed that the latter source is correct inasmuch as Li Kuo-chieh is also mentioned in connection with the C.M.S.N. Co. in Hummel, 1.471.

60. *YCTK,* 76.1a–2a, Sheng to Yang Shih-ch'i and Li Kuo-chieh, HT 2/5/9 (June 15, 1910).

61. *CTS-HCP,* 1.188, text of Yu-ch'uan pu reply.

62. *YCTK,* 76.4b–5b, Sheng to Li Kuo-chieh, HT 2/6/6 (July 12, 1910).

63. *CTS-HCP,* 1.188–189, text of petition.

64. *Ibid.,* 1.189, text of Yu-ch'uan pu reply.

65. *Ibid.,* 1.90, 202.

66. *Ibid.,* 1.161–164, text of revised regulations.

67. *NCH,* June 28, 1913, 944–945.

68. The *North-China Herald,* for example, expressed the following opinion of the C.M.S.N. Co. on August 8, 1874:

it is notorious that the whole affair is directly managed by the Viceroy of Chihli, and two or three officers more or less connected with the Tsungli Yamen. . . . it is equally notorious that were it not for the extravagant contract for the carriage of Government tribute rice to Tientsin, which in point of fact is but another name for a heavy subsidy, the Company could not run except at a heavy loss. . . . and pressure is placed on the principal native shippers to induce them to prefer shipping under the native flag, to sending their goods on board vessels sailing under foreign registration.

69. Between 1873 and 1911, a total of 37,704,386 piculs of tribute rice was shipped from Shanghai. The annual amount varied from a low of 244,734 piculs (1873) to a high of 1,758,570 (1909). For 1873–1895, the average annual shipment was roughly 800,000 piculs; for 1896–1911, 1,300,-000 piculs (China, Imperial Maritime Customs, *Returns of Trade at the Treaty Ports of China,* 1873–1911).

70. Harold Hinton, *The Grain Tribute System of China (1845–1911),* 86–87, Table D.

71. *LWCK-Memorials,* 36.33a, KH 6/3/27 (May 5, 1880); 56.2a–3a, KH 12/1/21 (February 24, 1886); *NCH,* March 9, 1887, 269–271.

72. Table 14 is compiled from the C.M.S.N. Co.'s annual reports: *NCH,* April 15, 1889, 405–406; May 16, 1890, 609–610; April 24, 1891, 506; April 14, 1892, 502–503; April 28, 1893, 605–606; April 13, 1894, 569–570.

73. *YCTK,* 7.32a–34a, memorial endorsed 28/9/? (October 2–31, 1902).

74. *CTS-HCP,* 1.265.

75. *Translations of the Peking Gazette,* September 1, 1877, 122–123.

76. *LWCK-Memorials,* 56.1b–2a, KH 12/1/21 (February 24, 1886).

77. *YCTK,* 2.31ab, memorial endorsed KH 25/7/27 (September 1, 1899).

78. *Translations of the Peking Gazette,* June 6, 1877, 83, a memorial from Li Hung-chang.

79. *LWCK-TLYM Correspondence,* 7.21b, KH 3/9/29 (November 4, 1877).

80. See *CTS-HCP,* 1.257–258, for an account of the rate wars between the C.M.S.N. Co. and foreign firms.

81. *LWCK-TLYM Correspondence*, 7.27b, KH 3/9/29 (November 4, 1877).

82. *LWCK-Memorials*, 30.33ab, KH 3/11/25 (December 29, 1877).

83. *Translations of the Peking Gazette*, August 24, 1886, 116.

84. 18th Annual Report, *NCH*, April 14, 1892, 502–503.

85. *Translations of the Peking Gazette*, February 11, 1894, 47; March 7, 1894, 59, reporting memorials from Li Hung-chang.

86. *CTS-HCP*, 1.274, 158.

87. Lo Yü-tung, "Kuang-hsü-ch'ao pu-chiu ts'ai-cheng chih fang-ts'e" ("The governmental policies of meeting the financial crisis during the Kuang-hsü period [1875–1908]"), 215–217.

88. *Ibid.*, 228–233.

89. *YCTK*, 3.5a, memorial endorsed KH 25/7/27 (September 1, 1899) quotes the edict and Hsü T'ung's memorial. Hsü, like Kang-i, was a pro-Boxer reactionary (see Hummel, 1.407, under Jung-lu).

90. *YCTK*, 3.5b–6a.

91. *Ibid.*, 3.6a–7a.

92. *Ibid.*, 4.18a–23a, memorial endorsed KH 26/2/19 (March 19, 1900); 4.24a–26a, supplementary memorial of the same date.

93. Compiled from data in *YCTK*, 1.21a and *passim; CTS-HCP*, 1.274–276; and C.M.S.N. Co. annual reports.

94. *CTS-HCP*, 1.275–276.

95. The Japanese steamship line Nippon Yūsen Kaisha, for example, sold its obsolete vessels and maintained adequate depreciation allowances (see the *Golden Jubilee History of Nippon Yusen Kaisha, 1885–1935*, 16).

96. Perhaps a third, purely economic, criterion should also be considered: that is, what was the hypothetical profitability of the company in the absence both of government subsidies and official exactions? Unfortunately the available data do not permit a conclusive answer to this question.

97. Source of Table 16: *CTS-HCP*, 1.271–273.

98. 3rd Annual Report, *NCH*, April 12, 1877, 370–374.

99. *LWCK–TLYM Correspondence*, 7.27b–28a, KH 3/9/29 (November 4, 1877).

100. Yen Chung-p'ing, *Chung-kuo mien-yeh chih fa-chan* (The development of the Chinese cotton industry), 124.

101. *LWCK-TLYM Correspondence*, 7.26a, KH 3/9/29 (November 4, 1877).

102. 9th Annual Report, *NCH*, October 18, 1882, 419.

103. *CTS-HCP*, 1.157, summarizes the text.

104. Annual reports of the C.M.S.N. Co., as printed in *NCH, passim.*

105. *CTS-HCP*, 1.271–273.

106. 20th Annual Report, *NCH*, April 13, 1894, 569–570.

107. *CTS-HCP*, 1.271–273.

108. *Ibid.*

109. *Ibid.*

110. *NCH*, August 17, 1912, 457, statement by Ch'en Yu.

111. In addition to arranging these investments by the shipping firm out of its surpluses, Sheng of course used his own earnings from the C.M.S.N. Co. to support his other enterprises.

112. 9th Annual Report, *NCH*, October 18, 1882, 420; 16th Annual Report, *NCH*, May 16, 1890, 609–610; 20th Annual Report, *NCH*, April 13, 1894, 569–570.

113. See Chapter 6.

114. *CTS-HCP*, 1.315–316; Hsü Jun, *op. cit.*, 119ab.

115. *Ibid.*

116. *CTS-HCP*, 1.315–316, 290–292.

117. *Ibid.*, 1.218.

118. *CWHK-Memorials*, 50.3a–8b, KH 25/6/17 (July 24, 1899); *NCH*, November 27, 1899, 1086–1087.

119. Hsü Jun, *op. cit.*, 119ab; *CTS-HCP*, 1.290–292.

120. K. C. Liu, "The Steamship Business in Nineteenth-century China, an Essay on Some Problems of Entrepreneurship," 13.

121. H. B. Morse to I. M. Daae, Letterbooks, December 31, 1886, enclosure headed "Statement of Number and Tonnage of European-type Vessels Flying the Chinese Flag and Belonging to the China Merchants S. N. Co."; *NCH*, May 2, 1914, 349–351.

122. *Golden Jubilee History of Nippon Yusen Kaisha, 1885–1935*, 1–18.

123. *Ibid.*, 135; British shipping firms in Chinese waters showed a steady growth comparable to the N.Y.K. Jardine's Indo-China Steam Navigation Company between 1883 and 1894 expanded its fleet from 13 ships totaling 12,571 net tons to 22 ships and 23,953 tons. Butterfield and Swire's China Navigation Company grew even more rapidly. Between 1874 and 1894, the China Navigation Company fleet increased from six steamers (10,618 net tons) to 29 steamers totaling 34,543 tons (K. C. Liu, "The Steamship Business in Nineteenth-century China," 31–33).

124. *Golden Jubilee History*, 14, 26–35.

125. 8th Annual Report, *NCH*, September 27, 1881, 320–322; *NCH*, October 4, 1881, 358.

126. 9th Annual Report, *NCH*, October 18, 1882, 417–420.

127. *Golden Jubilee History*, 163–167.

128. *The Chronicle & Directory for China, Corea, Japan . . . for the Year 1885*, 396–398.

129. *NCH*, July 7, 1893, 11–12.

130. *YCTK*, 3.20a–30b, C.M.S.N. Co. accounts appended to memorial endorsed KH 25/7/27 (September 1, 1899); *CTS-HCP*, 1.277–278.

131. *Golden Jubilee History*, 133.

132. C. F. Remer, *The Foreign Trade of China*, 76, 125.

133. C.M.S.N. Co. Annual Reports, 1877–1893.

134. *CTS-HCP*, 1.287–292.

CHAPTER 6

Three Kuan-tu Shang-pan *Enterprises*

1. *YCTK*, 4.22a, memorial endorsed KH 26/2/19 (March 19, 1900).

2. Li Chien-nung, *Chung-kuo chin-pai-nien cheng-chih shih* (Chinese political history in the last 100 years), 2.201–202.

3. *NCH*, February 7, 1900, 237.

4. *NCH*, March 7, 1900, 422–423. The accounts of the Telegraph Administration were kept in units of *yang-yuan*, "foreign dollars," that is, Mexican silver dollars which had considerable currency in the treaty ports of China. While the exchange between this dollar and the tael varied from time to time and from place to place, a fair general average for the period

we are discussing would be Tls. 1.0 equals $1.33 (See Julean Arnold, ed., *Commercial Handbook of China*, 1.265–266; 2.167, 180, 187).

5. *YCTK*, 4.15a–17b, memorial endorsed KH 26/1/12 (February 11, 1900).

6. *NCH*, January 21, 1903, 123.

7. *NCH*, May 30, 1900, 988; see also March 14, 1900, 475; March 21, 1900, 524; December 12, 1900, 1258.

8. *NCH*, September 24, 1887, 335–336.

9. There is no substantial study in any Western language of the telegraph in China. Two histories in Chinese are useful: Chang Hsin-ch'eng, *Chung-kuo hsien-tai chiao-t'ung shih* (A history of modern communications in China), and Hsieh Pin, *Chung-kuo yu-tien hang-k'ung shih* (A history of the post, telegraph, and aviation in China), 204–238. The most valuable survey, which reprints many documents, is *Chiao-t'ung shih* (History of communications [in China]), *Tien-cheng pien* (section on telegraphs, telephone, and radio); this is cited hereafter as *CTS-TCP*.

10. *LWCK-Memorials*, 38.16b, KH 6/8/12 (September 16, 1880).

11. H. B. Morse, *International Relations of the Chinese Empire*, 3.336–337. According to Li Hung-chang, Ambassador Tseng Chi-tse's telegrams took only one day to reach Shanghai from Moscow; but even by steamer it was six or seven days from Shanghai to Peking, and ten days by the official post (*LWCK-Memorials*, 38.16a, KH 6/8/12 [September 16, 1880]).

12. Sheng T'ung-i et al., [*Sheng Hsuan-huai*] *Hsing-shu*, 9a.

13. *LWCK-Memorials*, 38.17a, KH 6/8/12 (September 16, 1880).

14. *CTS-TCP*, 1.6–7.

15. Petition from Sheng Hsuan-huai quoted in *LWCK-Memorials*, 44.22b, KH 8/8/16 (September 27, 1882).

16. Text in *LWCK-Memorials*, 45.35a–36b, KH 8/12/8 (January 16, 1883); and *CTS-TCP*, 1.8–10.

17. The character *ch'üan* can be translated as "authority," "interests," and "rights" — all three.

18. Class I official telegrams included communications of the Grand Council, Tsungli Yamen, governors-general, and governors, as well as diplomatic representatives abroad, on matters of a military nature (*chün-wu*) or concerning Westernization projects and relations with foreigners (*yang-wu*).

19. This was made explicit in the imperial decree ordering the nationalization of the telegraphs (*NCH*, December 17, 1902, 1286):

The telegraph services in the various countries of the world are all administered and controlled by the Government, hence whenever important business of State regarding either the army or civil administration has to be transmitted by telegraph, to and fro, perfect secrecy can be maintained as well as promptitude and haste. In China, however, the telegraph service was begun as a commercial undertaking, whereby much inconvenience and obstruction have been experienced by the Government. It is therefore of urgent necessity for the Government to acquire the whole of the said telegraph service in order to safeguard the interests of the State.

20. *NCH*, August 17, 1889, 202.

21. *LWCK-Memorials*, 51.26a–27a, KH 10/8/1 (September 19, 1884).

22. *Ibid.*, 53.50a–52a, KH 11/5/10 (June 20, 1885). For other official

sections, *ibid.*, 55.5a–6a, KH 11/9/5 (October 12, 1885); 55.49ab, KH 11/12/20 (January 24, 1886).

23. *Translations of the Peking Gazette,* August 18, 1885, 116–117; November 16, 1886, 165.

24. *Ibid.,* December 30, 1888, 187. Another example is the line from Hankow to Yunnan via Szechwan; *ibid.,* February 11–12, 1886, 23.

25. *LWCK-Memorials,* 54.50a–51b, KH 11/8/15 (September 23, 1885); 53.21a–23a, KH 11/3/3 (April 17, 1885).

26. *Ibid.,* 45.32a–36b, KH 8/12/8 (January 16, 1883), including text of the regulations of the new line submitted by Sheng.

27. *Ibid.,* 55.5a–6a, KH 11/9/5 (October 12, 1885), including text of petition from Sheng; *CTS-TCP,* 1.19.

28. *LWCK-Memorials,* 54.53ab, KH 11/8/15 (September 23, 1885).

29. *Hsing-shu,* 13a–14a.

30. *LWCK-Memorials,* 60.24a–26b, KH 13/7/10 (August 28, 1887); *YCTK,* 4.19b, memorial endorsed KH 26/2/? (March ?, 1900).

31. *LWCK-Memorials,* 46.39ab, KH 9/6/14 (July 17, 1883); 55.49ab, KH 11/12/20 (January 24, 1886).

32. *LWCK-TLYM Correspondence,* 15.36ab, KH 10/5/25 (June 18, 1884); 15.39b–40b, KH 10/intercalary 5/11 (July 3, 1884).

33. Chang Hsin-ch'eng, *op. cit.,* 436–438.

34. *LWCK-Memorials,* 43.39a–44b, KH 14/11/12 (December 14, 1888). Note that Chang Chih-tung, then governor-general at Canton, in contrast to Li Hung-chang was strongly opposed to the agreement to join the Chinese line with the French (*CWHK-Memorials,* 25.3a–6b, KH 14/12/20 [January 21, 1889]).

35. *LWCK-Memorials,* 75.5a–6b, KH 18/7/18 (September 8, 1892).

36. *CTS-TCP,* 1.21.

37. See Chapter 3.

38. Hsü T'ung-hsin, *Chang Wen-hsiang kung nien-p'u* (Chronological biography of Chang Chih-tung), 166; *NCH,* December 17, 1902, 1286, text of decree.

39. *NCH,* January 21, 1903, 123, translation of text of imperial decree of January 15.

40. *Ibid.;* see *CTS-TCP,* 1.45–46 for the text of the new Regulations of the Telegraph Administration issued in April 1903.

41. *NCH,* June 6, 1908, 643. It was rumored in Shanghai that one of Wu Chung-hsi's first tasks would be to investigate Sheng Hsuan-huai's financial relations with the Telegraph Administration (*NCH,* March 12, 1903, 491). This could only be intended to benefit Yuan Shih-k'ai.

42. *NCH,* April 12, 1906, 82; April 20, 159; September 14, 634.

43. *NCH,* January 21, 1903, 123, translation of imperial decree.

44. *NCH,* February 4, 1903, 230.

45. *NCH,* April 12, 1907, 91.

46. *NCH,* July 5, 1907, 28.

47. The Peking correspondent of the *North-China Herald* reported (July 18, 1908, 195):

H. E. Sheng Kung-pao is in a very difficult position, for on one side he is the substantive Junior Vice-President of the Ministry of Posts and Communications, though the post is now temporarily held by Mr. Shen Yun-pai [Shen Yün-p'ei] in Peking, while on the other hand he was the original founder of the Imperial Chinese Telegraph Administration about thirty years ago, and most of the present shareholders are his relatives or friends who purchased the shares chiefly through his advice.

48. *NCH*, April 10, 1908, 92.

49. *NCH*, June 6, 1908, 643.

50. *YCTK*, 73.17b–18a, telegram from Sheng to the Yu-ch'uan pu, KH 34/5/8 (June 6, 1908); *NCH*, June 27, 1908, 816.

51. *YCTK*, 23.26b, memorial telegraphed KH 34/7/1 (July 28, 1908); *CTS-TCP*, 1.51.

52. *NCH*, June 13, 1908, 664–665.

53. See *YCTK*, 73.17b–18a, KH 34/5/8 (June 6, 1908); 73.18ab, KH 34/5/11 (June 9, 1908); 73.18b–19a, KH 34/5/12 (June 10, 1908); 73.19ab, 34/5/13 (June 11, 1908); 73.20ab, KH 34/5/16 (June 14, 1908); and *passim*.

54. *CTS-TCP*, 1.49–51, text of Ch'en Pi memorial.

55. *Ibid.*, 1.52; *NCH*, August 29, 1908, 534.

56. See note 4 above; dollar ($) throughout this section refers to the Mexican silver dollar.

57. *CTS-TCP*, 1.11.

58. *LWCK-Memorials*, 53.21b, KH 11/3/3 (April 17, 1885); *CTS-TCP*, 1.13, 16.

59. *YCTK*, 3.6b, memorial endorsed KH 25/7/27 (September 1, 1899); Sheng's version of the accounts of the Telegraph Administration from Kuang-hsü 8 through Kuang-hsü 23 which he appends to this memorial (3.12a–19a) shows only $400,000 under this heading; probably the balance was transferred in Kuang-hsü 24 or 25.

60. *Ibid.*, 3.18b–19a.

61. *NCH*, June 27, 1908, 816.

62. *YCTK*, 73.17b-18a, Sheng to Yu-ch'uan pu, KH 34/5/8 (June 6, 1908).

63. *NCH*, July 18, 1908, 195. In several places Sheng refers to the shareholders as including his friends and relatives: see for example, *YCTK*, 73.20ab, Sheng to Yu-ch'uan pu, KH 34/5/16 (June 14, 1908).

64. *YCTK*, 73.19ab, Yu-ch'uan pu to Sheng, KH 34/5/13 (June 11, 1908); 73.20ab, Sheng to Yu-ch'uan pu, KH 34/5/16 (June 14, 1908).

65. *Ibid.*, 3.6b, 12a–19a, memorial endorsed KH 25/7/27 (September 1, 1899).

66. *LWCK-Memorials*, 44.22a–24a, KH 8/8/16 (September 27, 1882), 55.5a–6a, KH 11/9/5 (October 12, 1885); *Translations of the Peking Gazette*, February 11–12, 1886, 23, December 30, 1888, 187.

67. For example, from the Liang-Chiang governor-general; see *Translations of the Peking Gazette*, August 18, 1885, 116–117.

68. Text of Regulations, *CTS-TCP*, 1.8–12.

69. *Ibid.*, 1.12–14; *LWCK-Memorials*, 45.35a–36b, KH 8/12/8 (January 16, 1883).

70. *LWCK-Memorials*, 52.25a–28b, KH 10/11/21 (January 6, 1885); 59.28a–29b, KH 13/2/9 (March 3, 1887); 62.5a–6a, KH 14/1/22 (March 4, 1888); 62.32a–33a, KH 14/4/27 (June 6, 1888); 67.11a–12b, KH 16/2/6 (February 24, 1890). I have estimated the amounts for 1882 and 1887, which do not appear in Li's collected papers, by extrapolating from the adjacent years.

71. *YCTK*, 3.12a–19a, accounts appended to memorial endorsed KH 25/7/27 (September 1, 1899).

72. *LWCK-Memorials*, 53.21b, KH 11/3/3 (May 17, 1885); *CTS-TCP*, 1.11.

73. Li Hung-chang reported that Tls. 6,559 was paid out of Chihli funds in 1888 to cover telegraph charges at one half the usual rate (*LWCK-Memorials*, 67.11a–12b, KH 16/2/6 [February 24, 1890]). Assuming approximately the same number of telegrams from year to year — there would have been more than usual in 1884–1885 because of the fighting with France — this would give a total of about Tls. 52,000 (8 × 6,559) in official telegrams accepted free from 1884 through 1887. However, this figure apparently includes only wires sent by Li as commissioner for the northern ports and excludes those sent by the Tsungli Yamen and the commissioner for the southern ports. Judging from the figures for 1899 cited below, the total value for 1884–1887 of the wires sent free by all three could conservatively be estimated to have been at least Tls. 50,000 annually, which would still be only one half of the nearly Tls. 100,000 in official business actually recorded for 1899.

74. *YCTK*, 4.20b, memorial endorsed KH 26/2/? (March ?, 1900).

75. *Ibid.*, 19ab; and 3.6b, memorial endorsed KH 25/7/27 (September 1, 1899).

76. Sheng stated in 1908 that in the previous five years the shareholders had paid over Tls. 200,000 as *pao-hsiao* (*ibid.*, 23.27b, telegraphic memorial of KH 34/7/1 [July 28, 1908]).

77. Also included under the heading *pao-hsiao* by Sheng and others are the contributions made by the Telegraph Administration to the two modern schools (the Pei-yang kung-hsüeh in Tientsin and the Nan-yang kung-hsüeh in Shanghai) which Sheng founded in 1895 and 1896 respectively. These payments cannot, however, be considered as official exactions. They amounted to approximately Tls. 90,750 (= $121,000) for the Tientsin school and Tls. 240,000 (= $320,000) for that in Shanghai between 1895 and 1902. In 1903 Yuan Shih-k'ai stopped the payments to the Nan-yang kung-hsüeh; apparently those to the Pei-yang kung-hsüeh (Tls. 14,000 or $20,000 annually) were continued for several additional years. See *YCTK*, 2.18a–26b, memorial endorsed KH 24/5/19 (July 7, 1898), 4.19ab, endorsed KH 26/2/? (March ?, 1900), and *passim;* also Shu Hsin-ch'eng, ed., *Chin-tai Chung-kuo chiao-yü shih-liao* (Historical materials relative to education in modern China), 1.23–40.

78. *LWCK-Memorials*, 45.33a, KH 8/12/8 (January 16, 1883); Yen Chung-p'ing, *Chung-kuo mien-yeh chih fa-chan* (The development of the Chinese cotton industry), 73.

79. *YCTK*, 10.36a–37b, memorial endorsed KH 31/1/6 (February 9, 1905), 12.38ab, endorsed KH 32/3/? (March 25–April 23, 1906); *NCH*, February 12, 1904, 290, June 2, 1905, 466, April 26, 1907, 198–199; *CTS-LCP*, 11.3105–3107.

80. *LWCK-Memorials*, 45.33a, KH 8/12/8 (January 16, 1883); Arnold Wright, ed., *Twentieth Century Impressions of Hong Kong, Shanghai, and other Treaty Ports of China . . . ,* 552.

81. *Translations of the Peking Gazette,* April 24, 1887, 58, April 18, 1890, 61, December 20, 1891, 180–181.

82. *Ibid.,* August 18, 1885, 116–117.

83. *Ibid.*

84. *LWCK-Memorials,* 55.31ab, KH 15/4/22 (May 21, 1889); 74.17a–18a, KH 18/3/11 (April 7, 1892).

85. *YCTK,* 4.13a–14a, memorial endorsed KH 25/12/? (January ?, 1900), 5.47a–48a, endorsed KH 27/9/? (October 12–November 10, 1901), 8.43a–45a, endorsed KH 28/9/18 (October 19, 1902).

86. *NCH,* November 14, 1900, 1045.

87. Sheng Hsuan-huai, *Sheng K'ang hsing-shu* (Biography of Sheng K'ang), 28a–29b; *NCH,* August 14, 1903, 340.

Thomas E. LaFargue (*China's First Hundred,* 90–92, 174–176) notes that perhaps twenty of the youths who studied in the United States with the "Chinese Educational Mission" were at some time associated with the Imperial Telegraph Administration. The absence of characters from his text combines with the use of Cantonese forms for the names cited (is it the "official" name [*ming*] or "courtesy" name [*hao*] that is employed?) to make it impossible to correlate his list with such names as I have found in other sources.

88. *NCH,* June 20, 1908, 750.

89. *YCTK,* 23.26a–28b, telegraphic memorial of KH 34/7/1 (July 28, 1908).

90. *Ibid.; CTS-TCP,* 1.51.

91. Text of Ch'en Pi memorial in *CTS-TCP,* 1.49–51.

92. *NCH,* June 13, 1908, 664–665.

93. *NCH,* July 5, 1907, 28.

94. *NCH,* June 20, 1908, 750.

95. *YCTK,* 4.3a–4a, memorial of KH 25/10/? (November 1899).

96. The best account of the cotton textile industry in China is Yen Chung-p'ing, *Chung-kuo mien-yeh chih fa-chen* (The development of the Chinese cotton industry) which first appeared in 1943. A revised edition under the title *Chung-kuo mien-fang-chih shih kao* (A draft history of Chinese cotton spinning and weaving) was published in Peking in 1955; some additional data are included.

97. Translations of P'eng's petition and of the regulations and financial estimates which he enclosed, of the replies from Li and Shen, and of a further petition from P'eng together with a reply from Li are printed in *NCH,* February 21, 1879, 168–171. Only the surname P'eng is given in these documents; no *ming* or *hao* is indicated. The Chinese texts have not been found.

98. P'eng to Li and enclosures, October 5, 1878, *NCH,* February 21, 1879, 168–170.

99. Li to P'eng, October 21, 1878, *ibid.,* 170. Shen Pao-chen also replied in the affirmative: Shen to P'eng, November 14, 1878, *ibid.,* 170–171.

100. Li alleged such actions by industrial promoters as the following:

Of late . . . the practice of making false estimates with intent to deceive has been prevalent, assertions are made that the share capital amounts to so and so and operations are begun. As soon as money ceases to come to hand, the thing halts just when it is en train, *and much loss is thereby caused.*

101. P'eng to Li, no date (evidently written in Tientsin), *ibid.,* 171.

102. Li to P'eng, no date, *ibid.,* 171.

103. Li to P'eng, October 21, 1878, *NCH,* February 21, 1879, 170.

104. *NCH*, April 4, 1879, 319.

105. P'eng to Li, *NCH*, February 21, 1879, 171.

106. Yen Chung-p'ing, *Chung-kuo mien-fang-chih shih kao*, 102.

107. P'eng to Li, *NCH*, February 21, 1879, 171.

108. *LWCK-Memorials*, 43.43a–44b, KH 8/3/6 (April 23, 1882).

109. *NCH*, December 6, 1881, 596. It should be noted that Li's memorial of April 1882 was reporting a *fait accompli* for which he was seeking imperial sanction. Obviously he had taken the actions which he proposed in this memorial well before referring them to Peking.

See also *NCH*, September 23, 1883, 366: "The cotton mill which is to be erected a few miles down the river . . . belongs to Chinese connected with officials and is consequently favoured by them, and is understood to have been started with sufficient capital."

110. *LWCK-Memorials*, 43.43a–44b, KH 8/3/6 (April 23, 1882).

111. Yen Chung-p'ing, *Chung-kuo mien-fang-chih shih kao*, 101, 103.

112. *Tseng Chung-hsiang kung tsou-i* (Memorials of Tseng Kuo-ch'üan), 31.13a, KH 15/10/2 (October 25, 1889). Tseng (1824–1890; see Hummel, 2.749–751), younger brother of Tseng Kuo-fan, in 1889, was ordered to investigate and report on the state of the Shanghai Cotton Cloth Mill in his capacity as Liang-Chiang governor-general. This memorial (cited hereafter as Tseng 1889 Report) represents the findings of this investigation. Sheng Hsuan-huai reported to Li Hung-chang in December 1893, after investigating the affairs of the razed mill, that "on the old shares, Tls. 70 per share at first was paid" (Sheng's petition to Li Hung-chang, translated in *NCH*, December 29, 1893, 1031–1032; cited hereafter as Sheng 1893 Report).

113. See Hummel, 1.404.

114. Yen Chung-p'ing, *Chung-kuo mien-fang-chih shih kao*, 102.

115. China, Imperial Maritime Customs, *Decennial Reports*, 1892–1901, 1.513.

116. Tseng 1889 Report, 13b.

117. *Ibid.*, 13a; Yen Chung-p'ing, *Chung-kuo mien-fang-chih shih kao*, 104, n. 5.

118. Tseng 1889 Report, 13a.

119. As early as the second moon of 1883, Kung Shou-t'u had petitioned requesting that his brother, Kung I-t'u, be dispatched to replace Cheng at the head of the company (*ibid.*, 13b).

120. *Ibid.*, 13a; on P'eng Yü-lin (1816–1890) see Hummel, 2.617–620.

121. Tseng 1889 Report, 13b-14a.

122. Yen Chung-p'ing, *Chung-kuo mien-yeh chih fa-chan*, 91, n. 9, quoting a Chinese work printed in 1897.

123. See *NCH*, August 4, 1888, 139–140, August 24, 1888, 225; the immediate occasion may have been the efforts of the English firm Boyd and Co. to open a machine cotton cleaning factory.

124. H. B. Morse "à M. Thévenet, Chef de la mission de l'industrie française en Chine, à Tientsin," Letterbooks, March 28, 1887, March 31, 1887, April 26, 1887.

125. Yen Chung-p'ing, *Chung-kuo mien-fang-chih shih kao*, 104; Tseng 1889 Report, 13b–14a; Sheng 1893 Report.

126. Sheng 1893 Report.

127. *Ibid.*

128. C.M.S.N. Co. 18th Annual Report, *NCH*, April 14, 1892, 502–503.

The report specifically states that the amount put into the Cotton Cloth Mill in 1891 was Tls. 100,000. No additional sum appears in later annual reports, but Sheng's figure of 1893 is undoubtedly accurate.

129. Sheng 1893 Report.

130. *Ibid.*

131. *NCH*, April 10, 1891, 443–444, a detailed description of the plant and its operations.

132. G. J. Morrison, "The Industries of Shanghai," *NCH*, November 24, 1893, 816–817.

133. *Decennial Reports*, 1891–1902, 1.513; *NCH*, October 20, 1893, 628.

134. *Decennial Reports*, 1891–1902, 1.513.

135. *LWCK-Telegrams*, 14.42a, KH 19/5/25 (July 8, 1893).

136. Strictly speaking, the Cotton Cloth Mill did not have an absolute monopoly. In 1891 the Shanghai taotai T'ang Sung-yen organized the New Chinese Spinning and Weaving Company (*Hua-hsin fang-chih hsin-chü*) as a joint official-merchant enterprise. Its origins are obscure, and it was later amalgamated with Sheng Hsuan-huai's textile interests. The New Chinese Company operated 7,008 spindles in 1891; despite its name it was only a spinning mill and produced no cloth until Sheng took it over (*Decennial Reports*, 1891–1902, 1.513; Yen Chung-p'ing, *Chung-kuo mien-fang-chih shih kao*, 342).

137. A translation appears in *NCH*, January 13, 1893, 53–54.

138. See C. F. Remer, *The Foreign Trade of China*, 86–87, 93–94 for an analysis of this phenomenon.

139. See Roswell Britton, *The Chinese Periodical Press, 1800–1912*, Chapter 6, "The Shun Pao and other Shanghai papers."

140. *NCH*, October 20, 1893, 628. The attitude of the Shanghai foreign community toward the mill is reflected in the refusal of the Shanghai Volunteer Fire Brigade to go to the fire. Among the arguments in support of this position — with which the *North-China Herald*, the leading English paper in Shanghai, did not agree — was the fact that the mill was outside of the International Settlement. But the principal reason given for the inaction of the Fire Brigade was the following (*NCH*, October 20, 1893, 609):

The mill belongs to Li Hung-chang and his friends, and as he has been and still is putting every possible obstacle in the way of foreigners being allowed to import machinery for ginning, spinning, and weaving cotton, it would be absurd for foreigners to try to save the mill which he is doing his best to make a monopoly, and which is interfering seriously with foreign trade.

141. Sheng 1893 Report.

142. The *North-China Herald* reported in a characteristic manner that the mill was not insured because "the mandarin in charge concluded that it was a waste of money, so that when the last policies ran out, he would not renew them, with the result that when he found the place on fire he attempted to throw himself into the flames" (October 20, 1893, 628).

143. *LWCK-Memorials*, 77.38ab, KH 19/10/26 (December 3, 1893); Sheng 1893 Report.

144. Sheng 1893 Report and appended reply from Li Hung-chang, dated December 4, 1893, agreeing in full.

145. Sheng to Li, *LWCK-Telegrams,* 15.14b, KH 19/12/30 (February 5, 1894).

146. In the telegram just cited, which is printed in Li Hung-chang's collected papers, the name of Sheng Hsuan-huai's younger brother appears as Sheng Chou-huai. *Decennial Reports,* 1892–1901, 1.513, gives the same name. However, the privately printed biography of Sheng K'ang, written by his sons Sheng Hsuan-huai and Sheng Shan-huai, calls Sheng K'ang's fifth son — the only one who held the title of expectant *chih-fu —* Sheng Hsing-huai (*Sheng K'ang hsing-shu,* 28a–29b). On the face of it, this source should be the more accurate and I have followed it in this instance.

147. See note 145 above.

148. *NCH,* August 14, 1903, 349.

149. See note 145 above.

150. *LWCK-Memorials,* 78.10b, KH 20/3/28 (May 3, 1894).

151. *Ibid.,* 11a.

152. *Ibid.,* 10b–11a.

153. *LWCK-Telegrams,* 15.14b–15a, Sheng to Li and Li's reply, KH 19/12/30 (February 5, 1894); *Decennial Reports,* 1892–1901, 1.513.

154. *YCTK,* 34.11b–13b, exchange of telegrams between Liu K'un-i, governor-general of Liang-Chiang, and Sheng Hsuan-huai, KH 25/3/17 (April 26, 1899).

155. *LWCK-Telegrams,* 15.14b–15a, KH 19/12/30 (February 5, 1894).

156. See Yen Chung-p'ing, *Chung-kuo mien fang-chih shih kao,* 153, 342–344.

157. Source of Table 22: *ibid.,* 114.

158. Li Hung-chang in 1894 estimated the daily capacity of the 400,000 spindles which he planned at 1,000 bales; the present estimate is based on his (*LWCK-Memorials,* 78.10b, KH 20/3/28 [May 3, 1894]).

159. Yen Chung-p'ing, *Chung-kuo mien-fang-chih shih kao,* 139.

160. *Decennial Reports,* 1891–1902, 1.514.

161. Yen Chung-p'ing, *Chung-kuo mien-fang-chih shih kao,* 151.

162. *Decennial Reports,* 1891–1902, 1.514.

163. Sheng to Li, *YCTK,* 28.11b–12a, KH 23/8/6 (September 2, 1897).

164. Li to Sheng, *Ibid.,* 28.12b, KH 23/8/7 (September 3, 1897).

165. *Ibid.,* 5.5ab, memorial endorsed KH 27/8/21 — the date actually printed in *YCTK* is KH 28, but the preceding and following memorials both are dated KH 27; 28 is probably an error, as Sheng's papers are normally arranged in strict chronological order — (October 3, 1901).

166. *Decennial Reports,* 1891–1902, 1.517.

167. *YCTK,* 5.4b, KH 27/8/21 (October 3, 1901).

168. *Decennial Reports,* 1891–1902, 1.516.

169. *Ibid.,* 1.517.

170. *YCTK,* 5.5b, KH 27/8/21 (October 3, 1901).

171. Yen Chung-p'ing, *Chung-kuo mien-yeh chih fa-chan,* 89, states: "But we now definitely know that this invitation to merchants to take over was really a ruse by Sheng to convert the government factory into his own private property. The shares of stock remained at all times in the hands of the Sheng family." See also Yen, *Chung-kuo mien-fang-chih shih kao,* 343, for a summary of the mill's later history. During the period after 1913 it was known as the San-hsin Spinning and Weaving Company and was headed by Sheng Hsuan-huai's son, Sheng En-i (b. 1892; *Who's Who in China,* 3rd edition, 1926, 661).

172. Yen Chung-p'ing, *Chung-kuo mien-fang-chih shih kao,* 342–344; *NCH,* January 8, 1902, 10.

173. *YCTK,* 28.11b–12a, KH 23/8/6 (September 2, 1897).

174. Yen Chung-p'ing, *Chung-kuo mien-yeh chih fa-chan,* 89.

175. A literal translation of the bank's name would be "Chinese Foreign Trade Bank"; I take it that *t'ung-shang* in the first instance implies foreign trade. However, before 1911 the bank was most commonly known to foreigners as the "Imperial Bank of China," probably because it had been organized under imperial auspices and until the establishment of the Hu-pu Bank in 1905 was the only modern national bank. The bank's translated name as it appears in several sources follows: "Imperial Bank of China" (Miyashita Tadao, "Hōgaki Shina ginkōgyō no bokkō" [The rise of modern Chinese banking], 83; *NCH,* March 12, 1897, 460; Wen Pin Wei, *The Currency Problem in China,* 53), "Imperial Bank of International Commerce" (Wen Pin Wei, *loc. cit.*), "Imperial Chinese Bank of International Commerce" (S. R. Wagel, *Chinese Currency and Banking,* 79–80; *NCH, loc. cit.*), "Commercial Bank of China" (for the Republican period) (Miyashita Tadao, *loc. cit.;* Tokunaga Kiyoyuki, *Shina chūō ginkō ron* [Central banking in China], 22).

176. See Lien-sheng Yang, *Money and Credit in China: A Short History,* 88–89.

177. *Ibid.,* 80–87; John C. Ferguson, "Notes on Chinese Banking in Shanghai," 55–82.

178. Text of Sheng's *shuo-t'ieh* in Mai Chung-hua, compiler, *Huang-ch'ao ching-shih-wen hsin-pien* (New collection of essays on statecraft of the Ch'ing dynasty), 13A.3b–6a.

179. Hsü T'ung-hsin, *op. cit.,* 105; and *YCTK,* 1.14a, memorial endorsed KH 22/9/26 (November 1, 1896):

Now we are building railways, which require a heavy initial investment. Unless we quickly establish a Chinese bank, we shall have no way to circulate the funds which serve as blood in our veins or to stop the control of our economic life by foreign merchants.

180. *YCTK,* 1.6b, memorial endorsed KH 22/9/26 (November 1, 1896).

181. *Ibid.,* 1.14a–15b, memorial endorsed KH 22/9/26; translated in part in S. Y. Teng and J. K. Fairbank, *China's Response to the West,* 213–215, whose wording I have followed with only minor changes.

182. According to Yung Wing (*My Life in China and America,* 234–246), Sheng was responsible for the failure of a scheme to establish a "National Bank of China" which Yung had presented to the Hu-pu in 1896. He claims that the president of the Ministry of Revenue, Weng T'ung-ho, was on the point of sending in a memorial seeking the appropriation of Tls. 10,000,000 for such a project. But Sheng got wind of it, and was able to get Weng to delay, "Ung [Weng] and Shing [Sheng] being intimate friends, besides being compatriots [more accurately, co-provincials; both came from Kiangsu]." Yung Wing then alludes to Sheng's "system of graft reaching even the Dowager Empress through her favorite eunuch, the notorious Li Ling Ying [Li Lien-ying]," which enabled Sheng to secure control of the scheme for a modern-style bank for himself. It is known that Yung Wing did in fact propose the establishment of a national bank in 1896 (see *Huang-ch'ao ching-shih-wen hsin-pien,* 10B.39b–45a, for the text of the regulations which

he drew up for this project; and *NCH,* July 24, 1896, 143, August 28, 1896, 355, which report the failure of his scheme). Also Sheng and Yung Wing later clashed on the matter of railroad development, Sheng believing that the north-south line from Shantung along the coast for which Yung unsuccessfully sought imperial sanction would harm his own Lu-Han project (*YCTK,* 30. *passim,* includes many telegrams exchanged at the beginning of 1898 among Sheng, Chang Chih-tung, Wang Wen-shao and others concerning the threat of Yung Wing's railroad proposals; also see Hsü T'ung-hsin, *op. cit.,* 112). Further, Sheng did have the favor of the eunuch Li Lien-ying. But, from the available evidence, Yung Wing is incorrect in asserting that Sheng "got away with the Tls. 10,000,000 of appropriations by setting up a bank to manipulate his own projects." As will be seen from the following, all that Sheng received from Peking in this instance was a loan for his bank of Tls. 1,000,000 from the Hu-pu.

183. *Ta-Ch'ing li-ch'ao shih-lu, Kuang-hsü ch'ao* (Veritable records of the Ch'ing dynasty, Kuang-hsü reign), 395.16b, KH 22/9/26 (November 1, 1896); 396.9b–10a, KH 22/10/8 (November 12, 1896).

184. *Ibid.,* 397.1b–2b, KH 22/11/2 (December 6, 1896).

185. *YCTK,* 2.30ab, memorial endorsed KH 24/5/20 (July 8, 1898).

186. Text of Sheng's draft Regulations in *Huang-ch'ao ching-shih-wen hsin-pien,* 10B.45b–48a; an English translation, sometimes garbled, appears in *NCH,* March 12, 1897, 460–461.

187. Miyashita Tadao, *op. cit.,* 81, states that the Chinese manager who worked with Maitland was one Hsieh Lun-hui who had formerly operated the Ch'en-yü money shop in Shanghai. Apparently Hsieh was the successor to Ch'en Sheng-hsiao; his name is signed as "Chinese manager" to the bank's report for the second half of KH 32 (August 20, 1906–February 12, 1907) (Tōa Dōbunkai, *Shina keizai zensho* [China economic series], 6.704–709).

188. The text reads *"pu-yü shih-ts'un yin-liang chih shu"* which the *North-China Herald* translates "will never exceed the amount of cash reserve in the Bank." From the context provided by Chang Chih-tung's memorial of July 16, 1897, which will be discussed below, it is certain, however, that what was meant by *shih-ts'un yin-liang* was the actual paid-up capital of the bank.

189. Text of Tsungli Yamen criticisms in *Huang-ch'ao ching-shih-wen hsin-pien,* 10B.48a–49a.

190. Text of Sheng's answer, *ibid.,* 10B.49a–52a.

191. Text of Tsungli Yamen communication to Sheng, *ibid.,* 10B.52ab.

192. *Ta-Ch'ing li-ch'ao shih-lu, Kuang-hsü ch'ao,* 403.10a–11a, KH 23/3/29 (April 30, 1897).

193. Hsü T'ung-hsin, *op. cit.,* 109.

194. *CWHK-Memorials,* 46.3b–9b, KH 23/6/17 (July 16, 1897).

195. See H. B. Morse, *The Trade and Administration of the Chinese Empire,* Chapter 5.

196. *CTS-HCP,* 1.315; Hsü Jun, *Hsü Yü-chai tzu-hsü nien-p'u* (Chronological autobiography) 119ab.

197. *YCTK,* 3.12a–19a, accounts appended to memorial endorsed KH 25/7/27 (September 1, 1899).

198. On Yen Hsin-hou: *YCTK,* 5.4a–8a, 7.35a–37b, memorials of 1900 and 1902 respectively; *NKSPTCP-I,* 2.27a, 4.3b, 5.3a, 9a, 18a, 28a, and *NKSPTCP-II,* 5.6b, 11a; *NCH,* March 12, 1897, 460–461; Yen Chung-ping,

Chung-kuo mien-yeh chih fa-chan, 122; idem, *Chung-kuo mien-fang-chih shih kao,* 153; Wright, ed., *Twentieth Century Impressions,* 540–544.

199. *NCH,* February 12, 1904, 290.

200. On Chang Chen-hsun: *YCTK,* 10.36a–37b, memorial endorsed KH 31/1/6 (February 9, 1905); Tseng K'un-hua, *Chung-kuo t'ieh-lu shih* (History of Chinese railways), 73; *NCH,* March 12, 1897, 460–461; *NKSPTCP-I,* 2.35a, 36a, 4.10a, and *NKSPTCP-II,* 4.24a.

201. On Chu P'ei-chen: *NKSPTCP-I,* 4.3b, 5.16b, 18a, 28a, and *NKSPTCP-II,* 5.6b, 10b, 11a; *NCH,* March 12, 1897, 460–461.

202. Miyashita Tadao, *op. cit.,* 81, describes Wang as assistant director *(fu-tsung-tung)* and Sheng as director *(cheng-tsung-tung)* of the bank.

203. The names of these men appear in Miyashita, *op. cit.,* 81 and in *NCH,* March 12, 1897, 460–461.

204. Sheng promised an auditor *(ch'a-chang)* independent of the managing directors in his reply to the criticisms of his draft regulations by the Tsungli Yamen; see *Huang-ch'ao ching-shih-wen hsin-pien,* 10B.49b–50a.

205. *Shina keizai zensho,* comp. by Tōa Dōbunkai, 6.704–709.

206. On Shen Tun-ho: *YCTK,* 10.36a–37b, memorial endorsed KH 31/1/6 (February 9, 1905); Wright, ed., *Twentieth Century Impressions,* 527–530; *CTS-LCP,* 11.3105–3107; *NKSPTCP-II,* 5.10b.

207. On Ku Jun-chang: *CTS-HCP,* 1.191; *NKSPTCP-I,* 3.64a, 5.9b.

208. Sheng Hsuan-huai, *K'ao-ch'a Jih-pen pao-kao* (Report of my observations in Japan), 18b.

209. A contemporary Japanese account asserts that there was mismanagement by the Chinese directors and staff; see Tōa Dōbun Shoin, *Shina seiji chiri shi* (Political and geographic gazetteer of China), 2.510.

210. See Tseng K'un-hua, *op. cit.,* 73–76.

211. *YCTK,* 2.34b–35a, memorial endorsed KH 24/6/10 (July 28, 1898).

212. *Ibid.,* 2.30a–32b, memorial endorsed KH 24/5/20 (July 8, 1898).

213. Text of Hu-pu memorial of KH 24/5 in Shen T'ung-shen, comp., *Kuang-hsü cheng-yao* (Important documents of the Kuang-hsü period), 24.21b–22a.

214. *Ta-Ch'ing li-ch'ao shih-lu, Kuang-hsü ch'ao,* 420.13ab, KH 24/5/25 (July 13, 1898).

215. *YCTK,* 2.66b–68a, memorial endorsed KH 25/10/16 (November 18, 1899).

216. Sources for Tables 23 and 24: *NCH,* March 6, 1899, 392, May 29, 1899, 969; *Shina keizai zensho,* 6.704–709; *Shina seiji chiri shi,* 2.511–512.

217. *YCTK,* 61.20ab, telegram from Sheng to the Wai-wu pu, KH 29/8/14 (October 4, 1903).

218. See Li P'ei-en, "Chin-pai-nien-lai Chung-kuo chih yin-hang" (Chinese banking in the last 100 years); Ray Ovid Hall, *The Chinese National Banks from their Founding to the Moratorium,* appendices.

219. *CTS-HCP,* 1.271–273.

220. Kuo Hsiao-hsien, "Shanghai ti nei-kuo yin-hang" (Chinese banks in Shanghai), 441, 490.

CHAPTER 7

Conclusion: Toward "Bureaucratic Capitalism"

1. See Joseph R. Levenson, *Liang Ch'i-ch'ao and the Mind of Modern China;* "The Attenuation of a Chinese Philosophical Concept: 'T'i-yung' in the Nineteenth Century"; "Redefinition of Ideas in Time: The Chinese Classics and History"; and " 'History' and 'Value': The Tensions of Intellectual Choice in Modern China."

Index

Acum (Lin Ch'in), 110
Adamson Bell and Company, 134
Agriculture, proposals for reform of, 34–35
American China Development Company, 69
Anhwei Army. See Huai-chün
Annual budget, proposed by Sheng Hsuan-huai, 92

Bank of Communications (Chiao-t'ung yin-hang), 7, 80, 239
Banks: foreign, in China, 226; modern Chinese, 87–88, 225–241; traditional Chinese, 226. See Bank of Communications; Ch'ien-chuang; Hong Kong and Shanghai Banking Corporation; Hu-pu Bank; Imperial Bank of China
Blackburn Chamber of Commerce, 54
Boxer indemnity, payment of, 45–47
Boxer Protocol, 46, 73
Boxer Rebellion, 44, 72–73, 272
British and Chinese Corporation, 69, 78
Bureaucracy, traditional Chinese, 22–23; in modern-type industries, 24–25, 33, 90, 123, 137–144, 213, 236
Bureaucratic capitalism, 20, 29, 251
Butterfield and Swire, 17, 33, 116, 128, 172, 205

Canton-Hankow (Yüeh-Han) railroad, 16, 29, 69, 77, 81, 117
Capital, shortage of, 18–19, 131, 246–247, 249
Carlowitz and Company, 67, 68, 182
Chambers of commerce, 53, 70–71
Chang Chen-hsun, 234
Chang Chien, 4, 10, 12, 15–16, 18, 21, 22, 38, 235
Chang Chih-tung, 2, 12, 28, 66, 72, 78, 90, 93, 244–245; and Hanyang Iron-works, 25, 79; and Imperial Bank of China, 227, 232–233; and railroads, 14, 77; and Sheng Hsuan-huai, 59, 65, 66 f., 89, 160; and telegraphs, 198; and textile mills, 15, 18, 25, 220
Chang Hung-lu, 113, 114, 129

Chang Ts'an-chen, 88
Chang Yao, 64
Ch'ang-chou hsien-che i-shu, 86
Chao Feng-t'ien, 31
Chao-hsin p'iao, "Sincerity Bonds," 45
Chartered Bank of India, Australia and China (Mai-chia-li yin-hang), 226
Chekiang Industrial Bank (Chekiang hsing-yeh yin-hang), 20
Ch'en Chih, 35–36
Ch'en Hsien, 235
Ch'en Li-fu, 70
Ch'en Pi, 200, 206–207
Ch'en Sheng-hsiao, 229
Ch'en Shu-t'ang, 125
Ch'en Yu, 119, 122, 143
Ch'en Yu-sheng, 122
Cheng Kuan-ying, 17; biographical sketch, 116; and C.M.S.N. Co., 87, 113, 116–117, 163; and Han-Yeh-P'ing, 116; on modern-type enterprises, 33–34; on officials in industry, 37–38; and Shanghai Cotton Cloth Mill, 209, 211–214; Sheng-shih wei-yen, author of, 17, 117; and telegraphs, 205
Cheng Tsao-ju, 155
Chi-ch'eng Spinning and Weaving Mill, 224
Chi-yü kung-ssu. See China Merchants' Holding Company
Chiang Kai-shek, 259
Chiao-t'ung yin-hang. See Bank of Communications
Ch'ien-chuang, money shops, 52, 113, 132, 134, 226
Chin-li-yuan wharves, 19, 99, 142–143
Ch'in Shih Huang-ti, 85
China: agriculture, 34–35; economic conditions in nineteenth century, 31–57; effect of foreign trade, compared with Japan, 51–56, 185–186; government and the economy, 37–39; impact of foreign manufacturers on, 36; industrialization, compared with Japan, 1, 2, 32–33, 37, 47–48, 84, 183–185, 246, 247; weakness of central government, 13, 22, 39–40, 47, 188, 246. See Bureaucracy,

BIBLIOGRAPHY OF WESTERN WORKS

Allen, G. C. and Audrey G. Donnithorne. Western Enterprise in Far Eastern Economic Development. 292 pp.; London, 1954.

Arnold, Julean, et al. Commercial Handbook of China (Department of Commerce, Bureau of Foreign and Domestic Commerce, Miscellaneous Series, No. 84). 2 vols., 630 + 470 pp.; Washington, 1919-1920.

Blackburn Chamber of Commerce. Report of the Mission to China of the Blackburn Chamber of Commerce, 1896-1897. 2 vols., xii + 152 + vii + 386 pp.; Blackburn, 1898.

Bland, J. O. P. Li Hung-chang (Makers of the Nineteenth Century, edited by Basil Williams). viii + 327 pp.; London, 1917.

------- Recent Events and Present Policies in China. xi + 481 pp.; London, 1912.

Bodde, Derk. "Authority and Law in Ancient China," in Authority and Law in the Ancient Orient (supplement to Journal of the American Oriental Society, No. 17, July-September 1954), pp. 46-55.

Braisted, William R. "The United States and the American China Development Co.," Far Eastern Quarterly, 11.2:147-165 (February 1952).

Britton, Rosswell S. The Chinese Periodical Press, 1800-1912. 151 pp.; Shanghai, 1933.

Carlson, Ellsworth. The Kaiping Mines (1877-1912). Harvard University, Chinese Economic and Political Studies, Special Series. vii + 174 pp.; Cambridge, Mass., 1957.

Chang Chung-li. The Chinese Gentry, Studies on their Role in Nineteenth-Century Chinese Society. xxi + 250 pp.; Seattle, 1955.

Ch'en, Gideon (Ch'en Ch'i-t'ien). Review of 1939 edition of Yü-chai ts'un-kao, The Yenching Journal of Social Studies, 3.2:242-247 (August 1941).

------- Tso Tsung-t'ang, Pioneer Promoter of the Modern Dockyard and the Woolen Mill in China. 91 pp.; Peiping, 1938.

Ch'en Huan-chang. The Economic Principles of Confucius and His School (Studies in History, Economics and Public Law, vols. XLIV,

XLV). 2 vols., xv + 756 pp.; New York, 1911.

Cheng Lin. The Chinese Railways, An Historical Survey. 214 pp.; Shanghai, 1935.

China, Imperial Maritime Customs. Decennial Reports on the Trade, Navigation, Industries, etc., of the Ports Open to Foreign Commerce in China and on the Conditions and Development of the Treaty Port Provinces, 1882-1891 (xii + 694 + lxxiv pp.; 1893); 1892-1901 (2vols., xi + 568 + xii + 601 + lxxiv pp; 1904-1906); General of Customs, Shanghai.

------- Returns of Trade at the Treaty Ports of China. Shanghai, 1870-1912 annually.

------- Salt: Production and Taxation (V. Office Series: Customs Papers No. 81). viii + 349 pp.; Shanghai: Statistical Department of the Inspectorate General of Customs, 1906.

The China Who's Who (Foreign): A Biographical Dictionary. Compiled and published by Carrol Lunt; Shanghai, 1927.

The Chronicle and Directory for China, Corea, Japan. . . for the Year 1885. Hongkong: The Daily Press, 1885.

Duckerts, Jules. La Chine en 1889, rapport de la mission commerciale de Jules Duckerts, Consul Général, Chargé d'affaires de Belgique. vi + 269 pp.; 2nd edition, Verviers, 1901.

Fairbank, John K. and Liu Kwang-ching. Modern China: A Bibliographical Guide to Chinese Works, 1898-1937. xviii + 608 pp.; Cambridge, Mass., 1950.

Ferguson, John C. "Dr. Charles D. Tenney," The China Journal, 13.1: 5-6 (July 1930).

------- "Notes on the Chinese Banking System in Shanghai," Journal of the North China Branch of the Royal Asiatic Society, 37:55-82 (1906).

Feuerwerker, Albert. "A Draft Biography of Sheng Hsuan-huai, Official and Industrialist (1844-1916), " Papers on China, Committee on International and Regional Studies, Harvard University, 8:1-37 (February 1954).

------- "From 'Feudalism' to 'Capitalism' in Recent Historical Writing from Mainland China," The Journal of Asian Studies, 18.1: 107-116 (November 1958).

Forke, A. "Das chinesische Finanz- und Steuerwesen," Mitteilungen des Seminars für orientalische Sprachen, 3:165-191 (1900); 4:1-75 (1901).

Frochisse, J. -M. La Belgique et la Chine: relations diplomatiques et économiques (1839-1909). 459 pp.; Bruxelles, 1936.

Great Britain. Parliamentary Papers, China: No. 3 (1900), Correspondence Respecting the Insurrectionary Movement in China.

------- Parliamentary Papers, China: No. 1 (1912), Correspondence Respecting Affairs in China.

Gulik, R. H. van. "Dr. John C. Ferguson's 75th Anniversary," Monumenta Serica, 6:340-356 (1941).

Hail, William James. Tseng Kuo-fan and the Taiping Rebellion, with a Short Sketch of his Later Career. 400 pp.; New Haven, 1927.

Hall, Ray Ovid. The Chinese National Banks from Their Founding to the Moratorium. 291 pp.; Berlin, 1921.

Hinton, Harold C. "The Grain Transport System of the Ch'ing Dynasty," Far Eastern Quarterly, 11.3:339-354 (May 1952).

------- The Grain Tribute System of China (1845-1911). vii + 163 pp.; Cambridge, Mass., 1956.

Ho, Franklin L. and Fong Hsien Ding. Extent and Effects of Industrialization in China (data paper, Biennial Conference of the Institute of Pacific Relations). 34 pp.; Tientsin, 1929.

Ho Ping-ti. "The Salt Merchants of Yang-chou: A Study of Commercial Capitalism in Eighteenth-century China," Harvard Journal of Asiatic Studies, 17.1-2:130-168 (June 1954).

Honjō Eijirō. The Social and Economic History of Japan. xii + 410 pp.; Kyoto, 1935.

Hummel, Arthur W., editor. Eminent Chinese of the Ch'ing Period. 2 vols., xi + 1103 pp.; Washington, 1943, 1944.

Hummel, Arthur William, Jr. "Yüan Shih-k'ai as an Official Under the Manchus." ii + 179 pp.; unpubl. M.A. thesis (University of Chicago), 1949.

Jamieson, George. Report on the Revenue and Expenditure of the Chinese Empire (British Parliamentary Papers, Diplomatic and Consular Reports, Miscellaneous Series, No. 415). 62 pp.; London, 1897.

Jansen, Marius B. "Yawata, Hanyehping and the Twenty-one Demands,"
Pacific Historical Review, 23.1:31-48 (February 1954).

Japan Year Book 1933. Tokyo, The Foreign Affairs Association of Japan.

Kent, Percy Horace. The Passing of the Manchus. xi + 404 pp.; London,
1912.

------- Railway Enterprise in China. ix + 304 pp.; London, 1907.

King, Paul. In the Chinese Customs Service, a Personal Record of
Forty-seven Years. London, 1924 (rev. ed., 1930).

LaFargue, Thomas E. China's First Hundred. xiv + 176 pp.; Pullman,
Wash.,1942.

Langer, William L. The Diplomacy of Imperialism 1890-1902. xxiv +

797 + xxii pp.; 2nd edition, New York, 1951.

Lawton, Lancelot F. and H. Hobden. "The Fall of Yüan Shih-k'ai,"
Fortnightly Review, old series, 93:420-434 (March 1910).

Levenson, Joseph R. Liang Ch'i-ch'ao and the Mind of Modern China
(Harvard Historical Monographs, 26). xii + 256 pp.; Cambridge,
Mass., 1953.

------- "'History' and 'Value': the Tensions of Intellectual Choice in
Modern China," in Studies in Chinese Thought, edited by Arthur
F. Wright, pp. 146-194; Chicago, 1953.

------- "Redefinition of Ideas in Time: The Classics and Chinese History," Far Eastern Quarterly, 15.3:399-404 (May 1956).

------- "The Attenuation of a Chinese Philosophical Concept: 'T'i-yung'
in the Nineteenth Century," Asiatische Studien, 1.4:95-102
(1955).

Levy, Marion J. "Contrasting Factors in the Modernization of China and
Japan," Economic Development and Cultural Change, 2.3:161-197
(October 1953).

Levy, Marion J. and Shih Kuo-heng. The Rise of the Modern Chinese
Business Class, Two Introductory Essays. viii + 64 pp.; New
York, 1949.

Lieu, D. K. (Liu Ta-chün). China's Industries and Finance.
xiv + 238 pp.; Peking and Shanghai, 1927.

------- The Growth and Industrialization of Shanghai. ix + 473 pp.;
    Shanghai, 1936.

List of Principal Foreign and Chinese Industrial Enterprises in China
    and Hong Kong (Revised to December 31, 1917). Compiled by
    H. M. Commercial Attaché with the assistance of H. M. Con-
    suls in China, 60 pp.; Shanghai, 1918.

Liu Kwang-ching. "Administering a Steam-Navigation Company in China,
    1862-1867," The Business History Review, 29.2: 157-188 (June
    1955).

------- "Financing a Steam-Navigation Company in China, 1861-1862,"
    ibid., 28.2: 154-181 (June 1954).

------- "The Steamship Business in Nineteenth-century China: An Essay
    on Some Problems of Entrepreneurship." MS., 48 pp.; August
    1956.

------- "Two Steamship Companies in China, 1862-1877." Unpubl. diss.
    (Harvard University), 1956.

Lockwood, William W. The Economic Development of Japan: Growth and
    Structural Change, 1868-1938. xv + 603 pp.; Princeton, 1954.

Lyon, Chambre de commerce. La mission lyonnaise d'exploration com-
    merciale en Chine, 1895-97. xxxvi + 473 pp.; Lyon, 1898.

Michael, Franz. "Military Organization and the Power Structure of
    China During the Taiping Rebellion," Pacific Historical Review,
    18.4:469-483 (November 1949).

Morse, Hosea Ballou. Chinese Bills, Notes, etc. Collected by Hosea
    Ballou Morse. Samples presented to the Harvard University
    Library, September 1886.

------- The International Relations of the Chinese Empire. 3 vols.,
    xxxix + 727 + xlv + 479 + xvii + 530 pp.; London, 1910-1918.

------- "Letter-books of H. B. Morse Containing Copies of his Corres-
    pondence While Commissioner with the Chinese Maritime Cus-
    toms, 1886-1907." 5 vols., MS., Houghton Library, Harvard
    University.

------- The Trade and Administration of the Chinese Empire.
    xi + 451 pp.; London, 1908.

Nippon Yusen Kaisha. Golden Jubilee History of Nippon Yusen Kaisha, 1885-1935. vii + 175 pp.; Tokyo, 1935.

Norman, E. Herbert. Japan's Emergence as a Modern State; Political and Economic Problems of the Meiji Period. xvi + 254 pp.; New York, 1940.

North-China Herald and Supreme Court and Consular Gazette (Shanghai, weekly edition of the North-China Daily News). File for 1872-1916 consulted.

Parker, Edward Harper. China, Past and Present. viii + 424 pp.; New York, 1903.

------- "The Chinese Revenue," Journal of the China Branch of the Royal Asiatic Society, new series, 30:102-141 (1895-1896).

------- "The Financial Capacity of China," ibid.; 74-101.

Pelcovits, Nathan A. Old China Hands and the Foreign Office. xi + 349 pp.; New York, 1948.

Pirenne, Henri. Les périodes de l'histoire sociale du capitalisme. 44 pp.; Bruxelles, 1914.

Powell, Ralph L. The Rise of Chinese Military Power, 1895-1912. x + 383 pp.; Princeton, 1955.

Reid, John Gilbert. The Manchu Abdication and the Powers, 1908-1912. 497 pp.; Berkeley, 1935.

Remer, C. F. Foreign Investments in China. xxi + 708 pp.; New York, 1933.

------- The Foreign Trade of China. 258 pp.; Shanghai, 1926.

Richard, Timothy. Forty-five Years in China. 384 pp.; New York, 1916.

Schumpeter, Joseph A. Business Cycles; A Theoretical, Historical and Statistical Analysis of the Capitalist Process. 2 vols.; New York and London, 1939.

------- "The Creative Response in Economic History," Journal of Economic History, 8:149-159 (November 1947).

Shanghai Steam Navigation Co. Minutes of a General Meeting of the Shareholders, and Report of the Board of Directors to the General Meeting: February 21, 1868, March 5, 1870, March 4, 1871, January 15, 1877. Widener Library, Harvard University.

Sheldon, Charles D. "Some Economic Reasons for the Marked Contrast in Japanese and Chinese Modernization as Seen in Examples of 'Premodern' Shipping and Trading by Water," Kyōto University Economic Review, 23.2:30-60 (October 1953).

Sheng Hsuan-huai. China's National Bank and Currency Reform, A Memorial by Sheng Hsuan-huai, Junior Vice-President of the Board of Posts and Communications. Translated by John C. Ferguson, Ph. D., 24 pp.; Shanghai, 1909.

Smith, Thomas C. Political Change and Industrial Development in Japan: Government Enterprise, 1868-1880 (Stanford University Publications, History, Economics, and Political Science, vol. X). viii + 126 pp.; Stanford, 1955.

------- "Landlords and Rural Capitalists in the Modernization of Japan," Journal of Economic History, 16.2:165-181 (June 1956).

So Kwan-wai. "Western Influence and the Chinese Reform Movement of 1898." Unpubl. diss. (University of Wisconsin), 1950.

Spector, Stanley. "Li Hung-chang and the Huai-chün." x + xi + 641 pp.; unpubl. diss. (University of Washington), 1953.

Stanley, Charles J. "Chinese Finance from 1852 to 1908," Papers on China, Committee on International and Regional Studies, Harvard University, 3:1-23 (1949).

------- "Hu Kuang-yung and China's Early Foreign Loans." Unpubl. diss. (Harvard University), 1951.

Steiger, G. Nye. China and the Occident; the Origins and Development of the Boxer Movement. xix + 349 pp.; New Haven, 1927.

Sun Zen E-tu. Chinese Railways and British Interests, 1898-1911. x + 230 pp.; New York, 1954.

Tan, Chester C. The Boxer Catastrophe (Columbia Studies in the Social Sciences, No. 583). ix + 276 pp.; New York, 1955.

Teng Ssu-yü and John K. Fairbank. China's Response to the West: A Documentary Survey, 1839-1923. x + 296 pp.; Cambridge, Mass., 1954.

Translations of the Peking Gazette (reprinted annually from the North-China Herald). Shanghai, 1873-1900.

U.S. Bureau of Statistics (Treasury Department). Commercial China in

1899... (From the Summary of Commerce and Finance for March 1899). iv + 150 pp.; Washington, 1900?.

Wagel, Srinivas Ram. Chinese Currency and Banking. 457 pp.; Shanghai, 1915.

------- Finance in China. 503 pp.; Shanghai, 1914.

Wang Yü -ch'üan. "The Rise of Land Tax and the Fall of Dynasties in Chinese History," Pacific Affairs, 9.2:201-220 (June 1936).

Wei Wen Pin. The Currency Problem in China. 157 pp.; New York, 1914.

Who's Who in China. 3rd edition, Shanghai, 1926, and supplement, 1928, published by The China Weekly Review.

Who's Who in the Far East, 1906-1907. Hong Kong, 1906, published by the China Mail.

Williams, Edward Thomas, translator. Recent Chinese Legislation Relating to Commercial, Railway, and Mining Enterprises. Shanghai, 1904.

Wilson, James Harrison. China; Travels and Investigations in the "Middle Kingdom." xxiv + 376 pp.; 2nd edition, New York, 1894.

Wright, Arnold, editor. Twentieth Century Impressions of Hongkong, Shanghai, and other Treaty Ports of China: Their History, People, Commerce, Industries, and Resources. 848 pp.; London, 1908.

Wright, Stanley F. China's Struggle for Tariff Autonomy, 1843-1938. xi + 775 pp.; Shanghai, 1938.

------- Hart and the Chinese Customs. xvi + 949 pp.; Belfast, 1950.

Wu, James T. K. "The Impact of the Taiping Rebellion upon the Manchu Fiscal System," Pacific Historical Review, 19.3:265-275 (August 1950).

Yang Lien-sheng. Money and Credit in China, A Short History (Harvard-Yenching Institute Monograph Series, No. 12). 143 pp.; Cambridge, Mass., 1952.

Yung Wing (Jung Hung). My Life in China and America. vi + 286 pp.; New York, 1909.

Asobe Kyuzō 遊部久藏 . "Chūgoku kindai kōgyō no hatten" 中國近
代工業 の 發展 (Development of Modern Industry in
China); in Niida Noboru 仁井田陞 , ed., Kindai Chūgoku no
shakai to keizai 近代中國 の 社會 と 經濟 (Society and
Economy of Modern China), pp. 167-203; Tokyo, 1951.

Chang Chih-tung 張之洞 . Chang Wen-hsiang-kung ch'üan-chi 張文
襄公全集 (Complete Papers of Chang Chih-tung). Edited
and published by Wang Shu-nan 王樹枬; 229 chüan in 120 ts'e;
Peiping, 1928. Includes memorials (tsou-i 奏議), 72 chüan;
telegraphic memorials (tien-tsou 電奏), 13 chüan; official correspondence (kung-tu 公牘), 36 chüan; telegraphic correspondence (tien-tu 電牘), 80 chüan.

Chang Hsiao-jo 張孝若 . Nan-t'ung Chang Chi-chih hsien-sheng chuan-
chi 南通張季直先生傳記 (Biography of Chang Chien).
649 pp.; Shanghai, 1930.

Chang Hsin-ch'eng 張心澂. Chung-kuo hsien-tai chiao-t'ung shih 中
國現代交通史 (A History of Modern Communications in
China). 7 + 618 pp.; Shanghai, 1931.

Chang Yen-chü 張延舉. "Wu-hsü pien-fa shih-ch'i wan-ku-p'ai chih
ching-chi ssu-hsiang" 戊戌變法時期頑固派之經
濟思想 (Economic Thought of the Conservative Party in
1898); Chung-kuo ching-chi 中國經濟 (Chinese Economics),
4.6:141-147 (June 1936).

Chao Feng-t'ien 趙豐田 . Wan-Ch'ing wu-shih-nien ching-chi ssu-
hsiang shih 晚清五十年經濟思想史 (Economic

Thought during the Last Fifty Years of the Ch'ing Period). 320 pp.; Peiping, 1939.

Ch'en Ch'iu 陳鍫．"Wu-hsü pien-fa shih fan-pien-fa jen wu chih cheng-chih ssu-hsiang" 戊戌變法時反變法人物之政治思想 (The Political Thought of the Anti-Reformers during the Time of the Reform Movement of 1898); Yen-ching hsüeh-pao 燕京學報 (Yenching Journal of Chinese Studies), No. 25, pp. 59-106 (June 1939).

Ch'en Kung-lu 陳恭祿．Chung-kuo chin-tai shih 中國近代史 (History of Modern China). 860 pp.; Shanghai, 1935.

Cheng Kuan-ying 鄭觀應．Sheng-shih wei-yen 盛世危言 (Warnings to a Seemingly Prosperous Age). 8 chüan; 1900.

Chiao-t'ung-shih 交通史 (History of Communications [in China]). Compiled by the Ministries of Communications and Railroads, Republic of China; 37 vols.; Nanking, 1930 ff. Includes vols. 6-11, Hang-cheng pien 航政編 (section on shipping); vols. 12-29, Lu-cheng pien 陸政編 (section on railroads and motor roads); vols. 30-32, Tien-cheng pien 電政編 (section on telegraph, telephone, and radio).

Chien Po-tsan 翦伯贊 et al., compilers. I-ho-t'uan 義和團 ([Source Materials on] the Boxer Uprising). 4 vols.; Shanghai, 1951.

------- Wu-hsü pien-fa 戊戌變法 ([Source Materials on] the Reform Movement of 1898). 4 vols.; Shanghai, 1953.

Chin Liang 金梁．Chin-shih jen-wu chih 近世人物志 (A Gazetteer of Modern Personages). 366 pp.; 1934.

Ch'ing-ch'ao hsü wen-hsien t'ung-k'ao 清朝續文獻通考 (Encyclopedia of the Historical Records of the Ch'ing Dynasty). Compiled by Liu Chin-tsao 劉錦藻 ; 4 vols.; Shanghai, 1936.

Ch'ing-shih kao 清史稿 (Draft History of the Ch'ing Dynasty). Compiled by Chao Erh-sun 趙爾巽 ; 536 chüan; 1927.

Ch'üan Han-sheng 全漢昇 . "Ch'ing-mo Han-yang t'ieh-ch'ang" 清末漢陽鐵廠 (The Han-yang Iron and Steel Works, 1890-1908); She-hui k'o-hsüeh lun-ts'ung 社會科學論叢 (Journal of Social Sciences), 1:1-33 (April 1950).

------- "Sung-tai kuan-li chih ssu-ying shang-yeh" 宋代官吏之私營商業 (Clandestine Commercial Enterprises of Sung Officials); Li-shih yü-yen yen-chiu-so chi-k'an 歷史語言研究所集刊 (Bulletin of the Institute of History and Philology), 7.2:199-253 (1936).

Chung-kuo tzu-pen chu-i meng-ya wen-t'i t'ao-lun chi 中國資本主義萌芽問題討論集 (Collected Papers on the Problem of the Incipiency of Capitalism in China). Edited by the Chinese History Seminar of the Chinese People's University; 2 vols., 8 + 1102 pp.; Peking, 1957.

Fan Wen-lan 范文瀾 . Chung-kuo chin-tai shih 中國近代史 (History of Modern China). Vol. 1, 543 pp.; Peking, 1950.

Fang T'eng 方騰 (pseud. ?). "Yu Ch'ia-ch'ing lun" 虞洽卿論 (On Yu Ho-te); Tsa-chih yueh-k'an 雜誌月刊 (Monthly Miscellany), 12.2:46-51(November 1943); 12.3:62-67 (December 1943); 12.4:59-64 (January 1944).

Feng-kang 鳳岡 . San-shui Liang Yen-sun hsien-sheng nien-p'u 三水梁燕孫先生年譜 (Chronological Biography of Liang Shih-yi). 2 vols.; 1946.

Feng Kuei-fen 馮桂芬 . Hsien-chih-t'ang kao 顯志堂稿 (Literary Works). 12 chüan; 1877.

Gendai Shina jimmei kan 現代支那人名鑑 (Biographies of Contemporary Chinese). Compiled by Gaimushō jōhōbu 外務省情報部 (Japanese Foreign Office Intelligence Section); Tokyo, 1928 edition.

Hashikawa Tokio 橋川時雄, compiler. Chūgoku bunkakakai jimbutsu sōkan 中國文化界人物總鑑 (Comprehensive Dictionary of Personalities in Chinese Cultural Circles). Peiping, 1940.

Hsia Yen-te 夏炎德 . Chung-kuo chin-pai-nien ching-chi ssu-hsiang 中國近百年經濟思想 (Chinese Economic Thought in the Last One Hundred Years). 6 + 202 pp.; Shanghai, 1948.

Hsieh Pin 謝彬 . Chung-kuo yu-tien hang-k'ung shih 中國郵電航空史 (A History of the Post, Telegraph, and Aviation in China). 7 + 262 pp.; Shanghai, 1928.

Hsü Jun 徐潤 . Hsü Yü-chai tzu-hsü nien-p'u 徐愚齋自敘年譜 (Chronological Autobiography). Published by the Hsü family of Hsiang-shan, 1927.

Hsü T'ung-hsin 許同莘 . Chang Wen-hsiang-kung nien-p'u 張文襄公年譜 (Chronological Biography of Chang Chih-tung). 1 ts'e edition, 229 pp.; Shanghai, 1946.

Huang Ta-shou 黃大受 . Chung-kuo chin-tai shih 中國近代史 (History of Modern China). 3 vols., 618 + 602 + 610 pp.; Taipei, 1953-1955.

Kindai Chūgoku kenkyū iin kai 近代中國研究委員會 (The Seminar on Modern China). Sei Sen-kai En Sei-gai sōgi mokuroku 盛

xii

宣懷袁世凱奏議目錄 (List of Memorials Presented to the Emperor by Sheng Hsuan-huai and Yuan Shih-k'ai). 2 + 90 pp.; Tokyo, 1955.

Kōsaka Torizō 上坂酉三. Chūgoku kōeki kikō no kenkyū 中國交易機構の研究 (A Study of Commercial Mechanisms in China). 356 + 5 pp.; Waseda University, 1949.

Ku Hung-ming 辜鴻銘 (Han-pin tu-i-che 漢濱讀易者, pseud.). "Yeh-chün chuan" 葉君傳 (A Biography of Yeh Ch'eng-chung 葉澄衷); in his Chang Wen-hsiang mu-fu chi-wen 張文襄公幕府紀聞(Notes from the Office of Governor-general Chang Chih-tung), 2.22-24; 1910.

Kung Chun 龔駿. Chung-kuo hsin kung-yeh fa-chan shih ta-kang 中國新工業發展史大綱 (An Outline History of the Development of Modern Industry in China). 302 pp.; Shanghai, 1933.

Kuo Hsiao-hsien 郭孝先. "Shang-hai ti nei-kuo yin-hang" 上海的內國銀行 (Chinese Banks in Shanghai); Shang-hai-shih t'ung-chih-kuan ch'i-k'an 上海市通志館期刊 (Journal of the Shanghai Gazetteer Office), 1.2:441-498 (September 1933).

Kuo-li Hua-pei pien-i-kuan kuan-k'an 國立華北編譯館館刊 (Bulletin of the National North China Compilation and Translation Bureau), December 1, 1942; Peking. Notice of 1942 reprint of Yü-chai ts'un-kao (see infra, Sheng Hsuan-huai).

Li Chien-nung 李劍農. Chung-kuo chin-pai-nien cheng-chih shih 中國近百年政治史 (Political History of China in the Last Hundred Years). 2 vols., 690 pp.; Shanghai, 1947.

Li Hsi-sheng 李希聖. Kuang-hsü k'uai-chi lu 光緒會計錄(Fis-

cal Statistics of the Kuang-hsü Period). 2 ts'e; Shanghai, preface dated 1896.

Li Hung-chang 李鴻章. Li Wen-chung-kung ch'üan-chi 李文忠公
全集 (Complete Papers of Li Hung-chang). Edited by Wu Ju-
lun 吳汝綸; 100 ts'e; Nanking, 1905. Includes memorials
(tsou-kao 奏稿), 80 chüan; letters (p'eng-liao han-kao 朋僚
函稿), 20 chüan; Tsungli Yamen correspondence (I-shu han-
kao 譯署函稿), 20 chüan; telegrams (tien-kao 電稿), 40
chüan.

Li Ku-fan 李孤帆. Chao-shang-chü san-ta-an 招商局三大案
(Three Major Cases relating to the China Merchants' Steam Navigation Company). 13 + 211 + 3 pp.; Shanghai, 1933.

Li P'ei-en 李培恩. "Chin pai-nien lai Chung-kuo chih yin-hang" 近
百年來中國之銀行 (Chinese Banking in the Last Hun-
dred Years); Hsüeh-lin 學林 (The Academic World), 9:1-14
(July 1941); Shanghai.

Liu Sheng-mu 劉聲木. Ch'ang-ch'u chai sui-pi 萇楚齋隨筆 (Miscellaneous Notes by Mr. Liu); in Chih-chieh-t'ang ts'ung-k'o
ch'u-pien 直介堂叢刻初編 (Chih-chieh-t'ang Collectan-
ea); ts'e 20-25; preface dated 1929.

Liu Yu-yün 劉嶽雲. Kuang-hsü k'uai-chi piao 光緒會計表
(Kuang-hsü Fiscal Tables). 4 ts'e; 1901.

Lo Yü-tung 羅玉東. Chung-kuo li-chin shih 中國釐金史 (History of the Likin in China). 2 vols., 15 + 649 pp.; Shanghai,
1936.

------- "Kuang-hsü-ch'ao pu-chiu ts'ai-cheng chih fang-ts'e" 光緒朝
補救財政之方策 (The Governmental Policies of Meet-

ing the Financial Crisis during the Kuang-hsü Period [1875-1908]); Chung-kuo chin-tai ching-chi-shih yen-chiu chi-k'an 中國近代經濟史研究集刊 (Studies in Modern Economic History of China). 1.2:189-270 (May 1933).

Ma Chien-chung 馬建忠 . Shih-k'o-chai chi-yen 適可齋記言 (Notes from the Shih-k'o-chai [Studio]); in Hsi-cheng ts'ung-shu 西政叢書 (Hsi-cheng Collectanea), ts'e 27. Preface dated 1897.

Mai Chung-hua 麥仲華 , compiler. Huang-ch'ao ching-shih wen hsin-pien 皇朝經世文新編 (New Collection of Essays on Statecraft of the Ch'ing Dynasty). 21 chüan in 24 ts'e; Shanghai, 1898.

Mao-hsin Fu-hsin Shen-hsin tsung-kung-ssu sa-chou-nien chi-nien ts'e 茂新福新申新總公司卅週年紀念冊 (The Thirtieth Anniversary Memorial Book, 1898-1928, Mow Sing and Foh Sing Flour Mills and Sung Sing Cotton Mills). About 200 pp.; Shanghai, 1929.

Matsushima Shūe 松嶋宗衛. Shinchō matsuro hishi 清朝末路秘史 (Secret History of the End of the Ch'ing Dynasty). 6 + 271 pp.; Tokyo, 1925.

Min Er-ch'ang 閔爾昌 , compiler. Pei-chuan-chi-pu 碑傳集補 . (Supplementary Collection of Memorial Inscriptions). 61 chüan in 24 ts'e; Peiping, 1931.

Miyashita Tadao 宮下忠雄 . "Rōgaki Shina ginkōgyō no bokkō" 萌芽期支那銀行業の勃興 (The Rise of Modern Chinese Banking); Shina kenkyū 支那研究 (Chinese Studies), 47:63-93 (July 1938).

Miyazaki Ichisada 宮崎市定. "Shōshōkyoku no ryakushi, Chūgoku no dokusenteki kisen kaisha" 招商局ノ略史，中國ノ獨占的汽船會社 (A Short History of the China Merchants' Steam Navigation Company, China's Monopolistic Steamship Company); Tōyōshi kenkyu 東洋史研究 (The Journal of Oriental Researches), 11. 2: 63-69 (March 1951).

Momose Hiromu 百瀬弘. "Shimmatsu no Keisei bumpen ni tsuite" 清末ノ經世文編ニ就ゐて (On the Ching-shih wen-pien of the Late Ch'ing Dynasty); in Ikeuchi hakushi kanreki kinen Tōyōshi ronsō 池内博士還曆記念東洋史論叢 (Essays on Oriental History Collected to Commemorate the 60th Birthday of Dr. Ikeuchi), pp. 877-892. Tokyo, 1940.

Morisawa Rakugoro 森澤磊五郎. "Shanhai ni okeru kyōiku" 上海ニ於ける教育 (Education in Shanghai); Shina kenkyū 支那研究 (Chinese Studies), 18:293-364 (December 1928).

Negishi Tadashi 根岸佶. Baiben seido no kenkyū 買辨制度ノ研究 (A Study of the Comprador System). 392 pp.; Tokyo, 1948.

------- Chūgoku shakai ni okeru shidōsō: kirō shinshi no kenkyū 中國社會ニ於ける指導層，耆老紳士ノ研究 (Leading Classes in Chinese Society: a Study of Elders and Gentry). 2 + 278 pp.; Tokyo, 1947.

Nung-kung-shang-pu hsien-hsing chang-ch'eng 農工商部現行章程 (Current Regulations of the Ministry of Agriculture, Industry, and Commerce). 13 ts'e; Peking, 1908.

Nung-kung-shang-pu t'ung-chi piao 農工商部統計表 (Statistical Tables of the Ministry of Agriculture, Industry, and Commerce): Ti-i-tz'u 第一次 (First Collection), 6 ts'e; Peking, 1909;

Ti-erh-tz'u 第二次 (Second Collection), 2 ts'e; 1910.

P'eng Yu-hsin 彭雨新. "Ch'ing-mo chung-yang yü ko-sheng ts'ai-
cheng kuan-hsi" 清末中央與各省財政關係 (The
Financial Relations between Central and Local Government in
the Tsing Dynasty); She-hui k'o-hsüeh tsa-chih 社會科學
雜誌 (Quarterly Review of Social Sciences), 9.1:83-110 (June
1947).

Shang-hai-hsien hsü-chih 上海縣續志 (Supplementary Gazetteer of
the Shanghai District). 32 chüan; Shanghai, 1918.

Shen Lei-ch'un 沈雷春, editor. Chung-kuo pao-hsien nien-chien 中
國保險年鑑 (Chinese Insurance Annual). 43 + 220 + 34 +
114 pp.; Shanghai, 1937 edition.

Shen Nai-cheng 沈乃正. "Ch'ing-mo chih tu-fu chi-ch'üan, chung-
yang chi-ch'üan, yü 't'ung-shu pan-kung'" 清末之督撫集
權,中央集權,與" 同署辦公 "(On the Powers of the
Viceroy and the Governor of the Provinces in the Last Years of
the Tsing Dynasty); She-hui k'o-hsüeh 社會科學(The Social Sciences), 2.2:311-342 (January 1937).

Shen Tsu-hsien 沈祖憲 and Wu K'ai-sheng 吳闓生. Jung-an ti-tzu
chi 容菴弟子記 (An Account of Yuan Shih-k'ai by his Disciples). 4 chüan; 1913.

Shen T'ung-sheng 沈桐生, compiler. Kuang-hsü cheng-yao 光緒
政要 (Important Documents of the Kuang-hsü Period). 34
chüan in 30 ts'e; Shanghai, 1909.

Sheng Hsuan-huai 盛宣懷. Sheng shang-shu Yü-chai ts'un-kao ch'u-
k'an 盛尚書愚齋存稿初刊 (Collected Drafts of Board
President Sheng Yü-chai [Hsuan-huai], first issue). Edited by

Lü Ching-tuan 呂景端 ; 101 chüan in 51 ts'e; Shanghai, 1939.
Includes Sheng's biography (Hsing-shu 行述), prefix vol.;
memorials, chüan 1-20; telegraphic memorials, chüan 21-23;
telegrams, chüan 24-100.

------- editor. Ch'ang-chou hsien-che i-shu ti-i-chi 常州先哲遺
書第一集 (Writings of Eminent Men of Ch'ang-chou, First
Collection). 64 ts'e; 1899.

------- K'ao-ch'a Jih-pen pao-kao 考察日本報告 (Report of My
Observations in Japan), in Yü-chai ts'un-kao, supra, as appen-
dix vol.

Sheng Hsuan-huai and Sheng Shan-huai 盛善懷. Sheng K'ang hsing-
shu 盛康行述 (Biography of Sheng K'ang). 1 ts'e, 31 pp.;
n.d. East Asiatic Library, Columbia University.

Sheng T'ung-i 盛同頤 et al. [Sheng Hsuan-huai] Hsing-shu 行述
(Biography [of Sheng Hsuan-huai]), in the prefatory vol.
(chüan-shou) of Yü-chai ts'un-kao, supra.

Shu Hsin-ch'eng 舒新城, compiler. Chin-tai Chung-kuo chiao-yü
shih-liao 近代中國教育史料 (Historical Materials relating to Modern Chinese Education). 4 vols.; Shanghai, 1928.

Sonoda Kazuki 園田一龜 , compiler; Huang Hui-ch'üan 黃惠泉
and Tiao Ying-hua 刁英華 , translators from the Japanese.
Fen-sheng hsin Chung-kuo jen-wu-chih 分省新中國人
物誌 (Personalities of the New China arranged by Provinces).
518 pp.; Shanghai, 1930.

Ta-Ch'ing Kuang-hsü hsin-fa-ling 大清光緒新法令 (New Laws
and Ordinances of the Kuang-hsü Reign). Compiled by the Commercial Press; 20 ts'e; Shanghai, 1909.

Ta-Ch'ing li-ch'ao shih-lu, Kuang-hsü ch'ao 大清歷朝實錄 光
緒朝 (Veritable Records of Successive Reigns of the Ch'ing
Dynasty, Kuang-hsü Reign [1875-1908]). 597 + 4 chüan [ts'e
1071-1180 out of 1220 ts'e]; Tokyo, 1937-1938.

T'ang Ch'ing-tseng 唐慶增. "Ch'ing-tai t'ai-hsi shu-ju wo-kuo chih
ching-chih ssu-hsiang" 清代泰西輸入我國之經濟
思想 (The Introduction of Western Economic Thought into
China during the Ch'ing Dynasty); in Chung-kuo ching-chih wen-
t'i 中國經濟問題 (Proceedings of Chinese Economic Association: Chinese Economic Problems), pp. 316-329. Shanghai,
1929.

------- Chung-kuo ching-chi ssu-hsiang shih 中國經濟思想史
(A History of Chinese Economic Thought). Vol. 1; Shanghai,
1936.

T'ang Hsiang-lung 湯象龍. "Min-kuo i-ch'ien kuan-shui tan-pao chih
wai-chai" 民國以前關稅擔保之外債 (The Foreign
Loans Secured on the Customs Revenue before 1911) ; Chung-
kuo chin-tai ching-chi-shih yen-chiu chi-k'an 中國近代經
濟史研究集刊 (Studies in Modern Economic History of
China), 3.1:1-49 (1935).

------- "Min-kuo i-ch'ien ti p'ei-k'uan shih ju-ho ch'ang-fu ti? 民國
以前的賠款是如何償付的 ? (A Study of the In-
demnity Payments before 1911) ; ibid. , 3.2 :262-291 (1935).

Teng Chih-ch'eng 鄧之誠. "Review" of Feng-kang's San-shui Liang
Yen-sun hsien-sheng nien-p'u , supra; Yen-ching hsüeh-pao
燕京學報 (Yenching Journal of Chinese Studies), No. 33,
pp. 292-302 (1947).

Tezuka Masao　手塚正夫．Shina jūkōgyō hattatsu shi 支那重工業發展史　(History of the Development of Chinese Heavy Industry).　548 + 14 pp.; Tokyo, 1944.

Tōa Dōbun Shoin　東亞同文書院　．Shina seiji chiri shi 支那政治地理誌 (Political and Geographical Gazetteer of China).　Compiled by Ōmura Kin'ichi 大村欣一; 2 vols., 1025 + 21 pp.; Tokyo, 1913-1915.

Tōa Dōbunkai　東亞同文會．Shina keizai zensho 支那經濟全書 (China Economic Series).　12 vols.; Osaka and Tokyo, 1907-1908.

Tokunaga Kiyoyuki　德永清行．Shina chūō ginkō ron 支那中央銀行論 (Central Banking in China).　609 + 41 + 15 pp.; Tokyo, 1942.

Tōyō rekishi daijiten 東洋歷史大辭典 (Encyclopedia of Oriental History).　9 vols.; Tokyo, 1937-1939.

Ts'ai Kuan-lo 蔡冠洛, compiler.　Ch'ing-tai ch'i-pai ming-jen chuan 清代七百名人傳　(Seven Hundred Ch'ing Dynasty Biographies).　3 vols.; Shanghai, 1937.

Tseng K'un-hua 曾鯤化．Chung-kuo t'ieh-lu shih 中國鐵路史 (History of Chinese Railroads).　46 + 954 pp.; Peking, 1924.

Tseng Kuo-ch'üan 曾國荃．Tseng Chung-hsiang-kung tsou-i 曾忠襄公奏議 (Memorials of Tseng Kuo-ch'üan).　Compiled by Hsiao Jung-cho 蕭榮爵; 32 chüan in 31 ts'e; Changsha, 1903.

T'u-shu chi-k'an 圖書季刊 (Quarterly Bulletin of Chinese Bibliography), 4.3-4:105 (1943); Chungking.　Notice of 1942 reprint of Yü-chai ts'un-kao, supra.

Tung-hua hsü-lu, Kuang-hsü-ch'ao 東華續錄, 光緒朝 (Continuation of the Tung-hua Records, Kuang-hsü Reign Period). Compiled by Chu Shou-p'eng 朱壽朋 ; 220 chüan in 64 ts'e; Shanghai, 1909.

Wan Kuo-ting 萬國鼎 . "Pei-ch'ao Sui T'ang chih chün-t'ien chih-tu" 北朝隋唐之均田制度 (The Equal Land Allotment System of the Northern, Sui, and T'ang Dynasties); Chin-ling hsüeh-pao 金陵學報 (The Nanking Journal), 1:269-300 (1931).

Wang Ch'in-yü 王勤堉 . "Chin-pai-nien lai chih Chung-kuo t'ieh-lu shih-yeh" 近百年來之中國鐵路事業 (Chinese Railroads in the Past Hundred Years); Hsüeh-lin 學林 (The Academic World), 2:69-103 (December 1940); Shanghai.

Wang Kuang 王洸 . Chung-kuo hang-yeh lun 中國航業論 (On the Chinese Shipping Business). 2 + 6 + 143 pp.; Nanking, 1934.

Wang Liang 王亮 , editor. Ch'ing-chi wai-chiao shih-liao so-yin 清季外交史料索引 (Index to Historical Materials on Foreign Relations in the Latter Part of the Ch'ing Dynasty). 12 ts'e; Peiping, 1933.

Wang Yü-ch'üan 王毓銓 . "Ch'ing-mo t'ien-fu yü nung-min" 清末田賦與農民 (Land Tax and Peasantry in the Late Ch'ing Dynasty); Shih-huo pan-yüeh-k'an 食貨半月刊 (Economic History Fortnightly), 3.5:43-54 (February 1936).

Wu Chao-hsin 吳兆莘 . Chung-kuo shui-chih shih 中國稅制史 (History of Taxation in China). 2 vols.; Shanghai, 1937.

Wu Ch'eng-hsi 吳承禧 . "Pai-nien-lai yin-chia pien-tung chih hui-ku" 百年來銀價變動之回顧 (The Price of Silver, a Review of its Fluctuations 1833-1931); She-hui k'o-hsüeh tsa-chih 社會科學雜誌 (Quarterly Review of Social Sciences), 3. 3:323-363 (September 1932).

Wu Ch'eng-lo 吳承洛 . Chin-shih Chung-kuo shih-yeh t'ung-chih 今世中國實業通志 (Handbook of Modern Chinese Industry). 2 vols., 22 + 252, 14 + 272 pp.; Shanghai, 1929.

Wu-chin Yang-hu chih 武進陽湖志 (Gazetteer of Wu-chin and Yang-hu Districts). Compiled by T'ang Ch'eng-lieh 湯成烈 ; 30 chüan in 20 ts'e; 1879.

Wu Ching-ch'ao 吳敬超 "Han-Yeh-P'ing kung-ssu ti fu-ch'e" 漢冶萍公司的覆轍 (The Lesson of the Han-Yeh-P'ing Company); in his Chung-kuo ching-chi chien-she chih lu 中國經濟建設之路 (The Path of China's Economic Reconstruction), pp. 17-30. Chungking, 1943.

"Wu-hsi Jung-shih ch'i-yeh chia-tsu chi ch'i ch'i-chia ti mien-fen-yeh " 無錫榮氏企業家族及其起家的麵粉業 (The Yung Family and Their Flour Industry); Hsin shih-chieh 新世界 (New World), November 1944, pp. 19-25; Chungking.

Wu To 吳鐸 . "Chin-t'ung t'ieh-lu ti cheng-i"津通鐵路的爭議 (Controversy concerning the Proposed Railway Line between Tientsin and T'ung-chou [1888-1889]); Chung-kuo chin-tai ching-chi-shih yen-chiu chi-k'an 中國近代經濟史研究集刊 (Studies in Modern Economic History of China),4. 1:67-132 (May 1936).

Yang Ch'üan 楊銓. "Wu-shih-nien-lai Chung-kuo chih kung-yeh"五十年來中國之工業 (China's Industrial Enterprises for the Past 50 Years) ; in Tsui-chin chih wu-shih-nien, Shen-pao-kuan wu-shih chou-pien chi-nien 最近之五十年，申報館五

十週年紀念　(The Past Fifty years, in Commemoration of the Shen Pao's Golden Jubilee, 1872–1922); Shanghai, 1922.

Yen Chung-p'ing 嚴中平　. Chung-kuo mien-yeh chih fa-chan 中國棉業之發展　(The Development of the Chinese Cotton Industry). 3 + 305 pp.; Chungking, 1943.

------- Chung-kuo mien-fang-chih shih-kao 中國棉紡織史稿 (A Draft History of Chinese Cotton Spinning and Weaving). 5 + 384 pp.; Peking, 1955. Revised edition of preceding item.

GLOSSARY OF CHINESE AND JAPANESE NAMES AND TERMS

Acum (Lin Ch'in) 林欽

Bakufu 幕府

ch'a-chang 查賬
ch'a-chang tung-shih 查賬董事
Chang Chen-hsun 張振勳
chang-ch'eng 章程
Chang Chien 張謇
Chang Chih-tung 張之洞
Chang Hung-lu 張鴻祿
Chang Tsan-chen 張贊宸
Chang Yao 張曜
ch'ang 廠
Ch'ang-chou-fu 常州府
Ch'ang-chou hsien-che i-shu 常州先哲遺書
ch'ang-shang 場商
Ch'ang-shu-hsien 常熟縣
Chao Feng-t'ien 趙豐田
Chao-hsin p'iao 昭信票
chao-shang 招商
Chefoo 芝罘 (Yentai 烟台)
Chekiang hsing-yeh yin-hang 浙江興業銀行
Ch'en Chih 陳熾
Ch'en Li-fu 陳立夫
Ch'en Pi 陳璧
Ch'en Shu-t'ang 陳樹堂

Ch'en Yu 陳猷
Cheng Kuan-ying 鄭官應 (鄭觀應)
Cheng Tsao-ju 鄭藻如
cheng-tso-pan 正坐辦
cheng-tsung-tung 正總董
Chengtu 成都
Ch'eng-yü 承裕
Chi-ch'eng 集成
Chi-p'ing 濟平
Chi-yü kung-ssu 積餘公司
Chia-ch'ing 嘉慶
chia-kung chi-ssu 假公濟私
Chia-ting-hsien 嘉定縣
Chiang-nan ta-ying 江南大營
Chiang-yin-hsien 江陰縣
Chiao-t'ung yin-hang 交通銀行
chieh-liu 節流
chieh-yen chü 戒烟局
Chien-p'ing 建平
ch'ien-chuang 錢莊
Ch'ien-feng 乾豐
Ch'ien-lung 乾隆
chih-chou 知州
chih-fu 知府
Chihli 直隸
chin-hsien pu-yung-tao 儘先補用道
Chin-li-yuan (Kin Lee Yuen) 金利源

xxiv

chin-shih 進士

Ch'in Shih Huang-ti 秦始皇帝

ching-p'ing 京平

Ching-shih wen-pien 經世文編

Ching Yuan-shan 經元善

ching-yü 淨餘

[Prince] Ch'ing (I-k'uang) 慶親王 （奕劻）

ch'ing-i p'ai 清議派

ch'ing-liu p'ai 清流派

Chinkiang 鎮江

Cho-yuan i-chuang 拙園義莊

Chou Chin-piao 周晉鑣

Chou-hsien 周線

Chou-li 周禮

chou-t'ung 州同

Chu Ch'i-ang 朱其昂

Chu Ch'i-chao 朱其詔

Chu Ch'i-shun 朱其蕕

chu-chü pan-shih 駐局辦事

Chu Hung-tu 朱鴻度

Chu Pao-k'uei 朱寶奎

Chu P'ei-chen 朱佩珍

chu-shih 主事

Chu Yu-hung 朱幼鴻

Ch'u Ch'eng-wei 褚成燁

[Prince] Ch'un (Tsai-feng) 醇親王 （載灃）

Chung-hsi hsüeh-t'ang 中西學堂

Chung-kuo t'ieh-lu kung-ssu 中國鐵路公司

Chung-kuo t'ung-shang yin-hang 中國通商銀行

Chung Wen-yao 鍾文耀

chü 局

chü-jen 舉人

chü-kuei 局規

chü-nei ching-fei 局內經費

chüan-shou 卷首

ch'üan 權

chün-wu 軍務

daimyō 大名

Edo 江戶

Fan Chung-yen 范仲淹

Fan Shih-yao 范世堯

Fang-chih chi-ch'a kung-so 紡織稽查公所

Fang-chih tu-hsiao kung-so 紡織督銷公所

fen-ch'ang 分廠

feng ch'i pu-k'ai 風氣不分

Feng Kuei-fen 馮桂芬

feng t'e-chih k'ai-she 奉特旨開設

fudasashi 札差

fu-mu-kuan 父母官

fu-tso-pan 副坐辦

fu-tsung-tung 副總董

Hai-chou 海州

hai-kuan kuan-yin-hao 海關官銀號

hai-kuan tao 海關道

hai-yün wei-yuan 海運委員

han 藩

Hanyang 漢陽

Han-Yeh-P'ing mei-t'ieh ch'ang-k'uang yu-hsien kung-ssu 漢冶萍煤鐵廠礦有限公司

hao 號

Heilungchiang 黑龍江

Ho Ch'ang-ling 賀長齡

Ho Ch'i 何啟

Ho Ch'i-t'an 何其坦

Ho-lan yin-hang 荷蘭銀行

Ho Ssu-k'un 何嗣焜

Hsi-hsüeh 西學

Hsiang-chün 湘軍

Hsiang Jung 向榮

Hsiang-shan-hsien 香山縣

Hsiao-ch'ing 小清

Hsieh Chia-fu 謝家福

hsieh-hsiang 協餉

hsieh-li 協理

Hsieh-lung (Yah Loong) 協隆

Hsieh Lun-hui 謝綸輝

hsing 姓

Hsing-pu 刑部

Hsing-shu 行述

Hsiu-keng-t'ang shu-tien 修綆堂書店

hsiu-ts'ai 秀才

Hsueh Fu-ch'eng 薛福成

Hsü Chieh 徐傑

Hsü Ch'un-yung 許春榮

Hsü Jun 徐潤

Hsü-ke-chuang 胥各莊

Hsü T'ung 徐桐

hsüeh 學

hsün-fu 巡撫

Hu-Kuang 湖廣

Hu Kuang-yung 胡光墉

Hu Lin-i 胡林翼

Hu Li-yuan 胡禮垣

Hu-pei chih-pu kuan-chü 湖北織布官局

Hu-pei fang-sha kuan-chü 湖北紡紗官局

Hu-pu 戶部

Hu Yü-fen 胡燏棻

Hua-an 華安

Hua-hsin 華新

Hua-hsing 華興

Hua-sheng fang-chih tsung-ch'ang 華盛紡織總廠

Huai-chün 淮軍

Huang-ch'ao ching-shih wen hsü-pien 皇朝經世文續編

Huang-ch'ao ching-shih wen-pien 皇朝經世文編

Huang Tsun-hsien 黃遵憲

hui-chang. 會長

Hui-feng yin-hang 匯豐銀行

hui-pan 會辦

Hui-pan shang-wu ta-ch'en 會辦商務大臣

Hwangpoo (Huang-p'u) 黃浦

I-cheng-hsien 儀徵縣

i-chuang 義莊

I-ho lun-ch'uan kung-ssu 怡和輪船公司

I-k'uang(Prince Ch'ing) 奕劻（慶親王）

Ili 伊犂

i-nien k'uai-chi 一年會計

i-shih tung-shih 議事董事

Itō Hirobumi 伊藤博文

Iwasaki Yatarō 岩崎彌太郎

Jen-chi-ho 仁濟和

Jung-lu 榮祿

Jung Tsung-ching 榮宗敬

K'ai-p'ing 開平

Kan-yü-hsien 贛榆縣

Kang-i 剛毅

K'ang Yu-wei 康有為

Katsuro Tarō 桂太郎

Kiangnan 江南

Kin Lee Yuen (Chin-li-yuan) 金利源

Kirin (Chi-lin) 吉林

Kōbe 神戶

k'o-chang 科長

K'o Hung-nien 柯鴻年

Ku Chao-hsi 顧肇熙

Ku Jun-chang 顧潤章

kuan 官

kuan-ch'ang 官塲

kuan-chü 官局

kuan-li 官利

kuan-liao tzu-pen 官僚資本

kuan-shang ho-pan 官商合辦

kuan-she yin-hang 官設銀行

Kuan T'ing-hsien 管廷獻

kuan-tu shang-hsiao 官督商銷

kuan-tu shang-pan 官督商辦

Kuan-tzu 管子

kuan wei hu-ch'ih 官為護持

kuan-wu 官務

kuan-yün shang-hsiao 官運商銷

Kuang-hsü 光緒

K'uang-wu t'ieh-lu tsung-chü 礦務鐵路總局

Kuei-ch'ih 貴池

Kuei Sung-ch'ing 桂嵩慶

Kung, H.H. (K'ung Hsiang-hsi) 孔祥熙

kung-i 工藝

Kung I-t'u 龔彝圖

Kung-pu tso-shih-lang 工部左侍郎

Kung Shou-t'u 龔壽圖
kung-ssu 公司
kuramoto 藏元
Kyōdō Un'yu Kaisha 協同運輸公司

lang-chung 郎中
li 利
Li Ching-fang 李經方
li-ch'üan 利權
Li Han-chang 李瀚章
Li Hsing-jui 李興銳
Li Hung-chang 李鴻章
likin (li-chin) 釐金
Li Kuo-chieh 李國杰
Li Lien-ying 李蓮英
Li P'ei sung 李培松
li-ts'ai 理財
li-shih-jen 理事人
li-yuan 利源
liang 兩
Liang-Chiang 兩江
Liang Ch'i-ch'ao 梁啟超
Liang-Hu 兩湖
Liang-Huai 兩淮
Liang-Kuang 兩廣
Liang Shih-yi 梁士詒
lien-chün 練軍
lien-ping 練兵
Liu Hsueh-hsün 劉學詢
Liu Jui-fen 劉瑞芬

Liu K'un-i 劉坤一
Liu Shao-tsung 劉紹宗
Lu-Han 蘆漢
Lu-kou-ch'iao 蘆溝橋
Lu-k'uang tsung-chü 路礦總局
Lun-ch'uan chao-shang chü 輪船招商局
Lun-ch'uan chao-shang kung chü 輪船招商公局
Lü Ching-tuan 呂景端
Lü Hai-huan 呂海寰
lü-ying 綠營

Ma Chien-chung 馬建忠
Mai-chia-li yin-hang 麥加利銀行
mai-pan 買辦
mai-pan tzu-pen 買辦資本
Matsukata Masayoshi 松方正義
Mitsui Bussan Kaisha 三井物產會社
mi-yüeh 密約
Mo-ho 漠河
mou 畝
mu-liao 幕僚

Nantung 南通
Nan-yang ch'üan-yeh yin-hang 南洋勸業銀行
Nan-yang kung-hsüeh 南洋公學
Nan-yang ta-ch'en 南洋大臣
Nan-yang ta-hsüeh 南洋大學
Nich-nichi shimbun 日日新聞

Nieh Ch'i-kuei 聶緝椝

nien-p'u 年譜

Ningpo 寧波

Nippon Yūsen Kaisha 日本郵船會社

nung-hui 農會

Nung-kung-shang-pu 農工商部

Ōsaka 大阪

pan-li tung-cheng chuan-yün 辦理東征轉運

pan-shih tsung-tung 辦事總董

pan-shih tung-shih 辦事董事

pao-hsiao 報效

Pao-ting-fu 保定府

Pao-yuan-hsiang 寶源祥

Pei-yang ta-ch'en 北洋大臣

Peiyang ta-hsüeh 北洋大學

P'eng Yü-lin 彭玉麐

pien-hsiu 編修

pin 稟

ping-pei tao 兵備道

P'ing-hsiang 萍鄉

pu-cheng shih 布政使

pu-yü shih-ts'un yin-liang chih-su 不逾實存銀兩之數

samurai 士

San-hsin 三新

san-p'in hsien 三品銜

san-yuan san-tung 三員三董

Satsuma 薩摩

sha-ch'uan 沙船

Shanhaikuan 山海關

shang 商

Shang-hai chi-ch'i chih-pu chü 上海機器織布局

Shang-hai shang-yeh hui-i kung-ssu 上海商業會議公司

shang-hui 商會

shang-pan 商辦

shang-pan li-pu 商辦隸部

Shang-pu 商部

shang-tsung 商總

shang-tung 商董

shang-wu 商務

shang-wu chü 商務局

shang-wu hui 商務會

shang-wu tsung-hui 商務總會

shang-wu tsung-kuan 商務總官

She Ch'ang-yü 佘昌宇

Shen-hsin 申新

Shen Pao 申報

Shen Pao-chen 沈葆楨

Shen Neng-hu 沈能虎

shen-shang 紳商

Shen T'ing-tung 沈廷棟

Shen Tun-ho 沈敦和

Shen Yün-p'ei 沈雲霈

Sheng Ch'ang-i 盛昌頤
Sheng Chou-huai 盛宙懷
Sheng Chün-huai 盛寓懷
Sheng En-i 盛恩頤
Sheng Hsing-huai 盛星懷
Sheng Hsuan-huai 盛宣懷
Sheng K'ang 盛康
Sheng Keng 盛庚
Sheng Kung-pao 盛公保
Sheng Lung 盛隆
Sheng-shih wei-yen 盛世危言
Shih I-chüeh 施亦爵
shih, nung, kung, shang 士, 農, 工, 商
shih-ta-fu 士大夫
Shih Tzu-ch'ing 施紫卿
shou-hui 收回
shui-li 水利
shuo-t'ieh 説帖
Soong, T. V. (Sung Tzu-wen) 宋子文
Ssu-ming 四明
ssu-p'in ching-t'ang 四京品堂
Sun Chu-t'ang 孫竹堂
Sun Yat-sen 孫逸仙
Sung Chin 宋晉
Swatow (Shan-t'ou) 汕頭

Ta-cheng 大正
ta-ch'eng kuan 達成館
Ta-ch'un sha-ch'ang 大純紗厰

Taku 大沽
Ta-li-ssu shao-ch'ing 大理寺少卿
Ta-pei kung-ssu 大北公司
Ta-sheng 大生
Ta-tung kung-ssu 大東公司
Ta-yeh 大冶
ta-yuan 大員
Tai Heng 戴恒
tai-li 代理
Taiping 太平
Tai Wŏn Kun 大院君
T'ai-ch'ang-ssu shao-ch'ing 太常寺少卿
T'ai-ku lun-ch'uan kung-ssu 太古輪船公司
T'ai-tzu shao-pao 太子少保
tan 擔
T'ang Shao-yi 唐紹儀
T'ang-shan 唐山
T'ang Shou-ch'ien 湯壽潛
T'ang Sung-yen 唐松岩
T'ang Te-hsi 唐德熙
T'ang T'ing-keng 唐廷庚
T'ang T'ing-shu 唐廷樞
    (Tong King Sing 唐景星)
T'ao Hsiang 陶湘
t'i-t'iao 提調
T'ieh-liang 鐵良
T'ieh-lu tsung kung-ssu 鐵路總公司
T'ieh-lu tu-pan 鐵路督辦
T'ieh-tao chü 鐵道局

Tien-pao tsung-chü 電報總局

Tientsin-Hochien 天津河間

Ting Jih-ch'ang 丁日昌

Ting Ju-ch'ang 丁汝昌

Tokugawa 德川

Tong King Sing (T'ang Ching-hsing) 唐景星 (T'ang T'ing-shu 唐廷樞)

Tsai-chen 載振

Tsai-feng (Prince Ch'un) 載灃醇親王

Tsai-tse 載澤

ts'ai-cheng 財政

Ts'ai-cheng shuo-ming-shu 財政說明書

Ts'ai Hung-i 蔡鴻儀

Ts'ai Yuan-p'ei 蔡元培

Ts'en Yü-ying 岑毓英

Tseng Kuo-ch'üan 曾國荃

Tseng Kuo-fan 曾國藩

Tsining (Chi-ning) 濟寧

tso-pan 坐辦

Tso Tsung-t'ang 左宗棠

tsu-shih tsu-ping 足食足兵

tsung-ch'ang 總廠

Tsung-jen-fu fu-ch'eng 宗人府府丞

tsung-kuan 總管

tsung-li 總理

Tsung-li ko-kuo shih-wu ya-men 總理各國事務衙門

Tsungli Yamen 總理衙門

tsung ssu-li jen 總司理人

tsung-tu 總督

tsung-tung 總董

Tu-chih pu 度支部

tu-pan 督辦

tu-pan ta-ch'en 督辦大臣

[Prince] Tuan (Tsai-i) 端郡王載漪

Tuan Fang 端方

Tung-fang yin hang 東方銀行

Tung-hua lu 東華錄

Tung-nan hu-pao 東南互保

tung-shih 董事

tung-shih hui 董事會

T'ung-chih 同治

T'ung-chiu-yuan 通久源

T'ung-chou 通州

T'ung-meng hui 同盟會

t'ung-shang 通商

Tzu-cheng yuan 咨政院

tzu-ch'iang 自強

Tzu-ch'iang ta-chi 自強大計

tzu-chin-ch'eng ch'i-ma 紫禁城騎馬

tzu-k'ou shui 子口稅

Tz'u-hsi 慈禧

Wai-wu pu 外務部

wan wai-i 挽外溢

Wang Ch'ung-hui 王寵惠

Wang Hsien-ch'ien 王先謙
Wang Jung-ho 王榮和
Wang K'ang-nien 汪康年
Wang Ko-ch'en 王閣臣
Wang P'eng-yün 王鵬運
Wang Ts'un-shan 王存善
Wang Wei 王惟
Wang Wen-shao 王文韶
wei-yuan 委員
Weng T'ung-ho 翁同龢
Woosung 吳淞
Wu-chin-hsien 武進縣
Wu Chung-hsi 吳重憙
Wu-hsi-hsien 無錫縣
wu-jen-erh 無人耳
Wusih 無錫
Wu T'ing-fang 伍廷芳
Wu Tso-ch'ing 吳佐清
Wu-wei yu-chün 武衛右軍

ya-hang 牙行
Ya-li tsung-chü 牙釐總局
yamen 衙門
Yawata 八幡
Yah Loong (Hsien-lung) 協隆
Yang Shih-ch'i 楊士琦
Yang Shih-hsiang 楊士驤
Yang T'ing-kao 楊廷杲
Yang Tsung-lien 楊宗濂
Yang Wen-chün 楊文駿
yang-wu 洋務

yang-yuan 洋元
Yeh Ch'eng-chung 葉成忠
Yeh Kung-cho 葉恭綽
Yeh T'ing-chüan 葉廷眷
Yen Fu 嚴復
Yen Hsin-hou 嚴信厚 (Yen I-pin 嚴義彬)
Yen Shu-shen 嚴樹森
Yen Tso-lin 嚴作霖
Yen Ying 嚴瀅
yin 引
yin-hao 銀號
yin-shui 印稅
ying-yü 盈餘
Yu-ch'uan pu 郵傳部
yu-shih-lang 右侍郎
Yuan Shih-k'ai 袁世凱
yuan-wai-lang 員外郎
Yung-p'ing 永平
Yung Wing (Jung Hung) 容閎
yung-yeh 庸業
Yü-chin sha-ch'ang 裕晉紗廠
Yü Ho-te 虞和德 (Yü Ch'ia-ch'ing 虞洽卿)
Yü Hsi-sheng 郁熙繩
yü-li 餘利
Yü-lu 裕祿
yü-ts'ai 育才
Yü-yuan sha-ch'ang 裕源紗廠
Yüeh-Han 粵漢
yün-shang 運商